★ ★ ★ ★ ★

TEXAS
EATS

★ ★ ★ ★ ★

TEXAS EATS

THE NEW
LONE STAR HERITAGE COOKBOOK
WITH MORE THAN 200 RECIPES

ROBB WALSH

FOOD PHOTOGRAPHY BY LAURIE SMITH

TEN SPEED PRESS
Berkeley

Hill Country peaches.

CONTENTS

Kettle frying chicken at the Moulton Town and Country Jamboree.

Dedicated to my son,
Robert Joseph Walsh

ACKNOWLEDGMENTS

Thanks to all the Texas food experts who gave me their time and assistance, including: Jim Gossen, Dr. Sammy Ray, Tracy Woody, Ben and Jeri Nelson, Misho Ivic, Johnny and Lisa Halili, Jon Rowley, Doug Sartin Jr., Dale Lee, Nathan Jean Whitaker "Mama Sugar" Sanders, Irma Leal, Raul Molina, William Little, Aaron Franklin, Gregory Carter, Lillie Brown, Lolo and Rose Garcia, Frank Crappito, Tony Leago, Alan Lazarus, John Broussard, Gary Beams, Carl Han, Frank Mancuso, Kaiser Lashkari, and Shubhra Ramineni. Without them, this book wouldn't have been possible.

Thanks to recipe contributors Rebecca Rather, Jody Stevens, and Jay Francis. Much obliged to University of Houston intern director Stephanie L. Witowski and Conrad Hilton College of Hotel and Restaurant Management interns Jake Lewis, Jessica Choate, Matthew Zentano, and Jervonni Henderson for their hard work testing recipes.

Special thanks to Texas experts Joe Nick Patoski, John Lomax, and Bud Kennedy. And many thanks to chef Bryan Caswell, my partner at El Real Tex-Mex Cafe, and to his mom and dad, Barbara and Mike Caswell, for their family recipes.

Thanks to Marvin Bendele and Elizabeth Englehardt for their help and advice.

Thanks to my agent, David McCormick, at McCormick & Williams, and to editor Emily Timberlake at Ten Speed Press for making this project a reality.

Thanks to photographer Laurie Smith and stylist Erica McNeish for camping out in Texas to get the food photos. I am also indebted to photographer Paul S. Howell for his photos and his ongoing help.

Thanks to my wife, Kelly Klaasmeyer, for her love, support, and insight. Thanks to my mom, Mary Ann Walsh, and to my brothers, Scott, David, Gordon, Rick, and Mike, for always being there. And thanks to my kids, Katie, Julia, Ava, and Joe, for giving me so many reasons to keep cooking.

Portions of this book first appeared in different forms in the *Houston Press* and on its website (www.houstonpress.com) and food blog. Thanks to Margaret Downing, Catherine Matusow, and my former employers for permission to use photos, text, and articles first published by the *Houston Press* (or www.houstonpress.com), a Village Voice Media publication.

INTRODUCTION

Texas has produced an amazing number of blues guitarists and singer-songwriters, but not so many opera singers. Likewise, the state is better known for its folk cuisine than its haute cuisine. Texas top chefs do well in those televised cooking contests against chefs from other parts of the country. But our real strengths are folk foods like barbecued brisket, cheese enchiladas in chili gravy, and chicken-fried steak, and in those categories, it's hard to find any state that can compete. Did I mention that chili con carne was invented in Texas?

The bicultural border cuisine called Tex-Mex is the most famous culinary hybrid in the state, but it's not the only one. There are thirty-some ethnic groups in Texas, each one with its own folk foods and each one contributing to our statewide potluck.

In Hallettsville, a Czech-Tex hot dog has both sauerkraut and chili con carne on top. In Arlington, Korean doughnut shops sell jalapeño kolaches. In Sugar Land, Indian immigrants put chutney on their fajitas. And that's part of the reason Texas food traditions are so fascinating.

The state's food history is a patchwork created by the resident ethnic groups and by an extremely varied geography. Texas has a long coastline, fertile farms in the river valleys, dense forests and swamps in the east, vast ranchlands and rugged mountains in the west, and a whole lot of empty space in between.

The food culture was shaped by the spirit of the frontier. Food was hard to find on the edges of civilization, and so were picky eaters. The French and Spanish didn't get along, and neither did the cowboys and Indians, but they all ate each other's cooking and borrowed each other's ingredients. Few modern-day Texans will turn down a bulgogi burger, a bun kebab, or a banh mi burger if you're offering to buy lunch.

For the last twenty years, I have been collecting stories about food in Texas. In this book, I have laid some of these accounts side by side in an attempt to sketch out a rough history of Lone Star cooking.

The title *Texas Eats* is a tribute to the unfinished *America Eats*, a book begun during the Great Depression by the Works Progress Administration. Writers in each state collected oral histories and local food lore and sent them to their editors in Washington. The intention was to create a book about our national food culture with a chapter for each state, but the Depression ended before *America Eats* was completed. The unfinished manuscript, which can be found in the Library of Congress, has spawned several other food books. The stories about folk foods like barbecue, ham sandwiches, and Tex-Mex recorded by the scribes of the Texas Writers Project were part of the inspiration behind this book.

Instead of organizing this book into chapters on appetizers, soups, salads, and so forth, I found it more helpful to sort the foods of Texas into categories, such as seafood, Tex-Mex, barbecue, and the like. Then I tried to put those categories into some kind of order.

The book begins on the water's edge with the accounts of the first Spanish observers of the 1500s, who reported that coastal Native Americans lived on seafood. I tried to sort the rest of the sections chronologically, but of course, things are never that neat. The timelines often overlap.

The borders of the state aren't very neat, either. That's because they have shifted frequently during its history. Some early maps show only the settled areas of East Texas; later maps include a lot of New Mexico and some of Colorado. Some contemporary maps divide up the state by its topography or its gardening zones. In fact, there are lots of ways to carve up the state. For this book, I have adapted a simple map of Texas regions that is often used by the state's tourism office, so that readers can find the places I have written about.

Every history is an incomplete record, told from a narrow point of view. I count myself lucky to have met all the people and gone to all the places I have described in this book. I am sorry if I left out your ethnic group, your part of the state, or your favorite old restaurant.

No doubt I'll cover your story in the sequel.

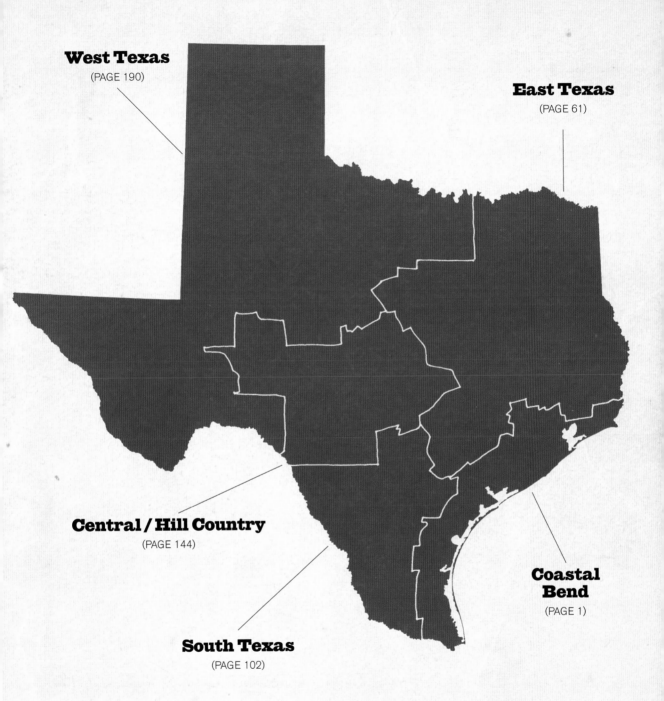

West Texas
(PAGE 190)

East Texas
(PAGE 61)

Central / Hill Country
(PAGE 144)

Coastal Bend
(PAGE 1)

South Texas
(PAGE 102)

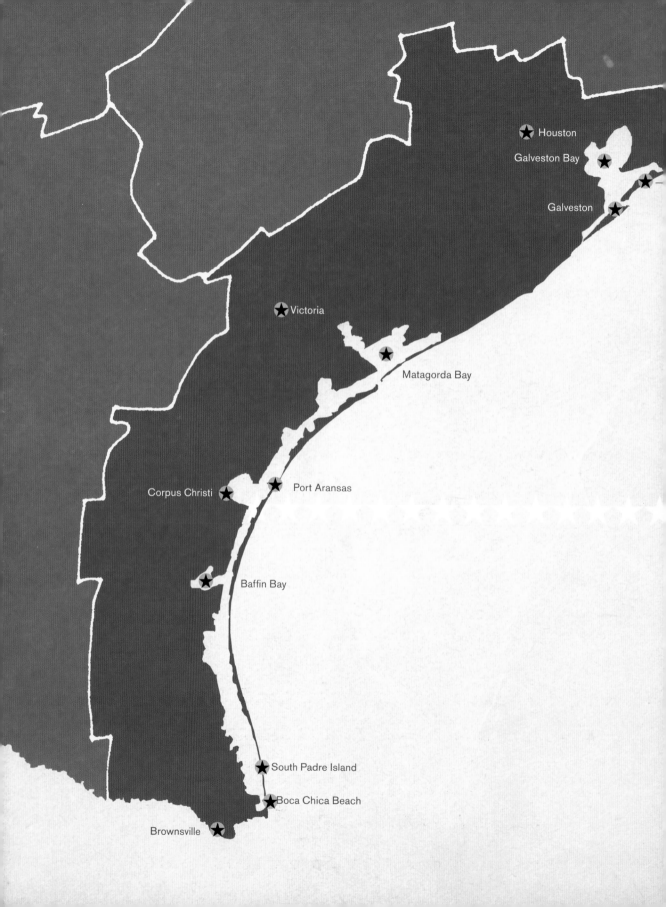

Beaumont

★ Sabine River LOUISIANA

★ Port Arthur

— Bolivar Peninsula

PART 1

LONE STAR SEAFOOD

The Coastal Bend

The Texas coast bends gently around the Gulf of Mexico for 367 miles, from Sabine Lake in Jefferson County to remote Boca Chica Beach on the Mexican border near Brownsville. The Coastal Bend includes the cities of Beaumont, Galveston, Houston, Victoria, Corpus Christi, and Brownsville.

The easternmost coastline in Jefferson County lies along a section of Texas Highway 87 that has been closed for decades due to constant battering by hurricanes. South of Galveston and Lake Jackson, a series of barrier islands protect the coast and create lagoons and bays that separate the mainland from the Gulf. From Corpus Christi the Padre Island National Seashore stretches for 113 miles to the south; it is the longest undeveloped barrier island in the world.

Beyond the Padre Island National Seashore lies South Padre Island, the state's most extensive beach resort. The southernmost beach in Texas is the remote shipwreck magnet and smuggler's haven known as Boca Chica Beach.

1

Broiled black drum (page 11) with Pope's Tartar Sauce (page 7).

ON THE BEACH
GALVESTON, TEXAS.

*Murdoch's Bathouse (left) was damaged by hurricanes in 1900, 1909, 1915, 1961, 1982, and 2008.
It was rebuilt each time and remains open today.*

CHAPTER 1

TARTAR SAUCE AND HURRICANES

★★★★★★★★★★★★★★★★

When I checked into the Lighthouse Inn in Fulton, I noticed some old black-and-white photos of elegant resort hotels hanging on the walls. The front-desk clerk told me those hotels were once nearby, but they no longer existed. I didn't have to ask why.

Many gorgeous spa hotels and upscale fishing lodges have been built along the Texas coast. Beachfront amusement parks that rivaled Coney Island once graced the sandy beaches, too. Most have been leveled by hurricanes.

But this was the first week of March, and the tropical storm season was months away. The Texas beachfront town of Rockport, with its charming crescent beach, and the neighboring fishing village of Fulton were putting on the annual celebration called Oysterfest. The event, which is a fund-raiser for the Fulton fire department, features the irresistible combination of cheap oysters on the half shell, draft beer, and live music.

Not many Texans realize that their home state is a leading oyster producer, ranking third behind Louisiana and Washington in total harvest most years. Texas is also a huge producer of crab and shrimp. But when you think of Texas you think of cattle, not mollusks or crustaceans. Is that because our cowboy image overshadows our prowess as fishermen? Or is it because most of our seafood is exported?

Giant junefish caught on a rod and reel.

Galveston fishermen.

After eating my fill of fat, juicy, eight-dollar-a-dozen oysters at the enormous festival tent, I walked back along Fulton's picture-book waterfront, with its handsome shrimp fleet and a marina with a huge bait shack at one end. The oyster lugs were tied up at their slips, with piles of oyster shells alongside them. I also passed another dock filled with expensive yachts and deep-sea fishing boats.

Named for a rock ledge along the waterfront, Rockport was once an important shipping center. In the late 1800s, the area was a major cattle-processing site and home to an international shipping industry. Those businesses were completely destroyed during the hurricanes of 1916 and 1919, and the port and cattle plants were never rebuilt.

The recorded history of the Texas coast is a litany of tropical storms, beginning with the one that washed the first European observer of Texas foodways, Cabeza de Vaca, up on the beach near Galveston Island in 1528. The expedition to Florida that he was a part of had met with several tropical storms. Cabeza de Vaca and his three surviving comrades, two other Spanish explorers and a North African servant named Esteban, spent two years with the Native Americans of Texas. On his return to Spain, Cabeza de Vaca published an account that provides the earliest insight into the indigenous diet. According to his book, the Karankawa tribe with whom he lived moved around South Texas following seasonal food sources.

In winter, from January to April, the coastal people lived almost entirely on oysters that they harvested from the Laguna Madre, the series of brackish bays that lie between the mainland and the barrier islands that hug the coast of Texas. When the wild dewberries ripened in May, the Karankawa moved inland to feast on them. In the summer, they migrated to an area south of what is now San Antonio, where they harvested prickly pears. When fall arrived, the tribe headed for the banks of what they called the "river of nuts" (probably the Guadalupe), where they ate pecans that fell from the trees. In the late fall and early winter, they harvested cattails and roots such as arrowroot along the coast and fished from their canoes and with fish weirs. And when the weather turned cold, the Karankawa went back to the oyster beds.

Archeological research indicates that the heaviest population concentrations of early aboriginal peoples occurred along the Texas coast at points where freshwater sources entered the Laguna Madre. These are the areas of brackish water where oyster reefs formed and where several marine species came to spawn. You would expect these areas to be heavily populated today. They aren't.

When you look at a map of the United States, you notice that all of the biggest cities of the East Coast and the West Coast are located on the water. But not in Texas. Houston, the biggest city in the state and the largest port on the Caribbean basin, is connected to the Gulf of Mexico by a long ship channel.

It's not that Texans didn't try to build their cities on the water. They did. The city of Galveston, eighty miles south of Houston, was once the biggest city in the state. It was built on Galveston Island, the barrier island directly facing the Gulf. The hurricane that hit Galveston without warning in 1900 covered the island with a storm surge that reached the upper floors of downtown office buildings. More than three thousand people died. The city never completely recovered. But at least Galveston still survives.

In its day, Indianola, the other major Texas port city of the 1800s, was said to be the best deepwater harbor on the Gulf and the port of call for the biggest steamships. As the arrival city for many European immigrants, it might have become a major city. But Indianola was leveled by a hurricane in September 1875. The town wasn't even completely rebuilt when it was hit again by another hurricane in 1886. Today, Indianola is a ghost town.

Much of the Texas coast is hauntingly beautiful. But longtime residents are prone to melancholy. They talk about the ruins of former homes and businesses lost to hurricanes the way war veterans talk about their battle scars. And every Texas beach resort and seafood restaurant seems to be built on the ruins of something more ambitious that no longer exists.

Consider, for instance, the sad case of Loyola Beach. The saga began three-quarters of a century ago, with Orlando Underbrink's dreams of grandeur. In 1935, Underbrink, a farmer who worked land not far from Baffin Bay, bought up the waterfront property and

A seafood feast at the King's Inn.

built a boardwalk, a fishing pier, rental cottages, and a restaurant he called Orlando's Café. He named the seaside resort Loyola Beach, and it got off to a good start, with lots of vacationers and fishermen taking advantage of its facilities. The town of Riviera built nearby was to be the gateway to the Texas version of a coastal paradise. But the would-be resort area was slammed by a pair of hurricanes—and then came World War II.

The clapboard café was the only business that survived the storms and the war. It was run by a French war bride, Blanche "Mom" Wright. She hired a cook named Cottle Ware, who had previously worked all over the state, including in the cafeteria at Texas A&M. When Mom Wright died in 1945, Cottle Ware and his wife, Alta Faye, inherited the business and renamed it the King's Inn. The name was no doubt inspired by the nearby town of Kingsville, headquarters of the historic King Ranch. The Wares made the restaurant a legend and ran it until their deaths. Their son Randy Ware took over in 1978. He changed the name over the entrance to The Famous King's Inn.

Like legions of fellow Texans, I count the King's Inn as one of my favorite restaurants. Perched on a lonely bluff overlooking Baffin Bay, miles from any major population center, the place sucked me in with its eccentric air of romantic tragedy. There is a quirkiness about it that gets under your skin. The King's Inn looks like a decrepit wooden beach house. The interior décor is appalling. The carpets are industrial gray and the acoustic ceiling tiles are stained and ill fitting. The trim near the bathroom is painted about as far as you can reach, and then the paint job ends.

It could be an incredibly depressing atmosphere, if it wasn't for the hordes of enthusiastic seafood eaters who always crowd the place. The last time I visited, my wife and I were seated next to a huge Christmas party. The participants were members of the train engineer's union, and it seems that the Brotherhood of Locomotive Engineers and their significant others know how to party. More than a hundred people were sitting at the long tables, drinking pitchers of beer, laughing loudly, and eating platter after platter of shrimp. One of the organizers stopped by our table to shoot the breeze. I felt like we were part of the festivities.

Shuckers at Fulton Oysterfest.

I ordered oysters on the half shell and a Bombay salad to start, but the waiter dropped a bombshell. He said that owner Randy Ware had decided not to serve raw oysters anymore.

When I got home, I called Randy Ware to ask why. He said that the King's Inn hasn't stopped serving oysters, he just hasn't been able to find any good ones since Hurricane Ike stirred things up in Galveston Bay, home to the state's biggest oyster reefs. When he finds some quality oysters to serve, he told me, he will start selling them again.

The paradox of Texas seafood is that the hurricanes that destroy the beach resorts, mess up the oyster reefs, and put our favorite seafood restaurants out of business are also the reason the Gulf Coast of Texas has such a bounty of seafood. Chesapeake Bay and New York Harbor were once blessed with enormous stocks of oysters and fish, but the seafood there is mostly gone. The Eastern Seaboard proved to be a perfect place to build mills, factories, and mighty cities. And so the wetlands were paved over and the waterways were polluted.

The Gulf of Mexico may go the same way soon. Oil spills like the BP Deepwater Horizon disaster disrupted some of the Louisiana oyster beds, shrimp-breeding areas, and fishing grounds. How long the marine ecosystem will be able to keep recovering from such devastating pollution events remains to be seen. But for now, the Gulf of Mexico is the most productive fishery in the United States and the home of the nation's last significant wild oyster reefs.

The settlers of Texas tried to build coastal towns and cities like the ones on the East and West Coasts, with disastrous results. Due to the frequent hurricanes, much of the coastline of Texas and Louisiana remains undeveloped, which is why such a large a percentage of the nation's remaining wetlands are found there. And the wetlands are a necessary part of the ecosystem that sustains the oysters, shrimp, and fish along the Gulf Coast.

It's easy to fall in love with the Texas coast and its desolate beaches, melancholy history, and succulent seafood. But think twice before you decide to build a resort there. I asked Randy Ware if he had any plans for the future of the King's Inn. "Yeah, I'm going to try and keep it open," he replied.

Galveston amusement parks
The Crystal Palace (top, center) was built in 1916. It featured a swimming pool filled daily with 300,000 gallons of salt water. The water was heated in the winter. The Electric Park (bottom) was one of the first businesses in Texas to use electric lights. Both parks were damaged by storms and demolished.

POPE'S TARTAR SAUCE

The original "tartare" sauce was invented in France in the mid-1800s and was served with steak tartare. In the 1950s, elaborate French-style tartar sauces (minus the *e*) were made famous in the United States by Antoinette Pope, who hosted one of the country's first television cooking shows, *Creative Cookery*, from 1951 to 1964. By this time the French had stopped serving the sauce with steak tartare, but Pope repurposed it by pairing it with seafood.

A French woman, Blanche Wright, was the original head cook at the King's Inn on Loyola Beach, though in those days it was still called Orlando's Café. I suspect she served a Gallic tartar sauce like the one Pope made famous in the 1950s. When Cottle Ware came along, he probably started doctoring up the French sauce with the obligatory Texas addition of hot chiles. But I'm just guessing. See photo on page 2.

MAKES ABOUT 2½ CUPS

2 cups mayonnaise
1 clove garlic, minced
½ cup chopped green onions (white and green parts)
2 tablespoons sweet pickle relish
2 tablespoons chopped pimiento-stuffed green olives
2 tablespoons freshly squeezed lemon juice, or as needed

In a bowl, using a wooden spoon, stir the mayonnaise until creamy. Fold in the garlic, green onions, relish, and olives. Thin with the lemon juice as needed. Serve immediately, or cover and refrigerate for up to 2 weeks.

BAFFIN BAY SEAFOOD SAUCE

Every meal at the King's Inn starts with a plate of sliced tomatoes and a dish of the restaurant's mysterious "tartar sauce." I usually eat huge gobs of the stuff on the tomatoes. It's more of a stiff, zesty spread than a tartar sauce. And it tastes weirdly wonderful—like an old-fashioned tartar sauce with chiles, chopped eggs, and Ritz crackers added.

The seafood at King's Inn is pretty straightforward: jumbo fried shrimp, black drum or redfish cooked on the grill, oysters on the half shell or fried. It's this tartar sauce, the curried avocado salad, and the homemade desserts that set the place apart. Proprietor Randy Ware says his father, Cottle Ware, concocted the sauce and that he used to make it with local chile pequin peppers, but now Randy uses serranos. The recipe is such a well-kept secret that when Ware makes the stuff, everyone has to leave the kitchen. So, this isn't the exact recipe for the famous seafood sauce at the King's Inn, but it tastes a lot like it. Serve with sliced tomatoes or seafood.

MAKES ABOUT 3 CUPS
Sleeve of Ritz crackers
2½ cups Pope's Tartar Sauce (page 7)
3 pickled jalapeño chiles, stemmed, seeded, and minced
2 hard-boiled eggs, minced
½ teaspoon curry powder
2 teaspoons anchovy paste

Put the crackers in a large ziplock plastic bag and crush them into fine crumbs. (A rolling pin works best.)

Put the tartar sauce in a bowl, add the cracker crumbs, chiles, eggs, curry powder, and anchovy paste, and stir well. Cover and refrigerate for at least 1 hour before serving so the cracker crumbs have time to soften. It will keep for up to 2 weeks covered in the refrigerator.

BOMBAY SALAD

This time-capsule dish will probably remind you of those curried egg salads and curried chicken salads that were once common to Southern cooking.

SERVES 2 GENEROUSLY
1 (1-pound) carton sour cream
1 avocado, halved, pitted, peeled, and mashed
¼ cup minced yellow onion
1 teaspoon onion powder
2 cloves garlic, minced
1 tablespoon curry powder
2 large tomatoes, thinly sliced
1 head iceberg lettuce, halved through the stem end
4 thin slices red onion
Salt
2 pickled jalapeño chiles

In a bowl, combine the sour cream, avocado, onion, onion powder, garlic, and curry powder and whisk until smooth.

Fan the tomato slices on 2 chilled salad plates. Remove several layers of leaves from the center of the cut side of each lettuce half, forming a cup. Place a lettuce cup atop the tomatoes on each plate. Fill the iceberg cup with the curried avocado mixture. Separate the onion slices into strands and scatter them over the top. Season with salt to taste and place a pickled chile across the top of each salad.

SAFARI CLUB BOMBAY DRESSING

If you'd like to experiment with another version of Bombay salad dressing, here's one from the Safari Club, a popular Houston eatery of the 1960s. The recipe was printed in the *Houston Chronicle*. Serve the dressing over iceberg wedges or your favorite mix of salad greens.

MAKES ABOUT 3 CUPS

3 cloves garlic, mashed

1-inch length anchovy paste from a tube, mashed

1 egg yolk

Juice of 1 lemon

1 tablespoon Worcestershire sauce

¼ cup dry white wine

¾ cup olive oil

3 avocados, halved, pitted, and peeled

Salt and white pepper

½ cup grated Parmesan cheese

In a bowl, whisk together the garlic, anchovy paste, and egg yolk until well blended. Add the lemon juice, Worcestershire sauce, and wine and whisk to combine. Slowly add half of the oil, whisking briskly until the mixture emulsifies. Press the avocado halves through a medium-mesh sieve into the bowl and whisk to combine. Whisk in the remaining oil. Season with salt and white pepper, then fold in the Parmesan. Serve right away.

SEAFOOD SEASONING

The favorite seafood seasoning in Texas is similar to a Cajun seasoning blend, but with more spices. Texans rarely use the popular Chesapeake Bay–born Old Bay Seasoning, which includes cloves, mace, and other aromatic spices that give a completely different flavor profile. You can use this on grilled or broiled fish or shellfish.

MAKES ABOUT ½ CUP

2 tablespoons salt

1 teaspoon dry mustard

2 teaspoons paprika

½ teaspoon cayenne pepper

½ teaspoon black pepper

½ teaspoon red pepper flakes

½ teaspoon ground dried thyme

½ teaspoon ground bay leaves

In a bowl, stir together all of the ingredients. The seasoning can be transferred to a small bottle or container and stored in a cupboard for up to 1 month.

FISH FLOUR

This is a good all-purpose flour for dredging fish for frying.

MAKES ABOUT 1 CUP

1 cup all-purpose flour

½ teaspoon salt

½ teaspoon black pepper

½ teaspoon white pepper

1 teaspoon garlic powder

Pinch of cayenne pepper (optional)

In a bowl, stir together all of the ingredients.

Griddled sea bream.

GRIDDLED WHOLE FISH

Red snapper is excellent cooked whole; so are sea bream, sheephead, and lots of other Gulf fish (see Trash Fish, page 27). Cooking the fish on the griddle is much easier if the fish is covered with a lid as it cooks. Putting a couple of ice cubes under the lid now and then adds some welcome steam.

SERVES 4

1 whole fish, about 3 pounds, cleaned

½ cup olive oil

1 yellow onion, minced

3 tablespoons freshly squeezed lemon juice

2 tablespoons seafood seasoning (page 9)

Ice cubes

Lemon slices, for garnish

Pope's Tartar Sauce (page 7), for serving

Rinse the fish and cut off the gill fins. Using a sharp knife, make 3 vertical slashes about 1½ inches apart on both sides of the fish, cutting all the way to the bone.

In a baking dish, stir together the oil, onion, lemon juice, and seasoning mix. Put the fish in the baking dish and bend it so that the slashes on one side spread open. Spoon the marinade into the slashes. Flip the fish and repeat on the other side.

Preheat a griddle to medium and spray with non-stick cooking spray. Remove the fish from the baking dish and put it on the hot griddle. Tuck a couple of ice cubes near the fish and cover the fish with a pot lid. Cook on one side for 7 minutes. Turn the fish over, add a couple more ice cubes, re-cover, and cook for 7 minutes on the second side. At this point, test the fish for doneness by slipping the tip of a sharp knife between the top fillet and the backbone. If it is still a little raw, transfer it to a roasting pan, place in a 350°F oven, and finish cooking for 5 to 10 minutes longer, or until the fish is done to taste.

Put the whole fish on a platter and garnish with the lemon slices. Carve the fish at the table. The flesh will fall away from the bone easily along the slash lines. Carefully remove any obvious pin bones. Serve with the tartar sauce.

BROILED FISH

Black drum fillets are excellent for broiling. Swordfish, shark, tuna, and other big Gulf fish are good for broiling too, either as fillets or as bone-in steaks. See photo on page 2.

SERVES 4
Juice of 2 limes
1 clove garlic, minced
½ cup seafood seasoning (page 9)
¼ cup vegetable oil
2 pounds fish fillets or steaks
Pope's Tartar Sauce (page 7), for serving

In a good-size shallow bowl, stir together the lime juice, garlic, seasoning mix, and oil. Add the fish and turn to coat evenly on both sides. Let marinate for 15 minutes.

Position an oven rack in the center of the oven, and preheat the broiler.

Transfer the fish to a broiler pan, place under the broiler, and broil, turning once. Plan on 5 minutes per side for a 1-inch-thick fillet or steak and 2½ minutes per side for a ½-inch-thick fillet or steak. Serve at once with the tartar sauce.

RED SNAPPER TOPPED WITH MUSHROOMS AND CRABMEAT

Battered and panfried snapper topped with a buttery seafood sauce is one of the most popular fish dishes on the Texas coast.

SERVES 6
1 egg
1½ cups milk
½ cup fish flour (page 9)
6 (6-ounce) red snapper fillets
¾ cup unsalted butter
2½ cups thinly sliced mushrooms
8 ounces lump crabmeat, picked over for shell fragments

In a shallow bowl, beat the egg until blended. Stir in the milk until combined. Put the flour in a separate shallow bowl. One at a time, dip the fillets into the milk mixture, allowing the excess to drip off, and then dredge in the flour, coating evenly and shaking off the excess. Set aside on a platter.

In a large cast-iron skillet, melt 6 tablespoons of the butter over medium to medium-high heat and heat just until it begins to brown. Add the battered fillets and cook for about 5 minutes, until browned on one side. Turn the fillets over, decrease the heat to medium-low, and cook for about 5 minutes more, until golden brown on the second side. Transfer the fillets to a clean platter and keep warm.

Add the remaining 6 tablespoons butter to the same skillet and melt over medium heat. Add the mushrooms and cook, stirring occasionally, for about 3 minutes, until just tender. Add the crabmeat and turn gently for about 3 minutes, until the crabmeat is warm.

Divide the fillets among 6 dinner plates. Spoon the mushrooms, crabmeat, and butter sauce evenly over the fillets. Serve piping hot.

*Grilled Oysters
on the Half Shell,
page 21.*

Galveston Island oyster roast, 1890.

CHAPTER 2

GALVESTON BAY OYSTERS

O n an April afternoon during the peak of the Gulf oyster season, oysters from a dozen different Galveston Bay oyster reefs were set out side by side at a special event at Tommy's Restaurant and Oyster Bar in Clear Lake. The bivalves were plump and more than three inches long, with perfect shells.

The oysters from Lost Reef and Old Yellow Reef were the fattest and sweetest, but they were a little lacking in saltiness. That makes sense because they come from near the San Jacinto River, where lots of nutrients enter the bay, but far from the opening to the Gulf, where the water is saltiest. The Lady's Pass oysters from the eastern part of the bay, closer to the Gulf, were the briniest. Oysters from Possum Pass in the middle of the bay had a nice balance of sweetness and saltiness. The most beautiful oysters were the Elm Grove Ruffles. Grown in a salty area with a very strong current, their shells develop a frilly curled edge.

When you buy a bag of Texas oysters, you usually get a hundred muddy bivalves in a burlap sack. In most of the rest of the world, oysters are sold by place-names. And when you buy a Blue Point, a Chincoteague, or a Belon, you pay more for the premium place-name.

In the 1800s, Galveston Bay oysters were sold by famous place-names, too. But the reefs were forgotten when Texas oysters became more valuable as substitutes for oysters from

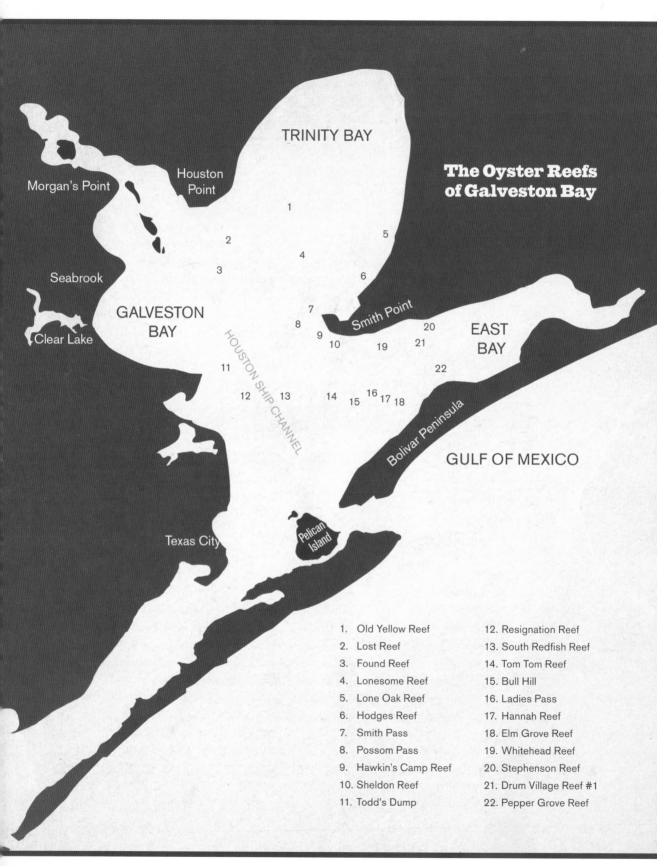

The Oyster Reefs of Galveston Bay

TRINITY BAY

Morgan's Point

Houston Point

Seabrook

GALVESTON BAY

Clear Lake

Smith Point

EAST BAY

HOUSTON SHIP CHANNEL

Bolivar Peninsula

GULF OF MEXICO

Texas City

Pelican Island

1. Old Yellow Reef
2. Lost Reef
3. Found Reef
4. Lonesome Reef
5. Lone Oak Reef
6. Hodges Reef
7. Smith Pass
8. Possom Pass
9. Hawkin's Camp Reef
10. Sheldon Reef
11. Todd's Dump
12. Resignation Reef
13. South Redfish Reef
14. Tom Tom Reef
15. Bull Hill
16. Ladies Pass
17. Hannah Reef
18. Elm Grove Reef
19. Whitehead Reef
20. Stephenson Reef
21. Drum Village Reef #1
22. Pepper Grove Reef

other places. Some three-quarters of the Texas oyster harvest is shipped by tractor-trailer to Virginia, Maryland, Florida, California, and other destinations, where they are never advertised as Texas oysters. But they are often passed off as Blue Points at oyster bars and as Maryland oysters by shucking houses.

The rediscovery of Galveston Bay's most famous oyster reefs began with the chance discovery of a newspaper article that appeared in the *Galveston Daily News* in September 1902. Written by John A. Caplen, the three-thousand-word essay described the whereabouts of Galveston Bay's best oyster reefs and provided a detailed description of the Texas oyster industry of that time. In February 2011, I read excerpts from the article as part of a presentation at the "Gulf Gathering" symposium, hosted by Foodways Texas in Galveston. I also projected a nautical map and pointed out the most popular oyster reefs of the turn of the last century.

At the time of the Civil War, Pepper Grove oysters, from a reef near Marsh Point, were considered the best in Galveston Bay. Elm Grove, Lady's Pass, Possum Pass, and Old Yellow Reef were also famous reef names. Working from old maps, Foodways Texas commissioned the three largest oystering companies in Galveston Bay—Jeri's Seafood, Misho's, and Prestige—to harvest oysters from the old reefs for a special oyster tasting.

An oyster bar with oysters from eight different Galveston Bay reefs was set up at the nearby Gaido's Restaurant following the lecture—probably the first time in one hundred years that Texas oysters were displayed this way. The differences in flavor from reef to reef amazed the oyster lovers present. The oystermen were impressed by how much excitement the tasting created.

In the weeks following, Jeri's Seafood, the Galveston Bay oyster concern with the most local customers, began to market hand-selected oysters from specific reefs to Texas restaurants. Along with the standard muddy burlap sack of one hundred commodity oysters, Jeri's now offers three or four reef-specific oysters to restaurants at a premium price.

And so far the program has been extremely successful. Hopefully, more upscale seafood restaurants will sell Texas oysters by their place-names in the future.

Maybe someday the sophisticated oyster-culturing methods of the nineteenth-century Galveston oystermen will also be revived. According to Caplen's article, "bayou oysters" were the most popular item in Galveston oyster bars of the late 1800s. These were wild oysters from the reefs that were relaid in shell-lined bayous to be fattened. The cultivation system was similar to the fattening done in the famed oyster-growing area near Marennes, France. Relaying Galveston oysters for fattening or to increase salinity could improve the flavor immensely.

Texas lost its sophisticated oyster industry shortly after the arrival of the railroad. Trains made it possible to ship oysters across the country. Texas oysters were substituted for Baltimore oysters and Long Island Blue Points in big-city oyster bars. And they sold for a lot more in Kansas City and St. Louis than they did in Galveston. It was much more profitable to sell oysters as a commodity product out of state than to sell local oysters by place-names or bother with cultivation.

But times have changed. The BP Deepwater Horizon oil spill hurt the Texas oyster industry despite the fact that none of the oil reached Texas. Consumers nationwide lost their confidence in Gulf seafood. Reviving the reef names and selling premium oysters for top dollar may help the Texas oyster industry survive these hard times.

Drawing attention to Texas oysters as a local product may help with political problems, too. Texas lags behind all other oyster-producing states in the return of empty oyster shells to the reefs. The Texas Shell Recovery Program needs a lot more funding. The state is also allowing water diversion from rivers upstream to create dangerously low freshwater flows to Galveston Bay.

Texas has long taken its oysters for granted. Many of the reefs on the old maps are gone now. In the 1800s, cattle ranchers could ford their herds across Galveston Bay at low tide by leading the

animals to walk on top of the oyster reefs. But the reefs were considered a hazard to navigation, so few complaints were heard when large sections of the reefs were removed.

The shells were sold to construction companies that used them to make concrete. Many of the streets and sidewalks of Galveston and Houston are composed of oyster shells that were stripped from Galveston Bay. The dredging was stopped in the 1970s. Today, the Texas Parks and Wildlife Department and the Nature Conservancy are spending millions of dollars to try to create new oyster reefs.

Many Texas consumers are suspicious of the pricier reef-specific oysters, so they will always be a niche market. Texans are used to paying ten bucks for a dozen Gulf oysters, and many have no desire to pay more for what they consider the same oysters in a different package. That means that commodity

oysters will continue to be the biggest segment of the half-shell business.

But there is more to this new oyster marketing than resorting the sacks. Currently, the largest select oysters harvested in Texas are being shucked and sold to restaurants for fried oysters and oyster gumbo. Shucked oysters are selling for as much as sixty dollars a gallon. The burlap sacks that go to the half-shell market are filled with undersized oysters that are too small to shuck. Many oyster eaters prefer the tiny oysters, but savvy oyster lovers prefer bigger ones.

Oysters that measure three to four inches are far more flavorful than the immature two-inch oysters currently found on the half-shell market. Creating a market for hand-selected premium oysters sold by place-names gives Texas oystermen an incentive to make their best oysters available to oyster bars. And I, for one, am willing to pay for better bivalves.

EATING OYSTERS IN MONTHS WITHOUT AN *R*

★ ★

I LEARNED A LOT about oysters from Dr. Sammy Ray, a marine biologist I contacted when I was working on an earlier book, *Sex, Death & Oysters*. The most important thing I learned was that oysters have a life cycle. This information proved to be the key to understanding the flavor of oysters, the months without an *r* logic, oyster lore, and the timing of the world's oyster festivals.

The season of the oyster goes roughly like this: In the fall or early winter, cold weather and falling water temperatures cause oysters to begin storing a carbohydrate compound called glycogen. To humans, glycogen tastes like sugar. As glycogen accumulates, oysters get plumper and taste sweeter. That's why eating oysters has always been associated with the midwinter holiday season.

In the Gulf, as the weather gets colder, the oysters keep tasting better, reaching their peak around Valentine's Day. In colder northern climates, glycogen production sometimes slows down in the coldest part of the winter, as food sources become scarce in the frigid waters. Hence, Washington State and Canadian oysters taste better in the "shoulder seasons" of late spring or late fall.

At the onset of warmer water temperatures, oysters begin to convert glycogen to reproductive material, known as gonad. As the season progresses, the oyster begins to lose its sweetness and becomes "fishy" tasting. It's not an unpleasant flavor—in fact, many oyster lovers like it—but it isn't sweet. As the oyster prepares to spawn, a milky white substance begins to form on it. It doesn't make the oyster dangerous to eat. But the flavor and texture of spawning oysters does make them "hard to swallow."

Sometime in the summer, when the water reaches a certain level of warmth, the oysters will spawn. The wild oysters of the Galveston Bay secrete sperm and eggs into the water, producing hundreds of millions of larvae. When summer ends and the water begins to cool in autumn, the cycle starts over again.

Once upon a time, you found oysters on the market in the winter and tomatoes in the summer. Today, both are available all year long. But it is important to remember that they are still seasonal foods. You can eat winter tomatoes and summer oysters if you want, but they certainly won't taste their best. Coincidently, summer is also when Gulf oysters contain the highest levels of *Vibrio vulnificus*, a naturally occurring bacteria that is, on very rare occasions, lethal. Because oysters were only harvested and transported in cold weather in the 1800s, *V. vulnificus* wasn't a problem. But today, leaseholders sell Gulf oysters year-round.

Where does an enlightened food lover draw the risk-and-reward line when it comes to raw Gulf Coast oysters? I once asked Gary Heideman, at the Seafood Safety Desk of the Texas Department of Health, for his advice. He explained that when the water temperature is below 65 degrees, little or no *V. vulnificus* is detectable. In Texas, the water temperature stays below 65 degrees from about December until April. (You can check the exact temperature in the marine forecast section of a weather website.) As it works out, Gulf oysters are the safest to eat during the same period that they taste the best. The Karankawa tribe had this figured out back in the 1500s. They lived on the barrier islands and ate almost nothing but oysters from January until April. Then, as soon as the dewberries ripened, they moved inland.

Following the example of the Karankawa, I eat raw Gulf oysters in the winter when the glycogen makes them sweet and the bacteria is scarce. And in the late spring, I switch over to Texas foods that have their peak season in warm weather, like dewberries, homegrown tomatoes, and blue crabs.

IN HIS OWN WORDS: MISHO IVIC

★ ★

I BECAME AN OYSTERMAN BY ACCIDENT. I was born in Zagreb, in what was then Yugoslavia, in 1950, and my father was a professor. He wasn't a communist, and the communists made his life miserable. He told me to get the hell out of the country. I was infatuated with America. I studied mechanical engineering in college and emigrated in 1972, when I was twenty-two. I got a job in Empire, Louisiana, as a deck hand on an oyster boat called the *Salona*, named after a town on the Dalmatian coast. I was paid twenty dollars a day.

In 1973, I bought my own oyster boat. I bought my first oyster lease in Galveston Bay in 1977. When you buy a new lease, you are buying mud. There are no oysters until you build a bottom with shells. I got a chance to buy out another guy's leases. They were very expensive, but it's a lot easier because there are already oysters.

How Croatians got into the Gulf oyster business is a long story. A group of Croatians came over to America for the California gold rush. There was no Panama Canal, so they landed in New Orleans. They didn't hit gold in California; they were too late. So they went back to New Orleans and started the Croatian oyster fleet.

A lot of the oystermen who came to join them kept their families in Croatia and lived on the boats while they worked. It's very normal for a Croatian fisherman to have a house and family in Croatia and work somewhere else. It's still like that. I have a house in Trpanj, and my wife and children go there in May and

Misho Ivic: Founder, Misho's Oyster Company, San Leon.

stay until the end of August. I go over and visit for a few weeks every year.

I eat between a dozen and sixty oysters every day. I ride a speedboat around and check all my boats—like a shepherd watching his flock. I eat a few oysters on each boat to see how they are.

What am I looking for? I like to see a lot of dark purple on the inside of the shell. That means the oyster is absorbing minerals. The perfect oyster grows between freshwater and saltwater. Oysters get fatter and sweeter as the water gets colder. January to April they are sweetest; in mid-May, they spawn and get a lot smaller.

I am the second largest shipper and the second largest processor of oysters in Texas. The state exports three to four times as many oysters as the residents consume. We ship to Florida, Virginia, and Maryland, and maybe 10 percent to California. The largest shipper in Texas is the Halilli family (Prestige Oysters), from Kosovo, another Adriatic country. The largest processor is the Nelson family (Jeri's Seafood), descendants of a Norwegian seaman.

Four of my six kids are in the oyster business. One of my daughters married a Croatian oysterman. Hurricane Ike really messed up the oysters by dumping silt and debris on them, so we are spending a lot of money to clean up. Rebuilding the oyster reefs in Galveston Bay isn't going to help me. This is for my children and my grandchildren.

JON ROWLEY'S WASHTUB OYSTER BAR

Seattle oyster entrepreneur Jon Rowley spends a lot of time shucking oysters at parties and praising their attributes. He came up with this excellent setup for a portable oyster bar, and I use it for oyster shindigs in my backyard. You need a small galvanized washtub and a soup pot. The shaved ice isn't necessary, but it sure looks good. Your local grocery store probably uses shaved ice in its seafood display. Ask the clerk in advance to set some aside for the appointed day.

YIELDS ABOUT 8 DOZEN OYSTERS

3 (10-pound) bags ice cubes
1 (10-pound) bag shaved ice or crushed ice
100 best-quality Galveston Bay oysters in the shell
6 lemons, cut into wedges

French Style

2 loaves caraway rye bread, thinly sliced
1 pound top-quality unsalted butter
Fleur de sel (the best French sea salt) or other sea salt
Plenty of good wine

Gulf Style

A couple of boxes of saltine crackers
Tabasco sauce
Cocktail sauce
Plenty of cold beer

Wash out a small galvanized tub and drain well. Turn a soup pot upside down in the bottom of the tub. This cuts down on the amount of ice required and the overall weight. Set the tub up so the top is at counter height. That's so you can display the oysters where people can see them. Fill the tub up with the big ice cubes to cover the soup pot, then cover the ice cubes with a layer of shaved ice. Shuck the oysters as people eat them. You don't want to shuck too far in advance because oysters are always best freshly opened.

Provide your guests with plates, oyster forks or toothpicks, napkins, and a place to dump the shells. Beyond that, you can make your oyster party as casual or as elegant as you like. I like to set up my oyster bar outside, with a nicely set picnic table nearby. Oysters taste great outdoors in cool weather.

For a French-style affair, put the lemon wedges in a bowl and place the bowl in the middle of the table along with a plate of rye bread and some premium butter and sea salt. Each diner should spread the rye bread with butter, sprinkle it with salt, and then eat it along with the oysters. Pour your favorite oyster wines.

For a Gulf-style party, substitute saltines for the rye bread, Tabasco for the butter, cocktail sauce for the sea salt, and cold *cerveza* for the wine.

GRAPEFRUIT OYSTER COCKTAIL

This is a classic recipe adapted from Fannie Farmer's 1918 *Boston Cooking-School Cook Book*. It's perfect with Texas red grapefruit.

MAKES 12 SHOOTERS

1 Texas red grapefruit
Freshly squeezed lemon juice
Tabasco sauce
Salt
12 oysters, freshly shucked, with liquor reserved

Section the grapefruit over a bowl to catch the juice. Combine the grapefruit juice and lemon juice and strain, then add the Tabasco and salt. Place 1 oyster and its liquor and 1 grapefruit section in each of 12 chilled glasses, then divide the juice mixture evenly among the glasses.

COCTELE DE OSTIONES (MEXICAN OYSTER COCKTAIL)

Cocteles, or seafood cocktails, are a favorite Texan way to eat oysters, either by themselves or mixed with shrimp and/or other seafood. This version features the traditional cocktail sauce of ketchup and lime juice.

SERVES 1

6 small oysters, freshly shucked, with liquor reserved
6 drops Tabasco sauce
1 tablespoon ketchup
1 tablespoon freshly squeezed lime juice
Salt
1 tablespoon finely diced avocado
1 teaspoon finely chopped red onion
1 teaspoon chopped fresh cilantro
Saltines or tortilla chips, for serving

Put a parfait glass in the freezer for at least 1 hour or up to overnight.

In a bowl, toss together the oysters and their liquor, Tabasco, ketchup, lime juice, and a little salt. Put the mixture in the chilled parfait glass. Top with the avocado, onion, and cilantro. Serve immediately with saltines or tortilla chips.

TEXAS BLUE POINTS

"On the Mexican Gulf, they [oysters] are definitely better cooked, although skilled gourmets have insisted otherwise to me, and one man from Corpus Christi once put his gun on the table while he stated quietly that anybody who said Texas blue points weren't the best anywhere was more than one kind of insulting liar."

—M. F. Fisher, *Consider the Oyster*

OYSTERS À LA BRYAN

Like the oyster cocktail on page 19, this recipe is adapted from a recipe in Fannie Farmer's 1918 *Boston Cooking-School Cook Book*. The original called for a Sauternes, but I have substituted Muscat Canelli dessert wine. Messina Hof Vineyards in Bryan, a town just a few miles from the main campus of Texas A&M, bottles a late-harvest Muscat Canelli that is excellent in the recipe.

SERVES 2

12 small oysters, freshly shucked and on the half shell
1 clove garlic, peeled but left whole
1 tablespoon unsalted butter, melted
1 teaspoon freshly squeezed lemon juice
1 teaspoon Muscat Canelli or other sweet white dessert wine
Several drops Tabasco sauce
Salt
Paprika, for seasoning
Finely chopped fresh parsley, for garnish

Preheat the oven to 350°F. Arrange the oysters in a roasting pan.

While the oven is heating, rub a small bowl with the garlic clove and discard the clove. Add the butter, lemon juice, wine, and Tabasco to the bowl and stir to mix.

Bake the oysters for about 10 minutes, or until the edges curl. Remove from the oven, divide the oysters between 2 plates, and spoon the butter sauce over the top. Season the oysters with a little salt and paprika and garnish with the parsley. Serve at once.

SCALLOPED OYSTERS

Texans love their Thanksgiving turkey served with oyster stuffing. This baked oyster dish is like an oyster stuffing without the turkey. It reminds me of oysters Mosca at Mosca's Restaurant in New Orleans. I have never been able to replicate Mosca's oysters, but I'll settle for these.

SERVES 2 OR 3

1 cup cracker crumbs
½ cup dried bread crumbs
½ cup unsalted butter, melted
1 pint shucked oysters, drained, with
**   4 tablespoons liquor reserved**
Salt and pepper
Several drops Tabasco sauce
Sherry, for seasoning (optional)
2 tablespoons milk or heavy cream

Preheat the oven to a 350°F. Butter an 8-inch square baking dish.

In a bowl, stir together the cracker and bread crumbs, then stir in the butter. Put one-third of the crumb mixture in the bottom of the prepared baking dish. Arrange half of the oysters in a single layer on top and season them with salt and pepper, a few drops of Tabasco, and a little sherry. Sprinkle evenly with 1 tablespoon of the milk and 2 tablespoons of the reserved oyster liquor. Cover with half of the remaining crumb mixture. Layer the remaining oysters on top, then season with salt, pepper, Tabasco, and sherry as before. Sprinkle evenly with the remaining 1 tablespoon milk and 2 tablespoons liquor, then cover evenly with the remaining crumb mixture. (Do not make more than 2 layers or the oysters won't cook through.)

Bake for 20 to 30 minutes, until the mixture begins to bubble. Serve hot.

GRILLED OYSTERS ON THE HALF SHELL

You want a little of the butter to spill onto the fire so that it will flare up and char the oyster shells. See photo on page 12.

SERVES 6

1 cup unsalted butter, melted
2 tablespoons chopped garlic
1 teaspoon salt
1 teaspoon pepper
36 oysters in the shell
Grated Parmesan cheese, for garnish
Chopped fresh parsley, for garnish

Prepare a hot fire for direct-heat grilling in a charcoal or gas grill.

In a small saucepan, melt the butter over medium heat, being careful not to let it brown. Stir in the garlic, salt, and pepper, then remove from the heat. (This can be done on the grill.)

You can shuck the oysters, leaving them on the half shell. Or, you can put the unshucked oysters on the grill grate, and when the shells pop open, remove the top shell from each oyster. Spoon the butter mixture evenly over the oyster meats and grill for 3 to 5 minutes, until cooked through. Transfer to platters and sprinkle with a little Parmesan and parsley. Serve at once.

Mrs. Thomas McCrary of San Antonio samples an oyster from the first shipment of the season in 1926.

KING'S INN FRIED OYSTERS

Try to fry oysters that are all the same size. That way they all get done at the same time. Many people like their oysters well done, but I like mine moist and gooey. If you are making fried oyster po'boys or oyster nachos, moister oysters will yield a better overall texture. Fry up a batch of French fries to serve alongside.

SERVES 2
Peanut oil, for deep-frying
1 teaspoon salt
1 teaspoon black pepper
Pinch of cayenne pepper
1 cup fish flour (page 9)
1 pint shucked oysters
Pope's Tartar Sauce (page 7), for serving

Pour the oil to a depth of about 1 inch into a heavy pot or fill a deep fryer and heat to 375°F.

While the oil is heating, in a small bowl or cup, stir together the salt, black pepper, and cayenne pepper. Put the fish flour in a small, shallow bowl. Drain off most of the liquor from the oysters, then pour the oysters and the remaining liquor into a bowl. Season the oysters, a handful at a time, with the salt mixture. Then toss the oysters, a few at a time, in the flour, turning them to coat well and then shaking them in a colander to remove the excess flour.

Working in small batches, drop the oysters into the hot oil and fry for 3 to 5 minutes, until golden brown and done to your taste. Using a slotted spoon, transfer to paper towels to drain briefly and keep in a warm oven until serving. Serve hot with the tartar sauce.

King's Inn Fried Shrimp: Substitute ½ pound of large shrimp for the oysters. Shell and devein the shrimp, leaving the tail intact, then proceed as directed. Cook for 3 to 5 minutes, or until the shrimp begin to curl.

FRIED OYSTER NACHOS

Oyster nachos were invented by Austin chef David Garrido, whose recipe first appeared in the 1995 cookbook we coauthored, *Nuevo Tex-Mex.*

MAKES 12 NACHOS
Peanut oil, for frying
About 1 cup buttermilk
1 cup fish flour (page 9)
12 oysters, freshly shucked
½ cup favorite salsa
12 large tortilla chips, preferably round

Pour the oil to a depth of 1 inch into a small skillet and heat to 375°F.

While the oil is heating, pour the buttermilk into a small, shallow bowl and put the fish flour in a second small, shallow bowl. One at a time, dunk the oysters in the buttermilk, allowing the excess to drip off, then dredge them in the flour, coating evenly and shaking off the excess.

Working in small batches, add the oysters to the hot oil and fry for 45 seconds to 1 minute, until lightly browned. Using a slotted spoon, transfer to paper towels to drain briefly.

Put 2 teaspoons salsa on each tortilla chip, then top with a fried oyster. Serve immediately.

OYSTERS ROCKEFELLER

Oysters Rockefeller are made with spinach in Texas, not the more traditional watercress or parsley. You can make them spicier by adding a little minced serrano or chile pequin if you like.

SERVES 6

36 oysters in the shell
6 tablespoons unsalted butter
6 tablespoons finely minced spinach
3 tablespoons finely minced yellow onion
3 tablespoons finely minced fresh parsley, plus
    sprigs for garnish
5 tablespoons dried bread crumbs
Tabasco sauce, for serving
½ teaspoon Pernod
½ teaspoon salt
Rock salt, for lining plates
Lemon wedges, for garnish

Using an oyster knife, pry open the oysters, discarding the top shells and putting the meats and their liquor in a bowl. Scrub and dry the bottom shells and set aside. Drain the oysters, reserving the oyster liquor, then set the oysters and liquor aside separately.

In a medium saucepan, melt the butter over medium heat. Add the spinach, onion, parsley, bread crumbs, Tabasco, Pernod, and salt and cook, stirring constantly, for 15 minutes, until the onions are soft. Remove from the heat, transfer to a food processor, and process until smooth. Let cool completely. (The spinach mixture may be made up to 3 days ahead. Cover and refrigerate until ready to use.)

Preheat the broiler. Line 6 ovenproof individual serving dishes with rock salt, layering it about 1 inch deep. Very lightly moisten the salt. Nest 6 oyster shells in the rock salt in each dish, making sure they are level, and place an oyster meat in each shell. Spoon a little of the reserved oyster liquor over each oyster. Spoon an equal amount of the prepared spinach mixture over each oyster and spread to the rim of the shell.

Broil the oysters for about 5 minutes, until their edges have curled and the topping is bubbling. Watch carefully. Garnish the plates with the parsley sprigs and the lemon wedges and serve immediately.

OYSTER STEW

In Texas, oyster stew is a bowl of oysters with a little milk, not a bowl of milk with a couple of oysters.

SERVES 1

1 pint shucked oysters and their liquor
½ cup water
½ teaspoon sea salt
½ teaspoon black pepper
Pinch of cayenne pepper
½ cup milk or half-and-half
2 tablespoons unsalted butter, cut into pieces,
    plus 1 pat
Tabasco sauce, for serving
Soda crackers, for serving

Pour the oysters and their liquor and the water into a small pot. Season with the salt, black pepper, and cayenne pepper. Place over medium heat and bring almost to a boil. Lower the heat to a simmer and cook until the edges of the oysters curl. Add the milk and heat until steaming hot. Do not allow to boil. Stir in the 2 tablespoons butter.

Pour the stew into a soup bowl and top with the butter pat. Enjoy piping hot. Season with Tabasco. As you eat the stew, crumble soda crackers into the bowl.

U-Shell-Em Mojo de Ajo Shrimp, page 30.

CHAPTER 3
ON A SHRIMP BOAT

★★★★★★★★★★★★★★★★★★★★★★★★★★★★★★★★★

One May morning at five o'clock, I kept an appointment to meet a shrimper named Dale Lee at the Port Aransas Municipal Harbor. I climbed aboard his thirty-five-foot shrimp trawler, *Cindy Lee*, in the predawn and we motored out to get into position for the opening of another day in the bay shrimping season. We were surrounded by other shrimp boats cruising in circles and waiting for six o'clock to drop their nets.

Dragging the East Flats of Corpus Christi Bay as the sun rose was a peaceful way to wake up. The only activity came as the nets were raised every hour or so and emptied onto the deck. It was a fascinating thing to see: piles of living seafood writhing and wet, glistening in the early light. The shrimp were mixed with seaweed, crabs, baby flounder, baby red snapper, moray eels, ribbon fish, and squid. The bycatch, as the stuff that isn't shrimp is known, is shoved overboard as the shrimp are sorted out. I grabbed a plastic laundry basket and, with Dale's permission, filled it with crabs before they were gone.

Fresh shrimp became an obsession of mine after trying to make the recipes in Paul Prudhomme's cookbooks. I was living in Austin at the time and couldn't find any fresh shrimp in the supermarkets, so I started buying them from the trucks that came up from the coast and parked at busy intersections in Austin on Saturday mornings. Sometimes they showed up and sometimes they didn't. The truckers told me they bought their product directly from shrimpers down in Port Aransas. My family often went to Aransas Pass and Mustang Island for beach weekends, so I tracked down the shrimp boats and made friends. I persuaded Dale Lee to let me go along for the ride and take some photos.

Fresh shrimp is hard to count on because when Texas shrimp boats go out in the Gulf, they stay away for three or four days. Many head for the Bay of Campeche in Mexico, and they freeze the shrimp on board. But during the bay shrimping season, shrimpers work the nearby bays and return with fresh shrimp every morning. The season runs on and off from May to October, with opening and closing days for Texas waters determined by authorities at Texas Parks and Wildlife. They drag test nets and determine the season by their samplings.

Boat owners like Dale Lee secure the licenses, deal with the game wardens, and hire crews to sort the shrimp. The deckhands sit amid the catch while seagulls buzz their heads, crabs pinch their fingers, and the shrimp shells puncture their skin. The day I went out, two of the deckhands were women from Michigan. One woman had gotten tired of her data-entry job and decided to extend her vacation to the Texas coast. The other woman, her sister, had been at it longer and was fighting a case of seafood poisoning that caused her hands to swell. They said they loved the work, but when I asked about shrimp recipes, the veteran sister gave me the finger down the throat signal for don't make me sick and the data-entry clerk nodded in agreement. After sorting shrimp all day, they eat pepperoni pizza.

Texans like brown shrimp and most of the catch is sold in the state. Brown shrimp (*Penaeus aztecus*) have a bold marine flavor, which some say tastes like iodine. (It's actually bromine, a flavor that comes from the wild kelp that the brown shrimp often feed on.) Elsewhere, consumers prefer the mild white shrimp (*P. setiferus*). White shrimp are often farmed. Both species are found in the bays during their respective seasons.

★ ★ ★

The earliest mention of shrimp fishing in the Gulf comes from the book *L'Histoire de la Louisiane*, by French explorer and naturalist Antoine-Simon Le Page du Pratz. He lived in Louisiana on and off from 1718 to 1734, and wrote about fishermen near New Orleans who used imported French throw nets to catch shrimp.

For a long time, shrimp was sold alongside oysters, crabs, and finfish in Galveston seafood markets. But the economics of shrimp fishing began to change when the Chinese introduced drying platforms in the late 1800s. Dried shrimp was a valuable commodity in Asia, and Gulf fisherman began drying shrimp to sell abroad. In 1880, an improvement in can liners made canning shrimp possible, and for the first time, shrimping became a major industry on the Gulf.

Early sailboats adapted to shrimping in the area followed the example of the Mediterranean *canot*, built with a centerboard. The Croatians probably introduced the lugger, a fishing boat with one huge forward sail called a lugsail. Both boats could operate in the shallow water of the bays and estuaries. When diesel engines were adapted to shrimp boats, it became possible for shrimpers to go out into international waters and stay out for several days. Today, there are two different classes of shrimpers and two different kinds of shrimp permits issued by Texas Parks and Wildlife.

Vessels of the Gulf shrimp fleet are typically steel-hulled craft between fifty-five and sixty-five feet. They are designed with living quarters and galleys and stay out for several days. Some are equipped with IQF (individual quick freezing) technology so shrimp can be carefully frozen and then stored in freezers on board. Bay shrimping licenses are issued to small boats like the *Cindy Lee* to fish in local bay waters. These boats go out in the morning and return within a few hours with fresh shrimp for the bait industry and seafood markets. Most of the boats in the bay shrimp fleet are between eighteen and forty feet.

TRASH FISH

★ ★

TYPICALLY, TWO-THIRDS of what winds up in the nets of a shrimp boat isn't shrimp. After the shrimp is sorted out, the bycatch, a wriggling mélange of finfish, crabs, and other creatures, is shoved off the back of the boat, where a flock of gulls waits to feed.

Bycatch is what fishermen call the sealife they don't set out to harvest. The commercial potential of utilizing the bycatch inspired P. J. Stoops to become a new kind of fishmonger. He got the idea after working in restaurants in the south of France and in Thailand. When he came home to Lake Jackson, Texas, a few years ago, he realized that some of what Gulf fishermen, oystermen, and shrimpers were throwing overboard was considered top-dollar seafood in the rest of the world. Chefs were paying high prices for imported white anchovies, for instance, while Texas shrimpers were shoving them back into the water.

P. J. Stoops and Bryan Caswell.

Stoops started asking boat captains to sell him some of the stuff that they would otherwise discard. Then he delivered the goods to interested chefs and farmers' market customers. He modeled his operation after a friend's artisanal poultry-farming business. If chefs were looking for unusual birds, like guinea fowl, squab, and partridge, why not offer them unusual fish, too, he reasoned. Stoops described his operation as an "artisanal fishery" business.

"Once the Vietnamese got into the shrimping business, the attitude about bycatch changed," Stoops says. "There is a lot less being thrown overboard now. But the Vietnamese fishermen aren't bringing the fish to the market. They are taking them home for dinner."

Boats that fish for snapper use rigs with lots of baited hooks. Along with the snapper, they catch other kinds of fish, like triggerfish, almaco jack, and porgy—all very tasty but in little demand in the local seafood business. These fish were all thrown back until P. J. Stoops started buying some.

At the Foodways Texas "Gulf Gathering" symposium in Galveston (see page 15), Stoops told the audience, "The Gulf of Mexico is the second most productive fishery in the world. But the way we eat seafood is not sustainable. We need to change our harvesting methods and stop throwing so much away. There is somebody interested in eating nearly everything caught in a fishing boat."

To demonstrate the point, Houston chef Chris Shepherd served the sea snails variously known as oyster drills, biganos, or whelks at the symposium lunch. Gulf oystermen find these miniature conchs in their dredges whenever there is a rise in the salinity level of the water. They are known as oyster drills because they bore into the shells of oysters and suck out the meat. In France, these same sea snails are often featured in the seafood assortments known as *plateaux de fruits de mer*.

Not surprisingly, the oystermen who used to throw oyster drills in the parking lot to kill them were delighted to find out that chefs were willing to pay for them. Braised until tender and then broiled in garlic butter in an escargot dish, Gulf whelks are tastier and a lot more interesting than the imported canned land snails usually served in restaurants.

Houston chef Bryan Caswell has been promoting underutilized Gulf fish for several years at Reef, his award-winning seafood restaurant. And he is not alone in using what was once discarded. Lots of cheap Gulf bycatch is being transformed Cinderella-like into rare and exotic seafood dishes by local chefs. For example, the baby squid that turn up in shrimpers' nets are tiny and difficult to clean, but a little patience yields a stunning appetizer of flash-fried baby squid tossed with minced garlic and chopped parsley. And Chris Shepherd has come up with a ceviche that uses both the catch—shrimp—and the bycatch (see page 29).

* * *

Before noon, Dale Lee limited out at 600 pounds of bay shrimp, which he would sell to the fresh shrimp houses at Aransas Pass for one dollar a pound, ungraded. Most of it would be sold for bait. Taking a full 600 pounds is not an everyday occurrence. One-third to one-half of that is the average, Dale said. One day in the previous week, the game warden had met Dale at the dock and weighed his catch. He had 609 pounds on board, and the warden ordered the entire catch seized. After several hours of pleading and cajoling, Dale convinced the warden that 9 pounds was too slight an infraction to impound his whole catch. He left operating under a warning.

On another morning, someone sabotaged Dale's nets. Some tension still exists between the Vietnamese and the crews of Cajun boats. The Vietnamese began to move into the business in the 1970s, after the fall of Saigon. Many of the Vietnamese who immigrated to the United States were employed in the seafood business in Vietnam, and they gravitated to the Gulf Coast to take up fishing. A lot of ugliness ensued for a while, with shrimpers vandalizing one another's boats. But Dale concluded that this time it was probably just an envious fellow shrimper who cut his nets.

The shrimp business looks easier than it is, he said, so lots of people get into it and then get pissed off because they don't catch much shrimp. Dale Lee has spent his whole life on the water. He used to be a crabber, and he bought his shrimp boat with money he made selling crabs. Like a seasoned hunter, he knows where the game is and he bags his limit more often than the novices. As a result, he is respected and resented.

Frozen shrimp is big business, and you can buy it any time of the year. Fresh Texas shrimp is a seasonal treat like homegrown tomatoes or corn on the cob. Sometimes you can get it, sometimes you can't. Be sure and take advantage of it when you see it.

In shrimp ports like Brownsville and Port Aransas, you'll find lots of seafood stores that sell fresh shrimp. In Rockport, the shrimp boats sell directly to consumers on the dock. In Old Seabrook, south of Houston, you can buy fresh shrimp from the Vietnamese seafood shacks for unbelievably cheap prices. "The secret to buying fresh shrimp is to remember that it turns black as it gets old," advises Dale Lee. "If you see heads-on fresh shrimp with loose heads that are turning black, don't buy it."

An Asian stir-fry, French bouillabasse, Italian American cioppino, and Cajun gumbo all taste better made with fresh shrimp. After shelling the shrimp, use the shells and heads to make a stock (see page 32). The heads contain an orange fat that is the most flavorful part of the crustacean.

CATCH AND BYCATCH CEVICHE

Houston chef Chris Shepherd recommends this tart ceviche with tortilla chips and cold beer on a hot summer day.

SERVES 12 AS AN APPETIZER

4 cups water

2 tablespoons salt

1 pound shrimp, peeled and deveined

2 pounds triggerfish, vermilion snapper, or
    other firm bycatch fish fillets

½ cup freshly squeezed lime juice

¼ cup freshly squeezed orange juice

1 tomato, diced

1 small red onion, diced

1 small bunch cilantro, chopped

1 small jalapeño chile, seeded and minced

Pepper

In a saucepan, combine the water and salt and bring to a simmer over medium-high heat. Add the shrimp and poach for about 2 minutes, just until they turn pink. Drain and refrigerate.

Cut the fish fillets into ¼-inch squares and place in a bowl. Add the citrus juices, cover, and refrigerate for 1 hour. Add the shrimp, tomato, onion, cilantro, and chile and stir to combine. Re-cover and refrigerate for another 45 minutes.

Season the ceviche with salt and pepper and serve chilled.

SHRIMP BOIL

Bowls of rémoulade and melted butter and bottles of hot sauce are traditional accompaniments to a shrimp boil—along with lots of cold beer.

SERVES 4 TO 6

8 cups water

1 cup crawfish or shrimp boil spice mix
    (page 56)

12 small red potatoes

4 ears corn, husked, silks removed, and snapped
    in half

2½ pounds shrimp in the shell

In a large pot, bring the water to a boil over high heat. Reduce the heat to medium, then add the spice mix, potatoes, and corn and cook for 15 minutes, until nearly done. Add the shrimp and cook for about 3 to 5 minutes, until they just begin to curl.

Drain the shrimp and vegetables. Serve them in a pile on trays or on newspaper in the middle of a picnic table. Let each diner peel his own shrimp.

Note: If you are cooking boiled shrimp for other uses, such as Pickled Shrimp (page 30), omit the potatoes and corn.

PICKLED SHRIMP

The first time I ever ate pickled shrimp, they were served in half-pint Mason jars with a little of the pickling liquid and some of the onions. You fished the shrimp out of the jar and ate them with a romaine and tomato salad. A friend of mine has a kumquat tree, so I get a free bag of kumquats every year and I pickle most of them. Pickled shrimp and pickled kumquat slices are a wonderful way to dress up a salad. Or, serve the shrimp as an appetizer.

MAKES 1½ QUARTS

2½ pounds shrimp

2 sweet onions (such as Texas 1015, Vidalia, or
    Maui), thinly sliced

3 cloves garlic, minced

1 tablespoon peppercorns

1 teaspoon celery seeds

1 teaspoon dill seeds

1 teaspoon mustard seeds

½ teaspoon powdered ginger

1 teaspoon sugar

1 teaspoon salt

2 bay leaves

1 cup cider vinegar

1 cup distilled white vinegar, or more if needed

3 tablespoons freshly squeezed lime juice

Boil the shrimp as directed in Shrimp Boil (page 29), omitting the potatoes and corn. Drain and cool, then peel the shrimp, leaving the tail segments intact.

In a large glass jar (1½ quarts) or 2 smaller jars, layer the cooked shrimp and onion slices, seasoning each layer with some of the garlic, peppercorns, celery seeds, dill seeds, mustard seeds, ginger, sugar, salt, and bay. (If using 2 jars, put 1 bay leaf in each jar.) Fill the jar(s) no more than about two-thirds full. Try to make at least 3 layers each of shrimp and onions. Combine the vinegars, lime juice, and any remaining seasonings, and pour the mixture over the layered shrimp and onions. The jar(s) should be nearly full.

Top with more white vinegar, if needed. Leave a little headspace so you can shake the contents of the jar(s).

Tightly cover the jar(s) and refrigerate for at least 48 hours before eating, shaking the jar(s) once a day. The shrimp will keep for up to 2 weeks. Serve chilled.

U-SHELL-EM MOJO DE AJO SHRIMP

For those summer days when it's too hot to spend more than a few minutes cooking, here's a lazy way to use shrimp at home or in the kitchen of your beachfront condo. This recipe is a cross between shrimp with *mojo de ajo* (sour orange and garlic sauce) and a peppery barbecued shrimp. It takes less than ten minutes to cook and serves three or four normal people or two guys like me. Accompany with crusty bread for sopping up the sauce and a green salad. See photo on page 24.

SERVES 3 OR 4

3 tablespoons olive ol

4 cloves garlic, crushed or minced

1 big unseeded jalapeño chile, minced

2 pounds head-on shrimp

Juice of 1 orange

Juice of 1 lime

Salt and pepper

In a large skillet, heat the oil over medium-high heat. Add the garlic and chile and sauté for about 45 seconds. Toss in the shrimp and sauté quickly for 2 to 3 minutes, until opaque. Squeeze or pour the orange juice and lime juice over the shrimp and cover the pan. Simmer for 3 or 4 minutes, until the shrimp just begin to curl. Do not overcook!

To serve, put the shrimp in a serving bowl with the pan sauce. Everyone spoons the shrimp and some of the sauce onto a plate and then peels and eats them. Don't forget to suck the heads. Diners can season the sauce with salt and pepper.

SHRIMP STOCK

Never throw away raw shrimp shells. They make a flavorful stock that you can use in soups, stews, grits, and all kinds of sauces. As you chop the vegetables for your soup, gumbo, or étouffée, toss the trimmings into the pot with the shells for flavor. If you want to adjust the yield here, figure on 1 cup water for every batch of shells from 1 pound of shrimp. I keep this stock in the freezer so I can make a small batch of gumbo at the drop of a hat.

MAKES 4 CUPS
4 cups water
Heads and shells from 4 pounds raw shrimp
Vegetable trimmings (see headnote)

In a stockpot, combine the water, heads, shells, and vegetable trimmings and bring to a boil over high heat. Lower the heat to a simmer. Cook for 20 or 30 minutes to extract the flavor.

Remove from the heat and strain through a fine-mesh sieve several times to remove any tiny shell or other bits. Use immediately, or let cool, cover, and refrigerate for up to a week or freeze for up to 3 months.

CORN AND SHRIMP CHOWDER

The sweetness of the corn and the creaminess of this soup are a wonderful foil for the bold iodine flavor of Texas brown shrimp. I once caught the cook at a Cajun restaurant sprinkling a packet of sugar into my bowl of corn and shrimp chowder to brighten the sweet flavor of the corn. It's a neat trick.

SERVES 8
4 pounds heads-on shrimp
½ cup unsalted butter
½ cup chopped green onions (white and green parts), plus more for garnish
½ cup chopped celery
½ cup chopped green bell peppers
½ cup chopped fresh parsley
1½ cups fresh corn kernels
1 (17-ounce) can creamed corn
½ teaspoon Worcestershire sauce
Pinch of ground nutmeg
Salt and pepper

Peel and devein the shrimp, then make the stock from the heads and shells as directed at left. Set the 4 cups stock aside.

In a Dutch oven or other heavy pot, melt the butter over medium heat. Add the green onions, celery, bell peppers, and parsley and cook, stirring, for about 5 minutes, until the vegetables are soft. Reduce the heat to low, add the corn kernels, creamed corn, Worcestershire sauce, and nutmeg, and stir to combine. Add the stock, bring to a simmer, and cook for 10 to 15 minutes, until thickened.

Stir in the shrimp and cook for a few minutes, until they turn translucent and begin to curl. Season with salt and pepper. Serve immediately, garnished with green onions.

SHRIMP BISQUE

In 1911, a twenty-four-year-old restaurant owner named San Jacinto Gaido opened Gaido's Seafood Café on Murdock's Bathhouse pier, in Galveston. It operated there continuously until Gaido passed away in the summer of 1939. In the 1940s, Gaido's son Mike opened the current Gaido's Seafood Restaurant at Thirty-ninth and Seawall in Galveston. Thanks to a succession of talented African American chefs schooled in the Louisiana Creole tradition, Gaido's reigned as the foremost seafood restaurant in Texas throughout the last half of the twentieth century. The restaurant is currently experiencing a renaissance under the direction of a new generation of the Gaido family. Young Casey Gaido, who recently graduated from the Culinary Institute of America, is restoring the kitchen to its former glory.

Here's an adaptation of Gaido's shrimp bisque. It's one of the richest seafood soups you'll ever eat.

SERVES 4

1½ pounds medium shrimp
3 tablespoons olive oil
¼ cup unsalted butter
1 large yellow onion, chopped
1 carrot, peeled and chopped
1 stalk celery, chopped
2½ cups water
1 cup dry white wine
¼ cup long-grain white rice
1 bay leaf
1 tablespoon salt
¼ teaspoon cayenne pepper
3 chicken bouillon cubes
2 (15-ounce) cans whole tomatoes, with juice
2 cups heavy cream

Peel and devein the shrimp, reserving the shells.

In 4-quart Dutch oven, heat the oil over medium-high heat. Add the shrimp shells and cook, stirring constantly with a slotted spoon, for about 5 minutes, until the shells turn pink. Using the spoon, remove and discard the shells, leaving the flavored oil in the pot.

Add the shrimp meat to the hot oil and cook over medium-high heat, stirring frequently, for about 3 minutes, until the shrimp turn pink. Using the slotted spoon, transfer the shrimp to a bowl. Lower the heat to medium and add the butter, onion, carrot, and celery. When the butter melts, cook, stirring occasionally, for about 15 minutes, until the vegetables are tender. Stir in the water, wine, rice, bay leaf, salt, cayenne, and bouillon cubes and bring to a boil, stirring to dissolve the bouillon cubes. Decrease the heat to low, cover, and simmer for about 15 minutes, until the rice is tender.

Remove from the heat and discard the bay leaf. Add the tomatoes and their juice and the cooked shrimp and stir to mix well. Add half of the mixture to a food processor or blender and process at high speed until smooth, then pour into a bowl. Process the remaining half of the mixture the same way.

Return the puréed mixture to the Dutch oven, place over medium heat, and stir in the cream. Heat the bisque, stirring occasionally, just until it comes to a boil. Ladle into bowls and serve immediately.

SHRIMP AND GRITS

The fisherman's dish of shrimp cooked in bacon grease and served over creamy grits is a traditional South Carolina Low Country preparation. Also known as "breakfast shrimp," it became the signature dish of upscale Southern cuisine after Craig Claiborne wrote about Bill Neal's version in the *New York Times* in 1985.

Ouisie's Table, Houston's first upscale Southern restaurant, serves shrimp and grits inspired by Bill Neal's version. Nowdays, shrimp and grits appears on the menu of almost every restaurant that features Southern regional cuisine. It's also a relatively easy dish to make at home.

SERVES 4

1 pound heads-on shrimp

Cheese Grits (page 74) or Herb Grits (page 73)

6 slices bacon, diced

Peanut oil, for frying

2 cups sliced white button mushrooms

1 cup minced green onions (white and green parts)

1 large clove garlic, minced

2 tablespoons chopped fresh parsley

4 teaspoons freshly squeezed lemon juice

1 or 2 dashes of Tabasco sauce

Salt and pepper

Peel and devein the shrimp, then make the stock from the heads and shells as directed on page 32, using only 1 cup water. Set the stock aside.

Prepare the grits as directed, substituting the 1 cup stock for 1 cup of the water. Set the grits aside in a warm place, or keep them warm over hot water in a double boiler.

In a skillet, sauté the bacon over medium heat until crisp, about 8 minutes. Using a slotted spoon, transfer the bacon to paper towels to drain, then crumble.

Return the skillet to medium heat and add enough oil to the bacon drippings so the fat is about ⅛ inch deep. When the fat is hot but not smoking, add the shrimp in a single layer. Turn the shrimp as they color. Add the mushrooms and sauté, stirring, for about 4 minutes, until the mushrooms are cooked through.

Add the green onions and garlic and cook, stirring, for about 1 minute more. Stir in the parsley and season with the lemon juice, Tabasco, salt, and pepper.

Divide the grits among 4 bowls. Spoon the shrimp on top, sprinkle with the bacon, and serve immediately.

HATTIE'S SHRIMP AND GRITS WITH TABASCO BACON PAN SAUCE

This is an adaptation of the shrimp grits served at Hattie's, a classy-looking American bistro in Dallas with a South Carolina Low Country spin. The coffee-flavored sauce reminds me of Southern red-eye gravy.

SERVES 8
Herb Grits (page 73)
8 slices bacon, diced
2 cups chopped yellow onions
40 large shrimp, peeled and deveined
4 tablespoons brewed strong coffee
1 cup chicken broth or shrimp stock (page 32)
Juice of 2 lemons
Tabasco sauce, for seasoning
Salt and pepper
8 ounces fresh goat cheese

Prepare the grits as directed and set aside in a warm place, or keep warm over hot water in a double boiler.

In a large skillet, fry the bacon over medium heat until the fat begins to render, then add the onions and cook, stirring often, for about 5 minutes, until the bacon is cooked and the onions are softened. Add the shrimp and cook for about 3 minutes, just until they begin to curl. Add the coffee and then the broth and stir well. Squeeze in the lemon juice and season with the Tabasco, salt, and pepper.

Divide the grits among 8 bowls. Spoon the shrimp and their sauce over the grits. Crumble an equal amount of the cheese over each serving and serve right away.

Caswell Family Barbecued Crabs, page 44.

CHAPTER 4

BARBECUED CRABS

★★★★★★★★★★★★★★★★★★★★★★★★★★★★★

Barbecued crab is Maine lobster's roughneck cousin from Beaumont. Invented in the corner of Texas that borders Louisiana and the Gulf of Mexico, it tastes like a cross between barbecue and Cajun deep-fried seafood. People who don't even like crab love barbecued crab.

Sartin's is the place that made barbecued crabs famous. And when you talk about hurricane-cursed eateries, the Sartin family takes the grand prize. Charles Douglas Sartin Sr. and Jeri Sartin founded the first location in the little waterfront town of Sabine Pass, near Port Arthur, in 1972. Along with their son, Doug Sartin Jr., and daughter, Kelli, they have opened a total of fourteen Sartin's Restaurants in the Beaumont and Houston area over the years, counting the two that are still in business. The rest were closed by hurricanes, collateral storm damage, and related calamities.

The first time I visited a Sartin's restaurant, a waitress dropped off a plate of six barbecued crabs, hot out of the deep fryer, at my table. I eagerly picked one up and juggled it trying not to burn my fingers. All that stood between me and a whole lot of luscious crabmeat was a little bit of hot crab shell. And I was hungry. I ended up burning my lips and tongue. It was a small price to pay. The rich marine flavor of the spicy crabmeat, slightly greasy from the deep fryer, was sensational.

Sartin's first opened as a retail seafood store. "My daddy was a pipe fitter at the Texaco refinery," Doug Sartin Jr. told me. "He fished for crab and shrimp on the side." In 1972, Doug Sr. set up his wife, Jeri, with a fish-market trailer on the dock at Sabine Pass.

But Jeri, who grew up in a family that owned several restaurants, decided that she would rather sell cooked seafood. And anyway, there was nowhere else to eat in Sabine Pass. So she started a little restaurant in front of the trailer, with four tables inside and another four outside in good weather. Things took off quickly.

As the restaurant expanded, Jeri Sartin hired a fry cook who had worked for a restaurant called Granger's in Sabine Pass. He brought along a recipe for a dish Granger's called barbecued crabs. Some old-timers report that Granger's got the recipe from an older Port Arthur eatery.

The Cajun crabs you get in Louisiana are boiled whole in highly spiced water with corn and potatoes, just like crawfish. On the East Coast, Maryland-style crabs are sprinkled with Old Bay seasoning and then steamed. Cajun crabs and Maryland crabs come to the table whole and the diner cracks the shell and cleans out the guts.

Texas barbecued crabs are much more civilized—at least for the diner. The crab has its top shell and guts removed while it is still alive. It is then dipped into a barbecue spice blend called Alamo Zestful Seasoning (see page 41). At Sartin's, the crabs are dropped into a deep fryer and brought to the table piping hot and crusted with barbecue seasonings. Other eateries and individuals like their barbecued crabs broiled or grilled after the spice dip.

All-you-can-eat barbecued crabs at Sartin's became a big part of the beachgoing tradition on the Bolivar Peninsula. Texas 87, the highway that used to run the length of the beach resort–studded peninsula, went right through Sabine Pass before it turned inland. Sunburned and salt-crusted beachgoers from Beaumont, Port Arthur, and Orange stopped off in their bathing suits to eat a mess of crabs on the way home from the beach.

The original Sartin's became enormously successful. The family added dining rooms several times, until the capacity of the restaurant eventually reached five hundred. On weekends, the lines were so long that the restaurant started setting out tubs of free beer for those who had to wait. The restaurants now sell beer for a penny when there's a line outside the door.

But the original Sartin's was open for only eight years before it developed a hurricane problem. In 1980, it was Hurricane Allen. In 1983, it was Alicia. The storms did some damage to the restaurant, but that wasn't the worst of it. What really devastated Sartin's business was the closure of Highway 87 between High Island and Sabine Pass. The beachfront road was washed out by the storm surge. Beachgoers were forced to use other routes. The road was finally reopened in 1985, and Sartin's began to make a comeback.

Three years later, in 1988, Hurricane Gilbert took out the road again. In 1989, after Hurricane Jerry hit the Texas coast, plans to repair the highway

were abandoned. On most highway maps, Texas 87 between High Island and Sabine Pass looks just fine. But don't try to drive it unless you are on a dirt bike. The road has been closed for two decades.

The senior Sartins' last restaurant in Beaumont was closed by Hurricane Rita in 2005. Two smaller Beaumont locations owned by Doug Jr.'s ex-wives remain in business.

★ ★ ★

Doug Sartin Jr. is a commercial fisherman these days. In 2006, he and I took his boat out one day and pulled up alongside a crab boat on Keith Lake, between Port Arthur and Sabine Pass, and climbed on board to check out the crabbing.

Crab boat captain Craig Ray is a burly bear of a guy with a crewcut and an anchor and ship's wheel tattooed on his enormous bicep. He might have been intimidating, except he was wearing shorts and goofy-looking white rubber boots. His boat was a bright white twenty-one-foot Carolina skiff, a shallow draft design built on a flotation hull that draws a mere six inches of water. The deck was shaded by a piece of bright blue vinyl stretched across a metal frame. The deck was always wet, but the water that washed over it didn't have to be bailed. It drained out of several holes in the aft.

Craig Ray had been crabbing for twenty-seven years when I met him in 2006. Most of the crabbers on Keith Lake used smaller boats, he said. The big skiff made his life easy. He steered the boat while his deckhand pulled up the crab traps marked by colored plastic floats. The first trap had fourteen crabs inside.

"Is that normal?" I asked.

"If they all had that many crabs, I would be home already," Ray chuckled. I asked him how Hurricane Rita affected the fishing.

"This is one of the best seasons I have ever seen," Ray said. Not that he was making a lot of money. The storm put the local restaurants that bought crabs out of business. It also closed down the distributors who needed electricity for refrigeration. There wasn't any

reason to go crabbing because no one was buying. But the storm did wonders for the crabs themselves.

"Hurricane Rita stirred things up," Ray continued. "The oxygen level of the water is way up. And so is the salt. I've heard that those dead zones out in the Gulf of Mexico were all shook up. It sure cleaned this area out. There used to be an oyster reef in the middle of the lake that I couldn't get my boat over. It's gone now. The oysters are spread out all over. All the sand bars and debris were washed out, too. The crabs sure like it. I am seeing more sponge crabs [egg-bearing females] than ever before."

Craig the crab man filled me in about the cycles of the crab season. The crabs hibernate under the mud when the water gets cold. Then, when the weather warms up, usually around April, they get active. That's when they spawn. The peak of the crab season is from May to August. A second spawning season occurs in August. When you eat crabs in the winter, you are eating previously frozen crabs. Add crabs to the long list of foods whose seasonality Americans have forgotten.

As the traps came on board the skiff, we drank our beers and watched. The crabs were dumped out of the traps and sorted according to size. If a crab measured less than five inches "point to point" (from the end of the spiky point that sticks out from one side of the crab's shell to the same point on the other side), it went overboard. If the crab measured between five and six inches, it went into the wooden crate with the #2s (number twos). A crab that measured over six inches went into the box with the rest of the prized #1s (number ones).

"Most of these crabs will go to Maryland where they sell for thirty dollars a dozen," Ray said admiring his #1s. "Here they sell for fifteen dollars a dozen."

Maryland, Virginia, and other crab-loving states have a lot of crab restaurants, but they don't harvest enough crabs locally to meet the demand. Seafood distributors buy crabs from Texas and sell them where they can get the most money. So although lots of premium crabs are taken in Texas, few are eaten here.

The way around this frustrating dilemma is simple: do your own crabbing. It's pretty easy. You can catch all the crabs you want with a chicken neck on a string and a fishing net. Or, you can get more sophisticated with an umbrella trap or a crab pot.

I told Craig Ray I planned to go crabbing near East Beach on Galveston Island. He didn't think that was such a great idea. "The best-tasting crabs come from brackish water," he said, picking up one of the largest #1s. "We call them sweetwater crabs." He turned the crab over and pointed to a fuzzy dark

CRAB SURPRISE
Port Arthur News, April 12, 1940

★ ★

BILL KEEFE, VETERAN SPORTS EDITOR of the *New Orleans Times-Picayune*, was taken to Sabine Pass to feast on barbecued crabs, which brought this comment in his *Times-Picayune* column under the headline "Port Arthur Surprises":

"You wouldn't think that a person would have to go from New Orleans to Port Arthur to find out a new way to cook crabs. And yet when Oscar Valeton and I were told that barbecued crabs not only were the best kind of crabs to eat but were obtainable–properly cooked–only in Port Arthur, why we just had to make the Wednesday night supper there.

"How the thing is done I couldn't find out. But barbecued crabs are just about the best way I ever tasted hard crabs cooked. They are a little greasy to handle as are barbecued pork ribs, but the flavor of the meat from which nothing is lost by being boiled out in water or cooking oil is incomparable.

"Oscar, who is a catch-as-catch-can trencherman as well as the game sort of cameraman, and who is far from being a novice at bisecting shellfish, went for more than a dozen of the barbecued bodies; I even went for a half a dozen, proving how delectable they must have been."

---

scum that stuck to the shell. "You want to see this black rusty color on the bottom. That's the sign of a really sweet crab."

"I always thought that was mud," I admitted stupidly. "So if I wanted to eat the ultimate barbecued crabs, I would start out by catching some #1 sweet-water crabs?" I asked Craig Ray.

"Here, let me get a bucket," he said to my surprise. "I'll give you some of the best crabs you'll ever eat." I was reluctant to take them. I was afraid they'd die before I could them back to Houston, and I didn't want to ruin such awesome crabs.

"I'll get them," Doug Sartin said, slipping Craig Ray some folded bills. "We'll cook them at the restaurant." So we headed back to the parking lot with a dozen #1 crabs in a bucket in the middle of Doug's little boat.

When were arrived at one of the last two Sartin's in Beaumont, we cleaned our crabs in the kitchen and then handed them over to the cook, a Vietnamese woman who has been with Sartin's since the early days in Sabine Pass. We waited in the dining room with some of Doug's friends. The subject turned to Rita and I told the group I was shocked by all the damage I had seen driving around Beaumont and Port Arthur. You didn't hear anything about this devastation from the national media, I remarked.

"You guys must be pretty tired of seeing New Orleans and Katrina coverage on television when your own hometown is in shambles," I said. The table went suddenly silent.

After a few seconds, somebody said, "You mean they had a hurricane in New Orleans, too?" And everybody cracked up.

Then the ultimate plate of barbecued crabs arrived and it was my turn to be silent for a while. There were six of them on the plate, and they were indeed the best I have ever eaten. I could barely believe the huge gobs of meat I was getting out of these sea monsters. The meat was sweeter than crabmeat usually tastes and very juicy. I sucked each body cavity clean and washed the spicy crabmeat down with one last beer.

STINGAREE BARBECUED CRABS

Stingaree Restaurant and Stingaree Marina are located in the little town of Crystal Beach on the Bolivar Peninsula. Each year, the town is the site of the Bolivar Peninsula Crab Festival, featuring seafood, beer, and live music. The first time I visited Stingaree was on a Saturday night in August 2001. I arrived just before sunset and ordered all-you-can-eat barbecued crabs. When they arrived, the slanting light cast a pink glow on the platter. I sucked a tangy claw and admired the still life with shellfish.

A bunch of people filed outside to take seats on the open deck, where they drank beer and faced west. It is one of those places that beachgoers like to go to toast the sunset. I was sitting in the air-conditioned dining room behind the partyers, looking over their shoulders and methodically disassembling barbecued blue crabs. I had eaten four crabs and about six were left on the table when the big red ball fell in East Galveston Bay. An hour and a half later, when I had finished my final crab, the fourteenth, the sky was covered with stars.

ALAMO ZESTFUL SEASONING

★ ★ ★ ★ ★ ★ ★ ★ ★ ★ ★ ★ ★ ★ ★ ★ ★ ★

ALAMO ZESTFUL SEASONING, a barbecue spice blend dominated by salt, sugar, and paprika, was originally marketed by John Sexton & Company. It began to appear in grocery-store advertising alongside seafood items in the 1950s. The brand was discontinued when Sexton was acquired in 1983. Sartin's developed its own "zestful seasoning" spice mix in cooperation with a San Antonio spice company, Bolner's Fiesta Products. Zestful Seasoning is now sold by Bolner's and several other spice suppliers. If you can't find it anywhere, you can make your own (see page 42).

The Stingaree I visited in 2001 is gone now. It was flattened, along with the rest of the town of Crystal Beach, by a twenty-foot storm surge when Hurricane Ike, the largest tropical cyclone in recorded history, hit the Bolivar Peninsula head-on in 2008. There is a new Stingaree now. And they still serve barbecued crabs.

"Crab shacks are going the way of the drive-in theater because neither one is a very good way to utilize space," Stingaree's owner once told me. Modern corporations look at restaurant tables as real estate. You make money by renting them out, and the shorter the stay, the more money you can make. Old-time Texas crab shack habitués will sit at a table for hours and eat twenty or thirty crabs.

Stingaree's crabs are especially delicious and made differently from the ones at Sartin's (see page 42). Instead of deep-frying raw crabs, Stingaree boils them, dips them in seasoning, and broils them.

MAKES 6 CRABS

8 cups water

6 live blue crabs

1 cup crawfish or shrimp boil spice mix (page 56)

1 cup Homemade Zestful Seasoning (page 42)

In a stockpot, bring the water to a boil. Add the crawfish or shrimp boil spice mix and simmer for about 10 minutes, until the spices dissolve and the stock has become fragrant. Add the crabs to the pot and cook until bright red and cooked through, about 10 minutes.

Preheat the broiler. Put the seasoning in a small, shallow bowl. If the crabs are no longer wet, dunk them briefly in the liquid in which you boiled them, then dip the whole crabs in the seasoning, coating them evenly. Place the crabs on a shallow pan and slip them under the broiler for 4 to 7 minutes, until the edges begin to char a little. Serve immediately.

SABINE PASS BARBECUED CRABS

Visitors to Texas seem shocked that Sartin's famous barbecued crabs are deep-fried and not prepared on a Texas barbecue smoker. Like the "barbecued shrimp" of New Orleans and the "barbecued oysters" of Tomales Bay in Northern California, barbecued crabs aren't slow smoked over a wood fire.

Cleaning the live crabs is the most difficult part of making barbecued crabs. First you have to leave them in ice water for several minutes to stun them enough so they stop fighting, then you have to rip the shell off and clean out the exposed guts and lungs.

MAKES 12 HALF CRABS
Peanut oil, for deep-frying
6 live blue crabs
1 cup Homemade Zestful Seasoning
   (recipe follows)

Pour the oil to a depth of about 2 inches into a deep, heavy pot or deep fryer and heat to 350°F.

While the oil is heating, immerse the crabs in ice water for 5 to 10 minutes until they are limp. Put 1 crab, shell side up, on a flat surface. Hold down a flipper on the bottom left side of the crab with the thumb of your nondominant hand and rip off the upper shell from left to right with your dominant hand. Don't be shy. It takes considerable force to get the shell started. Clean out the exposed guts and gills under running cold water, remove the reproductive parts, then break the crab in half with 1 claw on each half. This will expose the fleshy meat in the middle. Repeat with the remaining crabs.

Put the seasoning in a small, shallow bowl. Working in small batches, dip the crab halves, one at a time, into the seasoning and then lower them into the hot oil. Cook for 2 to 3 minutes, until the crabmeat is opaque and cooked through. If the spice mix begins to burn before the crabs are ready, lower the heat.

Scoop the crabs out of the hot oil with a wire skimmer. Let them cool just until they can be handled, then serve them right away with cold beer.

HOMEMADE ZESTFUL SEASONING

After experimenting with several home equivalent recipes for this iconic seasoning, I came up with my own blend. Only my version isn't really like the original. I omitted the cloves, because I don't like the aroma. And I substituted *pimentón de la Vera* for the paprika, because I like the smoky flavor that the Spanish paprika adds. I also added some tasty but expensive spices like mace and cardamom that you won't find in the commercial stuff.

MAKES ABOUT 1 CUP
2 tablespoons salt
1 tablespoon celery salt
1 tablespoon ground mustard
2 tablespoons smoked paprika (pimentón)
½ teaspoon ground mace
½ teaspoon cayenne pepper
½ teaspoon black pepper
½ teaspoon red pepper flakes
½ teaspoon ground cardamom
½ teaspoon ground bay leaves
About ½ cup sugar

In a large measuring cup, combine the salt, celery salt, mustard, paprika, mace, cayenne, black pepper, red pepper flakes, cardamom, and bay and mix well. (This should measure about ½ cup.) Add an amount of sugar equal to the total amount of spices and mix well. Store in a tightly capped jar or other airtight container for up to 3 months.

CASWELL FAMILY BARBECUED CRABS

Houston chef Bryan Caswell gave me his family recipe for barbecued crabs. His dad, Mike Caswell, told me, "When I started barbecueing crabs, I just brushed them with Tabasco ketchup while they were on the grill." But the Caswell family recipe has continued to evolve. By the time Bryan Caswell finished his culinary training and opened Reef, his famous seafood restaurant in Houston, the family recipe for barbecued crabs had gotten pretty complex.

The idea is to brush the crabs with the sweet-hot glaze when they are on the grill so that the glaze forms a crust. A little char is good, but keep the crabs far enough from the fire so they don't get black. See photo on page 36.

MAKES 24 HALF CRABS; SERVES 4

12 live blue crabs

2 tablespoons olive oil

¼ cup Homemade Zestful Seasoning (page 42)

Glaze

½ cup unsalted butter

2 cloves garlic, minced

1 jalapeño chile, minced

¼ cup Homemade Zestful Seasoning (page 42)

3 tablespoons dark brown sugar

½ cup tequila

¼ cup cider vinegar

¼ cup dark molasses

¼ cup soy sauce

¼ cup orange marmalade

2 tablespoons Worcestershire sauce

1 tablespoon Asian sesame oil

2 teaspoons kosher salt

1 teaspoon dry mustard

1 teaspoon white pepper

1 teaspoon black pepper

Grated zest and juice of 4 lemons

Mustard BBQ Sauce (page 45), for serving

Immerse the crabs in ice water for 5 to 10 minutes until they are limp. Put 1 crab, shell side up, on a flat surface. Hold down a flipper on the bottom left side of the crab with the thumb of your non-dominant hand and rip off the upper shell from left to right with your dominant hand. Don't be shy. It takes considerable force to get the shell started. Clean out the exposed guts and gills under running cold water, remove the reproductive organs, then break the crab in half with 1 claw on each half. This will expose the fleshy meat in the middle. Repeat with the remaining crabs.

In a large bowl, toss the crab halves with the olive oil and seasoning, coating evenly. Set aside until the fire is ready.

To make the glaze, in a saucepan, melt the butter over medium-high heat. Do not allow it to brown. Decrease the heat to medium-low, add the garlic, chile, and seasoning, and cook, stirring often, for 3 minutes, until the garlic begins to brown. Add the brown sugar and stir constantly for a few minutes, until the mixture caramelizes. Add the tequila and scrape up any brown bits from the pan bottom. Add the vinegar, molasses, soy sauce, marmalade, Worcestershire sauce, sesame oil, salt, mustard, white pepper, and black pepper. Increase the heat to high and cook, stirring constantly, for about 8 minutes, until reduced by half. Stir in the lemon zest and juice, remove from the heat, and let cool.

Prepare a grill for indirect grilling (with the heat on one side only). When the grill is heated evenly, put the halved crabs directly over the fire until they get hot and begin to sizzle. When the shells are hot, move the crabs to the cooler part of the grill grate and brush with the glaze. Grill the crabs, turning them every few minutes and brushing them with more glaze, until a crust begins to form. Move them closer or farther away from the fire to get the desired char. The crabs will be done in 10 to 15 minutes. Serve immediately with the BBQ sauce.

MUSTARD BBQ SAUCE

Mustard barbecue sauce is traditional with barbecued mutton in Kentucky. But in Texas, we are more likely to use it on barbecued crabs.

MAKES ABOUT 4 CUPS
1 cup sherry vinegar
½ cup pepper vinegar
½ cup rice vinegar
½ cup firmly packed dark brown sugar
½ cup firmly packed light brown sugar
1 cup Dijon mustard
1 teaspoon kosher salt
1 teaspoon Worcestershire sauce

In a saucepan, stir together all of the ingredients and place over medium heat. Bring to a boil, lower the heat to a simmer, and cook, stirring often, for 3 or 4 minutes, until hot and well blended. Use immediately or store covered in the refrigerator for up to 2 weeks.

GALVESTON CRAB CAKES

The 100-year-old seafood restaurant Gaido's made crab cakes famous on Galveston Island. Here's a favorite recipe. If serving the cakes as a main course, accompany with Bombay Salad (page 8).

MAKES 10 CRAB CAKES; SERVES 10 AS A FIRST COURSE OR 5 AS A MAIN COURSE
5 tablespoons unsalted butter
1 teaspoon finely chopped garlic
½ cup finely chopped celery
¼ cup finely chopped red bell peppers
¼ cup finely chopped yellow bell peppers
¼ cup freshly squeezed lemon juice
¼ cup white wine
1½ pounds jumbo lump blue crabmeat, picked over for shell fragments
1 cup fine dried bread crumbs

½ cup mayonnaise
1 teaspoon seafood seasoning (page 9)
½ teaspoon red hot-pepper sauce
Pinch of cayenne pepper
½ cup finely chopped green onions (white and green parts)
1 tablespoon finely chopped fresh parsley
Salt
Spicy Ravigote (page 53), Baffin Bay Seafood Sauce (page 8), and/or Pope's Tartar Sauce (page 7), for serving

In a skillet, melt 3 tablespoons of the butter over medium-low heat. Add the garlic, celery, and red and yellow bell peppers and sauté, stirring and gradually adding the lemon juice and wine, for about 10 minutes, until the vegetables are tender. Transfer to a good-size bowl and chill in the refrigerator.

When the mixture has cooled, fold the crabmeat and bread crumbs into the sautéed vegetables. In a small bowl, whisk together the mayonnaise, seasoning mix, pepper sauce, cayenne, green onions, and parsley. Season with salt. Add the mayonnaise mixture to the crab mixture and stir until well combined. Cover and chill for 1 hour.

Divide the crab mixture into 10 equal portions. Form each portion into a cake about 3 inches in diameter and 1 inch thick. In a large, heavy skillet, heat 1 tablespoon of the butter over medium heat. When the foam subsides, add half of the crab cakes and cook, turning once, for 2 to 3 minutes on each side, until golden brown on both sides. Drain well on paper towels and keep hot in a warm oven. Repeat with the remaining crab cakes and the remaining 1 tablespoon butter. (Or, if your skillet is large enough, you can cook all of the cakes at one time.)

To serve as a first course, put 1 crab cake on each plate and serve with the ravigote, Baffin Bay, or tartar sauce. To serve as a main course, put 2 cakes on each plate and accompany with 1 or more of the sauces.

GOODE COMPANY'S CRAB AND SHRIMP CAMPECHANA

SERVES 8 TO 12

Seafood "cocktails," so named because they were originally served in glasses designed for martinis and other such libations, became famous in the 1920s. Spicy ketchup was the original sauce and raw oysters were the most common seafood. Mexican seafood cocktails added lime juice, cilantro, and avocado. Campechana cocktail, a mixed seafood cocktail named after the favored fishing grounds of the Bay of Campeche, became the most famous of the Mexican seafood cocktails.

Goode Company Seafood, a Houston seafood eatery founded by a fanatical Texas fisherman named Jim Goode, serves its famous Campechana cocktail with both saltines and tortilla chips. It also comes with a bottle of Tabasco so you can "heat it up." The seafood cocktail tastes equally good with a frozen margarita or a cold beer. Maybe that's why it has become the quintessential Houston seafood appetizer.

FIRST BARBECUED CRABS

★ ★ ★ ★ ★ ★ ★ ★ ★ ★ ★ ★ ★ ★ ★ ★ ★ ★

THE EARLIEST MENTIONS OF barbecued crabs in print are these two newspaper items:

"Visit Le Blanc's Café, 526 Houston, for tempting barbecued crabs; best in town."

Port Arthur News, August 7, 1936 [classified ad]

"Tourists who flock to Treasure Island for the most splendid surf bathing take back with them lingering memories of the delicious stuffed and barbecued crabs served in the hotels and cafés of Galveston."

Galveston Daily News, January 18, 1938

Cocktail Sauce

¼ cup pitted green olives, chopped
1 cup Clamato juice
½ cup ketchup
½ cup chili sauce
⅓ cup extra-virgin olive oil
¼ cup freshly squeezed lime juice
¼ cup chopped fresh parsley
1 tablespoon chopped fresh oregano
1 teaspoon chopped serrano chile

½ cup seeded, diced tomatoes
½ cup peeled, seeded, and diced roasted long green chiles (page 129)
1 avocado, halved, pitted, peeled, and diced
¼ cup diced white onion
¼ cup chopped fresh cilantro
1 teaspoon minced garlic
½ teaspoon salt
8 ounces shrimp, boiled, peeled, and deveined
8 ounces lump blue crabmeat, picked over for shell fragments
24 pickled jalapeño chile wheels, for garnish
Saltines or tortilla chips, for serving

To make the cocktail sauce, in a bowl, combine all of the ingredients and mix well.

Add the tomatoes, chiles, avocado, onion, cilantro, garlic, and salt to the cocktail sauce and stir to mix well. Then gently fold in the shrimp and crabmeat, mixing until coated evenly with the sauce.

Spoon the seafood mixture into chilled martini or parfait glasses. Garnish each serving with 2 or 3 pickled jalapeño wheels. Serve with saltines.

Crawfish Boil, page 56.

CHAPTER 5

THE CAJUN INVASION

The French flag was the first of the six flags that have flown over Texas. After France claimed Texas in 1685, French explorers set up a few Indian trading posts and tried to blaze a trail between Louisiana and Mexico. Sadly, the French didn't add anything to the regional cuisine before turning Texas over to the Spanish in 1716.

Pirates and cowboys were the first French speakers to take up residence in Texas. The 367-mile Texas coastline was among the pirate Jean Lafitte's favorite waters. In 1817, Lafitte set up his headquarters on Galveston Island, which he named Campeche. It was home to around a thousand inhabitants at the height of his reign. Lafitte did a booming business smuggling slaves until his band was kicked off the island in the early 1820s.

The Spanish cattle-raising system had flourished in the South Texas Plains during the mission era of the 1700s. But at the end of the eighteenth century, after major defeats by the Apaches and Comanches, the Spanish abandoned the missions and retreated to interior Mexico. The remaining Spanish cattle ranches were concentrated in sparsely populated South Texas.

"About 1820, Cajun, Anglo, African, and assorted mixed-blood cattle raisers and cowboys began crossing the Sabine into the prairies of southeastern Texas [from Louisiana] bearing a herding system well preadapted for the western grasslands," wrote cowboy historian Terry Jordan. These Southern cowboys settled in the saltgrass plains between the Sabine and Trinity Rivers east of Houston. Although the Anglos among them continued their expansion westward, the Cajuns and Creoles (French-speaking blacks) never ventured past the Trinity, preferring to remain close to their fellow French speakers.

Worried that the incursion of French-speaking peoples might lead to a French takeover of Texas, the government of New Spain began recruiting settlers. But few residents of Mexico City had any desire to migrate to the desolate region of El Norte, as Texas was then known. And so the Spanish government recruited English-speaking American settlers and German-speaking immigrants to populate the state to keep it from becoming French—an ill-advised tactic that eventually resulted in Texas independence.

Few of the French-speaking Cajuns and black Creoles ever left Jefferson County. But they added a French accent to the cooking of Southeast Texas, and their love of game birds and seafood added such delicacies as wild duck and shrimp gumbo to Texas cuisine.

IN HIS OWN WORDS: JIM GOSSEN

★ ★

MY NAME IS JAMES GLENN GOSSEN and I was born on April 8, 1948, in Lafayette, Louisiana. I am three-quarters Cajun and one-quarter German. My German grandfather owned a lumber mill; my Cajun relatives were farmers. My mother and her sister spoke French when they didn't want us to know what they were talking about, but the kids spoke English. At school, you got in trouble if you spoke French.

I got into the restaurant business when I was twenty-three. I helped Floyd and Billy Landry open Don's Seafood in Morgan City. We worked hard and we had a helluva good time. When the oil business took off in the 1970s, a lot of Cajun oil-field companies moved to Houston, so we started scouting locations there in 1974. We opened Don's Seafood at 3009 Post Oak in Houston on April 15, 1976.

In some ways, Texas wasn't all that different from Louisiana. There were a lot of Cajuns over in Beaumont and Port Arthur, and there were a lot of rice farms in East Texas, just like my grandfather's. But there weren't any Cajun restaurants in Houston. We were the first ones and people didn't know what to make of us. When we started, flounder, specs [speckled sea trout], red snapper, and wild catfish were all anyone in Houston would eat. Except for shrimp and oysters—they were always big.

But then Paul Prudhomme came along. He took redfish, which was an underutilized species, and made it famous all over the country. We call them underutilized species now, but back then people called them trash fish. Everybody wanted blackened redfish after they saw Paul Prudhomme cook it on TV. Too bad he didn't come up with something to do with sheephead.

We tried serving crawfish when we first opened, but nobody would eat it, so we ended up using it as a garnish or throwing it away. I never sold that many crawfish in Houston until we opened Magnolia Grill. We set up boiling pots and played Cajun music outside on the patio, and the Cajun oil-field gang began coming in. On good weekends, we were selling seven or eight thousand pounds of crawfish. Not that that's any big deal now.

Jefferson County, which lies in the easternmost part of Southeast Texas, became a French stronghold and served as a transportation center for pirates and smugglers. It was nearly impossible to reach this area from Spanish-held Texas, but it was easily accessible by boat from French Louisiana.

After Texas won its independence in 1836, the fledgling state turned to France for assistance. In 1840, France and Texas signed a commercial treaty. A French chargé d'affaires was sent to the republic—he arrived with his chef in tow. He set up headquarters in Austin. The original hearth-centered French kitchen operated by his chef can still be seen at the French Legation museum just east of downtown.

In 1901, oil was discovered at the Spindletop Hill oil field in Beaumont, the biggest city in Jefferson County. The Lucas Geyser, the world's first gusher, produced one hundred thousand barrels a day. Huge fortunes were made in a matter of weeks, and the population of Beaumont rapidly grew from ten thousand to fifty thousand.

In the 1950s and 1960s, Cajuns from western Louisiana migrated toward the refinery center known as the Golden Triangle (Beaumont, Port

I started the Texas Crawfish Festival, where every year we cook thousands of pounds. And I cater a big crawfish boil for the annual OTC [Offshore Technology Conference] convention at Reliant Stadium. We cook seventeen thousand pounds of crawfish in one day for that event. We had giant boilers built to fit on the back of our truck. I believe that now more crawfish are consumed in Houston than are consumed in New Orleans.

We started a wholesale seafood business called Louisiana Foods. In the past, all of our seafood came from local Gulf fishermen, and I had personal relationships with all of the suppliers. The business was also a lot more seasonal than it is now. But the seafood market started changing in the late 1970s. Nobody cared about seasons anymore. Everybody wanted oysters year-round, regardless of quality. The personal relationships didn't matter, either. Instead, seafood started going to the highest bidder. The crab houses in Maryland get a lot more money

Jim Gossen:
Owner, Louisiana Foods.

for a dozen crabs than Gulf Coast seafood restaurants will pay. And so when Chesapeake Bay started running out of crabs, the wholesalers up there started buying up the #1 crabs from Louisiana and Texas. That ended the cottage industry of crab-picking plants on the Gulf Coast. I buy my crabmeat from Mexico now. Crab-packing plants in Matamoros sell blue crabmeat, and plants in Baja California sell swimmer crabmeat. We also buy pasteurized crabmeat from Malaysia.

Gulf shrimping has to compete with cheap farm-raised shrimp from Asia, so now 80 percent of the white shrimp we sell is imported. That's the problem with commodity marketing. Nobody asks the clerk at the seafood counter where the white shrimp are from. And he wouldn't know anyway. The shrimpers are lucky if they can get the grocery store to specify whether the shrimp is wild or farmed.

I'll tell you where we are going: Gulf seafood will become a boutique business. The quality stuff will sell to the highest bidders all over the world.

Arthur, and Orange) and the city of Houston in search of good-paying jobs in the petroleum industry. After the Arab members of OPEC prolaimed an oil embargo in 1973, another boom in oil drilling brought even more Cajuns to the area, as oil companies and oil-field service contractors consolidated their operations in Texas.

The culinary "Cajun invasion" started in 1976, when the Landry boys arrived from Lafayette. They brought in other partners as they opened and operated an extremely successful group of Texas Cajun restaurants, including Willie G's and Landry's. The

chain was eventually sold to Tilman Fertitta and is now part of Landry's Restaurants, Inc.

Cajun food became a hot new trend in the United States in the 1980s. At the same time, the Cajun population in Texas continued to climb. By the 1990s, there were an estimated 56,000 Cajuns in Texas (compared with 430,000 Cajuns in southwestern Louisiana). Although the fascination with all things Cajun has slowly ebbed in the rest of the country, boiled crawfish, seafood gumbo, po'boys, and boudin will always be a part of Texas food traditions.

CAJUN SEASONING

Tony Chachere's is the most famous Louisiana seasoning, but its main ingredient is salt and it contains MSG. You can buy dozens of other brands, too, including big names like Paul Prudhomme's, Zatarain's, and Luzianne and lesser-known labels like Cajun King, Dat Cajun Boy's, Cajun Chef, and Cajun Country.

Jim Gossen uses Guidroz's seasoning blend. He buys it in gallon jars at a little grocery store in Lafayette, Louisiana, called Guidroz's Food Center. If you want to buy a popular seasoning blend at the store or by mail order, Jim Gossen recommends Slap Ya Mama, which doesn't have MSG. Or, here's a Cajun seasoning blend you make yourself.

MAKES ABOUT ¾ CUP
3 tablespoons paprika
3 tablespoons salt
2 tablespoons garlic powder
1 tablespoon black pepper
1 tablespoon onion powder
1 tablespoon cayenne pepper
1 tablespoon ground dried oregano
1 tablespoon ground dried thyme

In a small bowl, stir together all the ingredients, mixing well. Store in a tightly capped jar at room temperature for up to 3 months.

CREOLE REMOULADE

Remoulade means seasoned mayonnaise, but it's also the name of the dishes you make with that mayonnaise, like shrimp remoulade and crab remoulade.

MAKES ABOUT 2 CUPS
1 teaspoon Creole mustard
2 cups mayonnaise
1 tablespoon Worcestershire sauce
Dash of Tabasco sauce

In a small bowl, stir together all of the ingredients, mixing well. Cover and chill before serving. It will keep for up to 1 week.

Crab Remoulade: Mix 1 pound (3 cups) crabmeat, picked over for shell fragments, with ½ cup Creole Remoulade. Serve over greens or an avocado half.

Shrimp Remoulade: Mix 3 cups chopped, cooked shrimp with ½ cup Creole Remoulade. Serve over greens and garnish with lemon wedges or grapefruit sections.

SPICY RAVIGOTE

Ravigote is a broad term. It can mean a warm seafood sauce, a spicy vinaigrette, or, in this case, sort of a Creole tartar sauce. Use ravigote sauce instead of remoulade to make a more elegant crab or shrimp salad.

MAKES ABOUT 2¹/₂ CUPS

2 hard-boiled eggs

2 cups Creole Remoulade (page 52)

2 tablespoons freshly squeezed lemon juice

3 tablespoons minced red onion

3 tablespoons capers, drained and coarsely chopped

2 tablespoons minced celery

1 tablespoon minced pickled jalapeño chile

1 teaspoon minced garlic

2 tablespoons chopped fresh parsley

1 teaspoon chopped fresh tarragon

2 teaspoons Cajun Seasoning (page 52)

Peel the eggs, then, using a spoon, force them through a coarse-mesh sieve into a bowl. Fold in the remoulade, lemon juice, onion, capers, celery, chile, garlic, parsley, tarragon, and seasoning mix. Cover and refrigerate until ready to serve. It will keep for up to 2 weeks.

Crab Ravigote: Mix 1 pound (3 cups) crabmeat, picked over for shell fragments, with ½ cup Spicy Ravigote. Serve over greens or an avocado half.

Shrimp Ravigote: Mix 3 cups chopped, cooked shrimp with ½ cup Spicy Ravigote. Serve over greens and garnish with lemon wedges or grapefruit sections.

MAQUE CHOUX

Pronounced "mock shoe," this spicy version of Indian succotash became popular in Cajun Louisiana. The word *maque* comes from the Choctaw word for "corn," and *choux* is French for "cabbage." In East Texas, this dish is often called corn pone.

SERVES 6

12 ears corn, husked and silks removed

3 tablespoons bacon drippings

1 large yellow onion, chopped

1 red bell pepper, seeded and chopped

3 jalapeños chiles with seeds, chopped

2 teaspoons salt

2 teaspoons pepper

1 cup heavy cream

Hold 1 ear of corn upright, flat end down, in a large, shallow bowl and, using a sharp knife, cut off the kernels, rotating the ear as you work. Then, using the back of the knife, scrape down the length of the cob to release the "corn milk" into the bowl. Repeat with the remaining ears.

In a Dutch oven, heat the bacon grease over medium-high heat. Add the onion, bell pepper, and chiles and cook, stirring occasionally, for 3 to 5 minutes, until soft. Add the corn and its liquid, salt, pepper, and heavy cream and stir well. Cook over low heat, stirring as needed to prevent the corn from sticking, for 20 to 25 minutes, until thickened. Serve hot.

ROUX

There's a joke that every Cajun recipe begins with the instruction, "First you make a roux." This roux calls for only two ingredients, flour and oil. All-purpose flour is the best choice. Don't try it with a fine flour like Wondra. Corn oil has a nice taste and is inexpensive, but peanut oil is a good choice, too. For some recipes, like the Turtle Soup on page 174, you will need a rich butter roux. The color of the roux is critical, so pay close attention to the roux as it cooks. If the flour sticks to the pan and you see black flecks as you stir, you have burned the roux. Throw it away and start over.

MAKES ⅔ CUP
⅓ cup all-purpose flour
½ cup corn oil or your favorite oil

In a cast-iron skillet, heat the oil over medium-high heat until it shimmers, then add the flour. Using a flat-headed wooden spoon or a whisk, stir the mixture constantly as it heats, scraping the bottom of the skillet. When it begins to brown, turn down the heat a little. Continue reducing the heat as you get closer to the color you are trying to reach.

Blond roux, peanut butter–colored roux, copper-colored roux, walnut-colored roux, and black roux are some of the descriptions you might hear. When the mixture is the desired color, turn off the heat but keep stirring. If the recipe calls for adding chopped vegetables to the roux, add them at this point and continue with the recipe as directed. Or, you can keep stirring the roux until it is completely cooled and store it in a sealed jar in the refrigerator for up to 2 weeks.

Add the roux carefully to gumbo, étouffée, or other dishes. Adding too much roux at a time will result in clumping; pouring the stock into the roux (instead of adding the roux a little at a time to the stock) will cause the entire sauce or soup to separate. Read the recipe carefully before adding the roux.

GRANDMA GOSSEN'S SHRIMP STEW

When Jim Gossen's grandma made this hearty seafood dish, shrimp were among the cheapest foods in the market in south Louisiana. The difference between shrimp stew and shrimp gumbo is all in the gravy.

SERVES 8
⅔ cup roux (at left)
¾ cup diced celery
2 cups diced yellow onions
½ cup diced green bell peppers
1 teaspoon salt
6 cloves garlic, finely minced
3 cups shrimp stock (page 32)
¼ teaspoon cayenne pepper
3 pounds shrimp, peeled and deveined
3 tablespoons chopped fresh flat-leaf parsley
3 tablespoons chopped green onion (white and green parts)
Cooked white rice, for serving

In a medium-large Dutch oven, make the roux as directed, cooking it until it is copper colored. Decrease the heat to low, add the celery, onions, and green peppers, stir to coat, and cook for 2 to 3 minutes. Add the salt and continue to cook, stirring, for about 15 minutes, until all of the vegetables are soft.

Add the garlic and 2 cups of the stock, turn up the heat to medium-high, and heat until the mixture comes to a low boil and looks like a brown gravy. Add the cayenne, turn down the heat to low, and simmer for 15 minutes, stirring occasionally.

Add the shrimp, stir to combine, cover, and cook, stirring occasionally to ensure even cooking, for 20 minutes. Add the remaining 1 cup stock, re-cover, and continue cooking for 3 to 5 minutes, until all of the shrimp are an even pink.

Just before serving, stir in the parsley and green onion. Spoon the rice into individual bowls and ladle the stew over the top. Serve right away.

CAJUN WHITE BEANS WITH FRIED FISH

White beans cooked with pork are more popular than pinto beans among Cajuns in Beaumont and Sicilians in Galveston. These spicy white beans are often served with fried fish or shellfish. The pork might be bacon, andouille, or other pork sausages, or tasso, the spicy-hot cured pork packed in sausage casings that is a staple of the Cajun kitchen. The secret of tender beans is long slow cooking. Simmering beans for hours on the stove top is not only tedious, but it also heats up the house—which is fine in the few months of cool weather we get in Texas, but not during the other nine months of the year. That's why slow cookers have become so popular for cooking beans. You put the beans in the ceramic insert, turn the appliance on, and slow cook your beans with a minimum of energy and no escaped heat. This recipe is written for the slow cooker, but feel free to cook your beans on the stove top.

SERVES 6

1 pound small dried white (navy) beans
1 tablespoon lard or bacon drippings
½ cup chopped yellow onions
2 (1-inch) cubes salt pork (optional)
½ cup chopped green bell peppers
1 cup diced tasso (¼-inch dice) or chopped
	cooked bacon
¼ teaspoon ground dried thyme
Pinch of cayenne pepper
2 bay leaves
1 clove garlic, minced
1 teaspoon Worcestershire sauce
1 tablespoon Cajun Seasoning (page 52)
5 cups boiling water, or as needed
Salt and pepper
Fried Catfish (page 87)
¼ cup chopped green onions (white and green
	parts), for garnish

Pick over the beans, discarding any misshapen beans or grit, then rinse well. Put the beans in a slow cooker.

In a skillet, melt the lard over medium-high heat. Add the yellow onions, salt pork, and green peppers and sauté for 5 minutes, until the onions are translucent. Add the tasso, thyme, cayenne, bay leaves, garlic, Worcestershire sauce, and seasoning mix and sauté for about 3 minutes, until well blended.

Add the onion mixture to the beans in the slow cooker, stir well, and then pour in enough boiling water to cover the beans by 2 inches. Turn on the cooker to the high setting, season with salt and pepper, cover, and cook for 2 hours. Turn down the cooker to the low setting and continue to cook for 6 to 8 hours or overnight, until the beans are meltingly tender.

To serve, divide the beans among 6 soup plates. Top each serving with an equal amount of the fish, garnish with chopped green onions, sprinkle with salt and pepper, and serve.

Cajun White Beans with Fried Oysters: Cook the beans as directed and divide among 6 soup plates. Substutite King's Inn Fried Oysters (page 22) for the catfish, topping each serving with 6 oysters.

Cajun White Beans with Fried Shrimp: Cook the beans as directed and divide among 6 soup plates. Substutite King's Inn Fried Shrimp (page 22) for the catfish, topping each serving with a few shrimp.

CRAWFISH BOIL

Stores that sell backyard gas grills often carry an outdoor Cajun cooking kit that includes a giant aluminum pot with a basket insert and a stand with a built-in propane burner. The pots generally have a 30-quart capacity. You have to supply your own propane tank.

SERVES 10

Bouquet Garni
20 bay leaves
¼ cup peppercorns
¼ cup mustard seeds
1 tablespoon dill seeds
1 tablespoon allspice berries
1 tablespoon red pepper flakes

30 pounds crawfish
6 gallons water
6 pounds medium red potatoes, halved
6 lemons, halved
12 ears corn, husked, silks removed, and broken
    in half
2½ cups crawfish or shrimp boil spice mix
    (recipe follows), plus more for sprinkling

To make the bouquet garni, combine all of the ingredients on a large square of cheesecloth, bring together the corners of the square, and tie securely with kitchen twine, or combine the ingredients in a muslin bag that can be tied closed. You can also just stir together all of the ingredients in a bowl and then add them loose to the pot.

Open the bag of crawfish and pour them into a galvanized tub or kiddie pool. Rinse them two or three times to rid them of dirt and debris. Pick through the crawfish and remove and discard any that are dead.

Pour the water into a 30-quart crawfish pot, and place on a propane burner. Light the burner. When the water comes to a raging boil, add the bouquet garni and boil for 5 minutes. Add the potatoes and lemons and boil for 5 minutes. Add the corn and continue to cook for 15 minutes. Remove the corn and potatoes to a cooler and sprinkle with spice mix to taste.

Add the 2½ cups spice mix and 10 pounds of the crawfish to the pot and cover the pot. When the pot begins steaming, let cook for 5 to 10 minutes, until the crawfish are bright red. Using a large wire-mesh skimmer, remove the crawfish from the pot, place in a cooler, and sprinkle with spice mix to taste. Repeat with the remaining 20 pounds of crawfish, 10 pounds at a time.

Combine the crawfish and vegetables. Serve them in a pile on trays or on newspaper in the middle of a picnic table with lots of ice cold beer. Let each diner peel his own crawfish. Be sure to provide somewhere to dump the shells and corncobs.

CRAWFISH OR SHRIMP BOIL SPICE MIX

Zatarain's has a popular line of seasonings for crawfish, shrimp, and crab boils. The company sells boiling spices loose, in giant "teabags," and in concentrated liquids. There is also an "extra spicy" option. It's a lot cheaper to make your own, though. If you want it extra spicy, increase the cayenne.

MAKES 5½ CUPS
3 pounds salt
½ cup cayenne pepper
½ cup paprika
¼ teaspoon ground cloves
1 tablespoon onion powder
2 tablespoons garlic powder
1 teaspoon lemon pepper

In a bowl, stir together all the ingredients. Store in a tightly covered container at room temperature for up to a month.

GREEN GUMBO

Green gumbo is a traditional Friday soup among the Catholic Cajuns of East Texas and western Louisiana. Feel free to add other greens, like radish tops, turnip greens, or chicory, to the mix. Panfish, such as bluegill, perch, or crappie, make a wonderfully sweet base for soups, or use redfish or sea trout if you are fishing in saltwater.

SERVES 4

1 big or 2 small whole fish (about 2 pounds total; see headnote), cleaned
2 carrots
1 yellow onion
2 stalks celery
6 cups water
2 tablespoons vegetable oil
1 cup chopped fresh parsley
1 teaspoon ground dried thyme
1 teaspoon black pepper
½ teaspoon white pepper
¼ teaspoon cayenne
2 bay leaves
Salt
1 potato, peeled and diced into ½-inch cubes
1 bunch mustard greens, chopped
1 bunch collard greens, chopped
Tabasco sauce, for serving

Fillet the fish and refrigerate the fillets. Put the bones and head(s) in a stockpot. Peel the carrots and onion and trim the celery, then add the peelings and trimmings to the stockpot. Cut the carrots, onion, and celery into small dice and set aside. Add the water to the pot and bring to a boil over medium-high heat. Decrease the heat to a simmer, cover, and cook for 30 to 45 minutes, until the fish head(s) disintegrates. Remove from the heat and strain the stock through a fine-mesh sieve placed over a bowl. Rinse out the pot and pour the strained stock into it.

In a skillet, heat the oil over medium heat. Add the carrots, onion, and celery and sauté for 10 minutes, until softened. Add the sautéed vegetables to the stock along with the parsley, thyme, the three peppers, and the bay leaves, then season with salt to taste. Place the pot over medium heat, add the potato and greens, bring to a boil, then reduce the heat to a simmer and cook for 20 minutes.

Dice the reserved fish fillets, add to the pot, and cook for 10 minutes longer, until the fish is cooked through. Discard the bay leaves. Serve piping hot. Pass the Tabasco sauce at the table.

GOSSEN'S WILD DUCK GUMBO

Duck are plentiful in the rice fields and salt marshes along the Texas coast. Every year around Thanksgiving, my brothers and I go duck hunting in the flats near Aransas Pass. In early morning, an enormous flock of ducks flies from the nearby rice fields out over the saltwater marshes. It's a breathtaking sight to see. The wild duck gumbo we make after our annual duck hunt has become more popular than the Thanksgiving turkey.

When I invited Jim Gossen over for duck gumbo, he wondered why I didn't put a guinea fowl or a speckled-belly goose in the pot. I ended up going over to Gossen's house to learn how to make wild bird gumbo the way a southern Louisiana rice farmer makes it. This is one of the richest gumbos you will ever eat.

MAKES ABOUT 10 QUARTS GUMBO; SERVES 20

6 wild duck breasts, plus 1 whole guinea fowl or chicken; or 4 whole wild ducks, 1 whole speckled-belly goose, and 1 whole guinea fowl or chicken
1 cup Cajun seasoning (page 52)
10 quarts water
3 cloves garlic, crushed and minced
1 small yellow onion, plus 8 cups diced onion
⅔ cup roux (page 54)

4 cups diced green bell peppers

4 cups diced celery

5 tablespoons Worcestershire sauce

2 tablespoons Tabasco sauce, plus more for serving

1 bay leaf

2 teaspoons dried thyme leaves

2 teaspoons dried oregano leaves

Pinch of cayenne pepper

½ teaspoon white pepper

Sea salt and freshly ground black pepper

10 cups cooked rice

5 sweet potatoes, baked and cut into 1-inch thick rounds

Filé powder, for serving

CAJUN RICE

★ ★ ★ ★ ★ ★ ★ ★ ★ ★ ★ ★ ★ ★ ★ ★ ★ ★

RICE FARMING IS AN OLD TRADITION in the Cajun areas of East Texas and southwest Louisiana. And Cajuns are picky about their rice. Some varieties that are popular in Cajun cookery are mostly unknown in other parts of the country.

Popcorn rice, also known as Della rice, is an aromatic long-grain rice that was developed in Louisiana. It cooks like long grain but gives off an aroma reminiscent of roasted nuts or popcorn. Della varieties include Della, Dellrose, Dellmont, and A-301.

Long-grain Toro rice also originated in Louisiana. Its kernels are the same size and shape as those of other U.S. long-grain varieties, but it cooks up like U.S. short- and medium-grain rice. Toro is a favorite of people who like the clingy cooked texture of the shorter grains in their long-grain rice. It's a favorite in gumbo.

Rub the birds generously inside and out with the seasoning mix. In a 20-quart soup pot, bring the water to a boil over high heat. Place the seasoned birds in the boiling water with the crushed garlic cloves and the small onion, reduce the heat to medium, and cook, uncovered, for about 1 hour. Check the birds for tenderness. If the meat is falling off the bones, remove the birds from the pot. If the meat is still tough, keep cooking it, adding water as necessary to keep the birds covered. (A goose will take as long as 3 hours to get tender.)

When all of the birds are out of the pot, strain the stock through a fine-mesh sieve and return it to the pot. Let the stock stand for a few minutes, then, using a large spoon, skim off all of the fat from the surface. (If you have the time, the easiest way to do this is to put the stock in the refrigerator overnight and lift off the solidified fat in the morning.) When the birds have cooled, remove the meat from the bones and discard the bones and skin. Cut the meat into bite-size pieces.

Make the roux as directed, cooking it until is walnut colored. Turn off the heat, add the diced onions, bell peppers, and celery, and stir for about 5 minutes, until the vegetables are wilted. Next, add the Worcestershire sauce, Tabasco sauce, bay leaf, thyme, oregano, cayenne, and white pepper to the roux and stir to blend.

Bring the reserved stock to a full rolling boil and slowly whisk the roux, a little at a time, into the stock, making sure there are no lumps. Cook over medium heat for 30 minutes. Add the duck meat and continue to cook for another 30 minutes. Season with salt and black pepper. The gumbo should be fairly thick.

To serve, mound ½ cup rice in the middle of each warmed bowl. Using a slotted spoon, divide the meat among the bowls. Ladle about 2 cups of the gumbo around the rice in each bowl. Put a sweet potato round in each bowl. Serve with filé powder and more Tabasco sauce on the side.

Texarkana ★

★ Dallas

★ Longview

Tyler ★

PINEY WOODS

★ Nacogdoches

★ Lufkin

PART II
EAST TEXAS
SOUTHERN

East Texas and the Piney Woods

Fort Worth is often described as "where the West begins." Dallas and everything east of Interstate 35 is on the East Texas part of the map.

The rolling plains between Interstate 35 and Interstate 45 are often called the Prairies and Lakes region. East of Interstate 45 lies the Piney Woods ecosystem that also includes part of northern Louisiana and southern Arkansas. The easternmost part of East Texas is called Deep East Texas and is the home to a dense underbrush and bayou system called the Big Thicket. Partially protected in a federal reserve, the Big Thicket is one of the most varied ecosystems in North America. As the forest thins out toward the Gulf Coast, the Coastal Bend region begins.

Clockwise from top left: Boardinghouse Biscuits (page 71), Sage Breakfast Sausage (page 72), Twoberry Jam (page 98), and Cheese Grits with Eggs Poached in Milk (pages 74 and 72).

Miss Bessie Beck of China Grove gives a home canning demonstration in 1943.

CHAPTER 6
BOARDINGHOUSE FARE

★ ★ ★ ★ ★ ★ ★ ★ ★ ★ ★ ★ ★ ★ ★ ★ ★ ★

Verdant East Texas was the best prospect for agricultural development in New Spain's El Norte region. It was well populated by the Caddo tribes, whose language gave the state its name—"Texas" is the Hispanicized form of the Caddo word *tejas*, meaning "friend." In 1690, the San Francisco de Espada mission was established in the Hasinai village of Nabedaches, near present-day Nacogdoches. But like most of the other Caddo-speaking tribes, the Hasinai were not easily subjugated.

Although the haciendas and plantations of colonial New Spain relied on peasant labor provided by the conquered natives, that pattern didn't work in Texas. The Hasinai fled from the Spanish missions following outbreaks of European diseases. After years of failure, the East Texas missions were dismantled in the early 1700s and moved to San Antonio.

It wasn't until the 1800s, in the era of the riverboat, that Spanish East Texas was developed. Ports on the Red River became the gateway for travelers from New Orleans and the United States. Two travelogues about East Texas written in the 1800s include opinions about the food. One was written by a Mexican spy and the other by a New York abolitionist. Neither one had a charitable view.

In 1834, two years before the war with Mexico, a Mexican diplomat named Juan N. Almonte entered East Texas from Louisiana and traveled to the Mexican border. He issued a report about the things he saw along the way, including, "Among the Americans, the most common food is bacon, and cornbread, coffee sweetened with bee's honey, because they have no cane sugar, butter, buttermilk, and sometimes crackers."

The chow was better in the Mexican part of the state according to the Mexican observer. "The food most generally used among the Mexicans in Texas is the tortillas, beef, venison, chickens, eggs, cheese, and milk, and sometimes coffee, chocolate, tea, and sugar may be secured."

Almonte also noted that although the Brazos Valley was the most successfully cultivated part of Texas, its pioneers offered the least comfort for outsiders. "Each settler lives independent of the whole world, having at home everything which he needs for himself but nothing for travelers," Almonte wrote of the cotton planters.

In its days as a colony of New Spain, all roads in Texas led to Mexico City. In San Antonio and South Texas, good supplies of imported Mexican foodstuffs like chiles and beans were available. But East Texas was cut off from the rest of the world; settlers there ate only what they could grow or gather in the wild.

Some twenty years after Almonte's trip, New Yorker Frederick Law Olmsted followed nearly the same route. He recounted the trip in his 1857 book, *A Journey through Texas*. His description of the difficulty of getting to East Texas explains a lot.

"Texas has but two avenues of approach—the Gulf and the Red River," wrote Olmsted. "Travelers for the Gulf counties and the West enter by the sea, for all other parts of Texas, by the river." Travelers to East Texas booked passage on riverboats from New Orleans. They entered the mouth of the Red River where it joined the Mississippi and then traveled a considerable distance upriver. Getting to Texas by horse from Louisiana was all but impossible.

"The roads leading into the state through Louisiana, south of Natchitoches, are scarcely used, except by residents along them and herdsmen bringing cattle to the New Orleans market," Olmsted wrote. "The ferries across the numerous rivers and bayous are so costly and ill-tended, the roads so wet and bad, and the distance from steam-conveyance to any vigorous part of the state so very great, that the current is entirely diverted from this region."

Once he got to East Texas, the New Yorker waxed poetic about the vast wilderness and isolation, but before long he began to complain about the food. He reported that close to the river port, some Texans made a living gouging travelers with overpriced meals and expensive accommodations. In the log cabins of rustic cotton plantations in the interior, Olmsted paid $1.25 a night for dinner, a bed, breakfast, and a dozen ears of corn for his horse. The standard fare for both lunch and dinner was unleavened cornmeal cakes, salt pork, and erstatz coffee.

"The bread is made of cornmeal stirred with water and salt and baked in a kettle covered with coals," wrote Olmsted. "The corn for breakfast is frequently unhusked at sunrise. A negro, whose business it is, shells and grinds it in a hand-mill for the cook. Should there be any of the loaf left after breakfast, it is given to the traveler, if he wishes it, with a bit of pork, for a noon-'snack,' with no further charge." To Olmsted's chagrin, wheat and wheat flour were nowhere to be found.

In 1849, East Texas produced six million bushels of corn. By 1859, more than sixteen million bushels of corn were grown. The Confederate government encouraged more corn production because a Northern blockade made it difficult to get cotton to market and corn was needed to feed the soldiers.

But after the Civil War, the importance of corn declined dramatically and the diet of East Texans changed. Wheat, soybeans, and sorghum were planted. Cattle raising rivaled cotton farming in importance. Beef and biscuits joined cornbread and bacon on the East Texas table, and the Texas version of Southern cooking was born.

Clearly, the smoky, falling-apart tender pork barbecue of the Carolinas is the granddaddy of the smoky, falling-apart tender beef brisket of Texas. The tangy barbecue sauce, the creamy mashed potato salad, and the cornbread on the other side of the barbecue plate came down to us from our Southern forebears as well.

The cattle ranchers, cotton planters, and slaves who came to East Texas from the Old South brought a food culture that was drastically different from that of the Spanish-speaking ranchers who settled South Texas. Catfish, fried chicken, sweet potatoes, black-eyed peas, and okra all came from Southern culinary culture, which remains one of the deepest currents in Texas foodways. But while no Texan would deny the importance of Southern food classics like pit-smoked barbecue and fried chicken to the state's cuisine, not all Texans agree that Texas is part of the South anymore.

Texas was a slave state, and part of the Confederacy, so it would seem its Southernness was pretty obvious. But at the time of the Civil War, only East Texas was settled. After the Civil War, when the buffalo were killed off and the Comanches were moved to reservations, the cattle-drive era began and West Texas became cattle country. The culture of the Wild West was very different from the culture of the Old South. Cowboys, who inherited their code of chivalry along with their equestrian traditions from the Spanish caballeros, became the stuff of American mythology. Dime novels, cowboy movies, and Buffalo Bill Cody's Wild West Show created a colorful image that captured the national imagination.

In 1936, at the suggestion of a New York advertising executive, Texas set about rebranding itself. The marketing campaign for a world's fair–size celebration of the Texas Centennial gave the state just the spotlight it needed. To promote the event, the governor donned cowboy boots and a ten-gallon hat and took the University of Texas Longhorn Band, a Texas ranger on a horse, and a bevy of beauties in chaps and cowboy costumes on a railroad train that toured the country giving away Stetsons and promoting the Texas Centennial. Texas was already synonymous with cowboys in the popular culture, and now it lived up to the perceptions.

The historical narrative was consciously rewritten to emphasize the state's Western image and downplay ties to the Confederacy. A Paul Bunyon–like cartoon character named Pecos Bill became the star of kids' stories about how the West was won. After the Texas Centennial campaign, former slaves, cotton plantations, the stars and bars, and all of the other embarrassing reminders of the Confederacy were swept under the rug in the interest of presenting a positive image. Rural East Texas didn't fit the cowboy image and so it was ignored; it still gets less media attention than the rest of the state.

The main industry of the Piney Woods region of East Texas is lumber. The federal Homestead Act of 1862 allowed settlers to claim up to 160 acres of land if they cultivated it for at least five years. Hundreds of thousands of pioneers headed for the midwestern prairies. To supply lumber for treeless Nebraska, Kansas, and the Dakotas, forests in other parts of the country were clear-cut. In East Texas, lumber barons like John Henry Kirby became wealthy shipping lumber, creating banks, and building railroads. At one point, the Kirby Lumber Company controlled some three hundred thousand acres of East Texas pine forests and ran thirteen sawmills.

Lumberjacks and sawmill laborers headed to the area seeking employment. Railroad spurs were built to provide access to large stands of timber. At the end of each spur, a camp for lumber-company employees, a sawmill, and a couple of small hotels with communal dining rooms for buyers and other visitors were built. These East Texas hotels were known as boardinghouses.

Kirby built his first sawmill in Silsbee, a town he named after one of his investors, Bostonian Nathaniel Silsbee. He also built a hundred company houses for workers, a commissary, and two boardinghouses where he could entertain friends and investors. The Kirby Mill Hotel and the Badders Hotel looked more like large private homes than big city hotels. As Silsbee grew in importance as a rail hub, it also became the home of a Harvey House.

Between the 1880s and 1930s, the railroads were the only reliable transportation in East Texas, and Harvey House restaurants operated in railroad stations. In remote communities like Silsbee, they provided the most elegant food available. The Silsbee Harvey House had a lunchroom, a dining room, a pool room, and a barber shop. It operated from the turn of the century until 1920, when it burned down. Harvey House also operated the dining cars on the Gulf, Colorado and Santa Fe Railway that ran through East Texas.

The lumber boom and the boardinghouse era ended with the Great Depression. Some of the villages that Kirby built, like Bessmay, home of the Bessmay Hotel, became ghost towns and were reclaimed by the wilderness from which they had been carved.

★ ★ ★

Today, interstate highways crisscross East Texas, and it's easy to find a McDonald's or an Applebee's. But tourists rarely venture very far beyond Dallas. And the feelings of isolation and disconnection linger in the countryside. Rural East Texas lags behind the rest of the state in economic development. The state's African American population is concentrated here. And for these very reasons, East Texas is the last place where old Southern food traditions still persist.

My wife's family lives in Arkansas, and we drive through the region several times a year on our way to visit them. I love roaming around in the time warp of East Texas. And every time I stop at a shade tree barbecue stand by the side of the road or pull over to admire a hand-painted sign on a roadside stand, my wife reminds me of the fine line between documenting folk culture and exoticizing rural poverty.

If I am occasionally guilty of romanticizing Southern culture in Texas, the early observers Olmsted and Almonte may have had the opposite tendency. Each was working to defeat the Southern cotton culture for different reasons. Almonte toured Texas just before the war with Mexico. He knew the Anglo pioneers wanted to secede and fight for independence, and he was spying on them on behalf of the Mexican government. Frederick Law Olmsted visited just before the Civil War. He was a vehement opponent of slavery and sought to convince Texans they could do without it. Simply put, the food of early East Texas probably wasn't as terrible as these two characters described it.

The Southern cooking of East Texas migrated to the rest of the state. After the Civil War, when West Texas was opened to ranchers, cattlemen of East Texas along with their slaves settled much of the northern part of the plains and the Panhandle. They brought their barbecue, fried chicken, hush puppies, and sweet potatoes with them. Chicken-fried steak is probably a hybrid of German Belt schnitzel and the East Texas batter-frying technique.

Today, East Texas is the last place you can still find mayhaw jelly sold at roadside stands, catfish camps where the chef catches your dinner when you order it, and log-cabin barbecue joints that open and close depending on the weather.

The boardinghouses of the lumber baron era are gone now. Some stories of the original boardinghouses along with a few recipes from their cooks have been preserved in a cookbook titled *Boardin' in the Thicket*. The author, Beaumont historian Wanda A. Landrey, is a descendant of East Texas boardinghouse keepers. Some of the recipes in this chapter were inspired by tales from those old boardinghouse cooks.

The simple, honest, made-from-scratch fare of the East Texas boardinghouses is what the Texas Southern kitchen is all about. Then and now, it's nothing fancy—just chicken and homemade biscuits, fresh green beans and field peas, yams baked in cane syrup, and a slab of pecan pie. It is the stuff of the Southern "meat and three" buffets and the backbone of Texas cooking.

CORN DODGERS

When the Spanish arrived in East Texas, they found the natives growing corn and eating it as mush, cooked corn pudding, and in many other dishes. Most of the simple "cornbreads" were more or less the same thing, regardless of whether they were called hoecakes, johnnycakes, or corn dodgers. Ground dried corn was cooked with water or whatever else was on hand that might improve the taste—eggs, milk, wild onions, bacon drippings—then fried or baked in a small oval cake.

Corn dodgers, better known now as hush puppies, are the surviving example of the corn cake genre, and they are extremely popular in East Texas. Consider making them when you are already heating oil for fried catfish or fried chicken.

MAKES ABOUT 20

Peanut oil, for deep-frying

2½ cups coarse-ground yellow cornmeal, plus more if needed

2 tablespoons sugar

2 tablespoons all-purpose flour

1 tablespoon baking powder

1 teaspoon baking soda

1 teaspoon salt

1 egg

2 cups buttermilk

3 tablespoons chopped yellow onion

"The universal food of the people of Texas, both rich and poor, seems to be corn-dodgers and fried bacon."

–Frederick Law Olmsted, *A Journey through Texas*, 1857

Pour the oil to a depth of about 2 inches into a deep, heavy pot or deep fryer and heat to 350°F.

While the oil is heating, make the batter. In a bowl, stir together the 2½ cups cornmeal, sugar, flour, baking powder, baking soda, and salt. In a small bowl, whisk the egg until beaten, then stir in the buttermilk and onion. Add the buttermilk mixture to the dry ingredients and stir until combined. The batter should be stiff enough to hold its shape. If it is too soft, add more cornmeal until it holds its shape.

Drop the batter by heaping tablespoons into the hot oil and fry for 3 to 4 minutes, until golden brown. Do not fry more than 5 or 6 cakes at a time. When the cakes are ready, using a slotted spoon, transfer to paper towels to drain briefly and keep hot in a warm oven. Serve hot.

Wild Onion Corn Dodgers: Substitute 3 tablespoons chopped wild onion or green onion (white and green parts) for the chopped yellow onion and proceed as directed.

Jalapeño Corn Dodgers: Add 1 tablespoon minced jalapeño chile with the onion and proceed as directed.

SKILLET CORNBREAD

When Frederick Law Olmsted visited East Texas in the 1850s, no one had any wheat flour. (It was impossible to store harvested wheat because weevils always got into it.) However, cornbread, in its many variations, was everywhere. This simple cornbread can also be used in cornbread stuffings and dressings.

SERVES 8 TO 10

2 cups yellow cornmeal

3 tablespoons sugar

1 teaspoon baking soda

2 teaspoons baking powder

1 teaspoon salt

2 eggs

2 cups buttermilk

½ cup unsalted butter, melted and cooled

1 teaspoon freshly ground pepper

Lightly grease a No. 8 10¼-inch cast-iron skillet, place it in the oven, and preheat the oven to 375°F.

To make the batter, in a large bowl, stir together the cornmeal, sugar, baking soda, baking powder, and salt. In a small bowl, whisk the eggs until blended, then stir in the buttermilk and butter. Pour the egg mixture into the center of the dry ingredients, sprinkle with the pepper, and then stir with a fork until the batter is well blended.

Carefully remove the hot skillet from the oven and pour the batter into it. Return it to the oven and bake for about 35 minutes, until the edges of the bread pull away from the sides of the skillet and the top is lightly browned. Let cool for 10 minutes before slicing into pie-shaped wedges.

Tamale Pie: Pour half the batter into the skillet, spread ¾ cup of Classic Chili con Carne (page 111) over it, top with the rest of the batter, and bake as directed.

DELUXE CORNBREAD

The creamed corn and onions keep this tasty cornbread moist. Sadly, it doesn't keep well.

SERVES 8 TO 10

1 cup all-purpose flour

1 tablespoon baking powder

2 tablespoons sugar

½ teaspoon salt

1 cup yellow cornmeal

2 eggs, slightly beaten

¼ cup lard, melted and cooled

1 cup canned creamed corn

¾ cup buttermilk or milk

½ cup finely diced yellow onions

3 jalapeño chiles, seeds and veins removed and minced

1 red bell pepper, seeded and finely diced

Lightly grease a No. 8 10¼-inch cast-iron skillet with oil, place it in the oven, and preheat the oven to 425°F.

In a large bowl, stir together the flour, baking powder, sugar, salt, and cornmeal. Add the eggs, lard, creamed corn, buttermilk, onions, chiles, and bell pepper and stir until well blended.

Carefully remove the hot pan from the oven and pour the batter into it, filling it about two-thirds full. Return it to the oven and bake for about 20 minutes, until firm to the touch and golden brown. Let cool for 10 minutes before slicing into pie-shaped wedges.

HOT AND COLD CORNBREAD

CORNBREAD IS BEST EATEN HOT. Cold cornbread can be reheated in a toaster oven. Day-old cornbread crumbled in a bowl, drenched with cold buttermilk, and topped with a little salt and pepper is a favorite East Texas breakfast or midnight snack.

A CORNUCOPIA OF DRIED CORN

★ ★

THE DIFFERENCES BETWEEN fine- and medium-grind cornmeal, grits, polenta, hominy, *nixtamal*, posole, and *masa* can be confusing. So here's a quick guide:

Cornmeal comes in fine and medium grinds. Fine-grind cornmeal is often called **corn flour** and is preferred for hush puppies, cornbread, and most other baked products. Medium-grind cornmeal can be used for old-fashioned black skillet cornbread and is preferred as a coating on fried fish and for dusting baking sheets before making pizza or rolls.

White, yellow, and blue cornmeal can be used interchangeably. Yellow cornmeal has an earthier flavor and blue cornmeal is higher in some nutrients. White cornmeal was preferred in wealthy households of the Old South because it more closely resembled European wheat flour.

Grits are coarsely ground dried corn. The cornmeal and grits popular in the American South are made from "dent corn," the dried corn types identified by the dent or dimple on the surface of each grain.

Traditional slow-cooking grits take longer to cook, but have the best texture. Some custom producers such as Anson Mills in South Carolina use heirloom varieties of corn such as "Pencil Cob" to make full-flavored heritage grits (see Resources). These grits are excellent, but they can take several hours to cook. The easy method is to simmer them overnight in a slow cooker. To substitute slow-cooking grits for the quick-cooking grits in the recipes in this book, follow the package instructions and cook the grits to the desired consistency (using whatever liquid is specified in the recipe's ingredients list) before adding the other ingredients.

Instant grits cook in one minute, but they don't develop a creamy texture.

Quick-cooking grits are the most popular kind of grits and are specified for use in the recipes in this book.

Polenta is an Italian cornmeal mush made by coarse grinding "flint corn," a type of corn that yields a tougher dried kernel than dent corn does. Most polenta lovers like a medium grind.

Nixtamal, **posole, or hominy** is dried corn that is treated with lime (calcium oxide, not the fruit), which swells and softens the kernels. You can buy hominy in a can, but posole is usually sold in a dried form that must be cooked. (See Texas Green Chile Posole, page 132).

Masa is *nixtamal* ground into a dough, which is then used to make tortillas and tamales. Fresh *masa* is available in many Mexican markets, especially during the holiday tamale-making season. It must be refrigerated and used within a few days.

Masa harina is an instant powder made by dehydrating the fresh *masa* dough. The *masa harina* powder is sold in 5-pound bags in grocery stores. It is made into tortilla dough by adding water and kneading. See Puffy Taco Shells (page 138).

INDIAN PUDDING

This sweetened corn pudding was one of the earliest American desserts.

SERVES 6

3 eggs

⅔ cup molasses or cane syrup

2 tablespoons unsalted butter, at room
   temperature

½ teaspoon ground cinnamon

¼ teaspoon ground mace

½ teaspoon powdered ginger

3 cups milk

½ cup coarse-grind yellow cornmeal

½ teaspoon salt

⅔ cup chopped raisins

Whipped cream or vanilla ice cream, for serving

You can cook this pudding in a slow cooker or in the oven. If you will be using a slow cooker, lightly spray a medium-size slow cooker insert with nonstick cooking spray. If you will be baking the pudding, preheat the oven to 300°F, and grease a 1½-quart baking dish with butter.

In a bowl, whisk the eggs until blended, then stir in the molasses, butter, and all of the spices. Set aside.

In a saucepan, scald the milk over medium-high heat (small bubbles appear along the edge of the pan). Add the cornmeal and salt, stir well, and immediately decrease the heat to low. Cook, stirring constantly, for 10 minutes, until the mixture thickens. Remove the pan from the heat. Gradually add the egg mixture to the hot cornmeal mixture while stirring constantly, then continue to whisk until smooth. Stir in the raisins.

If using the slow cooker, pour the batter into the prepared cooker, cover, and cook on the high setting for 3 hours or on the low setting for 6 hours or more, until the pudding has set. If using the oven, pour the batter into the prepared baking dish, place in the oven, and bake for 45 minutes, until the pudding has set.

Serve the pudding warm with whipped cream or ice cream.

BOARDINGHOUSE BISCUITS

These biscuits are easy to make and come out perfect every time. Be sure to crowd them close together in the cake pan. You can use self-rising flour, if you like. Just be sure to omit the baking powder and baking soda. White Lily is the favorite low-protein biscuit flour in the South.

MAKES 10 BISCUITS

½ cup unsalted butter, chilled

3 cups pastry flour, preferably White Lily brand

2 teaspoons baking powder

2 teaspoons baking soda

1 tablespoon sugar

½ teaspoon salt

1¼ cups buttermilk, or more as needed

Cane syrup or fruit preserves, for serving

Preheat the oven to 425°F. Butter a 9-inch cake pan.

Cut 1 tablespoon off the stick of butter and set it aside. Cut the rest of the butter stick lengthwise into quarters, then cut crosswise into small cubes.

In a large bowl, stir together the flour, baking powder, baking soda, sugar, and salt. Put 1 cup of the flour mixture into a pie pan and set aside. Scatter the butter cubes over the remaining flour mixture. Using a pastry blender or 2 knives, work the butter cubes into the flour mixture until it resembles coarse meal. Add the buttermilk and stir with a fork to mix. The dough should be wet. Continue to stir until the dough resembles cottage cheese, adding more buttermilk if needed to achieve the correct consistency. Do not overwork.

Butter an ice cream scoop and scoop up a ball of dough. Plop the wet ball of dough into the flour in the pie pan. Roll the ball in the flour, gently shaping it, then pick it up and roll it gently in your cupped hand, shaking off any excess flour. Place the ball in the prepared cake pan. Repeat until all of the dough is used, arranging the balls very close together in the cake pan. You should have 10 biscuits.

(Continued)

Bake for 20 minutes, until golden brown. Meanwhile, melt the reserved 1 tablespoon butter. When the biscuits are ready, remove from the oven and immediately brush with the melted butter. Allow to cool for a few minutes. Invert the pan onto a flat plate, then lift off the pan, releasing the biscuits. Place another plate on top of the upside-down biscuits and turn the plates over again so the biscuits are right side up on the serving plate. Serve immediately with cane syrup or preserves.

EGGS POACHED IN MILK

When you poach eggs in water, the whites tend to separate. The usual solution is to add a little vinegar to the water. For some reason, hot milk has the same effect on eggs as vinegar does. And the flavor of milk is often preferable to that of vinegar—especially if you are serving your eggs over cheese-laced grits. See photo on page 62.

SERVES 6
2 cups milk
6 eggs
Cheese Grits (page 74)

Pour the milk into a small skillet and heat over medium heat until it is steaming. Do not let it boil. Carefully crack 2 eggs into the milk and poach until the whites are set and the yolks are still runny, or to desired doneness. The timing will depend on how hot the milk is.

While the eggs are cooking, spoon some of the grits into 2 warmed bowls. When the eggs are ready, using a slotted spoon, put 1 egg in each bowl. (You don't have to worry about draining the eggs on paper towels because the milk tastes good with the grits.) Repeat with the remaining 4 eggs, in 2 batches, serving them on the remaining grits.

EGGS BLINDFOLDED

These griddle-poached eggs were invented by short-order cooks who didn't have time to carefully remove eggs from hot liquid with a slotted spoon. It's a great way to make "poached eggs" fast and easy. Serve the eggs with Cheese Grits (page 74) and Sage Breakfast Sausage (recipe follows).

SERVES 1
Vegetable oil, for the frying pan
2 eggs
3 or 4 ice cubes

Coat a griddle or a 9-inch skillet with a light film of oil and place over medium-high heat. When the skillet is hot, crack the eggs into the middle. When the whites are set, place the ice cubes next to the eggs and cover immediately with a concave pot lid. Allow the eggs to steam for about 2 minutes for medium, or until cooked to your liking. Serve at once.

SAGE BREAKFAST SAUSAGE

The best way to make sausage is with a meat grinder, but if you use a cut of pork without gristle, it's easy to whip up small batches in a food processor. Red jalapeño chiles look pretty, but pickled jalapeños give the sausage a nice vinegary kick. I like to make a few big patties, but you can also divide the mixture into several small ones. Serve with eggs and Cheese Grits (page 74).

MAKES ABOUT 1 POUND; 4 TO 8 PATTIES
10 ounces boneless pork loin, finely diced
6 ounces sliced bacon, finely diced
1 tablespoon light brown sugar
1 tablespoon chopped fresh sage
1 tablespoon minced fresh rosemary
1 teaspoon paprika

HERB GRITS

If you are making these tasty grits for Shrimp and Grits (page 34), use shrimp stock (page 32) in place of the chicken broth.

SERVES 8

1 tablespoon unsalted butter
½ cup chopped green onions (white and green parts)
1 clove garlic, minced
4 cups milk
4 cups chicken broth
2 cups Anson Mills quick-cooking organic yellow grits or other quick-cooking grits (not instant)
1 tablespoon chopped fresh thyme or other fresh herb
½ teaspoon pepper
Tabasco sauce, for serving

In a large saucepan, melt the butter over medium heat. Add the green onions and garlic and sauté for 3 minutes, until wilted. Add the milk and broth, increase the heat to high, and bring to a boil. Slowly add the grits while whisking constantly. When all of the grits are incorporated, decrease the heat to low and cook, stirring occasionally, for 20 to 30 minutes, until soft and creamy.

Remove from the heat, add the herbs and pepper, mix well, and allow to sit for a few minutes covered. Serve with fried eggs, bacon, and Tabasco sauce on the side, or use for Shrimp and Grits.

1 tablespoon minced fresh red jalapeño or pickled jalapeño chile, or to taste
1 teaspoon black pepper
½ teaspoon salt
Pinch of cayenne pepper

In a food processor, combine all of the ingredients and process for 10 seconds, until coarsely ground. Fry a small nugget of the mixture in a hot skillet and taste it, then adjust the seasoning of the mixture if necessary. Process for another 5 to 10 seconds, until well ground.

Shape the mixture into patties about ½ inch thick. In a skillet, cook the patties over medium heat, turning once, for 5 minutes total, until cooked through. Serve hot.

CHEESE GRITS

Cheese grits are great all by themselves or topped with Eggs Poached in Milk (page 72). See photo on page 62.

SERVES 4

2 cups chicken broth

2 cups water

1 cup Anson Mills quick-cooking organic
    yellow grits or other quick-cooking grits
    (not instant)

1 cup shredded Cheddar cheese

¼ cup grated Parmesan cheese

¼ cup unsalted butter

½ teaspoon salt

¼ teaspoon black pepper

Pinch of cayenne pepper

Tabasco sauce, for serving

In a saucepan, combine the broth and water and bring to a boil over high heat. Slowly add the grits while whisking constantly. When all of the grits are incorporated, decrease the heat to low and cook, stirring occasionally, for 20 to 30 minutes, until soft and creamy.

Remove from the heat and stir in the Cheddar and Parmesan cheeses, butter, salt, black pepper, and cayenne and stir just until mixed. Serve hot with Tabasco sauce on the side.

SPICY PIMIENTO CHEESE

When making pimiento cheese sandwiches for a fancy luncheon, it is customary to cut the crusts off the bread slices. Use good-quality white sandwich bread, and spread the slices thickly with the cheese. If not serving immediately, cover the sandwiches with a damp tea towel to keep them moist until serving.

MAKES 1¼ POUNDS

1 pound sharp Cheddar cheese, shredded

½ cup jarred pimientos or roasted red peppers

¼ cup pickled jalapeño chiles

1 teaspoon onion powder

½ teaspoon Worcestershire sauce

¼ cup mayonnaise, or more as needed

Sea salt and freshly ground pepper

In a food processor, combine the cheese, pimientos, chiles, onion powder, and Worcestershire sauce and process until well blended. Add the mayonnaise and process until well mixed, adding more as needed to achieve the desired consistency. Season with salt and pepper.

The cheese can be store in a tightly covered in the refrigerator for up to 2 weeks.

BUTTERMILK MACARONI AND CHEESE WITH HOMEGROWN TOMATOES

Here's a tasty tomato season variation on an old boardinghouse favorite.

SERVES 8

¼ cup unsalted butter

1 (16-ounce) package elbow macaroni

3 eggs

1 cup buttermilk

1 cup half-and-half

1 teaspoon dry mustard

¼ teaspoon salt

¼ teaspoon pepper

8 ounces Cheddar cheese, shredded

12 ounces Jack cheese, shredded

¾ cup dried bread crumbs

1 large tomato, sliced ¼ inch thick

Preheat the oven to 350°F. Using 1 tablespoon of the butter, grease a 3-quart baking dish.

Bring a large pot of salted water to a boil. Add the macaroni and cook until al dente. Drain well.

While the macaroni is cooking, in a large bowl, whisk the eggs until blended. Whisk in the buttermilk, half-and-half, mustard, salt, and pepper and continue to whisk until the mixture is light and fluffy. Add the drained macaroni and the cheeses and stir to incorporate all of the ingredients. Pour the macaroni mixture into the prepared baking dish.

In a small pan, melt the remaining 3 tablespoons butter over low heat. Remove from the heat, add the bread crumbs, and toss until all of the butter is absorbed.

Arrange the tomato slices in a single layer on top of the macaroni. Sprinkle the bread crumb mixture evenly over the tomatoes. Bake for 45 minutes, until the mixture is bubbly and the bread crumbs are golden brown. Allow to set for at least 15 minutes before serving.

GRAMMY'S CREAMY COLESLAW

Amber Reece, my next door neighbor, showed me how her grandma taught her to make coleslaw.

MAKES 3 CUPS; SERVES 6
3 eggs
¼ cup cider vinegar
1 tablespoon sugar
2 tablespoons mayonnaise
¼ teaspoon dry mustard
½ head cabbage, finely shredded
Salt and pepper

In a small bowl, whisk the eggs until blended, then whisk in the vinegar and sugar until the mixture is thick and free of lumps and the sugar is dissolved. In a small skillet over medium heat, cook the egg mixture for a few minutes until just set. Set aside to cool. Whisk together the mayonnaise and mustard

in the bowl, add the egg mixture, and whisk until combined.

Put the cabbage in a bowl. Pour the warm egg, vinegar, and mayo mixture over the cabbage and toss and stir to coat the cabbage evenly. Season with salt and pepper. Chill in the refrigerator for a few hours before serving.

GREEN BEANS WITH BACON

Kentucky Wonders are the favorite green beans these days, but in pioneer times, pinto pods were the most common green beans. To plant them, you stuck dried pinto beans in the soil, waited for them to sprout, and then tied up the vines to a pole or a fence.

SERVES 8
2½ tablespoons vegetable oil
4 slices bacon, chopped
1 large yellow onion, chopped
10 cups green beans (about 2 pounds), trimmed
1¾ cups chicken broth
Salt and pepper

In a large pot, heat the oil over medium-high heat. Add the bacon and onion and fry, stirring often, for 5 to 10 minutes, until soft. Add the green beans and broth and stir well. Season with salt and pepper, decrease the heat to low, and cook for 30 to 45 minutes, until the beans are soft.

Taste and adjust the seasoning and serve hot.

ROAST BEEF AND GRAVY

A roast beef dinner was reserved for Christmas and other special occasions once upon a time in the boardinghouses and family farms of the Piney Woods. Today, it has become a popular Sunday dinner for beef-loving Texans everywhere.

SERVES 6 TO 8

1 (3½-pound) USDA Choice beef rump roast

1 teaspoon salt

1 teaspoon paprika

3 tablespoons all-purpose flour

1 tablespoon granulated garlic

½ teaspoon ground dried thyme

2 tablespoons vegetable oil or bacon drippings

5 carrots, peeled and cut into 4-inch lengths

5 stalks celery, cut into 4-inch lengths

1 large yellow onion, quartered

6 red or white potatoes, quartered

Gravy

2 tablespoons warm water

2 cups cold water or beef broth

1 tablespoon prepared Creole mustard

1 tablespoon Worcestershire sauce

Salt and pepper

Remove the roast from the refrigerator and bring to room temperature. Preheat the oven to 350°F.

In a shallow dish, stir together the salt, paprika, flour, granulated garlic, and thyme. Roll the roast in the seasoning mixture, coating it on all sides. Reserve the leftover seasoned flour.

In a Dutch oven or a roasting pan, heat the oil over medium-high heat. Add the roast and brown on all sides. Transfer the roast to a platter. Spread the carrots, celery, and onion on the bottom of the pan to serve as a roasting rack. Place the roast on top of the vegetables; do not let it rest directly on the pan. Tuck the potatoes around the edges of the beef.

Roast for 1 to 1½ hours, until an instant-read thermometer inserted into the thickest part away from the bone registers 135°F for medium-rare, 140°F for medium, or to desired doneness.

Return the roast to the platter, tent with aluminum foil, and let rest for 15 minutes. If the vegetables aren't quite done, stir them in the pan so they are evenly coated with the pan juices, return the pan to the oven, and roast for 10 minutes, or until well browned. Transfer to a warmed serving dish and keep warm.

To make the gravy, in a small bowl, stir together the reserved seasoned flour and the warm water, forming a slurry that is free of lumps.

Place the roasting pan on the stove top over medium-high heat. Pour in the cold water and bring to a boil, stirring to scrape up any browned bits from the pan bottom. Reduce the heat to a simmer, add the slurry, and stir continuously over medium heat until the gravy reaches the desired thickness. Stir in the mustard and Worcestershire sauce and season with salt and pepper. Pour into a warmed gravy dish.

Slice the roast and serve with the roasted vegetables and gravy. Mashed potatoes and cornbread are favorite sides for gravy lovers.

STEWED CHICKEN

In the 1920s, chickens sold for around fifty cents apiece in East Texas. They were the most affordable meat on the market and very common on local tables.

SERVES 4

1 (4½- to 5-pound) whole chicken

2 yellow onions, chopped, with trimmings reserved

3 cups cold water

2 tablespoons olive oil

2 cloves garlic, crushed and minced

3 thyme sprigs, chopped, plus more chopped for the gravy (optional)

1 teaspoon salt

½ teaspoon black pepper

¼ teaspoon cayenne pepper

1 tablespoon red hot-pepper sauce

1½ tablespoons all-purpose flour

1 cup warm water

Cooked rice or Herb Grits (page 73), for serving

Place the chicken on a cutting board, back side up. Using a sharp knife or poultry shears, and starting at the cavity end, cut along one side of the backbone. Pull the chicken open and cut along the other side of the backbone and remove the back. Then cut the breasts and leg into quarters or smaller pieces as desired and place in a bowl.

In a small saucepan, combine the back, neck, wing tips, and any other unused chicken pieces. Add the onion trimmings and cold water, bring to a boil over medium-high heat, decrease the heat to a simmer, and cook for about 20 minutes to make a stock. Drain the stock through a fine-mesh sieve, let cool, cover, and refrigerate until needed.

While the stock is cooking, make the marinade. In a small bowl, stir together 1 tablespoon of the oil, garlic, thyme, salt, black pepper, and cayenne. Rub the chicken pieces with the marinade, coating them evenly. Cover and marinate the chicken in the refrigerator for several hours.

Remove the chicken from the marinade and reserve the marinade. In a Dutch oven, heat the remaining 1 tablespoon oil over medium-high heat. When the oil is hot, add the chicken and onions and brown the chicken, turning as needed, for 5 to 7 minutes, until nicely colored. Add the marinade, the pepper sauce, and half of the stock. Cover, decrease the heat to medium-low, and simmer, adding more stock as needed to maintain the liquid level, for about 20 minutes, until the chicken is fork-tender.

Transfer the chicken pieces to a plate. In a small bowl, stir together the flour and warm water, forming a slurry that is free of lumps. Increase the heat to high, add the remaining stock and the slurry to the cooking juices, and stir until the gravy thickens to the desired consistency. Season with thyme, salt, and black pepper. Pour the gravy into a warmed gravy dish.

Serve the chicken with the rice. Pass the gravy at the table for pouring over the rice.

Chicken Potpie: This is a great way to use up leftover stewed chicken. Remove the chicken meat from the bones, discard the bones and skin, and chop the meat into ½-inch dice. Put the chicken, cooked carrots, and other cooked vegetables of choice in a baking dish or deep pie pan. Pour the gravy over the chicken and vegetables, and then lay circles of biscuit dough on top (see Boardinghouse Biscuits, page 71). Bake in a preheated 400°F oven for about 25 minutes, until the biscuit dough is golden brown and cooked through.

COUNTRY MEAT LOAF

This hearty meat loaf tastes great hot with a mound of mashed potatoes or some sweet potato wedges alongside. But I like it even better sliced cold and served in a sandwich with lettuce, tomato, and mayonnaise.

MAKES 1 (3-POUND) MEAT LOAF; SERVES 6 TO 8

1 pound breakfast sausage, homemade (page 72) or store-bought

2 pounds ground sirloin

1 large yellow onion

¾ cup dried bread crumbs

2 eggs

½ cup heavy cream or half-and-half

2 cloves garlic

1½ teaspoons salt

1 teaspoon black pepper

1 teaspoon ground dried thyme

1½ teaspoons chili powder, homemade (page 110) or store-bought

½ jalapeño chile, seeded and chopped

6 slices bacon, or 2 large, thin sheets pork fat

Preheat the oven to 350°F. Spray a standard loaf pan with nonstick cooking spray.

In a large bowl, combine the sausage and sirloin. In a food processor or blender, combine the onion, bread crumbs, eggs, cream, garlic, salt, pepper, thyme, chili powder, and chile and process until a smooth puree forms. Add the puree to the meats and mix well. The mixture should be quite wet.

Transfer the meat mixture to the prepared loaf pan to shape it. Place 3 slices of the bacon or 1 sheet of pork fat on the bottom of a baking pan with high sides. Invert the loaf pan onto the bacon or pork fat and smooth the top of the meat loaf. Place the remaining 3 slices bacon or 1 sheet pork fat on top of the meat loaf.

Bake for 1½ hours, until an instant-read thermometer inserted into the center registers 160°F, or to desired doneness.

Mini Meat Loaves: Divide the meat mixture among 2 or 3 smaller loaf pans and decrease the cooking time to about 1 hour.

Glazed Meat Loaf: Spread ketchup or your favorite barbecue sauce on the top and sides of the meat loaf during the last 15 minutes of cooking.

Meat Loaf with Mashed Potato Icing: Frost the top and sides of the meat loaf with a ½-inch-thick layer of seasoned mashed potatoes during the last 15 minutes of cooking. Allow the potatoes to brown slightly.

CHAPTER 7

JUNETEENTH

Mrs. Nathan Jean Whitaker Sanders, known to her friends and family as "Mama Sugar," was wearing a bright red and yellow apron over her cotton dress and stirring a soup pot full of okra and tomatoes when I found her on the kitchen porch. The two-burner propane stove had been set up under the porch eaves to keep it out of the rain. Every burner on the stove inside her house was already occupied. Mama Sugar had been cooking all week.

"These are my own homegrown tomatoes," she bragged with a big smile, holding up a spoonful by way of a greeting. Her mood hadn't been so cheerful when I phoned her earlier in the day. A huge thunderstorm had moved across East Texas on the morning of Juneteenth, the biggest holiday in the state's African American community, with the possible exception of Christmas.

The television news showed cars stalling out in deep puddles on the highways. If it kept raining, the unpaved road that leads into Mama Sugar's 5 Bar S Ranch, a sixty-seven-acre horse farm in Fresno, about a forty-minute drive south of Houston, would turn to mud. And more flooding elsewhere would make it hard to even reach Mama Sugar's road. The Juneteenth parade in Galveston, forty-five miles away, had already been canceled because of rising water.

A canvas tent roof on aluminum poles out in Mama Sugar's front yard provided some shelter in case of a downpour. But by the time I arrived in the early afternoon, the rain had tapered off. The only showers now were when a gust of wind shook the cottonwood and pecan trees that shaded the yard. The afternoon turned cloudy and cool, which is as good as it gets on June 19 in East Texas.

I had been looking forward to this day ever since first meeting Mama Sugar about four months earlier. I had quizzed African American cultural historians around Houston about cooking, and they all recommended that I visit Mama Sugar, who had grown up on a farm in East Texas. So I had come to the ranch to see her, and as I copied down her recipes and marveled over the down-home flavors of her food, I wangled an invitation to her famous Juneteenth party.

Clockwise from top left: Just Like Moma's Fried Chicken (page 87), Dot Hewitt's Stewed Okra (page 89), and Fresh Field Peas (page 90).

With the threat of rain over, Mama Sugar's husband, Ron Sugar, set up the sound system and soon the 1980s disco hit "Funkytown" was blaring from the nightclub-size speakers on the big wooden front porch. Country, jazz, soul, and pop music would boom out over the ranch for the rest of the afternoon and into the night.

Gathered on the front lawn in a collection of mismatched benches, lawn furniture, and plastic chairs were some of the early arrivals to Mama Sugar's Juneteenth party. While their mothers were busy cooking and setting up the buffet, a gaggle of teenage granddaughters were roaring with laughter at the expense of their tall, muscular nineteen-year-old cousin Nathan Mitchell. The young women were all dressed Western style in blue jeans and cotton shirts, some with cowboy hats. They were making fun of cousin Nathan's hip-hop outfit of chartreuse baggy shorts and matching shirt accented with a backward baseball cap.

I asked LaDraun Campbell, a friend of the family who manned the two barbecue trailers parked under the carport at the edge of the lawn, what all the hilarity was about. "Nathan don't rodeo," he said. "He thinks he's a big-city boy now," he teased in a loud voice that made Nathan roll his eyes and the girls roar with laughter.

City boy or not, Nathan was one of the best horsemen in the family. Mama Sugar and most of the people invited to this Juneteenth party belonged to the Southwestern Trail Riders Association, an umbrella organization for black horseback riding clubs. Mama Sugar's gang, the Sugar Shack Trailblazers Riding Rodeo Club of Arcola/Fresno, was formed in 1983. Her kids all ride and her grandchildren grew up in the saddle.

★ ★ ★

June 19, 1865, was two and half years after the enactment of the Emancipation Proclamation. The delay in freeing the slaves in Texas was a result of the Union Army's slow progress in securing control of the entire South. The last slaves in the United States were freed when Major General Gordon Granger landed in Galveston. The Texas state holiday known as Juneteenth (short for June 19) commemorates the anniversary of the reading of the document known as General Order Number 3: "The people of Texas are informed that in accordance with a Proclamation

From left: Reverend Jeffrey's Fried Chicken at Just Like Moma's soul food restaurant, Mama Sugar, and field peas.

BARBECUE AND FREEDOM

★ ★

IN *THE SLAVE NARRATIVES,* a series of interviews with more than twenty-three hundred former slaves conducted in the 1930s by writers working for the Works Progress Administration (WPA), two former Texas slaves recall emancipation.

On learning the slaves had been freed on June 19, 1865:

"I kin remember w'en I was jes a boy about nine years old w'en freedom cum's ... w'en we commenced to have de nineteenth celebrations ... an' everybody seems like, w'ite an' black cum an' git some barbecue."

—Former Texas slave Anderson Jones

On being forced to leave the plantation where he grew up:

"So we jes' scatters 'round, here and yonder, not knowin' zactly what to do. Some of us works on one farm and some on another for a little co'n or some clothes or food. Finally I works 'round 'til I comes to San Angelo, Texas, and I cooks barbecue (at a barbecue stand) for a long time 'til I jes' finally breaks down."

—Former Texas slave Steve Williams

from the Executive of the United States, all slaves are free. This involves an absolute equality of rights and rights of property between former masters and slaves, and the connection heretofore existing between them becomes that between employer and free laborer."

At the time of emancipation, there were 180,000 slaves in Texas, 30 percent of the state's population. For more than a century, Juneteenth was celebrated among African Texans statewide with parades, pageants, and barbecues. Because blacks were barred from congregating in public parks, Juneteenth celebrations were often held out in the country on private ranches. Horseback riding and cowboy-riding gear became a part of the Juneteenth tradition.

The black holiday had largely died out by the early 1960s. But Juneteenth was revived on June 19, 1968, the final day of the Poor People's March on Washington when Reverend Ralph Abernathy called for people of all races to show solidarity. Since then, Juneteenth celebrations have spread across the country. The holiday is big in Milwaukee and Minneapolis, among other places. In 1980, it became an official state holiday in Texas.

The spirit of Juneteenth is sort of a cross between Martin Luther King Day, Passover, and the Fourth of July—a celebration of African American heritage, freedom from slavery, and barbecue blowout.

"We always celebrated Juneteenth in my family," LaDraun told me as we checked out the smoked meats in the barbecue smoker. He grew up in Lane City, Texas, a small farming community near Wharton, about a half hour southwest of Houston. "My daddy took us to the beach in Freeport every year." LaDraun remembers the vanilla ice cream made on the spot in an old-fashioned hand-cranked machine. He also remembers the barbecued brisket. The barbecue pit was a fifty-five-gallon oil drum with a grill welded inside, and it was carried to the beach in the back of a pickup truck.

LaDraun ran a company called L&D BBQ and Catering in Missouri City, Texas. He had been barbecuing since he was eleven or twelve, and he learned how to cook brisket from his mother. The rub was just salt and pepper, but that wasn't the only seasoning. "My mom poked a hole and stuck some garlic in it. She basted the brisket with a mop [sauce] of vinegar, lemon, and onion. Mama made me watch the meat. She seasoned it, I flipped it."

But at her Juneteenth party, Mama Sugar was doing the seasoning. LaDraun opened up the five-foot smoker and showed me Mama Sugar's margarita ribs, which were rubbed with tequila and then marinated in margarita mix. We cut off some little pieces of meat from the skinny end of the rack. The pork was still a bit tough, but the tart and peppery flavor made my cheeks tingle.

In the big barbecue trailer, a whole lot of briskets—I couldn't count them for all of the thick smoke—were cooking. LaDraun had rubbed them with a commercial seasoning, Bolner's Fiesta brisket rub, and he planned to smoke them, fat side up, at around 300 degrees for five hours. The wood was mostly oak, with some pecan wood added for its sweeter flavor, he said. After five hours of smoking, the briskets were wrapped in aluminum foil to hold them. The foil keeps the meat from getting too black and also traps escaping steam to accelerate the cooking process and make the beef come out falling-apart tender.

As the skies cleared, cars and pickup trucks started arriving, and soon people were milling around the broad expanse of St. Augustine grass that surrounds Mama Sugar's house. To the delight of the dozen or so small kids in the backyard, Ron Sugar led the two gentlest horses out from the barn and parked them under a shade tree. The bigger kids got to ride first. And then they put the littlest kids in the saddles in front of them. Soon, one of the older boys was charging around the backyard at a gallop. "This is all these kids want to do out here," said Ron Sugar with a laugh, "tear around on these horses."

Energized by the arrival of family and friends, Mama Sugar buzzed around supervising the cooking. She moved pretty fast for an older woman with a cane. The okra in the pot on the porch had come from the grocery store, she said, but now she needed

Galveston Juneteenth parade.

more okra for the black-eyed peas. I followed her as she waded into the green sea of her garden, walking carefully between the rows.

Gently pushing the spiked leaves of the young eighteen-inch-high okra plants back and forth, she found some fuzzy baby pods, no more than three or four inches long, and snapped them off their stems. "I usually let them get bigger than this," she said, rolling them in her palm. But the tender little okra pods would be perfect as an accent for the peas. She also picked a bright green, corkscrew-shaped cayenne pepper to cut up for the pea pot.

Mama Sugar has been celebrating Juneteenth since she was a small child. Born on June 6, 1939, she was raised from the age of six by an aunt and uncle on a farm in County Line, a tiny community east of Dallas near Sulphur Springs. Her cooking recalls the pure country flavors of her East Texas upbringing. The family ate what it grew. From an early age, she helped raise hogs, chicken, ducks, geese, and cattle.

Watermelon, tomatoes, and peanuts were sold for cash in town. Corn, okra, sweet potatoes, black-eyed peas, pole beans, and ribbon cane were harvested for the farmhouse kitchen. The ribbon cane was taken to a local mill, where it was crushed and cooked down into syrup. Cane syrup was the only sweetener available, and Mama Sugar grew up using it for everything.

Today, when she cooks sweet potatoes, she still sweetens them with cane syrup. And when she can't find cane syrup in the store, she makes her own using cane sugar and water. She makes her vegetables the same way they did on the farm, too, except she adds meat to her beans now.

I asked her what Juneteenth was like in her childhood. "We did the same thing we're doing here, except we did it at County Line Baptist Church," Mama Sugar said, looking over her front lawn as she recalled those early Juneteenth celebrations. She told me that between one hundred and two hundred people came to the celebrations on the church lawn. "My uncle would kill a goat and clean it and hang it in a tree until it was time for the barbecue," she said. She fondly recalled the desserts, too, which she simultaneously recited and ticked off on her fingers: "Peach cobbler, banana pudding, cakes, pecan pie, sweet potato pie, and sweet potato cobbler—nobody makes that anymore!"

As we looked out over the front yard, the buffet was being set out on a pair of tables under the canvas roof. The vegetables included black-eyed peas with ham hocks, baby okra and peppers, green beans, okra and homegrown tomatoes, pintos, and smoked corn on the cob. There was also white bread, jalapeño cornbread, pickles, onions, and barbecue sauce. Three sweet potato pies, one pecan pie, and a huge container of banana pudding made up the desserts.

As dinnertime approached, LaDraun started bringing barbecued meats up to the porch so Mama Sugar could do the carving. She unwrapped a brisket from its aluminum foil and put it on a cutting board she had set up on a card table, so she could carve while sitting down. I managed to sneak a few tidbits of brisket as she carved. The meat was juicy and had a deep smoke flavor. Mama Sugar was cutting it into nice thin slices with her favorite carving knife, but you could probably carve this brisket with a butter knife.

What did the preacher at County Line Baptist say Juneteenth was about? I asked Mama Sugar. "He said it was about being delivered from slavery," she replied. "About how we used to work in the fields and eat outside all the time." Then I asked her what she told her kids and grandkids Juneteenth was about.

Mama Sugar said that the days of slavery were hard for the kids to picture, so she tried to explain Juneteenth with stories from her own life. After she graduated from high school in rural East Texas, she moved to Houston and worked in restaurants and as a maid in people's homes while raising five daughters.

"I tell them that when I worked as a cleaning lady in Houston in the 1970s, people had a different set of dishes for the maid." Then she relates a moment in her life that explains emancipation and equality. "I remember the first day a woman I worked for asked me to sit down at the table with the family for dinner. I had my own dishes there, and I always ate in the kitchen. But one day she just changed her mind."

The sky showed a few patches of blue by the time the sun started to set, and the party was in full swing. Suddenly the music went dead and Ron Sugar's voice came over the sound system: "Are you ready to bless the food?"

The kids who were lined up on the lawn to ride the horses were shushed up. The men holding Budweisers over by the barbecue pit bowed their cowboy hats. The domino players at the card table under the porch put down their tiles.

"Heavenly and most gracious father, we come to you on this day that you have glorified, . . ." the Reverend Ron Sugar's eloquent invocation for Juneteenth began. When he said "amen" at the end of the grace, everyone in earshot gave a loud "amen" in response. Then he shouted, "Let's eat!"

MAMA SUGAR'S MARGARITA RIBS

Don't try to use the huge 4- or 5-pound slabs of spareribs sold in the average supermarket meat section. They will never get tender.

SERVES 8
4 slabs baby back ribs, or 2 slabs pork spareribs
    (no more than 3½ pounds each)
Scant 1 cup tequila plata (silver)
1 (1-liter) bottle Mr and Mrs T's Margarita Mix
    or your favorite
1 cup Basic BBQ Rub (page 214)
Your favorite barbecue sauce, for serving

Pull off the membrane on the bone side of each slab of ribs. Rinse the ribs in water and dry with a towel. Place the slabs in a large baking dish or plastic tub and rub them vigorously with the tequila. Let stand for 1 hour, turning often.

Reserve 1 cup of the margarita mix for use later. Transfer the ribs and tequila to an airtight container or plastic storage bag, add the remaining margarita mix, cover or close tightly, and marinate in the refrigerator overnight.

The next day, remove the ribs from the marinade, draining them well, and discard the marinade. Sprinkle the ribs on both sides with the rub and rub it in well. Start a fire in a barbecue smoker and add wood chunks. Close down the dampers and maintain the temperature between 225°F and 300°F.

Place the rib slabs in the smoker and smoke for 3 to 4 hours, until a knife inserted between the bones passes easily. Transfer the slabs to a large sheet of heavy-duty aluminum foil. Fold up the edges of the foil around the ribs, add the reserved 1 cup margarita mix, then seal the package tightly closed. Return the package to the smoker or place in a preheated 250°F oven for 30 minutes, until the ribs are very tender.

Cut the ribs apart and mound on 1 or 2 large platters. Serve with the sauce.

SMOTHERED STEAK

Smothered steak, smothered pork chops, and other "smothered" dishes are made by submerging battered meat in gravy and braising until extremely tender. These are the stars of the steam table in Texas soul food restaurants and very popular as dinner entrées.

SERVES 2 OR 3
1 pound round steak
1 cup seasoned flour (page 198)
¼ cup corn oil
1 large yellow onion, sliced
1½ cups beef broth
1 cup water
1 tablespoon Worcestershire sauce
1 tablespoon chopped fresh thyme

Preheat the oven to 350°F. Cut the steak into 2 or 3 serving-size pieces of 5 to 8 ounces each. Using a meat mallet, tenderize each piece. Put the flour in a small, shallow bowl and dredge the steak pieces in the flour, coating both sides and shaking off the excess.

In a large ovenproof skillet, heat the oil over medium-high heat. Add the steak pieces and cook, turning once, for about 3 minutes on each side, until both sides are a crisp golden brown. Transfer the meat to a plate. Turn the heat down to low and add the onion. Scrape up the browned bits of flour from the pan bottom and mix with the onion slices, separating the slices into rings as you go. Cook, stirring occasionally, for about 10 minutes, until the onion is soft. Add the broth, water, Worcestershire sauce, and thyme and stir well.

Return the steak pieces to the pan. Cover the skillet, transfer to the oven, and cook for 30 to 45 minutes, until the steak is tender and the gravy has thickened. Serve hot with gravy, mashed potatoes, and your favorite vegetables.

FRIED CATFISH

East Texas was part of the farm-raised catfish industry along with Mississippi. But the low price of catfish imported from Vietnam eventually put the catfish farms out of business. Mama Sugar says that the imported catfish isn't as sweet at local catfish. These days, she often substitutes whiting for the catfish. You can find whiting in the freezer case at many large supermarkets.

SERVES 6

6 catfish fillets, about 2 pounds total

1 egg

1 cup milk

2 teaspoons seasoning salt such as Lawry's

2 cups fish flour (page 9)

1 cup fine-grind yellow cornmeal

Vegetable oil, preferably peanut oil, for deep-frying

Cut the fillets lengthwise into manageable pieces. In a shallow bowl, whisk the egg until blended, then whisk in the milk and salt until combined. In a pie or cake pan, combine the fish flour and cornmeal, stir to mix well, then spread the mixture evenly in the pan.

Pour the oil to a depth of 2 inches into a deep, heavy skillet and heat to 325°F. One at a time, dip the fish pieces into the egg mixture, allowing the excess to drip off, then dredge in the flour mixture, shaking off the excess. Slowly place the coated pieces in the hot oil, being careful not to crowd the pan, and fry for about 6 minutes, until the fish floats. Cut into a thick piece to test for doneness. The fish should be flaky white and cooked all the way through. Using a slotted spoon, transfer to paper towels to drain briefly and keep in a warm oven until ready to serve. Serve hot.

JUST LIKE MOMA'S FRIED CHICKEN

Reverend Jeffrey opened a restaurant called Just Like Moma's near his Baptist church in Houston. "Yardbird" was his specialty. The restaurant is gone, but the memory of that chicken lives on. The recipe is simple, but the technique is tricky. If you don't use enough oil to fry the chicken, the temperature won't recover fast enough and the chicken will get greasy. So, count on using at least a couple of quarts of oil. See photo on page 80.

SERVES 4 TO 6

2 cups seasoned flour (page 198)

1 (4½- to 5-pound) whole chicken, cut into serving pieces

Peanut oil, for deep-frying

Spread the flour in a small, shallow bowl. One at a time, dip the chicken pieces in the flour and roll to coat evenly, then shake off the excess. As each piece is coated, set it aside on a large platter or tray. Let the coated chicken pieces sit at room temperature for 30 minutes. (This rest period helps the crust to adhere to the chicken when you fry it.)

Pour the oil to a depth of 3 inches into a deep, heavy skillet or a Dutch oven and heat to 300°F. Carefully slip the chicken pieces into the hot oil and fry for about 15 minutes, until the chicken is golden brown and cooked through. Remove with a slotted spoon and allow to drain on brown paper. Serve immediately, or hold in a warm oven until serving.

Edna's Fried Chicken: Brine the chicken for 24 hours (see Bock-Brined BBQ Chicken, page 220), then marinate it in buttermilk for another 24 hours, covered in the refrigerator. Substitute 1 pound lard plus ½ cup butter for the peanut oil, then proceed with the recipe.

PEARL'S CHICKEN AND FLUFFY DUMPLINGS

This recipe comes from Pearl Moses, who served it at Pearl's Country Kitchen, her soul food restaurant in the East Texas city of Lufkin. Her nephew Jervonni Henderson, a student at the Conrad N. Hilton College of Hotel and Restaurant Management, retested this recipe at my house several times until he was satisfied with the dumplings. (We enjoyed them every time.) But he says nobody's dumplings are as fluffy as Aunt Pearl's.

SERVES 6 TO 8

1 tablespoon olive oil

1 (4½- to 5-pound) chicken, quartered

1 large yellow onion, cut into ½-inch dice

3 stalks celery, cut into ½-inch pieces

4 carrots, peeled and cut into ½-inch pieces

4 cups chicken broth

2 quarts water

2 bay leaves

1 teaspoon salt

1 teaspoon ground dried thyme

1 tablespoon chopped fresh rosemary

Dumplings

2 cups pastry flour, preferably White Lily brand

2 teaspoons baking powder

¾ teaspoon salt, plus more to taste

¼ cup minced fresh herb (such as parsley, thyme, and/or rosemary)

2 tablespoons unsalted butter, melted

¾ cup milk

2 tablespoons dry sherry

1 tablespoon heavy cream

Pepper

¼ cup chopped fresh parsley

In a Dutch oven, heat the oil over medium-high heat. Add the chicken pieces, onion, celery, and carrots and sauté, turning the chicken as needed, for about 10 minutes, until the chicken is nicely browned.

After the chicken is browned, add the broth and 2 quarts water to the chicken and bring to a boil. Add the bay leaves, salt, thyme, and rosemary, adjust the heat to a simmer, cover partially, and cook for 45 minutes to 1 hour, until the chicken is extremely tender.

Remove from the heat. Transfer the chicken pieces to a large bowl and allow them to cool until they can be handled. Then, remove the meat from the bones and discard the skin and bones. Place the chicken in a bowl, cover, and set aside until needed. With a slotted spoon, check the broth for chicken skin, bones and unwanted solids. Then, using a large spoon, skim off the excess fat from the surface.

While the chicken is cooling, make the dumplings. In a bowl, stir together the flour, baking powder, salt, and herbs. Add the butter and milk and mix with a wooden spoon just until a stiff dough forms.

Transfer the dough to a well-floured work surface, divide it in half, and set half aside. Lightly roll out half of the dough to about ⅓ inch thick. This thickness will yield fluffy dumplings. (Some people prefer thinner dumplings.) Handle the dough as little as possible; you don't want to overwork it. If you do, the dumplings will be dense and chewy. Cut the dough into 1-inch squares for big dumplings or short, narrow strips for little dumplings and set aside. Repeat with the remaining dough.

To cook the dumplings, bring the chicken broth to a simmer over medium heat. Drop the dumplings into the simmering broth and cook for 40 minutes, until cooked through. To test for doneness, cut a dumpling in half to see if it is cooked. As the dumplings cook, they will thicken the broth.

When the dumplings are done, stir the sherry and cream into the broth and season with salt and pepper. Return the chicken meat to the pot and heat through. Ladle the broth, chicken, and dumplings into warmed bowls and serve with parsley sprinkled on top.

DOT HEWITT'S STEWED OKRA

A California food writer once asked me to help her find some great African American cooks to contribute to a cookbook she was writing. I introduced her to Dot Hewitt, who operates Dot's Place in Austin, and she asked for Dot's famous okra recipe.

Dot's cooking method is deceptively simple: you stew whole okra pods in tomato sauce. By keeping the pods whole, you all but eliminate the slime. When the book came out, I was distressed to find that the author had called for sliced okra in the dish, effectively ruining Dot's recipe. Whole okra stewed in tomato sauce is a wonderful vegetable dish. Sliced okra is good for thickening gumbo because it produces so much mucilage.

So if you don't want slimy okra, don't cut it up. If you don't think you like okra, this recipe will change your mind.

SERVES 4

2 tablespoons vegetable oil or bacon drippings

1 yellow onion, halved and sliced

½ pound okra pods

1 (14-ounce) can crushed tomatoes, with juice

1 teaspoon salt

1 teaspoon pepper

In a heavy saucepan, warm the oil over medium heat. Add the onion and sauté for about 5 minutes, until soft. Add the okra and sauté for 2 minutes, until the pods sizzle a little. Add the tomatoes and their juice and the salt and pepper and bring to a boil. Decrease the heat to low, cover, and simmer for 25 to 30 minutes, until the pods are tender but intact. Serve hot.

FRESH FIELD PEAS

Crowder peas, purple hull peas, Lady cowpeas, fresh black-eyed peas, and fresh pinto beans are among the many fresh "peas" you find at East Texas roadside produce stands in the summer. In the old days, people bought peas in the pod and hulled them themselves. These days we let hulling machines do the work.

SERVES 6

2 slices bacon, cut into ½-inch pieces

1 small yellow onion, chopped

2 cups chicken broth

3 cups shelled fresh peas (see headnote)

2 cups water

4 or 5 baby okra pods

1 fresh chile

Salt and pepper

In a large skillet, fry the bacon over medium-high heat until it begins to brown. Add the onion and

cook, stirring often, for about 5 minutes, until soft. Add the broth, stir, and remove from the heat.

Pick over the peas, rinse them, and place them in a large saucepan. Add the water, okra, chile, and the broth mixture, bring to a simmer over medium heat, and cook for about 15 minutes, until the peas are tender. Season with salt and pepper. Serve hot.

SWEET POTATOES BAKED IN CANE SYRUP

How long you bake this dish depends on how wet the potatoes are, cautions Mama Sugar Sanders. If the sweet potatoes give off a lot of water, increase the baking time until the liquid is reduced to a syrup.

SERVES 8

2 tablespoons unsalted butter

3 pounds sweet potatoes, peeled and cut into ½-inch-thick slices

1 cup cane syrup

½ cup granulated sugar

Preheat the oven to 350°F. Butter a 9 by 13-inch baking dish with about half of the butter.

Layer the sweet potato slices in the prepared baking pan. Pour the cane syrup evenly over the top, then cut the remaining butter into bits and dot the top.

Bake for 30 minutes. Remove the baking dish from the oven and, using a spatula, turn the sweet potato slices so the top slices are on the bottom and the bottom slices are on top. Sprinkle the top evenly with the granulated sugar and return the baking dish to the oven. Bake for 20 to 30 minutes longer, until the juices have thickened into a syrup.

Remove from the oven and press down on the sweet potato slices with the spatula to submerge them in the syrupy juices. Let cool for 30 minutes before serving.

MAMA SUGAR'S SWEET POTATO COBBLER

This old-fashioned Southern dessert is enjoying a revival. I had never heard of the dish until Mama Sugar told me about it. But I have since seen similar recipes in cooking magazines—usually attributed to elderly African American women from the Deep South. Adams Best, a blend of natural vanilla extract and artificial vanillin, is the favorite baking vanilla in Texas.

SERVES 8 TO 10

2½ pounds sweet potatoes, peeled and thinly
    sliced
4 cups water
¾ cup cane syrup
½ cup firmly packed light brown sugar
1 teaspoon ground cinnamon
½ teaspoon ground allspice
¼ teaspoon salt
2 tablespoons unsalted butter
1 teaspoon vanilla extract, preferably Adams
    Best brand

Dough
3 cups pastry flour, preferably White Lily brand
4½ teaspoons baking powder
¾ teaspoon salt
6 tablespoons unsalted butter, cut into
    ½-inch cubes
1¼ cups milk
Homemade Vanilla Ice Cream (page 240),
    for serving

In a 5-quart pot, combine the sweet potatoes, water, cane syrup, brown sugar, cinnamon, allspice, and salt and bring to a boil over medium-high heat, stirring to dissolve the sugar. Adjust the heat to maintain a gentle simmer, cover, and cook for 8 minutes, until the sweet potatoes are somewhat tender. Using a slotted spoon, transfer the sweet potatoes to a bowl.

Add the butter and vanilla to the sweet potatoes, stir to mix, and set aside.

Bring the liquid in the pot to a boil over medium-high heat and boil for about 20 minutes, until reduced to 2 cups. The liquid should be syrupy. Remove from the heat.

Preheat the oven to 375°F.

To make the dough, in a bowl, stir together the flour, baking powder, and salt. Scatter the butter over the top and, using a pastry blender or 2 knives, work the butter cubes into the flour mixture until it resembles coarse meal. Stir in the milk with a fork, mixing just until a dough forms. Gather the dough into a ball, transfer to a floured work surface, and knead lightly until it holds together well. Divide the dough in half and set half aside. Roll out the other half into a round about 14 inches in diameter and ¼ inch thick. Trim as needed to even the edges and reserve the scraps.

Drape the dough round over the rolling pin and transfer it to a 10-inch Dutch oven or deep-dish pie pan, pressing it onto the bottom and halfway up the sides. Roll out the remaining dough into a round about ¼ inch thick. Trim to a 12-inch round. Gather up the dough scraps from both rounds, press together, then roll out into a round about ¼ inch thick. It should be almost 10 inches in diameter.

Spoon half of the sweet potatoes into the dough-lined Dutch oven, then top with the round fashioned from the dough trimmings. It should almost cover the sweet potatoes. Spoon the remaining potatoes on top, then pour the reserved syrup evenly over the potatoes. Fit the 12-inch round over the potatoes and press the edges together with the bottom crust to seal. Using a paring knife, cut a few steam vents in the top crust.

Bake the cobbler for 40 to 45 minutes, until the top is light brown. Let cool for at least 30 minutes. Serve warm with the ice cream.

Harvesting mayhaws.

CHAPTER 8

MAYHAW JELLY AND DEWBERRY JAM

★ ★

I made the mistake of using a GPS navigation system to get to Jackson Fruit Farm in East Texas. The device, which unerringly sends you on the shortest route to your destination, doesn't know the difference between state-maintained highways and dirt roads on timber land. I ended up driving more than ten miles on lumber company tractor roads that were little more than wheel ruts. My Volkswagen Jetta bottomed out at every creek crossing.

Jackson Fruit Farm is in the Big Thicket, a loosely defined part of East Texas that is home to one of the most biodiverse collections of flora and fauna on the continent. It's actually pretty easy to get to the farm if you ignore your GPS system and take directions from Bill Jackson. It is in a clearing sandwiched between lumber company forests and the Big Thicket National Preserve.

"I tried growing peaches, but a virus got them," Bill Jackson told me as he stood under one of his mayhaw trees. "Then I heard that folks over in Louisiana were raising mayhaws. Well, there are wild hawthorn trees in the woods right over my fence line, so I figured mayhaws ought to do pretty well here. Mayhaw is slang for the fruits of the hawthorn. They got that name because the fruit is ripe in early May. I have been raising them for ten years now."

Beside the mayhaw orchard, Jackson grows vegetables in an extensive garden. His turnip patch was overgrown with more greens and vegetables than he and his wife could eat, so he pressed a bag of the roots into my hands to take home. The elderly Jackson lives on the remote farm with his disabled English wife, whom he met when he was stationed overseas during his military service. His wife loves turnips—especially mashed with carrots and seasoned with butter.

Jackson was born on the farm in 1932. It was 210 acres when his father bought it in 1928. In 1974, it got smaller when its eastern edge was purchased by the federal government for the Big Thicket National Preserve.

Mayhaw farmer Bill Jackson.

Like most of the longtime residents in the area, Jackson's family used to be in the logging business. His grandfather spent time in a lumber camp in nearby Silsbee. The only civilization in this part of East Texas were lumber camps where the loggers lived, boardinghouses where visitors stayed, and the community that surrounded the sawmills. The development of East Texas was centered on the railroad. The lumber companies built railroad spurs into the virgin timberlands and then hauled the trees out to the sawmills. When the lumber business waned, out-of-work loggers created farms in the clearings. Cotton was the cash crop, and the rest of the farmland was devoted to growing the family's food. "We picked all the cotton ourselves," recalls Jackson. "I was the youngest of ten brothers and sisters. When I was little, my brothers had me convinced that my acres were bigger than their acres and that's why I had to pick more cotton than they did. I wised up eventually."

Okra, tomatoes, greens, turnips, field peas, beans, onions, melons, and ribbon cane were among the most common field crops. "We had our own cane mill and a mule to turn it. Then we cooked down the syrup. That was our sweetener. There were cane mills all around here where you could take your cane if you didn't have one.

"The livestock was fenced out instead of fenced in," Jackson remembers. "Cattle and pigs were free-range; farmers had their own identification marks, so when you wanted to kill a pig or a steer, you had to go catch one. We killed a couple of pigs every year when it got cold. We had a smokehouse right over there," he said, pointing to a spot nearby.

We walked by two big depressions on our way to the fence line. "I tried raising catfish in these ponds," Jackson said. "But I never could get the flow high enough to keep the water clean." Just beyond the property line, Jackson pointed out several stunted hawthorns growing under the canopy of taller trees. One hawthorn wrapped around a black gum tree. The fruits were yellowish, mottled, and small in comparison to the ones from cultivated trees.

The red, orange, and yellow mayhaws are about the size of olives and look and taste like tiny crabapples. They are too tart to enjoy out of hand, and although birds eat them, most Native Americans ignored them. Early American botanists didn't bother with them either because of their impractical traits. Hawthorns grow in swamps and thickets along the Gulf Coast. The trees have large thorns, and the fruits ripen all at once and then start rotting.

Although mayhaws were impractical, their tart flavor was treasured in the Piney Woods where they were harvested in the wild and cooked down with sugar to produce jellies, sauces, sweets, and wine. Mayhaw jelly is still most commonly found at roadside stands along the back roads of the Old South. Clear-cutting by lumber companies has all but wiped out the hawthorn tree, however, and the wild fruits have become increasingly hard to find.

WATER-BATH CANNING ON YOUR HOME STOVE

★ ★

HERE IS ALL YOU NEED TO KNOW to put up the jelly, jams, and preserves in this book. First, assemble the equipment: a heavy, nonreactive saucepan or pot, canning jars, self-sealing lids with screw-down metal rings, jar tongs, a widemouthed (jar) funnel, a magnet lid lifter, and a ladle. You will also need a water-bath canner—a pot with a built-in removable rack that lifts the jars off the pot bottom, away from contact with direct heat, as they are processed. Alternatively, you can put together a makeshift canner with a large pot and a wire rack.

You can reuse jars—check to make sure they are free of chips or cracks, which can prevent a tight seal—but you must buy new lids for each batch. The first step is to sterilize the jars. Many new-model dish-washers have a "sterilize" setting that comes in handy for this step. If not, in a big pot, boil the jars in water to cover for 15 minutes, then turn off the heat and leave them in the hot water until you are ready to fill them. Put the lids in a small pot with water to cover, bring to a boil, and boil for 5 minutes, then turn off the heat and leave them in the hot water, too.

Prepare the recipe as directed. When it tests done, remove the jars from the hot water with the jar tongs. Then, using the funnel and ladle, fill the hot jars, leaving 1/4 inch headspace. Wipe each jar rim with a clean, damp cloth to remove any drips. Using the magnet lifter to prevent burned fingers, place a hot lid on each jar and screw on the metal rings.

Put the jars in the rack of the water-bath canner, making sure they don't touch one another. Add hot water to the canner to cover the jars by at least 1 inch, cover the canner, and bring the water to a boil. Start timing when the water is at a full boil and boil for 10 minutes, then turn off the heat. Place a large folded towel on a countertop near the stove. Using the jar tongs, remove the jars from the canner and place on the towel to cool. Let the jars stand overnight.

The next day, check for a proper seal by pushing down on each lid. If the lid clicks, the seal failed and you will need to refrigerate the jar and use the contents within 2 weeks. If it didn't click (that is, it remained slightly indented in the center), the seal is good. Label and date the properly sealed jars and store in a cool, dark place. They will keep for up to a year.

Mrs. Alfred Bohl and daughter Marle show off their canned goods at a pantry demonstration in Bigfoot in 1931.

In 1985, horticulturalists in several Southern states began experimenting with mayhaw cultivars in the search for wild mayhaw stock that would yield a productive orchard tree. Wild mayhaw cuttings are grafted onto various rootstocks to produce different kinds of fruits. Texas Superberry is one popular cultivar that yields a large, dark red berry of the kind favored by jelly makers. Most of the mayhaw production comes from Louisiana, Mississippi, and Georgia. East Texas is home to only a few orchards. Demand for berries is excellent and prices run as high as ten dollars a pound.

Jackson pointed out a few sturdier specimens deeper in the woods. "I took cuttings from the trees that produced the best fruit in the wild and grafted them onto the rootstock in my orchard," he explained. "That's how you produce new varieties of mayhaws."

I bought a couple gallons of Jackson's mayhaws. It's pretty simple to make the jelly: you just boil the fruit, strain it, and add sugar and pectin. But I was fascinated by the tart crabapple-like flavor of the syrup. So I took a gallon of mayhaws to Anvil, a Houston "craft cocktail" bar that makes lots of syrups, bitters, and tinctures to use in their old-fashioned cocktails.

When I came back a month later, the bartender served me a cocktail made with mayhaw syrup and mescal. He also let me taste a batch of mayhaw bitters he had brewed. Both were sensational.

There is no commercial market for mayhaws. All of Jackson's fruit is bought by home cooks who use it to produce mayhaw jelly and other home recipes. As the years go by, it seems that fewer and fewer people remember the mayhaw. I hope enough young people take an interest in the indigenous fruit to keep this Texas Southern food tradition alive. Maybe mayhaw margaritas (page 100) would help?

MAYHAW JELLY

Mayhaw berries have the aroma of overripe apples and pears with a tart finish. Once you add sugar, the tartness is balanced and makes a gorgeous red jelly. This is the legendary jelly sold at roadside stands in East Texas.

MAKES 2 TO 3 PINTS
6 cups mayhaw berries
4 cups water
1 (3-ounce) package liquid fruit pectin
5 cups sugar

In a heavy, nonreactive saucepan, combine the berries and water and bring to a boil over high heat. Decrease the heat to a simmer and simmer for 15 minutes. Remove from the heat, cover, and let steep for 15 minutes.

Pour the juice through a jelly strainer placed over a bowl, allowing it to drip undisturbed. (Or, use a colander lined with a double thickness of cheesecloth or even a clean pillowcase.) Do not press on the fruit or the juice will be cloudy.

Measure the juice. If you have less than 4¼ cups, add water to equal that amount. Pour the juice into a deep, nonreactive saucepan, add the pectin, place over high heat, and bring to a hard boil, stirring continuously. Boil for 1 minute. Add the sugar, return the mixture to a hard, rolling boil, and boil for about 1 minute to dissolve the sugar and to activate the jelling properties of the pectin. To test if it is ready, using a metal spoon, scoop up a spoonful of the hot mixture, lift it several inches above the pot, and then pour it back into the pot from the side of the spoon. If it "sheets" from the spoon, rather than falls in drops, the jell point has been reached.

Remove from the heat. Ladle into sterilized jars, seal with lids, process in a hot-water bath, and store as directed in Water-Bath Canning on Your Home Stove on page 95.

Mayhaw Jelly (at left), Texas Peach Preserves (page 99), and Twoberry Jam (page 98).

TWOBERRY JAM

Dewberries are wild blackberries. My kids don't like the gritty seeds in dewberries, so I puree the berries and strain the juice. But you don't get any chunky fruit texture in your jam if you use puree. Since strawberries are in season at the same time, I like to combine the two berries to make jam. That way, you get a chunky jam with the bright, tart flavor of dewberries.

MAKES 7 PINTS

4 cups dewberries or blackberries

Juice of 2 lemons

4 cups strawberries, hulled and quartered
　　lengthwise

2 (3-ounce) packages liquid pectin

7 cups sugar

In a blender, combine the dewberries and lemon juice and process until pureed. Strain the puree though a fine-mesh sieve into a large, heavy, nonreactive pot.

Add the strawberries to the dewberry juice in the pot, place over medium-high heat, and cook, stirring constantly to prevent scorching, for about 5 minutes, until the strawberries have softened. Then mash the berries to the desired consistency.

Add the pectin, increase the heat to high, and bring to a hard boil, stirring continuously. Boil for 1 minute. Add the sugar, return the mixture to a hard, rolling boil, and boil for about 1 minute to dissolve the sugar and to activate the jelling properties of the pectin. To test if it is ready, using a metal spoon, scoop up a spoonful of the hot mixture, lift it several inches above the pot, and then pour it back into the pot from the side of the spoon. If it "sheets" from the spoon, rather than falls in drops, the jell point has been reached.

Remove from the heat. Ladle into sterilized jars, seal with lids, process in a hot-water bath, and store as directed in Water-Bath Canning on Your Home Stove on page 95.

Dewberry Jam: Omit the strawberries and use 8 cups dewberries. Skip the pureeing and straining. (There will be a lot of seeds in this jam.)

TEXAS PEACH PRESERVES

When I lived in Austin, I thought that the best peaches in Texas came from the Hill Country. Then I moved to Houston and tasted East Texas peaches. That's when I realized that some years the Hill Country peaches are tops, other years the East Texas peaches are better, and still other years they are pretty equal. How good the peaches are depends on the weather during the growing season. A late-spring freeze, a drought, or too much rain can ruin a crop. Before you buy the peaches for this recipe, sample one to make sure the harvest was a good one.

MAKES 8 PINTS

8 pounds peaches

2 tablespoons freshly squeezed lemon juice

7 cups sugar

1 vanilla bean (optional)

1 (3-ounce) package liquid fruit pectin

Bring a large pot of water to a boil. Have ready a large bowl of cold water. Working in batches, drop the peaches into the boiling water and leave for about 1 minute. Scoop them out of the boiling water and immediately plunge them into the cold water. Then remove them from the cold water and, using a table knife, slip off the skins.

Halve and pit the peeled peaches, then cut into slices. Place the slices in a large, heavy, nonreactive pot and add the lemon juice. Place over high heat and bring to a hard, rolling boil, stirring continuously. Boil for 1 minute, then add the sugar and return to a hard, rolling boil. Add the vanilla bean. Adjust the heat to maintain a simmer and cook, stirring continuously, for 30 to 40 minutes, until the peaches are very soft.

Bring the mixture to a hard, rolling boil, add the pectin, and boil for about 1 minute to activate the jelling properties of the pectin. To test if it is ready, using a metal spoon, scoop up a spoonful of the hot mixture, lift it several inches above the pot, and then pour it back into the pot from the side of the spoon. If it "sheets" from the spoon, rather than falls in drops, the jell point has been reached.

Remove from the heat. Ladle into sterilized jars, seal with lids, process in a hot-water bath, and store as directed in Water-Bath Canning on Your Home Stove on page 95.

Brandied Peaches: Peel the peaches as directed, then halve and pit them but do not slice. Place the peach halves in the pot and add the lemon juice and sugar as directed. Once the sugar has been added, boil for only 10 minutes, until the peaches are just beginning to soften.

Remove from the heat. Using a slotted spoon, transfer the peaches to sterilized jars and add a shot of Cognac or other brandy to each jar. Ladle the syrup from the pot over the peaches, filling to within ¼ inch of the rim, then seal with lids, process in a hot-water bath, and store as directed in Water-Bath Canning on Your Home Stove on page 95.

FIG JAM

Houston was home to countless fig orchards, until they were paved over with suburbs. But the fig remains a popular backyard tree in East Texas. Figs are naturally high in pectin, so you don't need to add any to this jam.

MAKES 6 PINTS

5 pounds figs, peeled and quartered lengthwise

5 pounds sugar

1 orange, sliced

In a large bowl, combine the figs, sugar, and orange. Let stand at room temperature for 3 hours. Each hour, stir the mixture to help dissolve the sugar and create more juice.

Transfer the fig mixture to a large, heavy, nonreactive pot. Place the pot over high heat and bring

(Continued)

to a hard, rolling boil. Boil, stirring often to prevent the jam from sticking to the bottom of the pot, for 25 minutes, until very thick.

Remove from the heat. Ladle into sterilized jars, seal with lids, process in a hot-water bath, and store as directed in Water-Bath Canning on Your Home Stove on page 95.

Sweet and Savory Jam: Add 4 cups julienned yellow onions to the pot with the other ingredients, then proceed as directed.

PICKLED WATERMELON RIND

After you cut up a watermelon, you can use some of the rind to make watermelon pickles. Be sure to leave enough of the pink flesh on the rind so that both colors are visible in the jar.

MAKES 2 QUARTS
9 cups water
4 cups watermelon rind, cut into 1 by 4-inch spears
1 cup distilled white vinegar
2½ cups sugar
3 cinnamon sticks
1 tablespoon mustard seeds
1 tablespoon salt
½ teaspoon whole cloves
½ teaspoon allspice berries

In a large pot, combine 8 cups of the water and the watermelon rind and bring to a boil over high heat. Continue to boil for about 15 minutes, until the rind is tender but still crisp.

Drain the rind and then return it to the pot. Add the remaining 1 cup water, the vinegar, sugar, cinnamon, mustard seeds, salt, cloves, and allspice berries and bring to a boil over high heat. Lower the heat to medium and cook, stirring frequently, for about 20 minutes, until the liquid has thickened slightly.

Remove from the heat and let cool to room temperature. Transfer the pickled rind and syrup to an airtight container and refrigerate overnight before serving. The pickles will keep in the refrigerator for up to 2 weeks.

MAYHAW MARGARITA

If you are making Mayhaw Jelly (page 96), set aside a little of the juice for other uses, such as this surprising cocktail.

SERVES 1 GENEROUSLY
Ice cubes
2 jiggers tequila
2 jiggers mayhaw juice (see headnote)
2 jiggers simple syrup, or to taste
1 jigger freshly squeezed lime juice

Put a large martini glass in the freezer at least 5 minutes before you plan to serve the margarita.

Fill a cocktail shaker half full with ice cubes, add the tequila, mayhaw juice, simple syrup, and lime juice, cover, and shake vigorously. Strain into the chilled martini glass and serve immediately.

HERITAGE SYRUP FESTIVAL

★ ★

IN 2007, I DROVE TO HENDERSON, TEXAS, to attend the Heritage Syrup Festival. On the grounds of the Depot Museum, members of the Rusk County Syrup Team were busy making old-fashioned cane syrup. An eleven-year-old mule named Justice walked round and round an antique metal mill as two men continuously fed sugarcane stalks into one side of it. The crushed stalks emerged from the opposite side of the mill, while sweet cane juice flowed down into a bucket. The captured juice was strained through cotton pillow-cases and then poured into a long, narrow steel pan at the top of a sluice.

"Making syrup is an art form," team member Dale Weaver told me. Smoke from the wood fires under the pans stung our eyes as we watched the cane juice bubble and thicken on its way down the long steel channel. "You have to catch the finished syrup at just the right time. Not too thin, not too thick," Weaver explained. "We use half dried pine and half green pine to get the temperature right. In Louisiana, they use copper pots and cook in batches, but we do continuous cooking here. Van Zandt County, a little east of Dallas, was the center of the cane syrup business in the 1930s. There used to be a syrup mill every fifteen miles or so in East Texas. Today only a few are left."

PART III
VINTAGE TEX-MEX

South Texas

The region of South Texas includes the old Spanish missions of San Antonio and extends south to encompass the South Plains. This was once a grassland savannah and the southernmost range of the buffalo. In the eighteenth century, the South Plains served as a grazing area for the cattle, sheep, and goats introduced by the Spanish and tended by the mission inhabitants on horseback.

After the buffalo disappeared, the former grasslands were overgrown by brush and mesquite and became known as the Brush Country. The area was home to crude jacales, thatched-roof huts with stick-and-mud walls that were erected as temporary shelters at goat camps and hunting camps in the countryside.

The area closer to the Mexican border featured elaborate haciendas built by Mexican cattlemen who settled the area in the beginning of the eighteenth century. The Rio Grande was navigable as far upriver as Rio Grande City in the early 1800s, and habitations along the river often included wrought-iron adornments reminiscent of the New Orleans French Quarter.

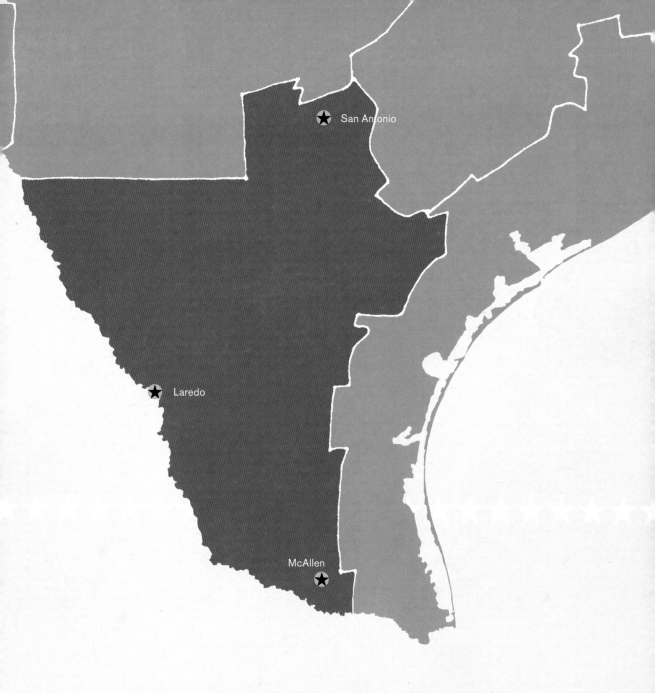

South Texas includes the cities of San Antonio, Laredo, and the Lower Rio Grande city of McAllen. It is the most Hispanic area of Texas. Some 90 percent of Lower Rio Grande Valley residents speak Spanish as their first language.

Enchiladas Dan Jenkins (page 113) with a fried egg.

CHAPTER 9

CHILI CON CARNE

★★★★★★★★★★★★★★★★★★★★★★

Latino-operated chili stands and tamale carts were the taco trucks of the 1800s. Laborers counted on them for quick, cheap sustenance. Adventurous eaters loved them. After visiting the chili stands of San Antonio and eating at a *fonda*, a restaurant located in a Tejano home, a tourist from Chicago named Otis Farnsworth was shocked that Anglos in fancy clothes were lining up to dine at such makeshift barrio eateries.

So Farnsworth came up with the idea of opening an elegant Mexican restaurant for Anglos in the commercial district and staffing it with Latinos. The Original Mexican Restaurant in San Antonio was built in 1899. Murals of Mexican peasants by a famous German artist named Herbert Bernard graced the walls. Gentlemen were required to wear jackets. The Original Mexican Restaurant in Galveston, like the Original in Houston and restaurants of similar names across the state, imitated the Farnsworth formula.

The Original in San Antonio became the most successful Mexican restaurant in the state. The "regular dinner" and "deluxe dinner" on the Original's menu became the proto-type for the many Tex-Mex combination plates that followed. The à la carte menu was divided into two parts. On the right were Mexican dishes like mole, chiles rellenos, and

TEJANO

★ ★

IN SPANISH, A TEXAN OF MEXICAN DESCENT is called a *tejano* or *tejana* (with a lower case *t*). Hispanics in Texas identified themselves as Tejanos as early as January 1833, when leaders at Goliad used the term. Contemporary historians use the term to distinguish Mexican Texans from residents of other regions, and to distinguish them from the Texians, as Anglo-American Texans were called, during the period between the end of the Spanish era in 1821 and Texas Independence in 1836.

> *"The term "Tejano" gained greater currency following the Chicano movement of the mid-1960s with corresponding changes in nuance and usage. It now encompasses language, literature, art, music, and cuisine. Tex-Mex is a related term that is not synonymous."*
> *—Adán Benavides from the* Handbook of Texas Online

The first Tejanos were Native Americans who learned the Spanish language and agricultural methods in the missions of San Antonio. They weren't Mexican-Texans because they didn't cross any borders to get to Texas—and Mexico wasn't a country yet anyway. During the Pueblo Revolt of 1680 in New Mexico, the buffalo-hunting Apaches and Comanches stole Spanish horses. These horseback-mounted warriors became a new threat to Texas and northern Mexico. Many of the Native Americans who entered the missions of San Antonio did so in part to seek protection from the raids of the mounted Plains tribes.

Mission San José, outside San Antonio, includes a wing with an interpretive exhibit of mission-era foodstuffs. The South Texas hunter-gatherers lived on nopals (prickly pear pads), tunas (prickly pear fruits), flour made from the beans of the mesquite tree, pecans, wild onions, and wild game, all of which they continued to eat after they moved to the missions. The chile pequin also grew wild in South Texas, as it still does today.

At the height of the mission era, around seven longhorn cattle were rounded up each week from outlying mission ranches and slaughtered for meat. Goats from Rancha de las Cabras, another nearby livestock ranch, supplemented the beef. Catfish and crawfish were abundant in the river. For their own use, the Franciscans imported chocolate, almonds, saffron, cloves, cinnamon, and copper plates and pots. The priests also imported large quantities of wheat for communion wafers. Tejano home cooking evolved from this mix of Native American and Spanish ingredients.

Tex-Mex is the gringo-friendly version of Tejano cooking that was first made famous by the chile queens of San Antonio.

sopa de fideo. On the left were Tex-Mex dishes, pairings of chili con carne with spaghetti, with scrambled eggs, or tamales, or other choices.

The Original coexisted with the chile queens and the tamale stands at first, but the high-minded citizens of San Antonio campaigned to ban the unsanitary street food vendors.

Tamales with chili con carne is the oldest dish on the menu at the Original Mexican Restaurant in Galveston, which, as far as I can determine, is the oldest extant Tex-Mex restaurant in the state. Raymond Guzman, who had worked at the popular outdoor Mexican Restaurant at Electric Park, a seaside amusement park, and at several other Galveston restaurants, opened it in 1916.

The tamales dish is so old-fashioned that people rarely order it anymore, but it was once the very definition of Texas Mexican food. I enjoy ordering it for its sense of nostalgia, but tamales just aren't what they used to be. Neither is the Original Mexican Restaurant in Galveston. The food is lackluster, but I'm glad it's open for the sake of history.

I wish the Original in Galveston were making tamales that were as rich and gelatinous as the ones they made ninety years ago, when the standard recipe for tamales included three or four times as much lard as it does today. But that's the Tex-Mex dilemma.

Modern Tex-Mex restaurants have cut back on the lard in the tamales and the refried beans in order to appease modern tastes and misguided health concerns. (Pure rendered lard is a lot better for you than butter or trans fat–laden margarine.) This is the main reason old-fashioned Tex-Mex food is in decline. Properly made, it includes lots of lard and processed American cheese, ingredients that send sophisticated food lovers into a tizzy.

"Was it health concerns that put the old Tex-Mex places out of business?" I asked eighty-four-year-old

Fort Worth sportswriter and Tex-Mex expert Dan Jenkins. "F✱!@ healthy. I've been eating lard for over sixty years," Jenkins railed. "What happened to Tex-Mex is the same thing that happened to all the other food. It got too fancy. Culinary institutes are turning out idiots who want to put ferns and cactus on everything—unfortunately, it has infected Tex-Mex, too."

Yellow cheese enchiladas served in chili con carne—not thin, meatless chili gravy, or authentic Mexican enchilada sauce—are the hallmark of vintage Tex-Mex, according to Jenkins. What else does he look for in a great Tex-Mex restaurant? "There isn't a goddamned fajita within ten miles of it," he told me.

"The first time I ate Mexican food was at the Mexican Inn in downtown Fort Worth when I was in junior high," he observed, when I asked for his advice about Fort Worth Tex-Mex. "Cheese enchiladas, rice, and beans. I'll never forget it. It was like an orgasm." Nowadays, Jenkins's favorite Fort Worth Tex-Mex restaurant is Mi Cocinita, a tiny operation located in a garage. He said the pork tamales there actually have some lard in them. He also likes the Original.

The Original of Fort Worth was once a favorite haunt of Fort Worth bluebloods, including Amon Carter and Franklin Delano Roosevelt's son Elliott. President Roosevelt raised the profile of Tex-Mex when he ate at the Original with his son Elliott during a visit to Fort Worth in 1937. If you want to sample real old-fashioned Tex-Mex, order what FDR ordered, now known as the Roosevelt Special. It's a fried-to-order *chalupa* shell topped with beans and cheese, a crispy beef taco, and a cheese enchilada in chili con carne topped with a fried egg.

★ ★ ★

I was still thinking about cheese enchiladas when I visited the Palmetto Inn on South Padre Island on a beach vacation. I usually ordered shrimp at the Palmetto Inn. After all, the biggest shrimp fleet in Texas docks right down the road in Brownsville. The Palmetto Inn's shrimp and avocado cocktail served in a traditional parfait glass, with chopped onion, cilantro, and serrano chile spicing up the red sauce, was its most popular shrimp dish. I also liked the Palmetto's shrimp fajitas, marinated in lime juice and garlic and served on a sizzling skillet with guacamole and hot flour tortillas.

"We started serving seafood in 1962, at the Palmetto Inn's Shrimp Boat restaurant in Brownsville," Christy Carrasco, one of the restaurant's owners, told me. Although I had eaten at the Palmetto Inn on visits to South Padre before, I was clueless about the chain's long history, until I interviewed the owners and waitstaff. But with Jenkins's exhortations about Tex-Mex ringing in my ears, I had to ask if the Palmetto served old-fashioned cheese enchiladas in chili con carne.

"Are you kidding?" Christy said in disbelief. Apparently, Palmetto Inn has always been much more famous for old-fashioned Tex-Mex than for new-fangled seafood. The menu featured such celebrated relics as tamales in chili con carne, chili by the cup or by the bowl, and a carne guisada dinner.

"Get a #10 Mexican Dinner," she advised. I could barely believe the sizzling-hot plate when it arrived. It held three "American-style cheese enchiladas" (the Palmetto Inn term for enchiladas in chili con carne) covered with a generous portion of oozy, neon yellow chile con queso. The #10 is also known as the Hangover Special and the Heart Attack on a Plate, Christy said.

The first Palmetto Inn was opened in Brownsville in 1945, by Christy's father-in-law, Moises M. Carrasco. He had six children, and as the family grew, they built restaurants in high-traffic locations in Harlingen, McAllen, Corpus Christi, Weslaco, and San Antonio. The northernmost Palmetto Inn

Nancy Reagan and Roger Staubach at Palmetto Inn.

was on The Circle in Waco, across from the Elite Diner. Christy showed me old photographs of what the Palmetto Inns had once looked like. I particularly liked a photo of Nancy Reagan eating with Roger Staubach, with a gaudy velvet painting on the wall behind them.

The chain was among the most successful in Texas, but business slumped at most locations when the interstate highway system opened. "When I-35 was completed, Moises started closing the restaurants," Christy said. "It was just like what happened to those wonderful diners along Route 66." The South Padre Island location was the last remnant of the once-proud chain. "It's the end of an era," she said.

Her words would prove prophetic. Two years after I talked to her, in June 2010, Hurricane Alex closed the Palmetto Inn on South Padre. It never reopened.

★ ★ ★

The oldest Tex-Mex chain in Houston is Molina's, which was founded in 1941. I had lunch there with Raul Molina Jr., the son of Molina's founder. When the waiter came by, Raul Jr. ordered a bowl of chili.

"Chili?" I queried him, flipping the menu back and forth. "I don't see chili on this menu." No, it wasn't on the menu, Raul agreed. But Molina's makes

TEJANOS AND MEXICANOS

★ ★

WHILE MANY MODERN MEXICAN TEXANS struggle to retain a connection with the culture of Mexico, many Tejanos feel a fierce loyalty to Texas. It's a tradition with deep roots. In 1835, when the Texas Revolution began, some Tejanos declared their independence and renounced their Mexican citizenship. One such Tejano was the legendary Juan N. Seguín.

The life of Juan N. Seguín illustrates the bicultural dilemma that Tejanos have faced throughout their history. A member of a long-established Tejano family, his father was the *alcalde* of San Antonio and an ally of Stephen F. Austin. When war with Mexico was declared, Seguin raised a company of sixty-five Tejanos and fought in the Battle of Gonzales in 1835, after which Stephen F. Austin granted him a captain's commission.

Seguin and his Tejano unit eventually joined up with Sam Houston's army to defeat the Mexicans at the Battle of San Jacinto. Seguín became the only Tejano in the Senate of the Republic. Despite his poor English, he was the chairman of the Committee on Military Affairs. Upon his return to San Antonio, he was elected mayor. But hostilities between Anglos and Mexican Texans began to erupt as the Anglos questioned the loyalties of anybody with a Spanish surname. Fearing for his safety, Seguin resigned as mayor in 1842, and crossed the border into Mexico with his family.

Seguin retired in Nuevo Laredo, where he died in 1890. His remains were returned to Texas in 1974 and buried in Seguin, the town named in his honor.

Mexican Chili Stands. San Antonio, Tex.

great chili con carne, he said, and you can always get a bowl of chili at Molina's whether it is on the menu or not.

In the beginning, the entire Molina family lived on the second floor above their first restaurant on West Gray. Mom did the cooking, dad was the waiter, and the kids bussed tables and washed dishes. In those days what they did was short-order cooking with lots of chili con carne. There was chili and scrambled eggs, chili over spaghetti, chili and crackers, chili and tamales, and chili with enchiladas. In other words, chili was at the heart of everything.

Considering Raul's lecture and my interview with Dan Jenkins, I went back to the oldest remaining Molina's location on Westheimer and looked for cheese enchiladas with chili con carne. I couldn't find the dish, until a waiter pointed it out on a separate part of the menu under the name enchiladas de tejas. Three enchiladas arrived smothered with chili and topped with a pool of yellow Cheddar. I poured a small dish of chopped raw onions over the top. It was the best meal I have ever eaten at Molina's.

1890S TEX-MEX

★ ★ ★ ★ ★ ★ ★ ★ ★ ★ ★ ★ ★ ★ ★ ★ ★ ★

"The Mexican cooking, though Americans have a prejudice against it, is exceedingly appetizing, but for most palates too highly peppered, chile entering largely into the composition of every dish. Yet it is a rare good feast one can have by ordering the following bill of fare: Sopa de Fideo, Gallina con Chile, Tamales, Frijoles Mexicana, Enchiladas, Chile con Carne, Tortillas, Salza de Chile, Pastel de Limon, Granadas de China, Café."

—Lee C. Harby, "Texan Types and Contrast," *Harper's New Monthly Magazine*, July 1890

Just like everybody else, I too often make the mistake of sitting down in an old-fashioned Tex-Mex joint and ordering the mole poblano or grilled beef and ignoring the vintage dishes that the kitchen does brilliantly. But that means eating more greasy taco shells, lard-laden tamales and refried beans, and processed cheese than doctors and nutritionists recommend. And that's one reason vintage Tex-Mex started to disappear.

HOMEMADE CHILI POWDER

In the old days, the first step to making a Tex-Mex meal was roasting the chiles and the cumin. It's a tradition worth reviving. Fresh-roasted cumin seeds and chiles make an incredibly flavorful chili powder. If you especially like the flavors of cumin and oregano, increase the amounts here.

MAKES ABOUT 1/4 CUP (1 1/2 OUNCES)
5 ancho chiles
1 teaspoon cumin seeds
1 teaspoon dried Mexican oregano
1/2 teaspoon garlic powder

Remove the stem and seeds from each chile and spread the chiles out flat. Place the chiles in a *comal* (flat cast-iron pan) or cast-iron skillet over medium heat and cook, flipping the chiles as needed to prevent burning, until lightly toasted. Transfer to a plate and let cool. Put the cumin seeds in the hot pan and stir and shake the seeds until fragrant. Pour into a small bowl and let cool.

Using scissors, cut the chiles into small strips. In a spice grinder or a clean coffee grinder, grind the strips in several batches into a powder. Pour into a bowl. Then grind the cumin seeds into a powder and pour into the bowl. Add the oregano and garlic powder and stir to mix. If the powder is still coarse, grind it in batches for an additional 2 minutes, until finely ground.

Store the chili powder in an airtight container at room temperature. It will lose much of its aroma after a month.

CLASSIC CHILI CON CARNE

Make this chili with your own chili powder and see what you've been missing by using the stale stuff that comes in bottles. If you like, once all of the ingredients have been mixed together, transfer the contents of the Dutch oven to a slow cooker, cover, and cook on the high setting for 1 hour. Puree the ancho chiles as directed, then return the puree to the slow cooker, stir well, and cook on the low setting for 4 to 6 hours to blend the flavors.

SERVES 8 TO 10

2 tablespoons cumin seeds

8 ounces sliced bacon

3 pounds boneless beef chuck, buffalo, or venison, cut into ¼-inch cubes

1 pound white onions, chopped

3½ tablespoons homemade chili powder (page 110)

2 teaspoons paprika

1 teaspoon dried Mexican oregano

1 teaspoon freshly ground black pepper

½ teaspoon dried thyme leaves

½ teaspoon salt

4 large cloves garlic, minced

1¾ cups beef broth

1 (28-ounce) can pureed tomatoes

1 cup water

2 ancho chiles, seeded

Put the cumin seeds in a Dutch oven over medium heat and stir and shake the seeds until fragrant. Pour the seeds onto a work surface and, using a small, heavy skillet, crush them coarsely. Set aside.

Return the Dutch oven to medium-high heat, add the bacon, and fry for 5 to 8 minutes, until crisp. Transfer the bacon to paper towels to drain.

Increase the heat to high, add the beef cubes in batches to the bacon drippings in the pot, and cook, turning as needed, for about 5 minutes, until well browned on all sides. Using a slotted spoon, transfer the beef to a bowl. Lower the heat to medium, add the onions to the remaining bacon drippings, and sauté for 8 to 10 minutes, until lightly browned.

Add the crushed cumin, chili powder, paprika, oregano, black pepper, thyme, salt, and garlic and cook, stirring often, for 1 minute. Crumble in the bacon and add the broth, tomatoes, water, anchos, and the browned beef. Increase the heat to high and bring to a boil, then decrease the heat to low, cover partially, and simmer for 2 hours, until the meat is very tender. Add water as needed to maintain a good chili consistency.

Remove the anchos, puree them in a blender, and then return the puree to the pot. Stir well, simmer for a few minutes to blend the flavors, and serve.

ORIGINAL CHILI GRAVY

Chili gravy is a cross between Anglo brown gravy and Mexican chile sauce. It was invented in Anglo-owned Mexican restaurants like the Original in San Antonio. Use it as a sauce for your homemade enchiladas.

MAKES ABOUT 2 CUPS

¼ cup lard or vegetable oil
¼ cup all-purpose flour
2 tablespoons chili powder, homemade
   (page 110) or store-bought
2 teaspoons ground cumin
1½ teaspoons garlic powder
1 teaspoon salt
½ teaspoon pepper
½ teaspoon dried Mexican oregano
2 cups chicken broth

In a skillet, heat the lard over medium-high heat. Stir in the flour and continue stirring for 3 to 4 minutes, until you have a very light brown roux. Add the chili powder, cumin, garlic powder, salt, pepper, and oregano and cook, stirring constantly and blending ingredients well, for 1 minute. Add the broth and stir until the sauce is smooth and has thickened. Decrease the heat to low and simmer for 15 minutes to blend the flavors, adding water as needed to achieve a gravy consistency. Use immediately.

CHILI CON CARNE SAUCE

Some Tex-Mex restaurants make this thin version of chili con carne to use as a sauce with tamales, enchiladas, and combination plates. Texas chili is typically made with hand-cut chunks of beef or venison, but ground chuck works best in the chili con carne that will be used as a sauce. This kind of chili is also great with chili dogs, chili burgers, and Frito pie. If you like the meat chunkier, ask your butcher to use a ¹/₂-inch chili plate on the grinder.

MAKES ABOUT 6 CUPS

1 teaspoon lard or vegetable oil
2 pounds ground chuck
1 cup chopped white onions
1 clove garlic, minced
1 cup tomato sauce
1 cup hot water
1 tablespoon chili powder, homemade
   (page 110) or store-bought
½ teaspoon dried Mexican oregano
½ teaspoon ground cumin
Several dashes of red hot-pepper sauce
All-purpose flour, for thickening
Salt

Heat the lard in a large skillet over medium-high heat. Add the meat, onion, and garlic and sauté, breaking up the meat with the side of a wooden spoon or spatula, for 5 to 7 minutes, until lightly colored. Add the tomato sauce, hot water, chili powder, oregano, cumin, and pepper sauce, stirring well, and bring to a boil. Decrease the heat to a simmer and simmer for about 1 hour, until the meat is tender. As the sauce cooks, skim off any fat that forms on the surface, and add water if needed to maintain a good consistency.

In a cup or small bowl, dissolve 1 tablespoon or so of flour in a little warm water to form a thin paste. Add the slurry to the sauce and stir constantly until smooth and thickened. Season with salt to taste. Use immediately, or let cool, cover, and refrigerate for up to 1 week.

ENCHILADAS DAN JENKINS

Dan Jenkins likes his cheese enchiladas with real chili con carne—not meatless chili gravy. Try these and you'll end up agreeing with him. Be sure to use yellow corn tortillas and not white ones, which are not sturdy enough. See photo on page 104.

MAKES 24 ENCHILADAS; SERVES 8 TO 12

½ cup lard

24 yellow corn tortillas

1 pound Velveeta cheese, cut into ½-inch cubes

2 large white onions, minced

6 cups Chili con Carne Sauce (page 112)

1 pound Cheddar cheese, shredded

Preheat the oven to 450°F.

In a small skillet, heat the lard over medium-high heat for 3 minutes, until it shimmers. Using tongs, place a tortilla in the hot fat. (If the tortilla does not bubble immediately, the lard is not hot enough.) Heat the tortilla for 30 seconds, until soft and lightly brown. Using the tongs, transfer the tortilla to paper towels to cool before handling. Repeat with the remaining tortillas.

Have the cheeses, onions, tortillas, and sauce handy for assembly. Place a tortilla flat on a work surface. Spoon about ¼ cup of the Velveeta cheese in a line down the center of the tortilla and top the cheese with about 1 tablespoon of the onion. Roll up the tortilla, enclosing the cheese and onion, and place seam side down in two 9 by 12-inch baking dishes.

Continue filling and rolling the tortillas until the baking dish is full, then repeat with the remaining tortillas and cheese, filling in the next baking dish. Pour an equal amount of the sauce into each dish, spreading it evenly over the enchiladas. Sprinkle the sauced enchiladas with the Cheddar cheese, dividing it evenly.

Bake for about 10 minutes, until the cheese on top begins to bubble. Remove from the oven, top with the remaining onion, and serve immediately.

Variation: Top with a fried egg.

BAN THE TAMALE STANDS!

★ ★ ★ ★ ★ ★ ★ ★ ★ ★ ★ ★ ★ ★ ★ ★ ★ ★ ★

"The Alamo Plaza, with its fine block pavement and splendid public buildings, is becoming the most select open space in our city. The city will, no doubt in time, sod the ground in the circle and thus relieve the eye of the unsightly pile of dirt. But there is needed some police regulations about the tamale stands which are still permitted to occupy the square. We are aware that any suggestion to the effect that the day or night of the tamale stand as an open-air institution is about over will be met with objection, and it will require a little more education to convince our people that all business avocations, including the restaurant business, should be put on a level and kept within proper limits and taxed equally. But there is one thing that should be done at once, that is, the old traps, stoves, tables, benches, etc., should he removed when morning comes and the glare of day exposes their unsightly appearance. Besides the unsightly traps, the streets about the stands are littered up with shucks and trash. A police regulation is much needed."

—"Unsightly Traps," *San Antonio Light*, December 11, 1889

PALMETTO INN #10

The #10, a dish of cheese enchiladas with chili con carne and chile con queso, was nicknamed Heart Attack on a Plate by the loyal patrons of the South Padre Island Palmetto Inn.

SERVES 4

½ cup lard or vegetable oil

8 yellow corn tortillas

4 cups shredded Velveeta cheese

1 cup chopped white onions

2 cups Chili con Carne Sauce (page 112)

Refried Beans (page 143, optional)

Green Rice (page 115, optional)

2 cups Crock-Pot Chile con Queso (page 121)

Preheat the oven to 450°F.

In a small skillet, melt the lard over medium-high heat for 3 minutes, until it shimmers. Using tongs, place a tortilla in the hot fat. (If the tortilla does not bubble immediately, the lard is not hot enough.) Heat the tortilla for 30 seconds, until soft and lightly browned. Using the tongs, transfer the tortilla to paper towels to cool before handling. Repeat with the remaining tortillas.

Have the cheese, onions, tortillas, and sauce handy for assembly. Lay a tortilla on a flat work surface. Spoon about ½ cup of the Velveeta cheese in a line down the center of the tortilla and top the cheese with about 1 tablespoon of the onion. Roll up the tortilla, enclosing the cheese and onion, and place it seam side down on an ovenproof dinner plate with a high lip. Fill a second tortilla the same way and add it to the plate. Ladle ½ cup of the sauce over the top. Repeat to assemble 4 ovenproof plates total.

Bake for about 10 minutes, until the sauce bubbles. Remove from the oven and add the beans and rice to the plates. Ladle ½ cup of the chile con queso over the enchiladas on each plate. Garnish the enchiladas with the remaining onions and serve immediately.

"WORLD'S BEST" CHEESE ENCHILADAS

Steve Wertheimer owns the Continental Club in Austin and Houston. He grew up in Rosenberg, a town south of Houston, where his father was once the mayor. There used to be a Mexican restaurant in the neighboring town of Richmond, right across the river from the famous Larry's Mexican Restaurant, Steve Wertheimer told me. He didn't remember the name of the place, but the sign out on the road said "World's Best Enchiladas." "My dad used to bring a big aluminum foil tray of those enchiladas home for dinner all the time. I think they were made with Velveeta. Those are the enchiladas I grew up with."

SERVES 4

½ cup lard or vegetable oil

8 yellow corn tortillas

1½ cups Original Chili Gravy or Chili con Carne Sauce (both on page 112)

2 cups shredded Velveeta cheese

1½ cups chopped white onions

1 cup shredded Cheddar cheese

Preheat the oven to 450°F.

In a small skillet, melt the lard over medium-high heat for 3 minutes, until it shimmers. Using tongs, place a tortilla in the hot fat. (If the tortilla does not bubble immediately, the lard is not hot enough.) Heat the tortilla for 30 seconds, until soft and lightly browned. Using the tongs, transfer the tortilla to paper towels to cool before handling. Repeat with the remaining tortillas.

Have the chili gravy, cheeses, onions, and tortillas handy for assembly. Ladle ¼ cup of the chili gravy onto an ovenproof dinner plate with a high lip. Lay a tortilla on a flat work surface. Spoon about ¼ cup of the Velveeta cheese in a line down the center of the tortilla and top the cheese with about 1 tablespoon of the onion. Roll up the tortilla, enclosing the cheese and onion, and place it seam side down on the gravy-covered plate. Repeat with a second tortilla and place it next to the first one. Pour another ¼ cup of the gravy over the top, and sprinkle with ¼ cup of the Cheddar cheese. Repeat to assemble 4 ovenproof plates total.

Bake for about 10 minutes, until the sauce bubbles and the cheese is completely melted. Garnish the enchiladas with the remaining onions and serve immediately.

GREEN RICE

Cilantro was once considered to have too strange a flavor for mainstream tastes. But nowadays it is popular, and herbed rice made with cilantro has become an alternative to the typical Spanish rice made with tomato sauce.

MAKES ABOUT 6 CUPS; SERVES 12

5 tablespoons unsalted butter
½ white onion, minced
2 cloves garlic, minced
2 cups long-grain white rice
2 bay leaves
2 teaspoons dried Mexican oregano
2 teaspoon chopped fresh cilantro
4 cups chicken broth or water
Salt and pepper

In a deep saucepan, melt the butter over medium heat. Add the onion and garlic and sauté for about 5 minutes, until the onion is wilted. Add the rice, bay leaves, oregano, and cilantro, stir well, decrease the heat to low, and cook, stirring often, for about 10 minutes, until the rice is opaque.

Add the broth, season with salt and pepper, cover, and cook for about 30 minutes, until all of the liquid has been absorbed and the rice is tender. Remove the bay leaves before serving.

A NINETEENTH-CENTURY FONDA

★ ★

"The old Dutch masters would have loved to perpetuate the interior of a Mexican restaurant, its patrons showing the cosmopolitan nature of the population of the State. A long, low-roofed room, with bare floor, an uncovered pine table, and hard bench, on which sit three noted politicians taking an evening lunch. . . . Each has a steaming platter of *chile con carne* before him, and a plate of *tamales* in their hot, moist wrappings of shuck. Behind them stands the Mexican host, tall, dark, dignified, and grave, yet watchful. . . . Over them flicker the dim rays cast by an oil lamp, deepening the shadows, throwing half-lights into the obscurity of the corners. A tiny hairless Mexican dog sits motionless on the doorstep, while the sign—written in both English and Spanish—swings creakingly above his head. . . . Only in the cities of Texas can be found that peculiar fusion of American civilization with Mexican life. . . ."

—Lee C. Harby, "Texan Types and Contrast," *Harper's New Monthly Magazine*, July 1890

Crock-Pot Chile con Queso, page 121.

Felix Mexican Restaurant on Westheimer in Houston opened in 1937 and closed in 2008.

CHAPTER 10

FELIX AND EL FENIX

★★★★★★★★★★★★★★★★★★★★★★★★★★

Within the short space of a few months, Felix Mexican Restaurant in Houston and Karem's in San Antonio went out of business, and the founding family of the El Fenix chain in Dallas sold out to a restaurant management corporation. Spanish Village and Cisco's Bakery in Austin closed shortly afterward. It was like a tectonic plate shift had taken place. The oldest family-run Tex-Mex restaurants in the state were suddenly gone.

I was shocked. I had included some of these places in *The Tex-Mex Cookbook*, and I knew the owners. I wondered whether times were equally bad for other old Tex-Mex spots. So I decided to drive around the state visiting the old Tex-Mex restaurants and documenting their cooking before they all disappeared.

I am glad I had a chance to visit Felix Mexican Restaurant on Westheimer before it went out of business. The chile con queso and cheese enchiladas served there were legendary. But it was Felix Tijerina's life story and his role in the larger sweep of Texas food history that I found most fascinating.

Felix was born in Mexico. His parents were farmworkers who came to Sugar Land, just south of Houston, to cut cane during the harvest season. In search of a better life, Felix walked to Houston at the age of fourteen and got a job as a busboy at The Original Mexican Restaurant on Fannin. Felix learned English on the job, worked hard, and became a manager.

In 1926, Felix built the first Mexican-owned restaurant for mainstream customers in Houston. It failed during the Depression, but Felix came back and tried again. Eventually he built a six-restaurant Tex-Mex chain and made a lot of money. His flagship restaurant on Westheimer near the corner of Montrose was a landmark.

Felix Tijerina was also a community activist. He was elected president of the League of United Latin American Citizens four times, came up with an educational program for Spanish-speaking children that inspired Lyndon Johnson's Head Start program, and became one of the most important Mexican American leaders of the last century.

Felix Tijerina (left), Houston's first Tex-Mex millionaire.

His wife, Janie Tijerina, ran the restaurants after Felix died in 1965. Janie passed away thirty-two years later in 1997, and the restaurants began to close. When the flagship Felix restaurant on Westheimer finally ceased operations in March of 2008, a wave of grief swept the city.

Felix Mexican Restaurant, which opened in 1948, was a museum of old-time Tex-Mex. Felix provided generations of Anglo Houstonians with their first taste of Mexican food, their first words of Spanish, and their first contact with Mexican Americans. "It was like a window on another culture," remembers journalist John Lomax, who ate there throughout his childhood. When the *Houston Press* food blog noted the closing, an outpouring of emotional comments were posted. Here is a sampling:

> I was first taken to Felix's in a car bed in 1945, and have gone at least once a week ever since. I am in mourning, as are my sister and many of my friends. —Nancy

> Our entire family is sad and grieving as if we have lost a family member. The queso and the cheese enchiladas were the best anywhere, hands down! It was my birthday spot for the last 20 years. So very sad! —Donna

> As a fourth generation [Felix patron] (my son is fifth and my grandson is sixth), I will deeply miss the food and staff. —Kathy

> I moved to Houston in 1954 as a very small child. Felix's was the first Mexican restaurant that my family had ever eaten at and has been our very favorite all these years. The queso is something to behold. I still have one quart in my freezer, and I will be extremely cautious with whom I share it! Only a true lover of Tex-Mex would deserve that honor! —Micaela

The menu at Felix was frozen in amber, and the most famous dish on it was the chile con queso.

Before there was Velveeta, old-fashioned queso was made with a flour-based tomato and paprika béchamel to which the cheese and cayenne were added. Felix's queso had an odd gravylike texture, and it tended to separate as it cooled, but it was one of the state's first Mexican cheese and chile dips and some Houstonians still crave the stuff.

Felix was also the last Tex-Mex place in Houston that served the nineteenth-century classic spaghetti and chili. It wasn't one of my favorite dishes. But some Houstonians told me they ate it all the time growing up. It was the best thing on Felix's menu for little kids, they explained. Spaghetti and chili is still popular in Cincinnati. It was also the inspiration for the chili and macaroni casserole called chili mac.

The Spanish sauce at Felix tasted like it was made with nothing but canned tomatoes. The salsa didn't have any heat. I took a lot of people to eat at Felix because of its historical significance, but it was hard to explain some of the food. I ended up telling my guests that eating at Felix was like listening to scratchy recordings of the Delta blues to understand the roots of rock and roll.

★ ★ ★

The last time I ate dinner at the El Fenix location in downtown Dallas, Albert Martinez, the eighty-four-year-old son of Mike Martinez, the founder of El Fenix, stopped by every table to ask diners if everything was alright. Albert and his siblings built the El Fenix chain and made it the place to see and be seen in Dallas in the 1960s. Dallas Cowboys football player Merlin Olsen loved the place. So did golfing great Lee Trevino.

El Fenix's iconic downtown Dallas location is a Tex-Mex masterpiece. The décor is dominated by elaborate trompe-l'oeil murals that cover two entire walls. Elsewhere, there are lots of old black-and-white photos of the Martinez family and its early restaurants.

Founded by Mexican immigrant Miguel Martinez in 1918, the El Fenix chain had been family run for five generations—until a few years ago, when it was sold to the Firebird Restaurant Group. The new owners promised not to change anything at El Fenix—and then immediately announced that they planned to expand statewide. But their short-term success will depend on their ability to hang on to El Fenix's regulars. And longtime patrons of Tex-Mex restaurants don't like change, which explains some of the bizarre food.

The soft cheese taco that came with the Special Mexican Dinner mystified me. It was stuffed with Cheddar and onions like a cheese enchilada, but the tortilla was steamed instead of fried and covered with chile con queso instead of chili gravy. It tasted like a cross between an enchilada and a soggy Tex-Mex grilled cheese sandwich. It has long been a signature item at El Fenix, but I have never understood why.

Susan Martinez, the former marketing manager of El Fenix, once explained to me over lunch that in the old days Dallasites liked their salsa mild and their enchiladas bland. At a former El Fenix location in Houston, they had to put processed cheese inside the taco, she said. It seemed that Houstonians liked Velveeta better than Cheddar. Some vintage Tex-Mex cooking has disappeared because mainstream tastes have changed. But altering the menu of an institution is dangerous.

When the thirty-year-old Los Tios chain in Houston was sold some years ago, the new owner, Gary Adair, figured it was time to replace the powdered cheese in the chile con queso with real cheese. Loyal patrons were furious about the change in flavor. Adair was accosted by irate regulars—including his mother. "She grabbed me by my lapels and said, 'Don't you change a single thing,'" said Adair.

Felix Mexican Restaurant

904 WESTHEIMER   PHONE JACKSON—
HOUSTON, TEXAS

Felix Mexican Dinner

50c

5c Extra with Tortillas—No Substitute

DINNER

65c

Tamales, Enchiladas, Frijoles,
Sopa de Arróz, Chile con Carne, Spaghetti,
Tortillas, Café.

WE SERVE OLEO.

SPECIAL DINNER

85c

Chile con Queso, Taco, Sopa de Arróz,
Tamales, Enchiladas, Frijoles, Chile con Carne,
Spaghetti con Chile, Tortillas, Café o Té.

WE SERVE ICE CREAM

FELIX DE LUXE DINNER

$1.25

Chile con Queso, Taco, Sopa de Arróz,
Tamales, Enchiladas, Frijoles, Chile con Carne,
Tostadas, Guacamole Salad, Candy o Piña
Tortillas, Café o Té.

Any Substitute On above Dinners Will Be 10c Extra

Chile con Carne	30c
Chile con Carne y Frijoles	30c
Chile con Queso	25c
Chiles Rellenos	60c
Tamales	25c
Tamales con Salsa de Chile	30c
Tamales con Salsa de Chile y Frijoles	40c
Tamales con Chile	45c
Envueltos de Picadillo	55c
Tacos	30c
Aguacate Salad	40c
Frijoles	20c
Frijoles Refritos	25c
Frijoles con Salsa de Chile	25c
Enchiladas	25c
Enchiladas con Huevos	50c
Huevos con Salsa de Chile	40c
Huevos con Chile con Carne	50c
Huevos Rancheros	50c
Spaghetti con Salsa de Chile	20c
Spaghetti con Chile con Carne	40c
Spaghetti con Queso	35c
Sopa de Arróz	20c
Cebolla Picada	10c
Sopa de Arróz con Chile con Carne	35c
Tortillas Fritas	10c
Tostadas Veracruzanas	30c
Chilaquiles con Huevo	50c
Huevos con Chorizo	50c
Leche	10c
Chocolate	15c
Té con Hielo	10c
Café	10c
Mexican Pecan Candy	10c
Piña	10c
Mole de Gallina (Special Order)	$1.50
Arróz con Pollo	$1.50

Beer of All Kinds at Popular Prices

USE OUR BANQUET ROOM FOR YOUR NEXT PARTY — CAPACITY 125

Felix's original menu, 1937.

FELIX'S CHILE CON QUESO

If this cheese dip isn't eaten immediately, it congeals and develops little pockets of grease. That said, those who grew up with it love it.

SERVES 4
½ cup all-purpose flour
1 cup water
¾ cup corn oil
1 small white onion, chopped
½ cup chopped fresh or canned tomatoes
¼ cup paprika
1 pound American cheese, shredded
½ teaspoon salt
½ to 1 teaspoon cayenne
Tortilla chips, for serving

In a small bowl, stir together the flour and water to make a paste. Set aside. In a saucepan, heat the oil over medium heat. Add the onion, tomatoes, and paprika and sauté for about 5 minutes, until the onion is translucent. Decrease the heat to low. Stir the flour paste briefly to recombine, add to the pan, and cook, stirring constantly, for about 5 minutes, until the onion-tomato mixture thickens. (The heat should be very low at this point.) Add the cheese and salt and stir until the cheese melts. Finally, add the cayenne, starting with the smaller amount and adding to taste.

Serve hot as a dip with chips, or spread on the chips and broil until bubbly.

CROCK-POT CHILE CON QUESO

It's easy to make and serve chile con queso in a slow cooker. You can ladle small amounts into a serving bowl as needed while the rest stays warm. See photo on page 116.

MAKES ABOUT 2 CUPS
1 pound Velveeta cheese, cut into 1-inch cubes
½ cup grated sharp Cheddar cheese
1 (10-ounce) can RO*TEL diced tomatoes and green chiles, with juice
1 teaspoon chili powder, homemade (page 110) or store-bought
Tortilla chips or Fritos corn chips, for serving

Combine the cheeses in a slow cooker, cover, turn on to the low setting, and heat gently until the cheeses melt. Add the RO*TEL tomatoes and juice from the can and the chili powder, mix well, and continue to heat for about 10 minutes, until hot and the flavors are blended.

Serve warm with tortilla chips for dipping. Any leftover dip can be covered and refrigerated for up to 1 week. Reheat gently to serve.

Salsa con Queso: Substitute 1½ cups homemade salsa such as Grilled Tomatillo Salsa (page 140) or 1 (16-ounce) jar Pace Picante Sauce for the RO*TEL tomatoes and chiles.

SOPA DE FIDEO

"We are out of rice. Would you mind if I gave you fideo?" the owner of Abuelitas restaurant on Galveston Island asked me. I was pleasantly surprised. Although fideo is a common dish in Tejano home cooking, it is seldom seen in Tex-Mex restaurants anymore.

Fideo is vermicelli that has been broken into small pieces. Q & Q brand fideo, which is manufactured in Fort Worth, is the standard among Tejanos. It's made with durum wheat and comes in 5-ounce packages.

SERVES 4

3 tablespoons lard or bacon drippings

1 pound ground beef

½ white onion, chopped

2 cloves garlic, minced

15 chile pequin peppers or 2 jalapeño chiles, chopped

1 tablespoon chili powder, homemade (page 110) or store-bought

1 teaspoon dried Mexican oregano

1 (15-ounce) can tomato sauce

5 ounces fideo

½ cup water

In a sauté pan or skillet, heat 2 tablespoons of the lard over medium-high heat. Add the beef, onion, garlic, chiles, chili powder, and oregano and cook, breaking up the meat with the side of a wooden spoon or spatula, for 5 to 7 minutes, until the meat is browned and the onion is soft. Add the tomato sauce and stir well, then lower the heat to a simmer.

In a separate skillet, heat the remaining 1 tablespoon lard over medium-high heat. Add the fideo and stir for about 3 minutes, until nicely browned. Add the browned fideo to the beef mixture, pour in the water, and stir well. Cover and simmer, uncovering and stirring often, for 5 minutes, until the fideo is soft. Add more water if the mixture becomes too dry. Serve immediately.

Sopa de Conchitas: Substitute small shell pasta for the fideo and adjust the cooking time as needed.

Sopa de Macaroni: Substitute small elbow macaroni for the fideo and adjust the cooking time as needed.

PECAN PRALINES

These simple pralines are the free dessert at many old-fashioned Tex-Mex restaurants. They recall an era when whole families of immigrants made a living as candy sellers.

MAKES ABOUT 24 PRALINES

1 cup firmly packed light brown sugar

1 cup granulated sugar

1 tablespoon light corn syrup

1 tablespoon unsalted butter

5 tablespoons water

1 cup pecans, chopped

Lay 1 or 2 large sheets of aluminum foil on a countertop and spray with nonstick cooking spray.

In a heavy saucepan, combine both sugars, the corn syrup, butter, and water over medium heat and bring to a boil, stirring frequently, until the mixture registers 238°F on a candy thermometer (soft-ball stage).

Remove the pan from the heat, add the pecans, and and stir vigorously with a wooden spoon for about 5 minutes, until the mixture begins to turn opaque and cools slightly. Quickly drop the still-hot mixture by the tablespoonful onto the sprayed foil. As the pralines cool, they will harden. Once they are firm, remove them from the foil and store in an airtight container at room temperature. They will keep for up to 2 weeks.

THE CANDY VENDOR

★ ★

"On every corner stand the candy-makers, selling their sweet wares. *Nueces dulces* and *queso de tuna* are prime favorites—the first a delightful compound of pecans, cinnamon, and sugar; the latter a very doubtful-looking sweetmeat, made of the juice and pulp of the fruit of the prickly-pear cactus. Then, too, they have a conserve of cocoa-nut and squares of pumpkin candied crisp without and soft within. . . . Following one of the vendors to his home, you come upon a scene which gives attractive variety to the city life which surrounds it. It is a low-roofed, dark shanty, the home of a family of candy-makers. A young man, slim, lithe, and dark-browed, sits on a raised threshold, cracking and shelling pecans. Behind him another stands at a stove, stirring a great kettle of boiling, seething syrup, the while a smooth-faced lad draws an inspiriting dance tune from the strings of his banjo, and a good-looking Mexican woman rocks slowly to and fro in her wide, low chair, and sings softly in unison. . . . No place but Texas could afford such a picture, and many subjects for the painter's art could be found in the homes of these people."

–Lee C. Harby, "Texan Types and Contrast," *Harper's New Monthly Magazine*, July 1890

Candy vendor, San Antonio.

Texas Green Chile Posole (page 132).

CHAPTER 11

THE GREEN CHILE LINE

When Texas entered the Union, it gave up its claim to New Mexico. But when the state lines were drawn, a large part of the old Santa Fe mission region, including its largest city, El Paso, remained in the state of Texas. The far western corner of Texas remains culturally connected to New Mexico.

That's why El Paso and far West Texas swear allegiance to the long green chile. Other towns west of the Pecos, like Presidio and Marfa, also have a long history of green chiles, as well as stacked enchiladas.

The word *enchilada* means "chilied," and the full name of the dish is tortillas enchiladas. The earliest enchiladas in Mexico consisted of nothing more than tortillas dipped in chile sauce, sometimes sprinkled with cheese and chopped onions. In most of the state, the Tex-Mex "enchilada plate" would evolve into a dish that featured a couple of tortillas wrapped around a stuffing. But old-fashioned West Texas enchilada purists still proudly served stacked enchiladas, usually in a sauce made of dried and pulverized long red chiles.

The Old Borunda Café in Marfa was the most famous bastion of West Texas Tex-Mex. It reached its heyday under the stern leadership of Carolina Borunda. Throughout its history, everything at the Old Borunda was cooked on a wood-burning stove, fueled exclusively with mesquite. Carolina was famous for her stacked enchiladas served with an egg on top. When you sat down at the table, you got a bowl of Fritos and a stack of white bread.

Marfa is part of the West Texas region known as the Trans-Pecos, made famous as the jurisdiction of Judge Roy Bean, a.k.a the Law West of the Pecos. The area is home to Big Bend National Park and an awesomely beautiful landscape. The movie *Giant* was shot here, and during its filming, one of its stars, James Dean, ate regularly at the Old Borunda.

Stephanie Spitzer, now eighty years old and the last surviving employee of the Old Borunda Café, told me that the history of the Old Borunda began in 1886, when Tulia Borunda opened Tulia's Café. Little is known about Tulia, except that she came from Mexico with her brother, probably via New Mexico. "Tulia's brother Cipriano Borunda had a *ranchito* where he grew chiles and produce for the restaurant," Stephanie Spitzer said. "His wife, my grandma Carolina, used to have to fight off the Indians." The Comanches were notorious for raiding farms and ranches and stealing food in those days. In 1910, Cipriano and Carolina took over Tulia Borunda's café and moved it from the train tracks out to the main road in town.

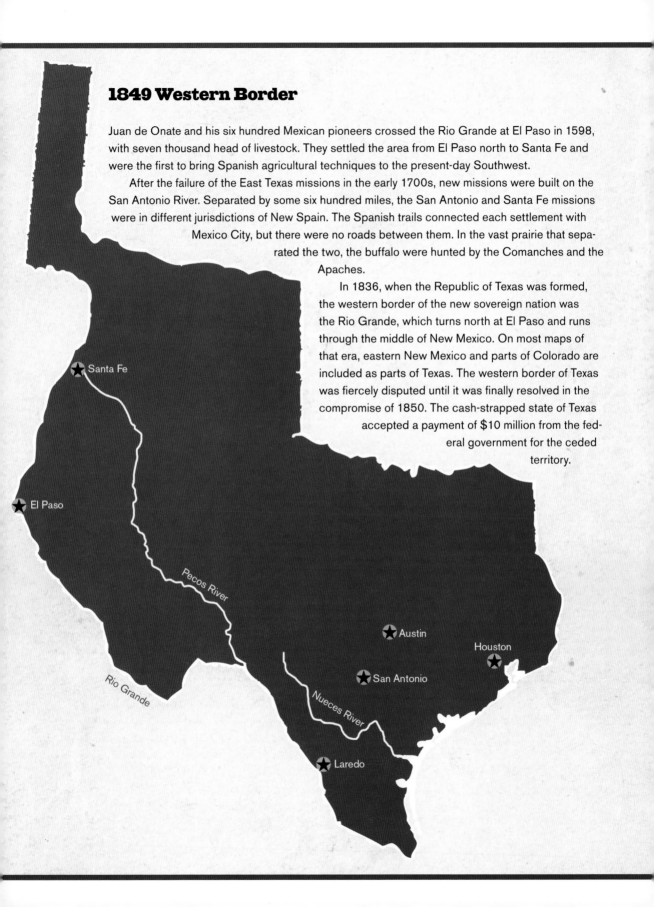

1849 Western Border

Juan de Onate and his six hundred Mexican pioneers crossed the Rio Grande at El Paso in 1598, with seven thousand head of livestock. They settled the area from El Paso north to Santa Fe and were the first to bring Spanish agricultural techniques to the present-day Southwest.

After the failure of the East Texas missions in the early 1700s, new missions were built on the San Antonio River. Separated by some six hundred miles, the San Antonio and Santa Fe missions were in different jurisdictions of New Spain. The Spanish trails connected each settlement with Mexico City, but there were no roads between them. In the vast prairie that separated the two, the buffalo were hunted by the Comanches and the Apaches.

In 1836, when the Republic of Texas was formed, the western border of the new sovereign nation was the Rio Grande, which turns north at El Paso and runs through the middle of New Mexico. On most maps of that era, eastern New Mexico and parts of Colorado are included as parts of Texas. The western border of Texas was fiercely disputed until it was finally resolved in the compromise of 1850. The cash-strapped state of Texas accepted a payment of $10 million from the federal government for the ceded territory.

Santa Fe

El Paso

Pecos River

Austin

Houston

San Antonio

Rio Grande

Nueces River

Laredo

Marfa had a growth spurt around that time, thanks in large part to Pancho Villa. His military campaigns consisted mainly of taking over haciendas in the Mexican state of Chihuahua, seizing all their horses and cattle, and trading the livestock in Texas for guns and money. The desolate river crossings in the Big Bend region, just south of Marfa, were perfect for this sort of activity.

After Villa set fire to the New Mexican town of Columbus in a 1916 raid, President Wilson ordered General John Jay "Black Jack" Pershing to pursue Pancho Villa into Mexico. During the hostilities, thousands of National Guard forces from as far away as Oklahoma were mobilized to protect the border. Because Marfa was the rail hub of all of this military activity, the town grew, and the fame of Old Borunda Café's enchiladas grew with it.

In 1932, when Cipriano and Carolina Borunda decided to retire, they turned the place over to their daughter, also named Carolina, who had grown up working in the restaurant. Carolina Borunda ran the Old Borunda Café for fifty-five years. It closed after its centennial in 1987.

★ ★ ★

Although the Old Borunda and other restaurants made the West Texas version of Tex-Mex famous, there is some question about how far the culture of the long green chile extends into Texas. "In my opinion, the green chile line is Balmorhea," Texas author and raconteur Joe Nick Patoski told me. "A restaurant there called Cuevo de Osso serves stacked enchiladas with your choice of red or green chile sauce. And that's my definition of long green chile country. I used to think that it ended at Sierra Blanca, a tiny village with four great restaurants. But I haven't found green chiles anywhere east of Balhorhea."

I pointed out that Leal's in Muleshoe was east of Balmorhea and that it serves excellent green and red chile enchiladas. Patoski conceded that the green chile line recrosses the border farther north.

Leal's, a fifty-one-year-old West Texas restaurant chain, serves some of the best western-style Tex-Mex I've ever encountered. On a recent visit, I ordered a deluxe plate and chatted with founder Irma Leal. The plate included a taco, rice and beans, a tamale, and enchiladas in red chile sauce. Leal's has two other locations just across the border in Clovis, New Mexico, a mere thirty miles away.

At Leal's, the tortillas are old-fashioned. Most of the tortillas you get in the United States and Mexico these days are made from the instant mix called *masa harina* (corn flour). Leal's tortilla factory is a throwback. It still buys dried white corn, slakes it with chemical lime to make *nixtamal*, and grinds it on giant lava stones into fresh corn dough. The difference between tortillas made with corn flour and those made with fresh *masa* is like the difference between instant coffee and fresh brewed.

"I grew up making tortillas," Irma Leal told me. And she means it literally. Her childhood home in the Lower Rio Grande Valley town of Mercedes was located next to her father's tortilla factory, El Arco Iris, where the whole family worked. Irma married Jesse Leal and the couple left the valley when Jesse got a job working for the Bracero Association in distant Muleshoe.

The bracero program of the 1950s was an immigration agreement between the United States and Mexico. By legalizing the influx of migrant Mexicans, the federal government was able to allocate workers to areas where they were needed and supervise their round-trip. In return, the government of Mexico negotiated some basic rights for the workers, including a guaranteed rate of pay, familiar food, proper shelter, and one day off a week.

When the program started, there wasn't any Mexican food in Muleshoe. Irma saw an opportunity. "I told Jesse, 'Let's buy a tortilla machine.'" They spent their savings bringing a tortilla machine up from the Rio Grande Valley and setting it up in a tin-roofed building on the east side of Muleshoe. When sales were slow, Jesse would peddle tortillas door to door. Before long, they were selling *barbacoa* on

TAXONOMY OF THE LONG GREEN CHILE

★ ★

THE NEW MEXICO CHILE was hybridized by Fabian Garcia at New Mexico State University beginning in around 1894. He crossed several chiles, including the pasilla chile and the colorado chile, to get the meaty, vegetable-like green chile he was trying to create. Known as the long green chile by New Mexicans and West Texans (until it turns red and becomes the long red chile), it has a pleasant vegetable flavor. You can buy them hot or mild.

There are countless cultivars, including Sandia, Big Jim, and others. Some are hotter, some are milder, some ripen early, some ripen late. Anaheims are the same chiles. Their name comes from a chile cannery opened in Anaheim, California, in 1900 by a farmer named Emilio Ortega, who carried the pepper seeds to California from New Mexico.

In New Mexico, the long green chile is further subdivided by region of origin. The two most common names encountered are Hatch and Chimayo. Hatch chiles are grown in the southern part of New Mexico (around the town of Hatch) from certified seed sources and are graded according to heat. Mild green specimens are often roasted and peeled and then eaten like a vegetable. It is rumored that Hatch chile growers have taken to sending their seeds across the border where they can grow chiles using cheaper Mexican water and labor. The "Hatch" chiles are then brought back into the United States. Anaheim and mild Hatch chiles are interchangeable in most recipes.

Chimayo chiles have been cultivated longer than their Hatch counterparts. They are grown in the northern part of the state (around the town of Chimayo) from seeds that have been saved from the previous harvest. Chimayo chiles are treasured for their superior flavor and unpredictable heat, but they are becoming increasingly rare. Most of the "Chimayo

Hatch chiles.

chiles" sold around the state (including on the steps of the chapel in the village of Chimayo) are actually cheaper Hatch chiles that hawkers pass off to tourists. The best place to buy certified Chimayo chiles is at the farmers' market in Santa Fe.

Long green chiles that are allowed to ripen are called long red chiles, which are typically strung on long strings and dried. The strings of drying chiles are called *ristras* and are often hung from the eaves of houses and barns or along fences. Chimayo chiles are nearly always sold dried, either whole or in powdered form. No Tex-Mex chili powder made from anchos contains cumin—New Mexico red chile powder is pure chile. New Mexican red chile is almost never seen fresh—neither are red anchos. If you cannot find the whole dried long red chiles or the chile powder, you can substitute whole or ground guajillo chiles, a popular ingredient in Mexican cooking.

weekends to go with the tortillas. Then they added a few tables and the tortilla factory was renamed Leal's Mexican Restaurant.

When I finished mopping up the red chile with tortillas, the tiny, soft-spoken Irma passed me a manila envelope. Inside I found a stack of handwritten letters from Leal's customers. The one written by Heriberto Mendoza, a former bracero, told the story of a day in 1960, when Mendoza's boss, a local farmer, dropped him off at Leal's on his day off. With no way to get back to the fields, Mendoza had to hitch a ride with Irma's husband, Jesse, who loaded him up with enough *barbacoa* and tortillas to last all week. Forty-eight years later, Mendoza, who is now a grandfather, still remembered that kindness. "I got married and made Muleshoe my home ...," the former farmworker wrote in his letter. "Now I take my children's children to Leal's."

The Muleshoe Leal's relocated to its current home on American Boulevard in 1968. There are now six Leal's Mexican Restaurants, all owned by members of the Leal family. Along with the one in Muleshoe, there are two in Clovis, New Mexico, one in Plainview, one in Henrietta, and one in Amarillo. All six locations serve tortillas and tortilla chips manufactured by Leal's Tortilla Factory in Muleshoe and green and red chile sauce.

The green chile border is getting blurry these days. Texas restaurants like Chuy's and Texas supermarkets like Central Market have brought the tradition of roasted green chiles to much of the rest of Texas. No one is talking about giving up jalapeños, of course, but people all over the state are cooking with long green chiles these days.

ROASTED LONG GREEN CHILES

In late August and early September, chile sellers set up their giant propane-fired rolling drum roasters at grocery stores and farmers' markets in Texas and New Mexico. Many people buy a whole year's supply of roasted peppers from these sellers and freeze them. If you don't have a handy chile roaster nearby, it's easy enough to roast your own chiles. You can use this recipe for roasting long green chiles, or for roasting poblanos.

5 or 6 fresh long green chiles

Using tongs or a fork, hold each chile over the flame of a gas burner and turn the chile as needed to blister the skin well on all sides. Don't allow the flame to burn too long in one place or you will burn through the chile. Alternatively, blister and char the chiles over the fire of a charcoal or gas grill or under a broiler. When most of the skin is well blistered, wrap the warm chile in a wet paper towel, put it inside a plastic bag, and set it aside to steam gently for 10 to 15 minutes.

When you remove the towel, most of the skin should come off easily. Scrape off the rest of the skin with a butter knife. If you are making chiles rellenos, make a lengthwise slit in the chile and remove the seeds carefully, trying to keep the pepper intact. (It's not easy.) Otherwise, remove the seeds and cut the chile as directed in individual recipes.

Oven Roasting: Preheat the oven to 350°F. Slit each chile open lengthwise and remove the stem and seeds. Lay the chiles, skin side up, on a baking sheet. Roast for 20 to 25 minutes, until the skin is loose. Wrap in wet paper towels and place in a plastic bag. You won't get quite as much charred flavor, but the method is easier.

GREEN CHILE SAUCE

For the brief time of the year when green chiles were available, the Old Borunda Café served a version of Frito pie featuring green chile sauce spooned over Fritos corn chips. This sauce is also good with *huevos rancheros*, grilled and braised meats, and enchiladas.

MAKES ABOUT 6 CUPS

5 tomatillos

4 cups vegetable broth

2 cups roasted long green chiles (page 129), peeled, seeded, then chopped

2 teaspoons minced white onion

1 teaspoon dried Mexican oregano

1 clove garlic, minced

½ teaspoon salt

¼ teaspoon white pepper

2 tablespoons cornstarch dissolved in 2 tablespoons water

Husk the tomatillos and rinse to remove dirt. In a medium saucepan over high heat, bring a quart of water to a boil and add the tomatillos. Reduce the heat to medium and simmer for 5 minutes or until the tomatillos are soft. Puree in a blender with a little of the cooking liquid.

In a saucepan, combine the pureed tomatillos, broth, chiles, onion, oregano, garlic, salt, and pepper and bring to a boil over medium-high heat, stirring occasionally. Cook for 10 minutes, until reduced slightly. Stir in the cornstarch mixture, lower the heat to a simmer, and cook for 5 to 10 minutes longer, until thickened.

Use immediately, or let cool, cover, and refrigerate. It will keep for up to 2 weeks.

RED CHILE SAUCE

Like the green chile sauce at left, red chile sauce is great with enchiladas, eggs, or Frito pie. When you order huevos rancheros or cheese enchiladas in some cafés in West Texas and New Mexico, the waitress will ask, "Red or green?" If you answer "Christmas," you will get red chile sauce over one half of the dish and green chile sauce over the other.

MAKES ABOUT 6 CUPS

4 cups vegetable broth

¾ cup New Mexico or guajillo chile powder

2 tomatoes, chopped, or 1 cup canned crushed tomatoes, with juice

2 teaspoons minced white onion

1 teaspoon ground cumin

1 clove garlic, minced

½ teaspoon salt

¼ teaspoon pepper

2 tablespoons cornstarch dissolved in 2 tablespoons water

In a saucepan, combine the broth, chile powder, tomatoes, onion, cumin, garlic, salt, and pepper and bring to a boil over medium-high heat, stirring occasionally. Cook for 10 minutes, until reduced slightly. Stir in the cornstarch mixture, lower the heat to a simmer, and cook for 5 to 10 minutes longer, until thickened.

Use immediately, or let cool, cover, and refrigerate. It will keep for up to 2 weeks.

ENCHILADAS BORUNDA (STACKED ENCHILADAS WITH PORK AND RED CHILE)

West Texans like stacked enchiladas. You stack the tortillas flat, with the filling between them. Don't use fluffy white corn tortillas. For enchiladas, you need the tough, old-fashioned yellow corn tortillas.

SERVES 2

8 ounces boneless pork loin chops, trimmed of fat and cut into short, narrow strips

Salt and pepper

1½ tablespoons vegetable oil

1 cup chopped white onions

3 cloves garlic, minced

3 cups Red Chile Sauce (page 130)

1 cup canned crushed tomatoes

1 teaspoon dried Mexican oregano

6 yellow corn tortillas

3 tablespoons crumbled Mexican cotija cheese

Preheat the oven to 350°F. Spray a shallow 9- by 13-inch baking dish with nonstick cooking spray.

Sprinkle the pork strips with salt and pepper and reserve. In a large skillet, heat the oil over medium-high heat. Add the onions and sauté for about 5 minutes, until they begin to turn translucent. Add the pork and the garlic and cook, stirring, for about 5 minutes, or until the pork is just cooked through. Add the red chile sauce, tomatoes, and oregano and mix well. Decrease the heat to low, cover, and simmer for 15 minutes, until the pork is very tender, adding water as needed to maintain a saucelike consistency.

Place 2 tortillas side by side in the bottom of the prepared baking dish. Spoon one-fourth of the meat and sauce onto each tortilla. Top each sauced tortilla with a second tortilla. Spoon the rest of the meat and most of the rest of the sauce (reserve a few spoonfuls) on top of the second layer of tortillas, saturating the tortillas as well as possible. Top with the remaining 2 tortillas. Add a few tablespoons of water to the sauce remaining in the pan and stir to incorporate. Spoon this mixture over the top layer of tortillas so that it is fully saturated. Scatter the cheese evenly over the top.

Bake for about 10 minutes, until the sauce bubbles. To serve, gently run a spatula under the bottom layer to loosen, then, using 1 wide spatula or 2 smaller spatulas, carefully move each stack to a dinner plate. (The bottom tortilla will be very soft.) Serve right away.

IN 1840, TEXAS PRESIDENT Mirabeau Lamar wrote a letter to the citizens of Santa Fe extolling the benefits of life in the Lone Star Republic. In 1841, he sent a commercial expedition hoping to charm the New Mexicans with Texan goods. Merchants drove twenty-one ox-drawn wagons full of goods for trade. Five infantry companies and artillery accompanied the expedition to protect the businessmen. Including guests and teamsters, the group numbered 321. The merchandise was valued at $200,000.

Sadly, the expedition met with several disasters. The party set out from Austin and traveled north through the Cross Timbers. Their first blunder was mistaking the Wichita River for the Red River. The group turned west too soon and found their route blocked by the cliffs of the Caprock. Turning north to correct the error, the expedition was harassed by the Comanches and deserted by its guide. Short of water and supplies, the wagons waited at the foot of the Llano Estacado while the military force went to look for New Mexican settlements.

The next mistake was assuming the New Mexicans were going to be friendly. In fact, an armed force of New Mexican militia overwhelmed the Texan soldiers near present-day Tucumcari without firing a shot. The Texan prisoners were marched to Mexico City, where they were tried and imprisoned.

TEXAS GREEN CHILE POSOLE

This dish falls somewhere between the South Texas squash casserole called calabacitas and New Mexican green chile posole. The squash gets cooked down to mush and becomes the thickener for the spicy stew. See photo on page 124.

SERVES 6 TO 8

4 slices thick-cut bacon, chopped

1 large white onion, chopped

1 pound boneless pork shoulder, cut into
1-inch chunks

3 cloves garlic, minced

6 cups water

2 cups long green chiles, roasted, peeled, and
seeded (page 129), then chopped

4 cups chopped summer squash (such as tatuma,
zucchini, or yellow crookneck)

1 (30-ounce) can pozole blanco (white hominy),
drained

1 teaspoon ground cumin

1 teaspoon dried Mexican oregano

1 tablespoon salt

Garnish Plate

Lime wedges

Sliced radishes

Chopped white onion

Chopped fresh cilantro

In a soup pot, fry the bacon over medium-high heat until it renders some of its fat. Add the onion and cook, stirring, for a few minutes, until just soft. Add the pork and garlic and cook, stirring, for a few minutes, until lightly browned.

Add the water, bring to a boil, and cook for 10 minutes. Lower the heat to a simmer and add the chiles, squash, hominy, cumin, oregano, and salt. Stir well, cover, and cook, stirring occasionally, for about 2 hours, until the pork is very tender. If the

stew begins to dry out as its simmers, add a little more water.

Taste and adjust the seasoning with salt. Serve the stew in shallow soup bowls. Pass the garnishes on a plate at the table for diners to add to their soup.

CARNE GUISADA

The sirloin and round steaks on a range-fed steer may taste great, but they are usually tough. This tomato and chile stew is simple to make and ensures the beef will be tender.

SERVES 6 GENEROUSLY

8 ripe Roma tomatoes (about 1½ pounds)

2 or 3 serrano chiles

1 teaspoon salt

1 teaspoon pepper

1 teaspoon ground dried Mexican oregano

3 tablespoons lard or bacon drippings

2 pounds beef sirloin or round steak, trimmed
of all fat and gristle and cut into strips
½ inch wide and 2 inches long

1 white onion, chopped

1 tablespoon all-purpose flour

Warm flour tortillas, for serving

With a paring knife, nip the stem end out of each tomato and cut the stem off of each serrano. Place the tomatoes and chiles in a dry skillet over medium heat and roast, turning as needed to darken evenly, for 10 minutes, until well charred.

Transfer the tomatoes and chiles to a bowl, cover with a clean, damp dish towel, and let steam for 10 minutes, until the skins of the tomatoes loosen and will slip off easily. Remove the tomato skins. (Don't worry if all of the skin doesn't come off.) Place the tomatoes and chiles in a food processor and process for about 20 seconds, until a chunky puree forms. Add the salt, pepper, and oregano to the puree, mix briefly, and set aside.

In a large skillet, heat the lard over high heat. Add the steak strips and cook, turning as needed, for 10 minutes, until browned. Add the onion and continue cooking, stirring occasionally, for 10 minutes, until the onion is soft. Add the tomato-chile puree and stir well. Decrease the heat to low, cover, and simmer for 1 hour, until the meat is very tender. If the stew begins to dry out before the meat is tender, add a little water. Taste and adjust the seasoning with salt and pepper.

Scoop 3 tablespoons of the cooking liquid into a small cup, add the flour, and stir to form a thin, smooth paste. Add the flour slurry to the stew and stir for a few minutes, until slightly thickened. Serve immediately with the tortillas.

ROASTED RED CHILE POTATOES

Red potatoes are the most common potatoes in Mexican cooking. They don't mash very well, but they are excellent roasted.

SERVES 6

2½ pounds red potatoes, quartered
3 cloves garlic, minced
½ white onion, chopped
1 tablespoon ground dried Mexican oregano
¼ cup sherry vinegar
2 tablespoons New Mexico chile powder
Salt

Preheat the oven to 375°F. Spray a baking pan with nonstick cooking spray.

In a bowl, toss together the potatoes, garlic, onion, oregano, and vinegar, coating the potatoes evenly. Spread the potatoes in a single layer in the prepared pan. Sprinkle the potatoes with half of the chile powder.

Roast for 15 minutes. Turn the potatoes with a spatula and sprinkle the remaining chile powder on top. Continue baking for 20 to 35 minutes, until the potatoes are crisp. Season with salt and serve hot.

CHARRO BEANS WITH BACON

If you add some beer to these *frijoles charros*, they become *frijoles borrachos*. *Charro* means "cowboy" in Spanish and *borracho* means "drunk."

SERVES 6

1 teaspoon lard or vegetable oil
4 slices bacon, minced
1 white onion, finely chopped
1 cup chopped celery
1 cup thinly sliced, peeled carrots
1 jalapeño chile, minced
8 ounces ham, diced
6 cups drained cooked pinto beans and 4 cups bean cooking liquid
1 tablespoon salt
½ teaspoon ground dried Mexican oregano
½ teaspoon ground cumin
1 (12-ounce) bottle or can Mexican beer (optional)

In a skillet, heat the lard over medium-high heat. Add the bacon, onion, celery, and carrots and cook, stirring, for about 5 minutes, until the onion is soft. Add the chile and ham and cook for 1 minute. Remove from the heat.

Place the beans and cooking liquid in a soup pot. Using an immersion blender or a potato masher, break up some of the beans to create a thick, chunky-textured soup. Add the cooked ham mixture, including some or all of the fat in the pan, and stir well. Then stir in the salt, oregano, and cumin. Place over high heat, bring to a boil, then reduce the heat to low and simmer for 10 minutes to blend the flavors. Add either water or beer as needed to achieve a good soup consistency. Ladle into bowls and serve immediately.

Salpicón with Chipotle Dressing (page 141).

Taco truck art.

CHAPTER 12

OLD-FASHIONED TACOS

★★★★★★★★★★★★★★★★★★★★★★★★★

In the 1930s and 1940s, tacos replaced tamales and chili con carne as the state's most popular Tex-Mex dish. The taco of that era was fried to order, often from a fresh *masa* disk that puffed up in the deep fryer. The late, great El Matamoros on East Avenue in Austin declared "Home of the Crispy Taco" on its neon sign. Queso-covered chalupas called "Crazy Tacos" were the rage at Old Mexico in Corpus Christi, and puffy tacos were a sensation at Rosarita's in Laredo, El Fenix in Dallas, and many other taco joints.

Puffed tacos have been featured at Caro's in Rio Grande City since 1937, when Modesta Caro opened the place. I visited the original Caro's a few years ago, and it served the best puffy tacos I had ever eaten. Unfortunately, Rio Grande City, which is situated on an isolated bend in the river across from Carmago, in the Mexican state of Tamaulipas, is a long way to drive for a taco.

But Modesta Caro's daughter Maria and her husband, John Whitten, opened another Caro's on Blue Bonnet Circle in Fort Worth in 1954. The Fort Worth Caro's preserved the same family tradition for fine Tex-Mex. Diners were greeted with a basket of piping-hot puffy chips as soon as they sat down. "No steam tables, microwaves, or can openers," was the restaurant's slogan. Sadly, John Whitten died in 2010, and the Fort Worth Caro's went out of business in 2011.

Today, made-to-order tacos are a rarity. Blame it on Taco Bell.

Taco Bell's originator, Glen Bell, had a hamburger stand in San Bernardino, California, in 1948, when the first McDonald's opened in town. After watching the success of the fast-food hamburger, he set out to create a fast-food taco. Instead of taking the time to fry tacos to order, Bell developed a preformed taco shell that fit his fast-food assembly line. He opened the Taco Bell chain in 1962.

Tacos were a crossover Mexican food that appealed to mainstream Californians. So Bell and other operators built their fast-food taco stands in suburban Los Angeles neighborhoods. Soon the inexpensive fast-food taco rivaled the hamburger in popularity. If a Tex-Mex restaurant has the word *taco* in its name, it's operated by gringos, a Mexican American writer once told me.

"Back in the 1940s, nice restaurants were in hotels and Tex-Mex restaurants were short-order cafés," Tex-Mex restaurant owner Raul Molina Jr. explained. But when the automobile became popular in the 1950s, everything changed. People wanted to go out driving and they wanted to eat in restaurants that catered to customers in automobiles.

Taco Bell entered Texas in 1967. To compete with Taco Bell and McDonald's, Tex-Mex restaurant owners began streamlining the cooking process and cutting prices. At Molina's, they started making preformed taco shells by fastening tortillas to a bent coffee can. Others followed suit. Soon Tex-Mex restaurants were buying mass-produced taco shells like

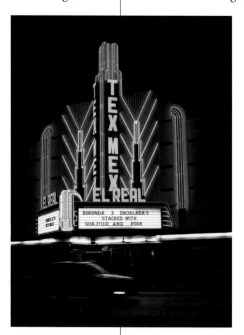

the ones you get in the taco kits at the supermarket. The fast-food taco was cheap, but like the fast-food hamburger, it was a pale imitation of the original.

Recently, the handmade hamburger has made a comeback, and so has the made-to-order taco. Just after sitting down at Matt's El Rancho in Austin a couple of years ago, my lunchmate asked me, "Have you ever tried the old-fashioned tacos here?" Matt's El Rancho had long ago fallen from its peak popularity, so I was a little dubious. But when we dug into those tacos, I was blown away.

Co-owner Matt Martinez Jr. told me he had invented the tacos for a Texas Beef Council promotion. A corn tortilla is dipped into hot oil and wrapped around several thick slices of smoked brisket. It is placed on a hot griddle with a bacon weight on top, and then flipped and griddled on the other side. It comes to the table crunchy but chewy, accompanied by chopped onions and cilantro, cold lettuce, tomatoes, and guacamole to shove inside. The wild variation in temperatures and textures is terrific. I have been back to eat those tacos at least a dozen times.

I have also eaten excellent crispy tacos at Amaya's Taco Village in Austin and wonderful puffy tacos at Henry's Puffy Tacos and Los Barrios in San Antonio. And now I am working in a Tex-Mex restaurant where puffy tacos are on the menu.

In 2010, after I quit working at the *Houston Press*, chef Bryan Caswell asked me to become a partner in a new Houston Tex-Mex restaurant that would pay homage to the old places. He wanted to create a menu of vintage Tex-Mex dishes from all over the state. I jumped at the chance. Our restaurant is called El Real Tex-Mex Cafe. It's located in the old

Tower Theater, a restored Art Deco movie theater on Westheimer, a few blocks west of the former Felix location.

While we were building El Real, Felix Tijerina Jr. was selling off the fixtures and furnishings at the restaurant his father built down the street. In the interest of preserving some of that restaurant's history, we purchased the distinctive caned chairs, carved wood display cases, and framed photos from Felix. These, along with items from other old Tex-Mex restaurants, are on display in an upstairs gallery at El Real.

Tex-Mex is an American regional cuisine that is appreciated around the world, and El Real Tex-Mex Cafe is an homage to Tex-Mex history. The menu includes recreations of some vintage dishes from the old temples of Tex-Mex, including puffy and crispy tacos.

But no matter how good restaurant tacos may be, the best tacos you'll ever eat are the ones you cook fresh at your house.

CRISPY TACO SHELLS

Tacos are a popular dinner at my house. On weeknights, I take the easy route. I fry a dozen yellow corn tortillas into shells and serve them with a whole roasted chicken from the supermarket, hacked into big pieces. I also cut up lettuce, avocados, limes, and tomatoes and set them all on the table. For the adults, I set out some salsa, chiles, and other spicy condiments. Then everyone makes his or her own pulled-chicken tacos at the table.

My chile-loving wife doctors her supermarket-chicken tacos with salsa, fresh chiles peppers from the garden, or Tabasco sauce. I like cilantro, raw onions, and pickled jalapeño slices on mine. It's fun to build them your own way, which is probably why the kids love them, too. One family friend who comes over for dinner a lot calls this kind of cooking "homemade junk food."

Frying your own taco shells with store-bought tortillas is easy. The darker, denser yellow corn tortillas work better than the fluffy white corn tortillas. If the tortillas are very fresh, air bubbles will form when you fry them, creating semipuffy taco shells. I like taco shells that are flexible and chewy, so I don't fry them too crisp. Other people like their taco shells super-crunchy. Feel free to experiment with the cooking times to find the taco texture you like best.

MAKES 10 TACO SHELLS
Peanut or vegetable oil, for frying
10 yellow corn tortillas or Fresh Corn Tortillas (page 138)

Pour the oil to a depth of ½ inch into a small skillet or sauté pan and place the pan over high heat. It will take 5 to 7 minutes for the oil to reach the optimum frying temperature of 350°F. A tortilla slipped into the oil at the proper temperature should bubble immediately. If the tortilla spits and bubbles violently, the oil is too hot. Control the heat to keep the oil at the right temperature. Preheat the oven to 250°F for keeping the shells warm until you serve them.

Line a baking sheet with a double thickness of paper towels. Slip a tortilla into the hot oil. Flip it after 5 seconds. After another 5 seconds, as the tortilla starts to harden a little, use a pair of tongs to pull one side up, forming a U shape. Hold it there for 10 seconds until it sets in that position. Flip the U over, and fry the side that had been elevated for 10 seconds. If the shell starts to close, spread the tongs on the inside of the U to keep it open. The taco shell is ready when it is golden brown. The whole process should take about 1 minute, if the oil stays at a steady 350°F. If a shell is getting too brown, turn down the heat. As you finish each taco shell, transfer it to the baking sheet and blot gently with paper towels, then put the pan in the oven to keep the shells warm. Rush the shells to the table as soon you have enough for everybody to make a taco, then start to fry another batch. Figure on at least 2 taco shells per person, 3 or 4 shells for big eaters.

PUFFY TACO SHELLS

The tortilla should puff up as soon as you put it in the oil. The spatula-crimping technique is tricky, so don't be discouraged if a few of your tortillas refuse to cooperate or get cut in half. There are usually a few mistakes in every batch.

MAKES 10

10 Fresh Corn Tortillas (recipe follows)
Peanut or vegetable oil, for frying

Preheat the oven to 250°F for keeping the puffy shells warm until you serve them.

Line a baking sheet with a double thickness of paper towels. Pour the oil to a depth of ¾ inch into a deep cast-iron skillet and heat to 325°F. The oil temperature must be steady throughout the frying, so make sure the tip of the thermometer is submerged in the oil and watch the temperature closely.

Slip a tortilla into the hot oil and hold it just under the surface of the oil by placing a metal spatula gently across the middle. After a minute or so, the tortilla will begin to puff up. Be sure to keep the spatula in place until the tortilla puffs so that a ridge forms in the middle. Release the tortilla, turn it over with a large slotted spoon, and cook for 45 seconds on the top side. Lift the tortilla from the oil with the slotted spoon, tilting it to drain any remaining oil, then transfer it to the baking sheet and blot gently with paper towels. Put the pan in the oven to keep the shell warm. Cook the remaining tortillas the same way. Rush the shells to the table as soon you have enough for everybody to make a taco, then start to fry another batch. Figure on at least 2 taco shells per person, 3 shells for big eaters.

FRESH CORN TORTILLAS

You can try to follow the instructions on the bag of *masa harina*, but I have found that it always takes more water than what is called for. (Maybe because I have hard water?) And I never get as many tortillas as they claim I should. (That's probably because I can never get them thin enough.)

MAKES 10 (5-INCH) TORTILLAS

2 cups masa harina (such as Maseca brand)
¼ teaspoon salt
1¼ cups warm water, plus more as needed

Cut two 8-inch circles out of a clean plastic shopping bag and set aside.

In a bowl, using your hands, mix together the *masa harina*, salt, and water. Then gradually work in more water, mixing a little at a time with your hands, until the ingredients are thoroughly combined and the mixture forms a ball. Knead in the bowl for a couple of minutes until elastic. The dough should be flexible, not stiff. Rest the dough for at least 20 minutes, covered with a damp tea towel.

Divide the dough into 10 equal portions, and form each portion into a ball. (Each ball should weigh 2 ounces.) Using a tortilla press, rolling pin, or the bottom of a heavy pot, flatten each ball between the circles of plastic, forming a tortilla 5 inches in diameter and ⅛ inch thick.

To cook tortillas for making Puffy Taco Shells:
Heat a stove-top griddle over high heat. Place the tortillas on the hot surface and cook, turning once, for 20 seconds on each side. They will look moist and be underdone. Transfer to a sheet of waxed paper to cool. Cook the remaining tortillas the same way, stacking them on the waxed paper. Use to make Puffy Taco Shells (at left). The tortillas will keep for a couple of hours.

(Continued)

Puffy Tacos with barbecue chicken.

To cook tortillas for Crispy Taco Shells (page 137) or for serving as is: Heat a stove-top griddle over medium-high heat. Place 1 or 2 tortillas on the hot surface and cook, turning once, for 1 to 2 minutes on each side, until cooked through and golden. Transfer to the center of a lightly dampened dish towel and drape the towel sides over the top to keep them warm. Cook the remaining tortillas the same way, stacking them on top of the first tortillas.

FLOUR TORTILLAS

Breakfast tacos are rarely seen in Mexico. That's because they are pure Tex-Mex. They generally consist of eggs fried with potatoes, sausage, bacon, chorizo, or some other breakfast food wrapped up in a hot flour tortilla. For great breakfast tacos, try making your own tortillas.

MAKES 18 (6- TO 8-INCH) TORTILLAS

4 cups all-purpose flour

1 teaspoon salt

½ teaspoon baking powder

¼ cup lard, at room temperature

¼ cup unsalted butter, at room temperature

1½ cups water, or more if needed

In a stand mixer fitted with the dough hook, combine the flour, salt, baking powder, lard, butter, and 1 cup of the water and mix on low speed for about 5 minutes, until well blended. The dough should be moist and pliable. If it is too dry, add ¼ to ⅓ cup additional water. Alternatively, use a food processor fitted with the dough blade to mix the dough, adding more water as needed, then knead the dough on a floured work surface and place in a bowl. Or, in a bowl, mix together the dry ingredients, work in the lard and butter until incorporated, mix in the water until the dough comes together, and then knead the dough on a floured work surface and return to the bowl. Cover the bowl with plastic wrap and allow the dough to rest for 30 minutes to 1 hour.

Divide the dough into 18 equal portions and form each portion into a ball. If the dough seems too sticky, dip the balls in a little extra flour. On a floured work surface, roll each ball into a 6- to 8-inch round about ¼ inch thick.

Heat a skillet, griddle, or *comal* (flat cast-iron pan) over high heat. When the pan is hot, add a tortilla and cook, turning once, for about 1 minute on each side, until puffy and freckled with brown spots on both sides. As the tortillas are ready, wrap them in a clean dish towel to keep them warm. Serve warm.

GRILLED TOMATILLO SALSA

This is my favorite all-purpose taco salsa. If you make this salsa just before serving, the tomatillos will still be hot from the grill, giving the salsa an appealing warmth. You can also make the salsa in advance, chill it, and serve it later—just hold off on adding the cilantro and green onion until dinnertime.

MAKES 1½ CUPS

10 tomatillos

½ cup chopped white onion

¼ cup freshly squeezed lime juice

1 clove garlic, crushed

1 or 2 serrano chiles, coarsely chopped

Pinch of salt

¼ cup chopped fresh cilantro

¼ cup chopped green onions (white and green parts)

Prepare a charcoal or gas grill for direct-heat grilling over medium heat. Remove the husks from the tomatillos and rinse well.

Place the tomatillos directly over the fire for 5 minutes, until charred on the underside. Turn and char the other side for a few minutes.

Remove from the grill, cut away the stem end, and place in a blender. Add the white onion, lime juice, garlic, chiles, and salt and process until smooth.

Pour into a bowl. If serving immediately, stir in the cilantro and green onions. If serving later, cover and refrigerate for up to 1 week, then stir in the cilantro and green onions just before serving.

SALPICÓN WITH CHIPOTLE DRESSING

Ground meat with some taco seasoning is the usual taco filling. But here's a beef filling for special occasions. Chilled salpicón looks sensational with lots of lettuce and other salad-style condiments on a decorative platter. It's a great recipe to make when you're throwing a party. See photo on page 134.

SERVES 10

4 pounds trimmed beef brisket
1 large white onion, chopped
4 bay leaves
3 cloves garlic, crushed
1 tablespoon salt
10 peppercorns
2 serrano chiles, coarsely chopped
8 cups water
4 cups beef broth

Dressing
¼ cup olive oil
¼ cup freshly squeezed lime juice
¼ cup red wine vinegar
2 cloves garlic, minced
Sea salt and freshly ground pepper
1 (7-ounce) can chipotle chiles in adobo sauce

Lettuce leaves, for serving
Chopped tomatoes, radish slices, cucumber slices, and chopped red onions, for garnish
20 Crispy Taco Shells (page 137) or 20 Puffy Taco Shells (page 138)

In a Dutch oven, combine the beef, onion, bay leaves, garlic, salt, peppercorns, and serranos. Pour in the water and broth and bring to a boil over high heat. Decrease the heat to low and simmer, covered, for about 3 hours, until the meat is falling-apart tender. An instant-read thermometer inserted into the thickest part of the brisket will register 190°F. Alternatively, bring to a boil as directed, then cover and cook in a preheated 350°F over for 3 hours. Or, combine all of the ingredients in a slow cooker and cook on the low setting for 6 to 8 hours.

Transfer the brisket to a cutting board and let cool. Meanwhile, strain the broth through a fine-mesh sieve and set aside. When the brisket is cool, trim and scrape away any fat and gristle. With your fingers or 2 forks, tease the meat into shreds. Cut the shreds into 1-inch-long threads and place in a bowl. Moisten the meat with ½ cup of the broth. Save the remaining broth for another purpose.

To make the dressing, in a blender, combine the oil, lime juice, vinegar, and garlic and sprinkle in a little salt and pepper. Drain the chipotles, pouring all of the adobo sauce into the blender. Then add the chipotles to taste: there are about 10 chipotles in a can. For a little heat, add just 1 chipotle; for a medium-hot dressing, add 2 or 3 chipotles; and for a spicy dressing, add 4 or more chipotles. Turn on the blender and process until you have a smooth dressing. Add the dressing to the shredded beef. The mixture should be moist but not soupy. Chop the rest of the chipotles and put them on the table as a condiment.

Salpicón is customarily chilled, then served at room temperature. To chill, cover and refrigerate for at least 1 hour or up to several days. When you remove it from the refrigerator, the top will be dry and the dressing will have collected on the bottom of the bowl. Just before serving, dump the mixture into another bowl and retoss it.

To serve, arrange a bed of lettuce leaves on a deep platter, and spoon the salpicón onto the lettuce. Garnish with the tomatoes, radish slices, and cucumber slices and top with a sprinkling of onion. Serve with the taco shells.

CRISPY PICKLED JALAPEÑO CHILES

Most canned or bottled pickled chiles have a mushy texture, so I make my own pickled chiles at home. I like to cook the jalapeños briefly to keep them crunchy. You can add other peppers from your garden to this recipe.

MAKES ABOUT 2½ QUARTS

2 tablespoons vegetable oil

1 small white onion (7 ounces), thickly sliced

1 pound carrots, peeled and sliced ½ inch thick (about 2 cups)

5 cloves garlic, quartered lengthwise

6 cups water

15 jalapeño chiles (about 1 pound)

1¼ cups distilled white vinegar, plus more as needed for the jars

1 tablespoon pickling salt, plus more as needed for the jars

1 teaspoon dried Mexican oregano, or more to taste

4 bay leaves

In a soup pot, heat the oil over medium-high heat. Add the onion and carrots and sauté for 3 minutes. Add the garlic and continue to cook for 1 to 2 minutes, until the onions are soft. Add the water and bring to a boil. Slit each jalapeño lengthwise with the tip of a sharp knife so the liquid can penetrate. Add the jalapeños to the boiling water and cook for 2 minutes, until slightly softened. (If you like softer chiles, cook for up to 5 minutes.)

Add the 1¼ cups vinegar, 1 tablespoon pickling salt, the oregano (you can up the amount if you prefer a stronger oregano flavor), and the bay leaves and simmer for 1 minute longer. Remove from the heat and let cool completely.

Using a slotted spoon, transfer the chiles, onion, and carrots to 6 pint jars. Ladle or pour the cooled cooking liquid over the vegetables, filling the jars three-quarters full. Add 1 tablespoon pickling salt to each jar, and fill the jars to the top with white vinegar. Cover the jars and refrigerate. The pickled chiles will keep for up to a month. Alternatively, fill sterilized jars without cooling the pickled peppers, seal with lids, process in a hot-water bath, and store as directed in Water-Bath Canning on Your Home Stove on page 95.

GUACAMOLE

Guacamole is the ultimate topping for chicken tacos. This is a very simple guacamole. But some people like it even simpler. Mashed avocado with a dash of garlic salt and lemon juice is the easiest recipe I've heard. Just don't try to make guacamole with underripe avocados.

MAKES ABOUT 2½ CUPS

3 ripe avocados

2 Roma tomatoes, peeled and minced

1 small white onion, minced

1 clove garlic, minced (optional)

½ teaspoon salt

Freshly squeezed lemon juice, for seasoning

Halve the avocados, pit them, and then scoop the flesh into a bowl. Add the tomatoes, onion, garlic, and salt to the bowl and mash well with a fork until you have the consistency you like. Mix in the lemon juice to taste.

You can use guacamole as a dip with tortilla chips, as a topping for your tacos, or serve it in iceberg "cups" on individual plates as a salad.

GREEN CHORIZO

When it comes to breakfast tacos, chorizo and scrambled eggs wrapped in a flour tortilla is my favorite. But I am not crazy about the chorizo you find in supermarkets. (You won't be, either, after you read the ingredients; the first item on the list is usually salivary glands.) Once you try this excellent and easy-to-make chorizo, you won't bother buying the stuff in the store anymore. This chorizo is also good combined with cooked potatoes (just add them to the pan after cooking the chorizo) or chile con queso (page 121) or used in *chilaquile* (fried tortilla strips simmered in salsa).

MAKES ENOUGH FOR 12 TACOS
8 ounces boneless pork chops or ground pork
¼ cup roasted long green chiles (page 129), seeded and cut into strips
1 tomatillo, husked removed, blanched for 5 minutes, and quartered
1 clove garlic, minced
1 serrano chile, seeded and chopped
2 tablespoons chopped fresh cilantro
2 tablespoons chopped green onion (white and green parts)
2 teaspoons chopped fresh parsley
1 teaspoon dried Mexican oregano
2 tablespoons cider vinegar
1 teaspoon salt
1 tablespoon olive oil

If using the pork chops, cut them into ½-inch dice, removing any gristle. In a food processor, combine the pork, roasted chiles, tomatillo, garlic, serrano chile, cilantro, green onion, parsley, oregano, vinegar, and salt and pulse until finely ground. (You want to pulse all of the ingredients at the same time so that the pork combines with all of the spices evenly.) In a skillet, heat a few drops of the oil over medium-high heat, add a small nugget of the chorizo, and fry until cooked through. Taste, then adjust the seasoning of the rest of the batch.

To cook the chorizo, in the skillet, heat the remaining oil over medium-high heat. Add the chorizo and fry, breaking up the meat with the side of a wooden spoon or spatula, for 3 to 5 minutes, until nicely browned and cooked through.

REFRIED BEANS

The first thing I put on a picadillo (ground meat) taco is a spoonful of refried beans. It gives the taco meat something to stick to. And it keeps a juicy taco filling from ruining the taco shell. Don't be shy with the lard. It's what makes the beans creamy.

MAKES ABOUT 3 CUPS; ENOUGH FOR 12 TACOS
½ cup lard or bacon drippings
3 cups drained cooked pinto beans and 3 cups bean cooking liquid, plus more liquid if needed
Salt

In a skillet, heat the lard over medium heat. Add the beans and their cooking liquid and cook, mashing the beans with a potato masher, until they are partially crushed and thick. You do not need to mash them completely smooth. The beans are ready when they are heated through and are a good consistency. If they seem too pasty, add more cooking liquid. Season with salt and serve.

PART IV
OLD WORLD FLAVORS

Central Texas and the Hill Country

Central Texas straddles the boundary between the rich farmlands of the Brazos Valley and the rugged Hill Country, the easternmost part of the Southwest. The dividing line is the Balcones Fault, where the black loam of the flat cotton-farming country to the east meets the rocky limestone upthrust of the Edwards Plateau and the Hill Country.

Limestone caves and natural pools abound in the Hill Country. It's also the home of the massive pink granite outcropping called Enchanted Rock. Although the region has a number of vineyards and peach orchards, the area is difficult to farm, with only a thin layer of topsoil covering the limestone.

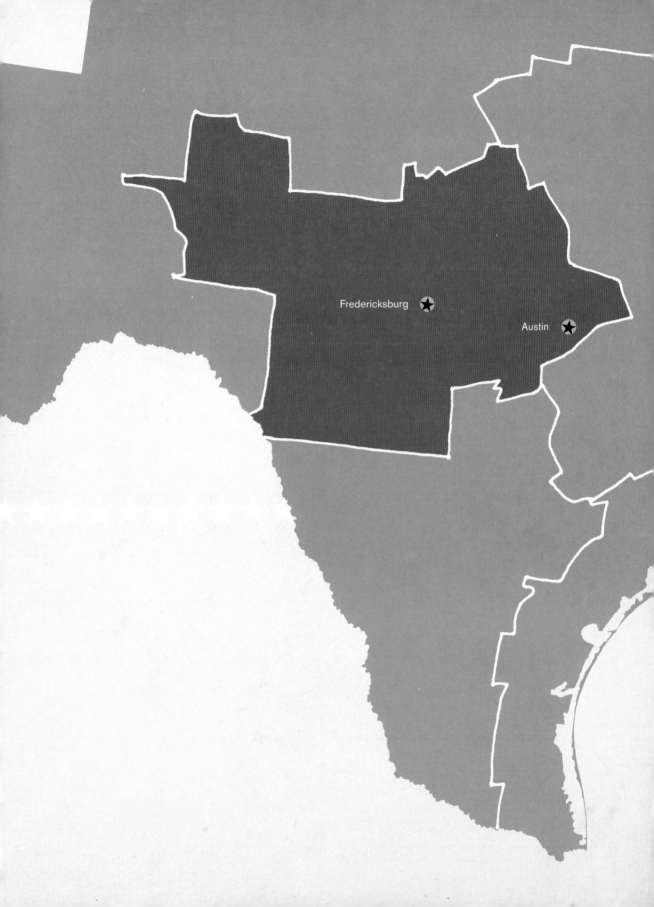

Homemade Pretzels (page 153) and
Shiner Bohemian Black Lager beer.

Turn-of-the-century German picnic near Salado Creek.

CHAPTER 13

THE GERMAN BELT

★★★★★★★★★★★★★★★★★★★★★★★★★

When the gates of Marktplatz opened on Friday evening, I made a beeline for the Shiner keg stand. The brewmaster tapped the ceremonial first keg, signaling the beginning of Fredericksburg's annual Oktoberfest. Free glasses of Shiner Helles, a German-style pale lager, were passed around. All of the beer was gone inside of fifteen minutes.

A food magazine had sent me to Oktoberfest to write about the German Texans. I roamed the Marktplatz fairgrounds for a while looking for edible clues. There were the usual turkey legs, fried dough, and cotton candy, but I was pleasantly surprised that so many food stalls were selling German treats. The Kiwanis pushed potato pancakes, sauerkraut, and sausage and something called a Dutchman burger, and the Jaycees had a bratwurst plate and sausage on a stick. My favorite Tex-Deutsch fusion item was a so-called German taco: a split sausage, sauerkraut, and mustard on a flour tortilla.

Outside the music tent, I watched one father in lederhosen and a Bavarian hat feeding his two sons, who were dressed much like their father. Inside the tent, the dance floor was crowded with whirling couples. About half of them hoofed it in cowboy hats and boots. The other half waltzed around in native costumes from various parts of Germany.

GERMAN TEXAS

★ ★

IN 1831, A GERMAN NAMED Johann Friedrich Ernst got a land grant of more than four thousand acres in present-day Austin County. The excited Ernst wrote letters to friends back home describing an earthly paradise of abundant fish and game, mild weather, and easy farming. He set off a steady stream of Germans immigrating to Texas that lasted for the next fifty years.

In the 1840s, a group of German noblemen brought German citizens to Texas by the thousands with the idea of founding a German colony. Many of these settlers were swindled out of their investment money and left to fend for themselves in the strange new land. Eventually, with the help of the Texas legislature, the early German immigrants established a colony at San Marcos.

The European revolutions of 1848 and the gold rush in California created another large group of German-speaking immigrants. Many of the forty-niners landed at Galveston, the westernmost port in the United States. After trying their hand at mining in California, some of the disillusioned Europeans returned to Texas to settle down.

These immigrants and more who followed after the Civil War created the Texas German Belt, a large swath of German farm communities dotted throughout the countryside from Houston to the Hill Country. By 1850, Germans made up 5 percent of the state's population. Some of them were middle-class farm folk hungry for land. Others were freethinkers and idealists who came to pursue lofty ideals.

The Forty, for instance, were college students who formed a utopian society in Germany and then sailed across the Atlantic to live out their dreams. They founded the communal settlement of Bettina on the Llano River in 1847. Followers of such socialist visionaries as Fourier and Cabet, they organized themselves around the principles of "friendship, freedom, and equality." The group included two musicians, an engineer, a theologian, an agriculturalist, two architects, seven lawyers, four foresters, and an army lieutenant. Unfortunately, the community was long on intellectuals and short on butchers and bakers. In less than a year, the settlement collapsed.

When the commune broke up, some of its members moved to Austin. Unionist Jacob Kuechler became commissioner of the state's general land office. Christof Flach and Johannes Hoerner founded Hill Country family dynasties that promoted the philosophy of free thought in everyday life for four generations.

I particularly liked the German singer's rendition of the Jimmie Rodgers song "Blue Yodel." Next, he started to sing "T for Texas, T for Tennessee," but he replaced Rodgers's twangy "yodel-ley-hees" with a superfast warbling alpine yodel.

Then the accordion player lifted his beer glass and sang the beginning of a toasting song, *"Ein Prosit, Ein Prosit …"* Suddenly the music and the dancers stopped and more than a thousand people in the music tent and the adjoining beer garden raised their glasses together.

"Ein Prosit, Ein Prosit, der Gemütlichkeit," they all sang in unison.

"Ein, zwie, drie, g'suffa," shouted the accordion player.

"Hoi, hoi, hoi," shouted the crowd in response, and then everyone chugalugged their beers. I had never seen anything quite like it. I felt like I had stumbled into a meeting of some secret society and didn't know the handshake.

When I sat down with the festival's director, Debbie Farquhar-Garner, I asked her about the singing toast. Farquhar-Garner, who was wearing a Bavarian peasant outfit, told me that *Ein Prosit* means "a toast," and that the word *Gemütlichkeit* is hard to translate. It can mean "friendliness," but it can also describe a communal sense of belonging. The toasting song was one of many traditions that the Fredericksburg celebration had borrowed from Munich's Oktoberfest, the largest public celebration in the world, she said. At the original Oktoberfest, the mayor of Munich taps the ceremonial first keg. That's why Shiner was invited to give away the first keg in Fredericksburg. "I wanted a Texas German brewery to kick off the party," she told me. "It's a Texas German festival, after all."

Beer garden in Comfort, Texas, 1896.

The Shiner Brewing Association was founded in 1908 by a group of German farmers in the town of Shiner, Texas. The earliest American breweries produced English-style ales and porters. These kinds of quick-fermenting brews are made with fast-acting yeasts that leave lots of residual sugars and malt flavors in the barrel. But the German settlers of Texas longed for the cleaner, crisper flavor of lager, the traditional beer of their homeland. Lager beers require aging at cool temperatures for a month or more while a secondary fermentation converts residual malt sugars into alcohol.

The first breweries in Texas appeared in German-settled areas around 1840. These tiny operations made highly individual beers in small quantities for local markets, much like the craft breweries of today. And because they lacked ice or refrigeration, they could only brew during the colder months.

In 1877, the king of German lager-style breweries, Anheuser-Busch of St. Louis, came to Texas. There were some seventy breweries in the state when it arrived. The national brewery sold a consistent lager beer, advertised heavily, and built many Texas icehouses. Undercapitalized and unable to compete, native Texas breweries began to decline. By the time

Prohibition arrived in 1918, there were only eighteen breweries left in Texas.

One of those survivors was Shiner. In 1914, the German farmers who started brewing in Shiner hired a German brewer named Kosmos Spoetzl. In 1915, Kosmos bought the business and changed the name to Spoetzl Brewery. Cigar-chomping Kosmos was a short man but a larger-than-life character. His earliest marketing strategy was to ride around the countryside with kegs of cold Shiner beer iced down in the back of a horse-drawn carriage. When he saw a farmer plowing his field, a cowboy riding by on a horse, or another wagon driver, he waved him down and poured him an ice-cold Shiner. When he started driving a car, he filled the trunk with ice and beer.

When Prohibition shuttered the brewery, Kosmos Spoetzl survived by continuing to run the ice factory and brew alcohol-free beer. The near beer is made just like regular beer, then the alcohol is boiled away. The tour leader who took me around the brewery told us that sometimes Kosmos forgot the alcohol removal step.

Although the formal name of the business is still Spoetzl Brewery, the labels on the beer bottles say "Shiner." Shiner Bock developed a cult following in Austin in the 1970s, when two hippies acquired the distribution rights for the price of an old beer truck. During the same years, it became the favorite beer at the Armadillo World Headquarters, Austin's legendary music hall. Willie Nelson and Shiner brewmaster John Hybner once played a high-stakes game of dominoes out at Willie's recording studio—the stakes were supposedly the title to the brewery against the title to the studio.

In 2008, as Shiner neared its one hundredth year in business, the brewery started counting down with a series of anniversary beers, including a Märzenbier (a medium lager), a Schwarzbier (dark lager), and a Czech-style pilsner. These microbrewery-style beers were part of a new marketing strategy.

Jimmy Mauric, Shiner brewmaster.

Young beer drinkers are now a big part of Shiner's target market. On a tour of the brewery, brewmaster Jimmy Mauric told me, "It used to be the old German guys that asked all the questions on the beer tours. Now it's the young kids. They want to know what kind of malt and what kind of hops we are using. These kids know their beer."

But Mauric says it is not just young people who are drinking the new Shiner brews. "The American palate has changed," he said. "People want some flavor in their beer. And so we are getting back to our roots as craft brewers."

The German Belt is mostly a memory these days. Most of the German population assimilated and adopted the English language, a process that was accelerated by anti-German sentiment during the two world wars. But a few communities in the rugged Hill Country have retained their Teutonic character. The best preserved of them is Fredericksburg, with its old-fashioned Main Street lined with German bakeries and beer gardens—and its annual Oktoberfest.

★ ★ ★

At eight thirty on Saturday morning, I was shuffling along in line with thirty other people at Dietz Bakery on Fredericksburg's Main Street. People get a faraway look in their eyes when they try to describe the hot-out-of-the-oven cinnamon rolls at Dietz Bakery, so I had to try one. They are hard to come by, as the bakery is open for only a few hours in the morning. Then they hang the Sold Out sign on the front door and lock up.

When it was my turn to order, I got several cinnamon rolls and a sampling of the fruit- and cheese-filled pastries. I ate a cinnamon roll out of the neatly folded cardboard bakery box while standing on the sidewalk out front. It wasn't one of those monstrosities like you get in the food court at the mall. In fact, it wasn't much bigger than a biscuit. It had a wonderful yeasty aroma, and because it was still warm from the oven, the icing was translucent and the layers of cinnamon-sweetened dough seemed to melt in my mouth.

The major flaw in this breakfast experience was the lack of coffee. So I walked across the street to the Fredericksburg Bakery, which has a café area. I was intrigued by what looked like pretzels covered in icing. When I asked the girl behind the counter if they were authentically German, she asked me to talk to the owner, Michael Penick.

"I guess they're authentic," Penick said. A young German baker named Luke Koh, who worked at the bakery for a few years, passed along the recipe, Penick explained. Then he invited me back to the kitchen where his wife and mother-in-law, Patsy Penick and Lola Mae Durst, dusted dough with cinnamon and sugar and rolled it out into dozens of pretzels. They handed me a broken one to sample. The pretzels weren't as sweet as they looked. I had another one with a cup of coffee at a table out front.

Opened in 1917, the Fredericksburg Bakery is the oldest continuously operating business on Main Street. For the past thirty years or so, it has been owned by Michael and Patsy Penick. When they first bought the place, they lived on the second floor above the business. "Main Street used to be the quietest place in town on Saturday and Sunday morning," Michael Penick said. But in the early 1980s, things began to change. "The majority of our business is the tourist crowd now."

Michael Penick and Donny Dietz, the current owner of Dietz Bakery, were in the same high-school class. "That's where we got our bread when I was a kid," Penick said. "Donny has the right idea. He sells out early every morning and goes home."

With a few hours to kill until Oktoberfest got going, I knocked on the back door of Fredericksburg's hippest restaurant, Rebecca's Table, next door to the Rather Sweet Bakery and Café. Baker and head chef Rebecca Rather wasn't in the kitchen that morning. But her assistant chef invited me in to watch him make something I'd never heard of before, rabbit sausage. The creamy emulsified meat filling made the fat links look like bratwurst. He plated up a serving and handed it to me. The sausage came on a bed of napa cabbage, apples, onions, and bacon braised in vinegar and chicken stock. I couldn't eat it all, but it was so good I couldn't part with it, either. So I got it wrapped up to go. Luckily, I always keep a cooler in my car.

My tour of Main Street continued at Fromage du Monde Fine Cheese, where I bought some spectacular Muenster. Then I looked in at Fredericksburg Winery, where samples of locally made wines were being poured. I also stopped in at Fredericksburg Brewing Company, the oldest brewpub in Texas. Business was booming at eleven o'clock. But before I started drinking beer, I decided to have a sit-down lunch.

The German food on Fredericksburg's Main Street ranges from stodgy sauerbraten and red cabbage at the enormous Friedhelm's Bavarian Inn to off-the-wall "Tex-clectic" at Silver Creek Beer Garden & Restaurant. I split the difference at Der Lindenbaum, a charming little restaurant not far from the Marktplatz gates. The old wooden floors and lace curtains lured me in. I sat down at a table near the bakery case and ogled the oversize dark chocolate cakes. I had spent all morning exploring and I hadn't covered even half of Main Street.

Lunch started out with a cup of goulash soup that was so loaded with paprika it reminded me of chili. My main course was a huge *Gurkensalat*. The crunchy wilted cucumbers were tossed in dill sauce

Fredericksburg Oktoberfest.

and served over a bed of lettuce, with a garnish of chopped parsley and green onions. The cukes were flanked by little piles of shaved carrots and cherry tomatoes. After lunch, I made my way back to Oktoberfest and roamed around the grounds for the rest of the sunny afternoon.

There was a homespun quality about some of the booths and the decorations. Flower arrangements seemed to festoon every fence pole and lamppost. And it seemed like more people in the crowd were in German costumes. In the tent where the outfits were sold, I actually found myself flipping through the lederhosen looking for my size. That would have been a bad idea.

Near the front gate, I saw two attractive, young women who stopped me dead in my tracks. They were in their late teens or early twenties and they were both wearing cowboy hats. But these were not just

THE GERMAN BELT CIRCA 1850

★ ★

ON HIS JOURNEY ACROSS TEXAS in the 1850s, Frederick Law Olmsted entered the German Belt after leaving Austin. In the Guadalupe River Valley, he met up with a German butcher from New Braunfels who had helped a neighbor dress some hogs and was now on his way home.

"He had been in this country eight years," wrote Olmsted. "He liked it very much; he did not wish to go back to Germany; he preferred to remain here. The Germans generally were doing well, and were contented. They had a hard time at first, but they were all doing well now—getting rich."

On entering New Braunfels in the company of the butcher, Olmsted observed that the place looked like a village in Germany. The houses had porches and gardens and were painted or stuccoed, and there were many workshops and small stores.

"'Here,' said the butcher, 'is my shop . . . and if you are going to stop, I will recommend you to my neighbor, there Mr. Schmitz.' . . . It was a small cottage of a single story, having a roof extended so as to form a verandah, with a sign swinging before it, 'Guadalupe Hotel, J. Schmitz.'

"I have never in my life, except, perhaps, in awakening from a dream, met with such a sudden and complete transfer of associations. Instead of loose boarded or hewn log walls, with crevices stuffed with rags or daubed with mortar, which we have been accustomed to see during the last month . . . instead, even, of four bare cheerless sides of whitewashed plaster, which we have found twice or thrice only in a more aristocratic American residence, we were—in short, we were in Germany.

"There was nothing wanting; there was nothing too much, for one of those delightful little inns which the pedestrian who has tramped through the Rhine land will ever remember gratefully. A long room extending across the whole front of the cottage, the wall pink, with stenciled panels, and scroll ornaments in crimson, with neatly-framed and glazed lithographic prints hanging on all sides; a long thick dark oak table with rounded ends; oak benches at its sides; chiseled oak chairs; . . . four thick-bearded men . . . all bow and say 'Good morning,' as we lift our hats in the doorway.

"The landlady enters, she does not readily understand us, and one of [the men] rises immediately to assist us. Dinner we shall have immediately, and she spreads the white cloth at an end of the table. . . . An excellent soup is set before us, and in succession there follow two courses of meat, neither of them pork, and neither of them fried, two dishes of vegetables, salad, compote of peaches, coffee with milk, wheat bread from the loaf, and beautiful and sweet butter—not only such butter as I have never tasted south of the Potomac before, but such as I have been told a hundred times it was impossible to make in a southern climate."

any cowboy hats: one had the word *Stetson* in big letters across the crown, and the other had the word *Texas* stenciled on it. I introduced myself and found out one of them was from Berlin and the other was from Austria. The two women were employed as au pairs near Washington, D.C., and they had chosen to spend their vacation visiting Fredericksburg's Oktoberfest.

A few minutes later, I bumped into Debbie Farquhar-Garner and we had a chuckle about the fact that the Texans were trying to look German and the Germans were trying to look Texan. Farquhar-Garner told me that the festival had set new records for attendance over the past few years, thanks in part to an upswing in culinary tourism. More and more food lovers were coming to visit the traditional German *Biergärten*, the artisanal sausage makers, the old German bakeries, and the Hill Country wineries, she said. And Oktoberfest was the biggest draw of all.

More than a dozen Oktoberfest gatherings are held in Texas annually. Wurstfest in New Braunfels is the largest, but Fredericksburg's Oktoberfest is the most traditional. The festival was founded by a local arts cooperative and the proceeds provide art scholarships for Hill Country students and pay for public music performances in Marktplatz throughout the year. The festival organizers welcome the attention the event is getting as a Texas food and beer festival, Farquhar-Garner told me. But its roots go much deeper.

Many German Texans feel the time has come to challenge the image of villainous Germans in the popular culture by celebrating their heritage. That's part of the reason why more than a thousand volunteers from the Hill Country come together to make this festival happen. These are the people who erect the tents, hang the banners, weave the wreaths and flower arrangements, and dress in native costumes. And these are the folks to thank if Fredericksburg's Oktoberfest teaches you the meaning of *Gemütlichkeit*.

HOMEMADE PRETZELS

Making pretzels is less daunting if you make the dough in a bread machine and then boil and bake them. If you don't have a bread machine, you can make the dough in a stand mixer fitted with a dough hook, using one 3/4-ounce package of active dry yeast. Beat on low speed until a stiff dough forms.

MAKES 12 PRETZELS

4 cups bread flour
1 tablespoon malt powder or sugar
1½ teaspoons salt
2½ teaspoons bread machine yeast
1 cup milk
½ cup warm water
Baking soda, for boiling

Glaze
2 egg whites, lightly beaten
Coarse sea salt or kosher salt

Prepared mustard, for serving

Following the manufacturer's directions, put the flour, malt powder, salt, yeast, milk, and warm water in a bread machine and set on the dough cycle.

Line 2 baking sheets with parchment paper. When the dough is ready, divide it into 12 equal portions and shape each portion into a ball. On a floured work surface, flatten 1 ball and then roll it back and forth with your palms to form a rope 18 inches long. Shape the rope into a U with the curved end away from you. Lift both ends of the rope and twist them together once, leaving about 1 inch beyond the twist on each end. Then fold the ends over and press them onto the curved end of the U; the twist should fall at the midpoint. Place the pretzel on the prepared baking sheet. Repeat with the remaining dough balls. Let the pretzels rise in a warm spot for 20 minutes.

Preheat the oven to 400°F. If you want to make hard pretzels, skip this next boiling step. If you want

(Continued)

to make soft, breadlike pretzels, fill a saucepan two-thirds full of water, then measure the water. Add 2 tablespoons baking soda for each cup of water to the pan and bring to a boil. With a slotted spoon or wire-mesh skimmer, lower a pretzel into the boiling water for 45 seconds, until the dough turns golden or yellow. Using the spoon, return the pretzel to the baking sheet. Repeat with the remaining pretzels.

To glaze the pretzels, brush them with the egg white and sprinkle them with sea salt. Bake for 16 to 20 minutes, until deep brown. Serve with mustard—and cold beer, of course.

HILL COUNTRY GOULASH

German-born William Gebhardt saw his ancho-based chili powder as an American equivalent to the paprika of his homeland. In 1917, he published his first cookbook, which included a recipe for so-called American goulash using his Eagle Brand chili powder. That recipe called for beef chunks, butter, onion, garlic, and chili powder.

With the addition of tomato sauce, that same goulash recipe is still common in German Texan households today. When I asked a German Texan woman what the difference was between Texas goulash and chili con carne, she said, "Goulash is served over elbow macaroni."

SERVES 4

8 ounces elbow macaroni
1 tablespoon bacon drippings or vegetable oil
1 pound ground beef
1 yellow onion, chopped
1 clove garlic, minced
1 (15-ounce) can tomato sauce
1 tablespoon paprika or chili powder, homemade (page 110) or store-bought
Salt
Sour cream, for garnish (optional)

Bring a large pot of salted water to a boil. Add the macaroni and cook until al dente, following the instructions on the package.

While the water is heating, in a skillet, heat the bacon drippings over medium-high heat. Add the beef and cook, breaking up the meat with the side of a wooden spoon or spatula, for 5 to 7 minutes, until the meat is browned. Add the onion and cook, stirring often, for about 3 minutes, until wilted. Add the garlic and continue to cook for about 1 minute, until the garlic is lightly cooked. Add the tomato sauce and paprika and season with salt. Stir well and cook, stirring occasionally, for about 15 minutes to blend the flavors.

When the macaroni is done, drain well. Divide the macaroni among dinner plates and spoon the goulash over the top. Garnish each serving with a dollop of sour cream and serve immediately.

REHWURST (VENISON SAUSAGE)

According to early histories of the Hill Country, German immigrants had a tough time in their first few years for two reasons, crop failures and because they weren't good with firearms. Luckily, they were great butchers, so they ended up specializing in processing wild game for others. In the old German towns of the Hill Country, some meat markets will offer to turn your scrap into *Rehwurst* (venison sausage) instead of venison "hamburger."

You can also make this sausage at home out of scraps and tough cuts like shoulder, or you can start with ground venison if you already have some in your freezer. Just thaw it and add it to the freshly ground pork.

Hog casings are sold salted, and are generally only available in large quantities—often enough for 15 pounds of sausage. So you'll have a lot of hog casings left over.

MAKES ABOUT 3¹/₂ POUNDS

2 pounds boneless fatty pork shoulder

1½ pounds boneless venison shoulder

4 cloves garlic, coarsely chopped

⅓ cup loosely packed fresh rosemary leaves

3 tablespoons prepared mustard

2 tablespoons minced jalapeño chiles

2 teaspoons coarsely ground pepper

3 tablespoons kosher salt

1 teaspoon vegetable oil

1 package medium-size natural hog casings

Cut the pork and venison into strips, trimming away any gristle or other tough pieces. Fit a meat grinder with the ¼-inch plate. Pass the pork and the venison through the grinder, capturing the coarsely ground meat in a large bowl. Add a little of the garlic and rosemary to the grinder as you go so the seasonings will become well incorporated with the meat. Add the mustard, chiles, pepper, and salt to the ground meat and knead the mixture with your hands until everything is well blended.

In a small skillet, heat the oil over medium heat. Scoop up a meatball-size portion of the mixture, flatten it into a patty, and fry it in the oil until cooked through. Taste, then adjust the seasoning of the rest of the batch.

Soak the hog casings in lukewarm water. Then, using a sausage stuffer or a pastry bag fitted with a large-size plain tip, stuff the casings with the meat mixture. As each casing length is filled, tie off one end with kitchen twine, then twist the filled casing into 4- to 6-inch links, forcing out any air bubbles and making the links tight. Finally, tie off the other end. Wrap well and store in the refrigerator for up to 4 days or freeze for up to 2 months.

Sausage is a "batter" of meat, fat, and other ingredients. If you put uncooked sausages over high heat, you will melt the fat and it will all run out, leaving the cooked sausages dry. The trick to cooking raw sausages is to heat them up very slowly to set the mixture, and the best way to do that is in a hot-water bath. Combine the raw links with tepid water to cover and heat slowly over low heat until the water registers 140°F on an instant-read thermometer. At this point, the sausage "batter" will have set and you can grill, broil, fry, or bake the sausages.

GERMAN BARBECUE

★ ★ ★ ★ ★ ★ ★ ★ ★ ★ ★ ★ ★ ★ ★ ★ ★

IN THE EARLY DAYS OF THE GERMAN BELT, local butchers turned scraps into smoked meats and sausages, just as they had done in Germany. Their regular customers took the sausages and pork home and served them with traditional German accompaniments, such as red cabbage and potatoes. But to a casual observer (especially a hungry one), the difference between these German smoked meats and Southern barbecue was pretty subtle.

Itinerant farmworkers who came through town during the harvest bought the smoked meats at the butcher store and ate them on the spot, right off the butcher paper. Side dishes were what they could find on the store's shelves. Crackers and pickles were usually about it. And thus began the German meat market barbecue tradition.

Some of the most famous barbecue joints in Texas, like Schmitty's Market in Lockhart and Southside Market in Elgin, are still butcher shops as well as barbecue joints.

GERMAN CUCUMBER SALAD WITH DILL

The key to the success of this salad is to let the salted cucumber slices sit for about 30 minutes, to allow all the excess moisture to drain out. This ensures the cucumbers will be crunchy.

MAKES 2 CUPS; SERVES 6 AS A SIDE DISH OR 3 AS A MAIN COURSE

3 English cucumbers, peeled and sliced
    paper-thin
1 tablespoon salt
1 tablespoon sugar
1 cup sour cream
1 tablespoon chopped fresh dill

In a bowl, combine the cucumber slices and salt, toss well, and let sit for 30 minutes.

Drain the cucumbers well in a colander or a sieve and transfer to a bowl. Add the sugar and toss to coat the slices. In separate small bowl, stir together the sour cream and dill. Add the sour cream mixture to the cucumbers and fold gently to coat evenly. Serve chilled over lettuce as a side dish, or with shredded carrots and other salad vegetables as a main course.

GERMAN POTATO SALAD

Serve this traditional sweet-and-sour potato salad warm with a garnish of crumbled bacon.

MAKES 6 CUPS; SERVES 8 TO 10

2½ pounds baby red potatoes
15 thin slices bacon
1 cup diced red onions
½ cup firmly packed light brown sugar
2 tablespoons cider vinegar
¾ cup olive oil
Kosher salt and freshly ground pepper

In a large saucepan, combine the potatoes with water to cover by 1½ inches and bring to a boil over high heat. Lower the heat to a simmer and cook for 20 minutes, until the potatoes are tender when tested with a knife.

While the potatoes are cooking, in a large skillet, fry the bacon over medium-high heat until crisp and brown. As the slices are ready, transfer them to paper towels to drain and cool. Crumble the cooled bacon. You should have 1 cup, plus a little to set aside for garnish.

Pour off all but 2 tablespoons of the bacon drippings from the pan and return the pan to medium-high heat. Add the onions and sauté for about 5 minutes, until soft. Remove from the heat.

When the potatoes are ready, drain them well. In a large bowl, whisk together the brown sugar and vinegar until the sugar dissolves. Slowly add the oil while continuing to whisk. Season with salt and pepper, then add the onions and the 1 cup bacon and stir to mix. Add the hot potatoes and toss to coat with the dressing. Let the salad sit at room temperature for 30 minutes.

Garnish the salad with the reserved bacon and serve warm.

RED CABBAGE

Working the cabbage in a salt brine with your hands before cooking it will give the finished dish a beautiful deep red-purple color. The sweet-and-sour flavor of this cabbage dish is an interesting alternative to barbecue sauce with a simple smoked pork loin, smoked pork chops, or grilled sausages. If you like a particularly intense sweet-and-sour taste, you will need to increase the sugar and vinegar.

MAKES ABOUT 8 CUPS; SERVES 16 AS A SIDE DISH

1 large head red cabbage (about 2 pounds)
1 tablespoon plus 2 teaspoons salt

2 tablespoons unsalted butter

1 large yellow onion, chopped

2 tablespoons all-purpose flour

2 tablespoons sugar

1 cup red wine

1 cup cider vinegar

1 cup beef broth

2 bay leaves

¾ cup strawberry jam

1 teaspoon freshly ground pepper

Quarter the cabbage through the stem end, cut away the core ends, and peel off any discolored leaves. Thinly slice the cabbage quarters crosswise. Fill a large bowl or a nonreactive pot with warm water and dissolve 1 tablespoon of the salt in it. Put the cabbage in the salted water and work it with your hands until the water turns an intense red-purple. Allow the cabbage to sit in the colored water for several hours or up to overnight.

If the cabbage has been soaking in a bowl, transfer the cabbage and water to a nonreactive pot. Put the pot over high heat, bring to boil, and cook for 5 to 7 minutes, until the cabbage is crisp-tender. Drain the cabbage in a colander in the sink.

In a Dutch oven, melt the butter over medium-high heat. Add the onion and sauté for 5 to 7 minutes, until soft. Add the cooked cabbage, sprinkle the flour and sugar over the top, and turn the cabbage to coat evenly. Add the wine, vinegar, broth, and bay leaves and bring to a simmer. Adjust the heat to maintain a simmer and cook for 15 minutes, until the cabbage is soft and the mixture thickens.

Remove the bay leaves. Add the jam, the remaining 2 teaspoons salt, and the pepper and mix well. Taste and adjust the seasonings, then serve.

APFELKRAUT

This sweet-and-sour kraut is one of the many ways that sauerkraut can be turned into a delicious side dish. When you eat this dish with smoked sausages, you will be reminded of the sweet-and-sour flavor of a good barbecue sauce.

SERVES 10 TO 12

3 pounds fresh-packed sauerkraut

2 slices bacon, cut into 1-inch squares

2 yellow onions, coarsely chopped

3 small cooking apples, peeled, cored, and cubed

1 (750-ml) bottle German Riesling wine

1 cup chicken broth

2 bay leaves

1 teaspoon freshly ground pepper

In a colander in the sink, rinse the sauerkraut under cold running water, then press to remove as much liquid as possible. Leave the sauerkraut in the colander until ready to use.

In a Dutch oven, sauté the bacon over medium heat for a few minutes, until it begins to render its fat. Add the onions and cook, stirring often, for 5 minutes, until they begin to soften. Add the apples and cook, stirring, for another 5 minutes, until the onions are limp and the bacon has released all of its fat.

Add the sauerkraut to the bacon mixture and mix thoroughly. Add the wine and broth, increase the heat to high, and bring to a boil. Add the bay leaves and pepper, lower the heat to a simmer, and cook, uncovered, for 45 minutes to 1 hour, until the liquid has been absorbed and the sauerkraut is very tender. Scoop out and discard the bay leaves. Serve hot.

PANFISH SOUP WITH MUSTARD AND BACON

Inspired by the seafood soups of Hamburg and Berlin, this fish soup has a Northern German flavor. Try it with caraway rye bread and cold beer.

SERVES 8

3 pounds panfish (such as bluegrill, perch, or
    crappie), cleaned
1 bunch dill (about 1½ ounces)
20 peppercorns
1 bunch parsley
6 cups water
3 tablespoons vegetable oil
1 leek, white and green parts, finely chopped
1 yellow onion, finely chopped
2 tablespoons all-purpose flour
2 potatoes, peeled and cut into 1-inch cubes
4 carrots, peeled and sliced
6 bay leaves
1 heaping tablespoon juniper berries
1½ teaspoons salt
1 teaspoon freshly ground pepper
6 slices bacon
2 tablespoons balsamic vinegar
1 teaspoon coarse-grain German mustard
1 cup German Riesling wine

Fillet the fish and refrigerate the fillets. Put the bones and head(s) in a stockpot. Add the dill, peppercorns, half of the parsley, and the water and bring to a boil over medium-high heat. Decrease the heat to a simmer, cover, and cook for 30 minutes. Remove from the heat and strain the stock through a fine-mesh sieve placed over a bowl. Discard the solids in the sieve and reserve the stock.

In a large skillet, heat the oil over medium heat. Add the leek and onion and sauté, stirring frequently, for about 20 minutes, until the leek is soft. Sprinkle the flour over the hot vegetables, increase the heat to medium-high, and cook, stirring constantly, for 3 minutes. Add half of the reserved stock to the vegetable mixture and stir well. Transfer the contents of the skillet to a soup pot and add the remaining stock to the pot.

Place the soup pot over medium heat and add the potatoes, carrots, bay leaves, juniper berries, salt, and pepper. Bring to a simmer, decrease the heat to low, and cook, uncovered, for 25 minutes, until the potatoes and carrots are tender.

While the soup is simmering, in a skillet, fry the bacon over medium heat until crisp and brown. Transfer to paper towels to drain.

Cut the fish fillets into 2-inch squares, and finely chop the remaining parsley. When the potatoes and carrots are tender, add the parsley, vinegar, mustard, and wine to the soup pot. Increase the heat to high and bring the soup to a full boil. Add the fish pieces, immediately decrease the heat to low, and cook for about 5 minutes, until the fish begins to fall apart.

Ladle the soup into bowls. Crumble a bacon slice over each serving and serve immediately.

German picnic, 1901.

GRILLED SPRING CHICKEN

German spring chickens are the same size as our Cornish game hens. They are delicious grilled and served in halves. Cold grilled chicken is a great idea for a picnic.

SERVES 6

3 Cornish game hens, split
½ teaspoon salt
½ teaspoon pepper

Glaze
¼ cup coarse-grain German mustard
2 tablespoons German Riesling wine
1 tablespoon honey
½ teaspoon freshly ground pepper
¼ teaspoon ground mace
¼ teaspoon ground cloves

Apfelkraut (page 157), for serving

Prepare a charcoal or gas grill for indirect-heat grilling over medium heat. While you wait for the fire, carefully remove as much skin as possible from the game hen halves. Work carefully; they are fragile and will come apart if you pull too hard. Season the halves with the salt and pepper and set aside.

To make the glaze, in a bowl, combine all of the ingredients and mix thoroughly.

When the fire is ready, put the hen halves, bone side down, directly over the fire until lightly browned. Then move them to the cooler part of the grill grate, cover the grill, and let the birds cook, turning once at the midpoint, for 20 to 25 minutes. Prick a thigh with a fork to test for doneness. If the juices run clear, move the hen halves back over the fire, brush them on both sides with the glaze, and finish them, turning them often, for a few minutes, until nicely browned on both sides.

If serving hot, accompany with the Apfelkraut. Or, serve cold with your favorite picnic side dishes.

PARISA, THE ALSATIAN TEXAN STEAK TARTARE

★ ★ ★ ★ ★ ★ ★ ★ ★ ★ ★ ★ ★ ★ ★ ★ ★

AN ALSATIAN IMPRESARIO named Henri Castro brought two thousand Alsatian immigrants to Texas between 1843 and 1846. By the 1860s, the Alsatian Texan town of Castroville was the twelfth largest town in the state, and several of its original Alsatian-style buildings are still standing today. Although today Alsace is a region of France, it bounced back and forth between France and Germany in the past, and the historical language is a dialect of German.

Two Alsatian dishes, coriander-seasoned sausages and a variation on steak tartare called parisa, have become a part of Texas culinary tradition.

Castroville parisa is a humble blend of ground meat, chopped onion, minced garlic, and shredded Cheddar. The concoction is usually homemade, but Dziuk's Meat Market and other meat counters in Castroville sell it by the pound. The butcher I talked to told me that while the Dziuk family is Polish, they make parisa because it is in demand in Castroville, especially around the holidays.

Parisa
SERVES 4

1 pound lean ground beef (preferably freshly ground, see page 228)
½ pound cheddar cheese, cut into ½-inch cubes
1 yellow onion, finely chopped
1 clove garlic, minced
Salt and pepper to taste
1 jalapeño pepper, minced (optional)
Juice of one lemon (optional)

Combine all the ingredients in a mixing bowl. Serve with saltines.

Stuffed Cabbage, Ruthenian Style, page 168.

Texas Czech wedding celebration near Eagle Lake, 1912.

CHAPTER 14

CZECH TEXAN

★ ★ ★ ★ ★ ★ ★ ★ ★ ★ ★ ★ ★ ★ ★ ★

On August 15, 2010, I took my family to the little Texas town of Praha (Czech for "Prague") for the 155th annual St. Mary's church picnic. It's the oldest Czech gathering in Texas and one of the largest. We got in line at the dining hall and joined more than five thousand people for lunch. There was fried chicken, the Czech version of goulash called Praha stew, and sauerkraut thickened with roux.

The cooking crew prepared three thousand pounds of Praha stew in giant cast-iron kettles. The kettles were once set over live fires, but in modern times the eighteen giant pots are heated over gas burners in the St. Mary's church hall kitchen. The secret recipe for Praha stew, sometimes called Shuster stew after the caterer who invented it, includes beef chuck, potatoes, ketchup, tomato sauce, and spices. In the past, little old Czech ladies gathered at the back door of the kitchen while the stew was simmering, waiting to suck the marrow-bones as they were extracted from the kettles.

My mom, who drove down from her home in Georgetown, Texas, was in heaven. Her family immigrated to western Pennsylvania from Ruthenia, one of several eastern European ethnic areas that were part of Czechoslovakia at one time.

Czechoslovakia and the Czech Republic didn't exist when the first "Czechs" immigrated to Texas in the mid-1800s. Many Czech Texan immigrants came from the villages of Bohemia and Moravia, but there were Slovaks, Silesians, and Ruthenians, as well. The migration of Czechs to Texas started as a trickle in the 1850s and accelerated in the 1870s. The largest influx arrived just before World War I, when the Austro-Hungarian Empire took over the Czech homelands of eastern Europe.

The Czech families who migrated to Texas were attracted by news of the thriving German population, the cheap farmland, and the growing Czech community. Tight-knit families and small family farms remain the most distinguishing characteristic of Czech Texan communities. Whereas the German settlers gathered in secular groups like singing clubs, garden clubs, and rifle clubs, Czech settlers were all Catholics and their social events revolved around the local church.

For dessert at the Praha picnic, you get to choose from a huge table of homemade baked goods. I chose a poppy seed kolache. After lunch we all drank beer and watched the musicians perform. The small band struck up a lively tune and the accordion player sang the lyrics in Czech. My mom took her grandkids out on the dance floor and taught them how to polka. The scene reminded me of the big family weddings of my childhood.

The unique fluffy pastries called kolaches are the most famous Czech contribution to Texas cuisine. Buying kolaches at a combination Czech bakery–gas station is a Texas road-trip tradition. Czech Stop in the town of West on Interstate 35 near Dallas and Weikel's Bakery on Highway 71 in La Grange are

Janak's Country Store.

perhaps the two most famous kolache stopovers. But aficionados of the pastry will debate the merits of many other Czech bakeries.

Texas kolaches have evolved into something different from their central European originals, which were—and still are—large fruit pastries traditionally served at weddings. In Texas, the kolache is closer to a Danish pastry. Fruit fillings such as apricot, peach, and prune are common. So is sweetened farmer cheese. But the height of the Czech Texan kolache makers' art is the poppy seed kolache. Sausage-stuffed versions of the kolache, known as pigs in a blanket in English, are popular, too, though they are not really kolaches. They are more accurately called klobasniky (klo-bas-SNIK-ee) in Czech-speaking Texas. *Klobása* is the Czech word for "sausage."

Czech Texans are also famous for their sausage, which is found in many barbecue restaurants. Czech sausage is distinguished from German sausage by the liberal use of garlic. The Czechs are also fond of summer sausages and of dried sausage that is eaten like jerky. Czech sausage factories like Janak's in Hallettsville and Prasek's Hillje Smokehouse in Hillje have country stores attached where you can buy sausages, sandwiches, and such Czech specialties as barrel-fermented sauerkraut.

If you venture past the Czech Stop gas station on the highway and into the center of West, you can find more Czech bakeries and restaurants. The Village Bakery on East Oak claims to have introduced the sausage-stuffed klobasniky to Texas. Several other bakeries in town turn out a wide selection of fruit-filled kolaches and the Czech cakes called butchas. Sulak's restaurant, which opened in 1923, offered a Czech-Tex menu with both veprova pecene (roast pork) and kureci rzky (chicken-fried steak). The Czech-American Restaurant serves stuffed cabbage rolls, roast pork, and a *klobása* (sausage) platter.

West, Praha, and Flatonia all have major Czech Texan celebrations: Westfest, on Labor Day weekend, features polka bands, Czech food, and traditional dance performances by Czech and Slovak troupes; Czhilispiel in Flatonia is a Czech chili cook-off; and the church picnic in Praha is celebrated every year on August 15, the Feast of the Assumption.

While I love barbecue and Tex-Mex, Czech-Tex cuisine, with its sauerkraut, garlic, and sausage, is just like my grandmother's cooking. And poppy seed kolaches will always remind me of home.

MUSHROOM SOUP

Mushroom soup was always one of the main dishes of our Ruthenian Christmas Eve dinner. Wild mushrooms are plentiful in Texas. In the spring, morels grow in the creek bottoms of the Hill Country, and in the rainy summer season along the Gulf Coast, golden chanterelles bloom on the roots of live oak trees. Puffballs and wood ears grow all over the state. The state is also a leading producer of commercial mushrooms. The town of Madisonville, home of a major mushroom operation, holds an annual Mushroom Festival to celebrate the town's main agricultural product.

SERVES 6

⅔ cup fresh wild mushrooms, or ⅓ cup dried
    porcini mushrooms

5 cups water

3 tablespoons olive oil

1 cup chopped fresh white mushrooms

1 small yellow onion, chopped

¼ cup diced, peeled carrot

¼ cup diced celery

1 tablespoon pearl barley

½ cup drained, cooked white beans

1½ tablespoons all-purpose flour

½ teaspoon dried thyme

½ teaspoon garlic powder

½ teaspoon white pepper

About ¼ cup red wine vinegar

Salt

If using fresh wild mushrooms, clean them with a soft brush, trim the stem ends, and chop them coarsely. If using dried mushrooms, in a small saucepan, combine the mushrooms and water, bring to a gentle simmer over low heat, and simmer for 30 minutes, until fully rehydrated. Remove the mushrooms from the liquid, chop coarsely, and set aside. Pour the liquid through a cheesecloth-lined fine-mesh sieve placed over a bowl, or carefully pour the liquid into a bowl, leaving the grit in a little of the liquid behind in the bottom of the pan. Reserve the strained liquid.

In a soup pot, heat 2 tablespoons of the oil over medium-high heat. Add the white mushrooms and onion and cook, stirring occasionally, for 3 minutes, until the onion is lightly browned. Add the wild mushrooms, carrot, celery, and barley and cook, stirring, for 5 minutes, until the vegetables are wilted. Add the mushroom liquid or 5 cups of water if you're using fresh mushrooms, and cook for 30 minutes, until all the vegetables are tender. Stir in the beans.

In a small skillet, heat the remaining 1 tablespoon oil over medium heat. Whisk in the flour and continue to whisk for about 3 minutes, until the flour mixture is light brown. Mix in the thyme, garlic powder, and pepper. Ladle a little of the broth from the soup pot into the browned flour and stir until the mixture is smooth. Stir the flour mixture into the soup, then season with the vinegar and salt to taste. Simmer for 15 minutes to blend the flavors. Serve piping hot.

CLAUDIA MATCEK'S POPPY SEED KOLACHES

The Burleson Kolache Festival is one of several kolache festivals held around the state. Claudia Matcek won the Burleson County kolache-baking championship in 1986 and 1987, and she went on to win the state championship in 1987. Here is her recipe.

MAKES 20 PASTRIES

Dough
2¼ cups milk
½ cup unsalted butter, plus 3 tablespoons melted
2 egg yolks, lightly beaten
½ cup sugar
1 tablespoon rapid-rise yeast
1 teaspoon salt
5¼ cups bread flour, sifted

Poppy Seed Filling
1½ cups milk
1 cup ground poppy seeds
1¼ cups sugar
1 tablespoon all-purpose flour
1 teaspoon unsalted butter
1 teaspoon vanilla extract

Glaze
2 cups confectioners' sugar
½ teaspoon vanilla extract
2 tablespoons unsalted butter, melted
¼ cup milk

To make the dough, in a saucepan, heat the milk over low heat until it is hot to the touch (160°F on an instant-read thermometer). Remove from the heat, add the ½ cup butter, and stir until melted.

Add the egg yolks, sugar, yeast, and salt to the cooled mixture and stir to combine. Transfer the mixture to a stand mixer fitted with the dough hook. Add the flour and beat on medium speed for 7 minutes. The dough should be moist, elastic, and tacky to the touch. If it seems too dry and not pliable, add water, 1 teaspoon at a time, and continue to beat on medium speed until the dough is the right consistency.

Transfer the dough to a lightly floured work surface and knead by hand for 2 to 3 minutes, until it is smooth and pliable. Spray the mixer bowl with nonstick cooking spray and return the dough to the bowl. Cover with plastic wrap and let rise in a warm spot for 1 hour, until doubled in size.

Grease 2 baking sheets with nonstick cooking spray. Turn the dough out onto a floured work surface and roll out ½ inch thick. Using a floured knife, cut the dough into 3 by 5-inch rectangles. Brush the sides and top of each rectangle with the melted butter. Place them close together, but not touching, on the prepared pans. Cover with plastic wrap and let rise in a warm spot for 1 hour.

While the pastries are rising, make the filling. In a saucepan, heat the milk over medium heat. When it comes to a boil, add the poppy seeds, sugar, flour, and butter while whisking continuously to prevent lumping. Cook over medium heat, whisking often, for about 4 minutes, until the mixture thickens. Remove from the heat, stir in the vanilla, and let cool completely before using.

Preheat the oven to 375°F. Using your finger, make an indentation in the center of each rectangle and fill with 1 to 3 tablespoons of the filling. Pinch the dough together over the filling.

Bake the pastries for about 25 minutes, until browned. Transfer the pans to wire racks.

Just before the kolaches are ready to come out of the oven, make the glaze. In a bowl, whisk together all of the ingredients until smooth. Spoon the glaze over the warm kolaches. Allow the glaze to set for 5 minutes and serve warm. The kolaches will keep in the freezer for several months.

Store-Bought Filling: If you are pressed for time, substitute canned poppy seed filling for the homemade and melted butter for the glaze.

PORK RIBS IN SAUERKRAUT

You can find fresh sauerkraut in the refrigerator case of the grocery store. Boar's Head and Claussen both make a decent version. Substitute pork spare-ribs or pork steaks in this recipe, if you like.

SERVES 6

1 tablespoon garlic powder

1 teaspoon coarsely ground pepper

½ teaspoon salt

3 pounds country-style pork ribs (about 4 boneless strips)

5 tablespoons vegetable oil

2 quarts (about 2 pounds) fresh-packed sauerkraut, undrained

1½ cups chicken broth

¼ cup all-purpose flour

1 cup chopped yellow onions

Mashed Potatoes (page 203), for serving

Preheat the oven to 350°F.

In a small bowl or cup, stir together the garlic powder, pepper, and salt. Rinse the pork and pat dry with paper towels. Sprinkle the seasoning mix on all sides of the pork. You may have some seasoning mix left over.

In a Dutch oven, heat 1 tablespoon of the oil over medium-high heat. Add the pork ribs and brown well on all sides. This should take about 10 minutes. Transfer the ribs to a plate and set aside. Decrease the heat to low, add the sauerkraut and its brine, and stir to dislodge any browned bits from the pot bottom. Add the broth and stir to mix well. Put the pork ribs on top of the sauerkraut, cover, and place the pot in the oven.

Cook for 1 hour, then remove the cover. The pork should be tender. Continue cooking for 15 to 30 minutes, or until the pork is browned on top and the liquid is slightly reduced.

Remove the pot from the oven. With a slotted spoon, transfer the pork to a plate, being careful not to break it up too much. Keep the pork warm.

In a sauté pan, heat the remaining 4 tablespoons oil over medium heat for 2 to 3 minutes, until hot. Add the flour, whisking constantly to prevent burning. Continue cooking and whisking until the roux is the color of a dark gravy, then remove the pan from the heat and stir in the onions with a wooden spoon. Add any remaining seasoning mix to the flour mixture.

Place the Dutch oven over medium heat and stir the sauerkraut to loosen any browned bits on the pan bottom. The sauerkraut should be soupy. If it is too dry, add a little water. When the roux has cooled a little and the sauerkraut has come to a simmer, add the roux, a tablespoon at a time, to the sauerkraut, stirring well to incorporate. When all of the roux has been added, continue stirring constantly until the sauerkraut thickens to the consistency of gravy. Adjust with a little more broth or some water if the mixture is too dry, then taste and adjust the seasoning.

Put the sauerkraut in a serving bowl and arrange the roasted pork on top. Serve the sauerkraut and pork over the potatoes.

CARAWAY PORK ROAST

This was a frequent Sunday dinner when I was growing up. Mom put a lot of garlic powder and salt on the fat to form a thick crust. My brothers and I fought over the crusty parts.

SERVES 8 TO 10

1 (4- to 5-pound) boneless pork loin roast
1 tablespoon caraway seeds
1 teaspoon garlic powder
1 teaspoon onion powder
1 teaspoon sea salt
Sauerkraut Gravy (recipe follows), for serving

Preheat the oven to 325°F. Using a sharp knife, score the fat on the top of the pork roast in a crisscross pattern. Rub the caraway seeds into the fat. In a small bowl or cup, stir together the garlic powder, onion powder, and salt. Sprinkle the seasoning over the top of the roast. Place the pork loin in a roasting pan and add water to the pan to a depth of ½ inch.

Roast for 35 minutes per pound, until an instant-read thermometer inserted into the center registers 145°F. Serve with Sauerkraut Gravy.

SAUERKRAUT GRAVY

You can put sauerkraut under a pork roast or a chicken and then make sauerkraut gravy following the directions in Pork Ribs in Sauerkraut (page 166). Or, you can make this sauerkraut and roux gravy with pan drippings or chicken broth whenever you want and serve it over potatoes.

SERVES 8 TO 10

3 tablespoons lard, bacon drippings, duck fat, or vegetable oil
2 cups chopped yellow onions
2 quarts (about 2 pounds) fresh-packed sauerkraut, undrained
About 2 cups pan drippings from a roast or chicken broth
¼ cup vegetable oil
¼ cup all-purpose flour
Salt and pepper
Mashed Potatoes (page 203), for serving

In a Dutch oven, heat the lard over medium heat. Add the onions and cook, stirring often, for 3 to 5 minutes, until wilted. Stir in the sauerkraut and its brine and add enough pan drippings to make the sauerkraut soupy. Decrease the heat to low and simmer for 10 minutes.

In a sauté pan, heat the vegetable oil over medium heat for 2 to 3 minutes, until hot. Add the flour, whisking constantly to prevent burning. Continue cooking and whisking until the flour turns light brown. Remove from the heat and season with salt and pepper.

Add the flour mixture, a tablespoon at a time, to the sauerkraut, stirring well to incorporate. When all of the flour mixture has been added, continue stirring constantly until the sauerkraut thickens to the consistency of gravy. Adjust with a little chicken broth or water if the mixture is too dry, then taste and adjust the seasoning and transfer to a serving bowl.

At the table, spoon the sauerkraut over the potatoes.

STUFFED CABBAGE, RUTHENIAN STYLE (HOLUPKI)

My grandmother would throw a couple of uncut heads of cabbage into the sauerkraut barrel in the basement and then, after they fermented, she would use the leaves to make stuffed cabbage. In Houston, I can buy the same whole fermented cabbage leaves at ethnic groceries like the Russian General Store. If you can find them, substitute fermented cabbage leaves for the fresh cabbage in this recipe.

SERVES 6 TO 8

1 cup long-grain white rice

1 cup boiling water

1 teaspoon salt

1 large head green cabbage, cored

¼ cup bacon drippings or vegetable oil

1 yellow onion, chopped

1 pound ground beef, or 8 ounces each ground beef and ground pork

1 egg, lightly beaten

Salt and pepper

1 quart (about 1 pound) fresh-packed sauerkraut

1 (46-ounce) can tomato juice

Dash of distilled white vinegar

Bread and butter, for serving

In a saucepan, combine the rice, boiling water, and salt and bring to a boil over high heat. Boil for 1 minute. Cover, remove from the heat, and let stand until the rice has absorbed the water.

Fill a large pot two-thirds full of water and bring to a boil. Add the cabbage, submerging it in the water. Remove from the heat and let the cabbage soak for 10 minutes, until the leaves are easily rolled.

While the cabbage is soaking, in a sauté pan, heat the bacon drippings over medium heat. Add the onion and cook, stirring often, for 5 to 7 minutes, until the onion is tender. Transfer the onion and fat

to a bowl and allow to cool. Add the beef, rice, and egg and mix well. Season with salt and pepper.

Remove the cabbage from the hot water and gently peel off the soft outer leaves. If the inner leaves are still hard, return the cabbage to the hot water for a while. When all of the large cabbage leaves have been removed, cut up the remaining cabbage and put it in the bottom of a large pot to keep the rolls from burning.

You can cook the rolls in the oven (be sure to use an ovenproof pot) or on the stove top. If cooking them in the oven, preheat it to 350°F. To make each cabbage roll, place ¼ cup of the meat-rice mixture in the middle of a softened cabbage leaf and gently roll up the leaf around the filling, folding in the sides. Arrange a layer of cabbage rolls on top of the bed of cabbage in the ovenproof pot. Top the rolls with some of the sauerkraut. Repeat until all of the rolls are layered in the pot, topping each layer with sauerkraut. Pour the tomato juice over the rolls, stopping

when they are still barely visible. You may not need all of the juice. Add the vinegar.

Cover the pot and place in the oven for 1 hour, until the filling is cooked. Or, place the pot on the stove top over low heat, bring to a gentle simmer, and cook for 1 hour. To test for doneness, remove a roll and cut into it. Serve the rolls hot with buttered bread.

JANAK'S HOT DOGS "ALL THE WAY"

Texas chili con carne and barrel-fermented sauerkraut are two of my favorite things. But I never thought of eating them together. In fact, they sound like two foods that should never, ever be combined. So imagine my amazement when a request for a hot dog "all the way" at Janak's Country Market in Hallettsville yielded a fabulous Janak's homemade Czech sausage on a bun spread with mustard and topped with both chili and Janak's own house-made sauerkraut. Now that's what I call Czech-Mex!

SERVES 2
2 hot dog buns or bolillos (Mexican rolls)
2 thin ready-to-eat Czech sausages or
    frankfurters
Mustard, for spreading
1 cup drained fresh-packed sauerkraut
1 cup Chili con Carne Sauce (page 112)

Split the buns and toast them. Cook the sausages in simmering but not boiling water or on a griddle until heated through. Spread the buns with the mustard. Place a sausage on each bun and top with the sauerkraut on one side and Chili con Carne Sauce on the other.

JANAK PACKING

IN 1938, PAUL AND MARK JANAK opened a small grocery store and meat market near Hallettsville. Neighboring farmers asked Paul to come out to assist at pig-killing time and to make his famous sausages out of the pork. Czech farmers from miles around brought their hogs to the meat market to have them processed into sausages. From this humble beginning, Janak Packing, Inc. expanded into a statewide operation. The company is now run by the second generation of Janaks.

Turtle Soup, page 174.

The Menger Hotel in the horse and buggy era, 1877.

CHAPTER 15
THE MENGER HOTEL

The mango ice cream was slick with the rich tropical fruit. Ted Lopez, the head chef of the Colonial Dining Room at the Menger Hotel, told me that it was actually halfway between an ice cream and a sherbet and that the dessert had been on the menu for more than a hundred years. I am guessing that the pastel walls of the Colonial Dining Room were painted to match the color of its famous ice cream.

The Colonial Dining Room doesn't get a lot of business these days. No more than a dozen patrons stopped by during my early evening dinner. But hotel restaurants aren't what they used to be. Over the years, this dining room has served such notables as Ulysses S. Grant, Robert E. Lee, Sarah Bernhardt, and Presidents Harding, Taft, and McKinley.

A MENGER BANQUET

★ ★

Menu

Canapes aux Anchois

Celerie, Olives

Tartines de Caviare

Consommé de Gibier

Soft Shell Crabs Americaine

Cailles en Aspic, Belle-Vue

Ris d'Agneau aux Pointres d'Asperges

Grouse Farci aux Truffes

Salade Jardinière

Glace Diplomate

Fraises

Gateaux Assortis

Fromage Roquefort

Beverages

APOLLINARIS • SHERRY EMPERADOR • CHÂTEAU YQUEM
ROYAL SCHARZBERG • CHÂTEAU LAROSE
LOUIS ROEDERER, GRAND VIN SEC
CAFÉ NOIR

EL PRINCIPE DE GALES [CIGARS]

Adolph Mitrovich, a Croatian from the Dalmatian Coast, worked as a chef at the Menger Hotel from 1902 to 1911. This is a banquet menu chef Mitrovich prepared for Teddy Roosevelt and the veterans of the Charge of San Juan Hill at the hotel in 1902.

Menger's Colonial Room, 1912.

The Menger was once the best hotel in the Southwest and its restaurant was legendary. It was founded by William Menger, a German immigrant who moved his San Antonio brewery to the Alamo Square in 1855. In 1857, he employed architect John Fries to design a two-story hotel on an adjacent site. The Menger Hotel opened on February 1, 1859.

Almost immediately, William Menger began work on an additional wing to attach the hotel to his brewery. The Colonial Dining Room was part of the new addition, and it quickly became legendary for its elegant presentation of local food. Its menu included such famous appetizers as turtle soup made from snapping turtles caught in the San Antonio River and main courses featuring Hill Country wild game.

In a June 21, 1929, article in the *San Antonio Express*, Gus Groben, a longtime steward at the Menger, was interviewed about the early menu. The author concluded, "Fine liquors and wild game comprised the best part of the menu in the early days. Fancy vegetables were scarce. . . ." The elegant desserts were made by pastry chefs from Germany and

Croatia, and wild game was hung in the cottonwood trees in the hotel courtyard. "There still exist a number of pictures of the old courtyard, with deer, wild turkeys, wild geese, partridge and quail hanging in the trees awaiting the artistic touch of the chef," the article reported.

On February 16, 1877, rail service reached San Antonio. The Galveston, Harrisburg and San Antonio Railway connected San Antonio to the coast for the first time. Oysters and fish delivered the same day from the Gulf became the rage in the city's establishments. Within a few years, several more railroads reached San Antonio, providing service to the north and south as well as to Corpus Christi.

Food historians such as James Beard and Larry Forgione have theorized that the heyday of American cooking may have been in the years between the beginning of the railroad era and the start of World War I, roughly 1880 to 1915. By 1880, the railroads had connected distant cities with rapid transportation. A barrel of fish on ice could be put on the train in Galveston and arrive in Dallas the same day. And in those days, the oceans and estuaries were still brimming with giant crabs, oysters, sea turtles, and other seafood that are no longer available.

It is easy to imagine that this era might have also been the heyday of great ingredients in Texas. Wild ducks and geese flew in clouds over the rice fields and swamps of Louisiana and Southwest Texas. Quail, dove, plover, and sandhill crane appeared on restaurant menus. So did elk, bison, and many other now-endangered species. Country hams were vastly superior in quality to the water-injected stuff we eat today. And domestic animals like chickens and pigs were free-range and flavorful. Wild mushrooms were common, and so were wild berries, nuts, and pequins.

After the hurricane of 1900 ended Galveston's reign as the largest city in Texas, San Antonio held the title for many years. Thanks to the Menger and other grand hotels, San Antonio dominated the fine-dining scene in Texas. With its colorful outdoor chili stands and flirtatious chile queens, the Alamo City was also the center of Tex-Mex cuisine. Otis Farnsworth's Original Mexican Restaurant (see page 105) was the first establishment to present that everyday fare in a fine-dining environment.

Between 1873 and 1880, Dallas became the major intersection for rail routes going both east and west and north and south. It quickly became a hub of new commercial and shipping activity, and banks and insurance companies soon followed. Not surprisingly, Dallas gradually took over the title of the premier fine-dining city in Texas.

When Adolphus Busch built the twenty-one-story Beaux-Arts Hotel Adolphus in downtown Dallas in 1912, it was the tallest building in Texas. In the era of the hotel restaurant, the Adolphus became the state's most famous place to see and be seen. In the 1930s and 1940s, Benny Goodman, Glenn Miller, and Tommy and Jimmy Dorsey brought their wildly popular acts to the Adolphus ballrooms. Today, the French Room at the Hotel Aldophus, which was refurbished in 1981, is one of the state's most elegant and sophisticated French restaurants.

TURTLE SOUP

The Menger made its famous turtle soup from snapping turtles harvested from the San Antonio River. Most commercially available turtle meat comes frozen, but it is still harvested from wild snapping turtles. Look for it at specialty seafood stores. (I buy mine from Louisiana Foods in Houston.) Don't skip the grinding step, or the tough turtle meat will be too hard to chew. Because of the butter roux, turtle soup is extremely rich, so keep the portions small if serving as a first course. See photo on page 170.

SERVES 8 AS A FIRST COURSE
4 cups venison stock (page 175) or beef broth
1 cup chopped celery
2 cups chopped yellow onions
2 pounds turtle meat
1 cup unsalted butter
1 cup all-purpose flour
1½ cups canned tomato puree
3 bay leaves
½ teaspoon ground dried thyme
½ teaspoon ground dried oregano
1 teaspoon freshly ground pepper
4 hard-boiled eggs, finely chopped
Juice of 1 lemon
3 tablespoons minced fresh parsley
Sherry, for serving

Put the stock in a small stockpot and bring to a simmer. As you trim the celery and onions for the soup, toss the trimmings into the soup pot. Trim the turtle meat, cutting away the worst of the gristle, and add the gristle to the soup pot. Cut the meat into strips and pass it through a meat grinder fitted with the fine plate. Set the meat aside.

In a large cast-iron skillet, melt the butter over medium heat. Add the flour and stir constantly with a flat-headed wooden spoon, scraping the bottom of the skillet, until the mixture begins to brown. As the mixture darkens, gradually decrease the heat, continuing to stir constantly, until the roux is the color of a copper penny. Add the turtle meat, remove from the heat, and stir for 1 minute. Add the celery and onions and keep stirring until the meat is brown and the vegetables are wilted. Add the tomato puree, bay leaves, thyme, oregano, and pepper, return the pan to low heat, and cook, stirring often, for 15 minutes.

Remove the simmering stock from the heat and strain it though a fine-mesh sieve into a soup pot. Place the pot over high heat and bring the stock to a boil. Add the turtle-roux mixture, a little at a time, stirring after each addition. If the soup is too thick after all of the turtle-roux mixture has been added, add a little stock or water. Decrease the heat to a simmer and cook, uncovered, stirring frequently, for 30 to 40 minutes, until the turtle meat is tender. If the soup thickens too much before the meat is tender, thin with stock or water.

Just before serving, stir in the eggs, lemon juice, and parsley. Ladle into bowls and add a shot of sherry to each bowl. Or, pass the sherry at the table for diners to add to their own bowls.

VENISON STOCK

In the central European kitchen, making a stock is the vital first step in wild-game cookery. The flavorful stock becomes the base for gravies, sauces, soups, and stews. If you butcher your own deer, it is easy to get the bones. If you take your deer to a processor, you will need to ask for the bones to be saved. If the butcher cuts the bones into pieces and freezes them in packages, this recipe will be pretty simple to follow. If you have more than 8 pounds of bones, increase the ingredients proportionally.

I make venison stock outdoors in cool weather while I am making venison sausage. That way I can throw the meat trimmings in with the bones. It also avoids smoking up the kitchen. I put the roasting pan on a hot gas grill. Then I boil the stock in a Cajun boiling pot (see Crawfish Boil, page 56) over propane so I can keep an eye on it while I work.

MAKES ABOUT 8 CUPS

8 pounds meaty venison bones
1 large onion, cut into eighths
3 carrots, peeled and coarsely chopped
3 tablespoons tomato paste
3 tablespoons red currant or berry preserves
1 (750-ml) bottle hearty red wine (such as Zinfandel)
4 bay leaves
10 juniper berries (optional)

Preheat the oven to 500°F, or preheat a gas grill to high.

In a large roasting pan, combine the venison bones, onion, and carrots. Place in the oven or on the gas grill and roast, turning the bones and vegetables every 15 minutes, for about 45 minutes, until the onions and carrots are browned. (Be forewarned that your oven will probably smoke at this temperature unless you have cleaned it recently.) Smear the tomato paste and preserves onto some of the bones and continue roasting for another 15 minutes, until the bones are very brown. Do not allow the tomato paste to burn.

Texas hunting party, 1879.

Transfer the contents of the roasting pan to a stockpot. Place the roasting pan on the stove top over high heat, pour in the wine, and scrape up the brown bits on the pan bottom. Pour the wine into the stockpot and add the bay leaves, juniper berries, and water to cover. Bring to a boil over high heat, adjust the heat to a simmer, and cook, uncovered, skimming any foam as it forms on the surface, for 1½ to 2 hours.

Pour the stock through a fine-mesh sieve and discard the solids. If the flavor of the stock lacks intensity, rinse out the stockpot, return the strained stock to the pot, and boil it until is it dark and flavorful. Remove from the heat and use immediately, or store in the refrigerator for up to 1 week and in the freezer for up to 3 months. (For convenient storage, pour the stock into ice-cube trays, freeze, and then put the cubes in a plastic container in the freezer.)

Venison Demi-glace: Boil 4 cups of the stock until reduced to about 1½ cups; it should coat a spoon. Pour into an ice-cube tray, freeze, then store the cubes in a plastic container in the freezer. Use the demi-glace cubes to add flavor to stews, gravies, and soups.

ROASTED VENISON HAUNCH

Present the whole venison roast on a platter surrounded by roasted potatoes and carrots and carve it at the table. Don't worry if the roast separates into sections as you carve; just slice the sections and serve lots of small slices to each diner.

SERVES 6

1 (3- to 5-pound) bone-in venison haunch roast
1 pound mixed wild mushrooms, trimmed
1 ancho chile, seeded and chopped into wispy strips
2 large sheets pork caul fat (optional; see note)
½ cup unsalted butter
1 cup red wine vinegar
1 teaspoon ground dried thyme
6 shallots, unpeeled
2 cups hearty red wine (such as Zinfandel)
3 cups venison stock (page 175)
3 tablespoons all-purpose flour
3 tablespoons warm water
Salt and freshly ground pepper

Preheat the oven to 450°F.

Bone the roast, or ask the butcher who processes your deer to do it for you. Trim away as much of the sinew and silver skin as possible. Slice the mushrooms if they are large. In a bowl, toss together the mushrooms and chile strips. Lay the roast flat on a work surface, spread the mushroom-chile mixture over it, and then roll up the meat and tie with kitchen twine to secure. Alternatively, lay caul fat on the counter and place the roast on top, add the stuffing, and roll the caul fat up around the roast to secure it in place. Place in a roasting pan.

In a small saucepan, combine 4 tablespoons of the butter and the vinegar and heat over low heat until the butter melts. Stir in the thyme and remove from the heat.

Roast the venison, basting with the butter mixture every 10 minutes, for 30 minutes. Add the shallots to the pan and continue to roast and baste, until an instant-read thermometer inserted into the center registers 140°F for medium or 150°F for medium-well. Plan on about 12 minutes per pound.

Transfer the roast to a platter and let rest for 10 minutes. Slip the skins off of the shallots, crush the shallots into a paste, and place in a small saucepan. Add the wine to the roasting pan and scrape up the brown bits on the pan bottom. Pour the wine into the saucepan with the shallot paste. Add the stock, bring to a boil, and cook for 10 minutes, until it reduces enough to coat a spoon. In a small bowl or cup, stir together the flour and the warm water, forming a slurry that is free of lumps. Add the slurry, a little at a time, to the wine sauce and stir until thickened to a good sauce consistency. When ready to serve, stir in the remaining 4 tablespoons butter, a little at a time, to finish the sauce. Season with salt and pepper. Pour into a warmed bowl.

Carve the roast into slices at the table. Pour a little of the sauce onto each dinner plate, and arrange the stuffed venison slices on top. Serve at once.

Note: Caul fat is a lacy sheet of fat taken from the abdomen of a pig. It is a handy way to secure a rolled roast in place of kitchen twine. As the roast cooks, the caul fat melts slowly, basting the meat as it holds it together. Look for frozen caul fat at specialty butchers or some Asian markets.

VENISON RAGOUT

Venison was the most common meat served at the Menger in the old days. The backstraps or tenderloins were grilled rare, the haunches were served as roasts, and the rest of the meat was made into elegant stews like this one.

SERVES 6

4 pounds boneless venison shoulder, cut into
   1-inch cubes
3 cups Zinfandel red wine
4 yellow onions, quartered
4 carrots, peeled and thickly sliced
10 peppercorns
1 large bay leaf
15 juniper berries
2 teaspoons sea salt
1 rosemary sprig, coarsely chopped
3 tablespoons all-purpose flour
½ cup vegetable oil
6 cups venison stock (page 175)
Cooked egg noodles or boiled potatoes,
   for serving

In a large bowl, combine the venison, 2 cups of the wine, the onions, the carrots, and all of the herbs and spices. Cover and refrigerate for 24 to 72 hours.

Remove the meat from the marinade, draining it well, and set aside. Strain the marinade, reserving the vegetables, herbs, and spices, then discard the liquid.

Toss the meat with the flour, coating it evenly. In a Dutch oven, heat the oil over medium-high heat. Add the meat and cook, turning as needed, for about 5 minutes, until well browned on all sides. Add the remaining 1 cup wine, the stock, and the reserved vegetables, herbs, and spices and bring just to a boil. Decrease the heat to a simmer, cover, and cook for 30 minutes, until the meat is very tender.

Discard the bay leaf and juniper berries and transfer the ragout to a serving bowl. Serve immediately with the noodles.

QUAIL IN MUSHROOM SAUCE

Wild quail are getting hard to find in Texas, but most of the bird hunters I know have white-winged doves in their freezer.

SERVES 3 OR 4

2 pounds quail or doves
1 large portabello mushroom, sliced
½ cup chopped yellow onion
½ cup chopped red bell pepper
¼ cup chopped celery
4 cups water
4 slices bacon
3 tablespoons all-purpose flour
2 cloves garlic, thinly sliced
2½ teaspoons ground cumin
1 teaspoon salt
1 teaspoon pepper
1 tablespoon brandy or whiskey
1 tablespoon light Worcestershire sauce
1 cup canned crushed tomatoes
Cooked rice, for serving
Chopped green onions (white and green parts),
   for garnish

(Continued)

Cut the breast meat from the carcasses of the birds. Refrigerate the meat, and put the bones in a saucepan. As you trim the mushroom, yellow onion, bell pepper, and celery for the soup, toss the trimmings into the saucepan. Add the water, bring to a boil over medium heat, and simmer for 20 minutes to create a flavorful stock. Drain the stock through a fine-mesh sieve and set aside. You should have about 4 cups. Discard the solids.

In a large nonreactive frying pan, fry the bacon over medium-high heat for about 5 minutes, until brown and crisp. Transfer the bacon to paper towels to drain. Pour off all but 3 tablespoons of the drippings from the skillet.

Dust the quail meat with the flour. Place the skillet with the bacon drippings over medium-low heat. Add the quail meat and cook, turning as needed, for about 5 minutes, until lightly browned on both sides but not fully cooked. Add the onion, bell pepper, celery, garlic, cumin, salt, and pepper and sauté for several minutes, until the onions are wilted. Add the mushroom, decrease the heat to low, and sauté for 5 minutes, until the mushroom is soft. Add the brandy and Worcestershire sauce and toss for 30 seconds to mix. Add the reserved stock and the tomatoes, stir well, cover, and simmer over low heat for 45 minutes, until the meat is tender. If the sauce appears to be getting too thick, add a little water to thin it to a good consistency.

Spoon the rice onto individual plates, then spoon the sauce over the top. Crumble the bacon and garnish each serving with the bacon and the green onions. Serve immediately.

MENGER SPINACH PUDDING

Texas was once a major spinach-producing state. Elaborate spinach preparations like this soufflé roll were popular offerings in hotel dining rooms in the early decades of the twentieth century.

SERVES 10

3 cups well-drained, cooked spinach (about 2 large bunches uncooked)
½ yellow onion
½ green bell pepper, seeded
2 cloves garlic, minced
4 eggs
1 teaspoon salt
¼ teaspoon pepper
Pinch of ground nutmeg
2 cups fine dried bread crumbs
½ cup unsalted butter, at room temperature

In a food processor, combine the spinach, onion, green pepper, and garlic and process until you have a smooth puree. Add the eggs, salt, pepper, and nutmeg and process until thoroughly combined. Transfer the puree to a bowl, add 1½ cups of the bread crumbs, and mix well.

Lay a clean dish towel or similar finely woven cloth on a flat work surface. Spread the butter in an 8 by 10-inch rectangle on the center of the towel. Sprinkle the remaining ½ cup bread crumbs evenly over the buttered area. Drop the spinach mixture onto the crumb-covered area and shape it into a roll about 1½ inches in diameter and 10 inches long. Wrap the roll loosely in the towel, then tie the ends securely with kitchen twine.

Bring water to a boil in the bottom of a steamer pan, then reduce to a simmer, place the wrapped spinach roll on the steamer rack, cover, and steam for 20 minutes. Remove the pudding from the steamer and let stand for about 10 minutes, until set.

Carefully unwrap the pudding, slice into 10 equal portions, and serve.

MANGO ICE CREAM

The Menger Hotel's mango ice cream recipe is a secret, but this one tastes a lot like it.

MAKES ABOUT 1½ QUARTS

2 large, ripe mangoes

1¼ cups sugar

2 tablespoons freshly squeezed lime juice

5 egg yolks

2 cups milk

1 cup heavy cream

Working over a bowl to catch any juice, peel each mango and cut the flesh away from the pit. Cut the flesh into ¼-inch dice. Add ½ cup of the sugar and the lime juice to the flesh in the bowl, stir to mix, cover, and refrigerate for 1 hour.

To make a custard, in a bowl, whisk together the egg yolks and the remaining ¾ cup sugar until the sugar dissolves. In a saucepan, scald the milk over medium-high heat (small bubbles appear along the edge of the pan). Remove from the heat and pour the hot milk into the egg mixture in a thin, steady stream while whisking constantly. Return the milk-egg mixture to the saucepan and cook over medium heat, stirring constantly, for about 3 minutes, until thick enough to coat the back of a wooden spoon. Do not let it boil. Pour the custard into a heatproof bowl and let cool completely.

Stir the mango mixture into the cooled custard mixture, then stir in the cream. Taste for sweetness and add more sugar, if desired. Transfer to an ice cream maker and freeze according to the manufacturer's instructions. If the ice cream is still loose, finish freezing it in your freezer before serving.

FIRST TEXAS RESTAURANT REVIEW

★ ★ ★ ★ ★ ★ ★ ★ ★ ★ ★ ★ ★ ★ ★ ★ ★

IN MOST OF TEXAS before the Civil War, the only food offered to the public was served family style in boardinghouses and hotels that catered to travelers. The food at these establishments was erratic. In his 1857 book, *A Journey Through Texas*, Frederick Law Olmsted reported that he stayed in the best hotel in Austin at the time—the name of the hotel was not revealed. But he described the food in what may be the earliest Texas restaurant criticism on record: "Never did we see any wholesome food on that table. It was a succession of burnt flesh of swine and bulls, decaying vegetables and sour, moldy farinaceous glues, all pervaded with rancid butter."

In contrast, he gave rave reviews to the food at the German boardinghouse in which he stayed in New Braunfels (page 152).

Steak au Poivre, page 189.

CHAPTER 16
FANCY FRENCH RESTAURANTS

French food and wine have been popular in Texas for a century and a half. In the mid-1800s, Galveston was the largest city in Texas and one of the most important ports in the world. Wines from Bordeaux, Champagnes, Cognacs, and imported delicacies were found in Galveston's best stores. And, of course, seafood was abundant.

In an 1861 advertisement for Restaurant Francais "L'International" in the *Galveston Daily News*, owner B. Abbadie pledged "to have always on hand the best the market affords together with fresh oysters daily procured from the Bay and served in every style; also fish, venison and game of all kinds, served appropriately to order at every hour from 6 am to 12 midnight, every day of the week."

The French food served in Galveston cafés of the 1800s was inspired by New Orleans restaurants like Antoine's, which opened in 1840. The chefs at Antoine's were following classic French recipes but substituting local ingredients. Gulf sea trout replaced brook trout in the trout meunière and seafood soups got creolized into gumbos. Legend has it that when a chef at Antoine's invented oysters Rockefeller he was looking for a substitute for the snails in escargots à la bourguignonne.

New Orleans Creole restaurants defined French food for Texas diners until a new kind of French restaurant appeared in the late 1940s. Americans serving in Europe during World War II developed a taste for the European cooking and fine wines they encountered. In the same years, waves of European refugees fleeing the Nazi occupation had entered the United States. After the war, fancy French restaurants began popping up across the country.

In Dallas, La Vieille Varsovie, better known as The Old Warsaw, opened in 1948, serving Continental cuisine. With its oil paintings and candelabra, it was considered the most romantic restaurant in the city. On weekends, Vin Lindhe, a famous musician and radio star of the time, played classical music on the dining room's grand piano.

The Old Warsaw was founded by Stanislaw Slawik, who liked to describe himself as a former Polish diplomat. After fleeing Europe, he did indeed work at the Polish consulate in New York for a brief period, until the Russians occupied Poland. After that, he sold air conditioners in New York for a while. He and his glamorous Polish wife, Janina, a former actress, ended up working as butler and maid in Florida.

Seeking a better life, the couple headed for California. Their car broke down near Dallas, and Stanislaw went to work selling cars and Janina got a job at Neiman Marcus. Although neither of them could cook, they knew fine dining and they could see that Dallas was ready for a European-style restaurant. So they hired a French chef and opened La Vieille Varsovie on Cedar Springs with money borrowed from friends. When the sailors on the Polish ship

Sobieski defected in New York, Stanislaw hired the entire crew to work in the restaurant. None of his Polish waiters spoke English, but there were lots of them, and they operated with the formality of a military unit.

Duck bigarade, lamb Provençal, and tournedo grille Helder were among the restaurant's famous main courses. The food was Continental, the wine list and the chef were French, and the pastry chef was

IN HIS OWN WORDS: RONNIE BERMANN

★ ★

PEOPLE USED TO SAY THAT MY DAD showed Houstonians how to eat with a knife and fork—that he taught Houston the difference between bourbon and Bordeaux. Before Maxim's opened, most of the best Houston restaurants were steak houses. Maxim's was the only place serving things like capon with sherry and rack of lamb.

When dad came over on a ship from France in 1939 to work at the New York World's Fair, his cabin mate was Salvador Dalí. I was born in New York in 1944, while my dad was waiting tables. There is a photo around here somewhere of the whole staff of Le Pavillon, including my dad and Henri Soulé.

We moved to Houston when I was five. I wasn't very good at schoolwork, so when I was thirteen, my parents took me out of school and I started working at the restaurant as a busboy. In 1960, when I was sixteen, I went to France for two years to learn the restaurant business. I worked for a year in the vineyards with Alexis Lichine at Château Lichine in Margaux. And then I worked in the kitchens of a couple of different fine-dining restaurants as an apprentice chef. When I got back to Houston in 1962, I went to work as a captain at the restaurant.

The food at Maxim's wasn't really French. It was Creole French—plus a little touch of Mexican. There

was a pinch of chili powder in the soups and sauces. The kitchen staff was Creole (French-speaking African American) and Mexican. Dad was a member of Les Amis de Escoffier, but there was never a French chef in the restaurant. There were two black Creole women working in the kitchen of the Peacock Grill when Dad took over. He kept them both. They made a wonderful gumbo. Dad also kept the *taramasalata* that the Greek guys used to put on the tables as a spread for the bread. We served that right up until the end—it was one of our trademarks.

Lots of dishes were prepared tableside. Steak tartare was my specialty, and I always did it at the table—it wasn't on the menu. There was also a cart for Caesar salad and a carving-station cart with a giant roast beef. We finished the sautéed sliced beef with mushroom sauce and made pepper steak tableside. We sliced the chateaubriand and the capon tableside, too. There were whole fish like sea trout that were poached or baked. The chef would come out and debone the fish tableside and then finish it in two skillets, one with brown butter and one with demi-glace.

There were trout meunière and trout amandine made from Gulf sea trout and crab cakes and red snapper. My favorite fish dish was red snapper excelsior, with artichokes and mushrooms. On the

Polish. In 1963, *Pageant* magazine named The Old Warsaw one of the top six restaurants in the nation; the other five were in New York, Chicago, Los Angeles, and New Orleans.

The restaurant suffered after moving from its charming Cedar Springs location to a much more pretentious space on Maple. By 1974, the kitchen was getting panned by *Texas Monthly* for putting iceberg lettuce in the salad, using dried herbs instead of fresh in the béarnaise sauce, and serving "pâté de maison" out of a can. Stanislaw Slawik sold the place and retired, but The Old Warsaw is still open under new management.

★ ★ ★

Not long after Stanislaw Slawik introduced fine dining to Dallas, Camille Bermann began serving fancy

lunch menu, we had an item called "oil field trash." It was a breaded tenderloin with gravy, and our customers called it chicken-fried steak. Dad once said that French food made him famous, but chicken-fried steak made him rich.

We served beluga caviar in a four and a half pound can. You ate all you wanted and then we weighed it afterward. We got our caviar from the '21' Club in New York. It sold for three dollars an ounce when Dad first opened. It was twenty-one dollars an ounce in the 1970s.

In the early days, you couldn't serve cocktails in a restaurant, so we opened a private club on one side of the building where people could bring in their own bottles. The oilmen had some lavish parties in the club. They hired entertainers and the party went on all night. We also catered a lot of parties in private homes.

Dad wasn't a snob. He liked to make everyone feel welcome and special. Maxim's had customers who wanted to sit at their favorite tables, and Dad took care of them. VIPs like the de Menils and the oil executives got special treatment. But everybody had to wear a coat and tie to get in. And in Houston, only people who were fairly well-off were going to put on a coat and tie for dinner.

In the 1970s, fashions began to change and we started admitting men in turtlenecks with jackets and women in pants. Then we moved to Greenway Plaza

in the 1980s, and we started getting customers in casual clothes coming in before and after the Rockets games. The whole dress code kind of ended then. It was never really the same again.

My dad passed away in 1991, and I took over. Business slowly declined. I guess our kind of fine dining went out of style. Maxim's never got into the elaborate presentations. We had nice china and crystal wineglasses and elegant surroundings, but the food was just garnished with a sprig of parsley and a lemon wedge.

People started to say that our food wasn't presented very well—that we were serving white fish with white crabmeat on a white plate. And the waiters didn't always know what was in the dish. Customers started to complain that we used the same brown butter sauce on just about everything. It was a simpler time.

Now when you go out to dinner, it's a contest to see how many ingredients you can list. And everything you order comes to the table in a pyramid or tied in green onions or something. There are a lot more fine-dining restaurants now, but the *fine* part has been left out. The elegance is gone. I am not sure the generation of today even knows what they are missing.

From left: Camille Bermann, Grand Duke Jean of Luxembourg, and Houston mayor Louie Welch.

Menu from the original Fannin Street location.

French food to Houston residents. Bermann was a waiter at New York's best French restaurant until 1945, when he got an offer to move to New Orleans to run a food and beverage operation at a country club. In 1949, he moved to Houston and went into business with two Greek partners at an eatery called the Peacock Grill. He quickly bought out his partners and changed the name to Maxim's.

Houston was the headquarters of twelve oil companies, including Humble Oil, known today as ExxonMobil. But although Houston had grown in affluence, it lagged behind Dallas in sophistication. At its heart, it remained a blue-collar town and its best restaurants were steak houses. Maxim's would change all that.

Bermann came to the United States to work at the 1939 New York World's Fair. On the Flushing fairgrounds, the French government had re-created a Parisian fine-dining restaurant, Le Restaurant du Pavillon de France, that could seat four hundred. "The team of men who would work at this restaurant

had been put together in France like specialists for a heist," Patric Kuh wrote in his book *The Last Days of Haute Cuisine*. The fish cook, Pierre Franey, would become one of America's best-known chefs. The head of day-to-day operations was a maître d'hôtel named Henri Soulé, who was "unknown as yet, but soon to be mythical in the American restaurant world."

After the fair was over, Henri Soulé opened his own restaurant, Le Pavillon, on East Fifty-Fifth Street in New York, across from the Saint Regis. Fine French food was already available elsewhere in New York. What Soulé imported was something new: Parisian snobbery.

Le Pavillon was a restaurant for the upper class. There was a special section in the front with seven tables that Soulé called Le Royale and the waiters called "the blue blood station." It was gauche to pay in cash, and the waiters put anyone who tried through a tedious and embarrassing ritual. Credit cards hadn't been invented yet.

In order to eat at Le Pavillon in comfort, you needed a house account. And to get a house account, you had to submit your application to Henri Soulé. He judged applicants not just on financial stability but also on social standing. As he put it, he was trying to protect his clientele by "keeping the four flushers out." Soulé was following a European model in which select restaurants did not welcome the common people.

When the World's Fair was over, many of the staff who had come from France followed Soulé to his new restaurant. Some of them, including Camille Bermann, went on to found restaurants of their own.

Bermann was known as "Frenchie" in Houston, thanks to his thick European accent. But he wasn't really French. He had been born in Luxembourg and was waiting tables in Paris when he was hired to work at the New York World's Fair. When he opened Maxim's, the most popular restaurant in town was Sonny Look's Sir Loin, a cavernous steak house. Houston didn't seem ready for a fancy French restaurant, but as luck would have it, the city's most socially prominent couple at the time had been born in Paris.

Two French brothers, Marcel and Conrad Schlumberger, who had founded the world's largest oil-field services company, opened a company office in Houston in 1934. A few years earlier, in 1930, Conrad Schlumberger's daughter Dominique met fellow Parisian John de Menil at a party in Versailles and they wed shortly after. During the Nazi occupation of France, both the company headquarters and the de Menils moved to Houston. Soon after Bermann opened Maxim's, the couple became dining-room regulars and they introduced the movers and shakers of the Houston oil industry to French food. They gave haute cuisine and fine wine a new importance on the social scene.

Maxim's and the de Menils changed fine dining in Texas. In 1999, *Texas Monthly* named Maxim's the Restaurant of the Century. Camille Bermann's son Ronnie, who grew up in the restaurant, took over the business after his father passed away.

Maxim's closed in 2001.

DUCK BIGARADE

Bigarade is the French name for the Seville or bitter orange. If you can find Seville oranges, you can omit the lime juice.

SERVES 4

2 boneless half duck breasts (about 2 pounds total)
Salt and freshly ground pepper
1 tablespoon duck fat or olive oil
1 jigger Grand Marnier
1 tablespoon sherry vinegar
¼ cup demi-glace or venison demi-glace (page 176)
Juice of 1 orange
Juice of 1 lime
1 tablespoon grated orange zest
Thin orange slices, halved, for garnish

Sprinkle the duck breasts on both sides with salt and pepper and let sit at room temperature for 30 minutes. Preheat the oven to 250°F.

In a skillet, heat the duck fat over medium-high heat. Lay the breast halves, skin side down, in the hot fat and cook, undisturbed, for 5 to 7 minutes, until the skin is crispy. Turn the breasts over and cook on the second side for 3 to 4 minutes longer, until the meat is cooked through but still rosy. Transfer the breasts to a heatproof platter, tent loosely with aluminum foil, and place in the oven. Place 4 dinner plates in the oven to heat.

To make the orange sauce, return the skillet to medium heat, add the Grand Marnier, vinegar, demiglace, and citrus juices, and deglaze the pan, stirring to scrape up any brown bits from the pan bottom. Add the orange zest, being careful the sauce doesn't splatter. Cook for a few minutes to burn off the alcohol. Season with salt.

To serve, transfer the duck breasts to a cutting board and carve on the diagonal into thin slices. Ladle an equal amount of the sauce on each warmed dinner plate. Divide the duck slices evenly among the plates. Garnish with the orange slices and serve.

SCHLUMBERGER SALAD

Camille Bermann named this salad in honor of Houston's most famous French family.

SERVES 4

Dressing
3 tablespoons sherry vinegar
2 tablespoons Creole mustard
1 clove garlic, minced
1 tablespoon minced celery
1 tablespoon minced fresh chives
½ teaspoon salt
¼ teaspoon freshly ground pepper
¾ cup olive oil

8 ounces torn romaine lettuce leaves
3 hard-boiled eggs, quartered lengthwise
1 avocado, halved, pitted, peeled, and cut into thin lengthwise slices
2 tomatoes, diced

To make the dressing, in a small bowl, whisk together the vinegar, mustard, garlic, celery, chives, salt, and pepper. Add the oil in a slow, steady stream, whisking to emulsify.

In a bowl, combine the lettuce, eggs, avocado, and tomatoes. Drizzle with the dressing and toss gently to coat evenly. Divide among chilled salad plates and serve at once. Alternatively, to serve banquet style, arrange the ingredients on a chilled platter with lettuce on the bottom and other ingredients placed on top. Drizzle half of the dressing over the top. Serve the remainder of the dressing in a small bowl on the side for diners to add as desired.

POMPANO EN PAPILLOTE

Pompano is one of the most highly prized fish in the Gulf of Mexico. Some say pompano has a flavor that reminds them of lobster. Whether you agree or not, you will agree it tastes good with lots of butter. It's fun to bring the whole paper package to the table and tear it open in front of your guests.

SERVES 2
2 small whole pompano, heads on (about 1 pound each), cleaned
Salt and pepper
3 tablespoons olive oil
2 tablespoons chopped garlic
2 cups julienned leeks
½ cup unsalted butter, chilled
6 shrimp, peeled and deveined
½ cup chopped shallots
½ cup freshly squeezed lemon juice
½ cup chopped fresh flat-leaf parsley, plus 2 sprigs
2 lemon slices

Preheat the oven to 400°F. Grease a baking sheet with nonstick cooking spray.

Trim the fins and tail off the fish. Make 3 deep incisions from the top fin to the belly on both sides of each fish, spacing them evenly between the head and the tail. Season the fish on both sides with salt and pepper.

In a large sauté pan, heat the oil over medium-high heat. When the oil is hot, add the fish to the pan and cook, turning once, for 2 minutes on each side, until lightly cooked on both sides. Transfer the fish to a platter. Add the garlic and leeks to the hot oil and cook, stirring over medium-high heat for a few minutes, until the garlic browns a little and the leeks wilt. Add 2 tablespoons of the butter and turn down the heat to low. Cook the leeks in the butter for about 10 minutes, until soft. Remove from the heat.

Lay 2 sheets of parchment paper large enough to enclose the fish on a work surface (2 sheets each about 9 by 13 inches should work fine). Fold each sheet in half lengthwise, then unfold. Place 1 fish on one half of each sheet. Divide the leek-garlic mixture evenly between the fish, mounding it on top of each one. Place 3 shrimp on top of each mound of leeks. Fold the other half of the paper over each fish and fold up the edges, making a tight double fold, to seal securely.

Place the parchment packages on the prepared baking sheet and bake for 10 minutes.

While the fish is baking, in a small saucepan, melt the remaining 6 tablespoons butter over medium heat. Add the shallots and cook, stirring, for about 3 minutes, until wilted. Add the lemon juice and parsley and simmer for a few minutes. Pour the sauce into a warmed sauceboat.

Remove the fish packages from the oven and place each package on a warmed dinner plate. Garnish each plate with a parsley sprig and a lemon slice, then carry the plates to the table. With a knife or decorative scissors, cut open the top of each package to expose the fish. With a spoon, ladle some of the sauce into the bag over the fish. The fish should be eaten out of the paper.

THE NEW SOUTHWESTERN CUISINE

★ ★

IN THE 1980S, AMERICAN CHEFS, inspired by the French nouvelle cuisine movement that began in the late 1960s, decided to attempt something similar. Hackneyed traditional fine-dining dishes made with previously frozen proteins were jettisoned in favor of fresh, indigenous ingredients and a return to the roots of regional cooking.

In the Southwest, a group of chefs that included Mark Miller, Robert Del Grande, Bruce Auden, Stephan Pyles, and Dean Fearing created a cooking style they called New Southwestern Cuisine. Beans, chiles, and corn were among the primary ingredients and enchiladas, tacos, and tamales were the favored forms. The style became famous in the 1990s and was taken to other parts of the country by high-profile chefs like Bobby Flay at Mesa in New York.

The movement produced such memorable dishes as Robert Del Grande's coffee-rubbed tenderloin, Stephan Pyles's cowboy rib eye, Dean Fearing's tortilla soup, and Mark Miller's lobster enchiladas. In the late 1990s, southwestern became generic, diluting the once-positive trend. Grocery stores stocked frozen southwestern items and convenience stores sold southwestern-style snack foods.

In their new twenty-first-century restaurants, Robert Del Grande, Stephan Pyles, and Dean Fearing still offer dishes inspired by the region but without the dogma. "In the beginning, everything had to be an enchilada or a tostada. We don't think about all that stuff anymore," Robert Del Grande told me. Mark Miller sold his interest in the Coyote Café in Santa Fe. "I couldn't find young chefs who wanted to cook southwestern anymore," he said. "When I asked them what they did want to cook, they said 'local organic' food. That's not a cooking style—that's a shopping list."

If you are looking for recipes, you can find dozens of good cookbooks dedicated to Southwestern cuisine.

TROUT MEUNIÈRE

The dish is classically made with brook trout, but French Creole chefs in Louisiana and Texas substituted speckled sea trout, which were once plentiful along the Gulf of Mexico. Speckled sea trout are no longer commercially available, but if you can get some from a fisherman, use them for this recipe.

SERVES 4

½ cup fish flour (page 9)
4 (6-ounce) trout fillets
¼ cup unsalted butter
2 tablespoons olive oil
Juice of 3 lemons
1 tablespoon grated lemon zest
½ cup minced fresh parsley, plus 4 sprigs
Sea salt and freshly ground pepper
4 lemon slices

Preheat the oven to 250°F. Spread the flour in a pie pan or shallow bowl. Dredge the fish fillets in the flour until well coated, shaking off the excess.

In a large skillet, heat 2 tablespoons of the butter with the oil over medium heat. Decrease the heat to medium-low, add the fillets, and fry, turning once, for 3 to 5 minutes on each side, until cooked through. (The cooking time varies with the thickness of the fillets; plan on 10 minutes per inch of thickness.) Transfer the fish to a heatproof platter and place in the warm oven.

Add the remaining 2 tablespoons butter to the skillet and melt over medium heat. Add the lemon juice, lemon zest, and minced parsley and whisk together for about 1 minute to combine. Season with salt and pepper.

Divide the fish fillets among 4 warmed dinner plates, pour the sauce over the fish, and sprinkle with pepper. Garnish each plate with a lemon slice and a parsley sprig.

RED SNAPPER EXCELSIOR

Excelsior recipes, like baked chicken excelsior, are generally made with mushrooms. This Maxim's dish probably came from Louisiana.

SERVES 4

1 cup fish flour (page 9)
4 (6-ounce) red snapper fillets
¼ cup unsalted butter
2 tablespoons olive oil
2 cups sliced mushrooms
1 cup jarred or canned artichoke hearts, chopped
Juice of 3 lemons
½ cup white wine
½ cup minced fresh parsley, plus 4 sprigs
Sea salt and freshly ground pepper
4 lemon slices

Preheat the oven to 250°F. Spread the flour in a pie pan or shallow bowl. Dredge the fish fillets in the flour until well coated, shaking off the excess.

In a large skillet, heat 2 tablespoons of the butter with the oil over medium heat. Decrease the heat to medium-low, add the fillets, and fry, turning once, for about 5 minutes on each side, until cooked through. (The cooking time varies with the thickness of the fillets; plan on 10 minutes per inch of thickness.) Transfer the fish to a heatproof platter and place in the warm oven.

Add the remaining 2 tablespoons butter to the skillet and melt over medium-high heat. Add the mushrooms and sauté for a minute or two to coat them with the butter. Then cover and cook for a few minutes, until the mushrooms give up their liquid. Uncover, add the artichokes, lemon juice, wine, and minced parsley, season with salt and pepper, and cook, stirring, for a few minutes, until the mushrooms are tender.

Divide the fish fillets among warmed dinner plates, spoon the artichokes and mushrooms over top, pour the sauce over the fish, and sprinkle with a little fresh ground pepper. Garnish each plate with a lemon slice and a parsley sprig.

Trout Amandine: Substitute ½ cup blanched slivered almonds for the minced parsley. Melt the butter in the skillet as directed, add the almonds, and toast them in the butter for a few minutes. Spoon the butter and almonds evenly over the fish fillets and garnish as directed.

STEAK AU POIVRE

At Maxim's, the pepper cream sauce was made tableside. Flaming the brandy in the copper cooking pan was part of the show. The sauce was then applied to the steaks with a flourish. See photo on page 180.

SERVES 4

4 (8-ounce) filets mignons

Coarse sea salt

3 tablespoons crushed peppercorns

2 tablespoons unsalted butter

1 teaspoon olive oil

½ cup brandy

1 cup heavy cream

¼ cup store-bought demi-glace or venison demi-glace (page 176; optional)

Sprinkle the steaks on both sides with coarse salt. Spread the peppercorns on a plate. One at a time, roll the steaks in the pepper to coat evenly.

In a large skillet (or copper sauté pan), melt the butter over medium heat and add the oil. When the butter begins to smoke, add the steaks and cook for 5 minutes. Turn the steaks and cook for 3 minutes. Then roll the steaks in the pan to sear their sides. To test for doneness, insert an instant-read thermometer into the center of a steak; it should register 125°F for rare or 130°F for medium. Transfer the steaks to a platter and tent with aluminum foil to keep warm. Remove the pan from the heat.

Add the brandy to the hot pan and ignite it with a firestick or a long match to burn off the alcohol. Return the pan to medium heat, add the cream and demi-glace, and simmer, stirring occasionally, for about 3 minutes, until the sauce thickens.

Transfer the steaks to 4 warmed dinner plates. Spoon the sauce over the steaks at the table and serve.

PART V
COUNTRY AND WESTERN

★ El Paso

On early maps, West Texas is dominated by the "Apacheria" and "Comancheria," the homelands of the Apache and Comanche Indians. After the Civil War, when the Apache and Comanche were confined to reservations, the prairies of West Texas that had formerly been grazed by wild buffalo were opened to cattlemen. Anglo cattlemen and their slaves settled the northern prairie and the panhandle, while Spanish-speaking cattlemen of South Texas set up ranches along the border.

Fort Worth is on the eastern edge of West Texas. Amarillo, Abilene, Lubbock, and Odessa are the other West Texas cities of note. Big Bend National Park is a magnificent reserve of desert and mountains, and Marfa is a notable town nearby. Paradise is also located in West Texas; it has a population of fewer than 500.

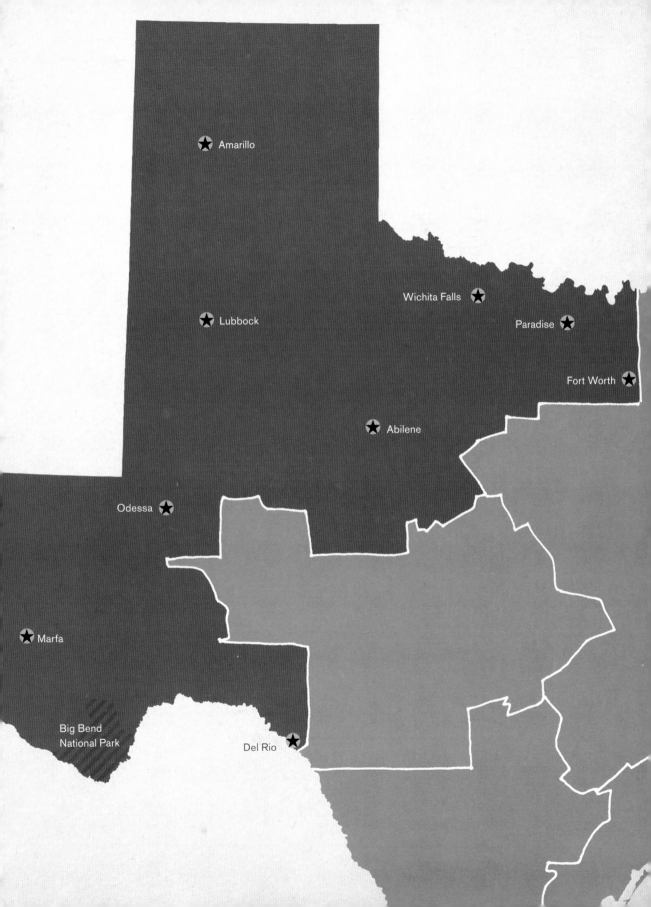

Southern-Style Chicken-Fried Steak (page 198) with Black Pepper Gravy (page 201) and Mashed Potatoes (page 203).

Lunch at a food truck in Brownwood, 1940.

CHAPTER 17

CHICKEN-FRIED STEAK IN PARADISE

★★★★★★★★★★★★★★★★★★★★★★★★★★

The crust on the chicken-fried steak (CFS) at the Frisco Shop on Burnet Road in Austin tasted bland. The meat was overtenderized. The mashed potatoes still held the shape of the ice cream scoop. "Soft and bland, that's the way this crowd likes it," joked my booth mate, Alan Lazarus, one of Austin's top chefs. When we walked in at dinnertime on Saturday night, he predicted we would be the youngest people in the restaurant, and he was right—by a long shot.

We had joined the senior-citizen set for dinner at the Frisco Shop to sample the last of the Night Hawk's chicken-fried steaks and to bid a sentimental goodbye. Walgreen's had purchased the lot and the fifty-five-year-old Frisco Shop was scheduled for demolition. It was the last location of the Night Hawk chain, which once ran the most prestigious restaurants in Austin.

Alan and I recited the familiar litany of dearly departed Austin chicken-fried steak restaurants. The Stallion, Hank's on the Drag, Virginia's on South Lamar, Jake's on Fifth—the list went on and on. "When we were in college, we used to live on chicken-fried steaks," Lazarus said. "But college kids nowadays don't eat that kind of food. Chicken-fried steak is outdated, it's not healthy, and it's not what people want to eat anymore."

"Well, not in trendy Austin, anyway," I said.

Alan Lazarus was right. Chicken-fried steak is out of favor in urban Texas. And so, I decided to go looking for chicken-fried steak in the country.

★ ★ ★

The crust on Granny's chicken-fried steak was so thick, it looked like the meat was coated with corn-flakes. The varying shades of gold and brown were accented here and there with flecks of black pepper. The tenderized round steak was tender but still chewy. Every bite carried a nice crunch. It was served with a side of home fries—hand-cut fries with bits of peel still attached—and I got the cream gravy on the side. It was the fourth chicken-fried steak I ordered at the Finish Line Café in Paradise that afternoon, and I think it proved my point.

In Houston, Dallas, and Austin, chicken-fried steak is now a nutritionally questionable throwback served mainly in cafeterias and diners that cater to mossbacks and "country cooking" restaurants decorated with branding irons and other such cowboy memorabilia. But in small-town Texas, chicken-fried steak is doing better than ever.

When I set out on this chicken-fried steak road trip, I thought I might publish some rankings. But after eating scores of great chicken-fried steaks in small-town cafés, I gave up on rating them. I loved them all. That's when I came up with the Chicken-Fried Steak Belt (CFSB) theory.

The theory postulates that Texas has a Chicken-Fried Steak Belt and within its confines, every small-town café serves a CFS that rates somewhere between very good and excellent. The exact borders of this belt have yet to be determined, but I decided to start the random sampling.

I was on my way to West Texas, which some would argue is the spiritual home of the chicken-fried steak. So one night before retiring, I got out a road atlas and looked for a hamlet that I had never visited on the next day's route from Denton to Abilene.

Paradise sounded like a nice place (it's on Highway 114 between Bridgeport and Boyd), so I drove there and looked around for a place to eat. That's when I discovered the Finish Line, housed in a funky metal building in a gravel parking lot. It's the oldest café in Paradise, and it had a chicken-fried steak and a pan-fried steak on the menu. I ordered both.

The chicken-fried steak was made from a frozen patty and it was pretty awful. The panfried steak, on the other hand, was an excellent hand-breaded tenderized round steak with a crunchy crust. The waitress told me the tenderized meat was first dipped in seasoned flour, then in buttermilk, then dipped a second time in seasoned flour, and finally fried in a deep fryer. It was served with previously frozen fries and cream gravy. "Why do you call this a panfried steak?" I asked the waitress. She explained that a panfried steak was what folks in Paradise called a hand-breaded chicken-fried steak.

I wanted to take a picture of the panfried steak,

CHICKEN-FRIED HISTORY

★ ★ ★ ★ ★ ★ ★ ★ ★ ★ ★ ★ ★ ★ ★ ★ ★

THE EARLIEST MENTION in print of chicken-fried steak that I have found is this June 19, 1914, classified ad in the *Colorado Springs Gazette*: "A Summer Dainty Chicken Fried Steak at Phelps 111 E. Bijou."

The earliest Texas mention is a classified ad in the *Grand Prairie Texan* on July 31, 1925: "DINTY MOORES CAFE PLATE LUNCH SATURDAY Chicken Fried Steak Blackeyed Peas Mashed Potatoes String Beans Sliced Tomatoes 35 Cents."

THE SEMI-TOUGH CFS

★ ★

THE GRAVY-SODDEN, greasy, chicken-fried steak was already out-of-date when Julia Child and JFK's White House chef made French food popular in the early 1960s. But the CFS made a comeback in the 1970s.

"I take full credit for reinventing the chicken-fried steak," Dan Jenkins told me on the phone from his home in Fort Worth.

In 1972, Jenkins, who has enjoyed a long career as one of America's favorite sports writers, published *Semi-Tough*, a novel about pro football. In it, former Texas Christian University football star Billy Clyde Puckett is horrified to discover that he can't get a chicken-fried steak in New York City after being drafted by the Giants.

"*Semi-Tough* was a best-seller and it reintroduced the chicken-fried steak," said Jenkins. "I was living in New York at the time and none of my friends up there knew what it was." But back in Jenkins's hometown of Fort Worth, the book set off a chicken-fried frenzy.

In May 1974, just a year after its founding, *Texas Monthly* magazine published "The Best Little Old Chicken-Fried Steak in Texas." Early statewide rankings always paid tribute to Massey's Restaurant on Eighth Avenue in Fort Worth. The restaurant, which was immortalized in print by Dan Jenkins, was owned by Herb Massey. It appears under the pseudonym of Herb's Café in Jenkins's novels.

"The reason it was so good was that it was a little cube steak tenderized all to hell served on toast with cream gravy over the top," Jenkins told me. "We got the bright idea of putting it on biscuits instead of toast and that tasted pretty good, too."

After Herb Massey passed away, the restaurant was taken over by new management. I asked Jenkins what makes a great chicken-fried steak. "It has to have the living shit tenderized out of it," he said. "You should be able to cut it with a fork."

but I had neglected to order the cream gravy on the side. So I ordered another steak for photography purposes. It was so good, I ate most of it.

By now, most of the lunch crowd had cleared out and the waitress returned to the table and asked what I was up to in Paradise. When I told her I was driving around Texas comparing chicken-fried steaks, she said that I ought to try Granny's. My waitress, Jenny Herrington, was the daughter of the Finish Line's owner and head cook, Rayanne Gentry. Rayanne's mother and Jenny's grandmother, Marie Brown, was also working in the kitchen.

"When I'm going to eat a chicken-fried steak, I have Granny make it," the third-generation CFS fan whispered. "And I get it with the home fries." Granny adds beaten egg to the buttermilk for a richer batter, Herrington told me. And she cuts the potatoes to

order. With a recommendation like that, I ordered a fourth chicken-fried steak. If you like the Southern fried version of the CFS, Granny's was the best one of the bunch.

"That's the last one we're going to make you," Rayanne Gentry yelled from the cash register. "Four chicken-fried steaks ought to be enough for anybody."

I was definitely in the thick of the Chicken-Fried Steak Belt.

★ ★ ★

The chicken-fried steak at Mary's Café in Strawn has a dense, flat flour coating that is darker in some places than others. It lacks the crispness of the bread crumbs found in the German-inspired chicken-fried schnitzels of Central Texas, and it doesn't have the richly battered southern-style crust of its cousins served in East Texas. This is the cowboy "panfried" version of the chicken-fried steak, and Mary's Café in Strawn is the mother church of the style.

Cowboys didn't have toasted bread crumbs and they didn't use eggs for a rich batter, which is why the West Texas panfried steak is the simplest of the Texas CFS styles. The coating is dry, which also makes the flavor of the CFS more dependent on the gravy. Thank goodness Mary's gravy is peppery and rich.

The dining room at Mary's was lit by the blue neon of a giant beer sign. In fact, beer signs made up most of the interior decoration in this ramshackle little roadhouse. Many of the other customers were middle-aged Harley drivers. Flossie's, a café across the street, is also famous for its CFS. In fact, the whole area is famous for chicken-fried steaks.

"Palo Pinto County's main industries are cream gravy and methamphetamines," said *Fort Worth Star-Telegram* columnist Bud Kennedy, who joined me at Mary's for lunch. "This used to be the only place within fifty miles where a student at Tarleton State University could get a beer," Kennedy said. "But then some other towns near the college went wet."

"A couple of generations ago, Strawn and nearby Mingus were known as places for college students to go howl at the moon for cold beer and country music," wrote Art Chapman in the *Fort Worth Star-Telegram*. "Now, older and wiser, they travel to Strawn for its chicken-fried steak."

★ ★ ★

I had heard that the Texas Restaurant Association (TRA) did a survey in the 1980s that revealed 80 percent of its members served CFS and that some eight hundred thousand of them were consumed daily in Texas. I called Wendy Saari, the association's director of communications, and asked her if these figures were correct.

"I am afraid that's an urban legend," she reported.

The TRA did conduct a member survey that included a market segmentation study in the 1980s, she said. While everyone remembers that a

From left: Tenderizing hammer, Dutch oven frying, and chicken-fried tenderloin.

surprisingly large number of the respondents served chicken-fried steak, nobody at the TRA can quote any statistics because they can't find the original study. Besides, the number of restaurants replying was only a tiny fraction of all the state's restaurants, so the numbers wouldn't mean much anyway. "It's safe to say that chicken-fried steak was really popular," Saari concluded.

Back home in Houston, I dug into a chicken-fried steak lunch special at Lankford Grocery. It was a petite patty that looked like a slightly flattened piece of southern fried chicken. The crust was heavenly. It was crispy and chewy at the same time, with plenty of salt and pepper and maybe a dash of cayenne in the batter. I admired the light sheen of the fryer grease and the way the crust pulled away from the meat while I ate it. I could have sworn there was some chicken skin under there.

Lankford Grocery is an old-fashioned country restaurant in a part of the city where old buildings are getting leveled to make way for townhouses. It won't be around much longer. As I sat there taking in the scene, I thought about how much the falling-down building and eccentric decorating scheme reminded me of Virginia's, which used to be my favorite chicken-fried steak joint when I was a college student in Austin. Virginia's was a small-town Texas café on the outskirts of town when it was built, but as Austin grew, the city swallowed it up. It's the same story with Lankford Grocery, which was built as a grocery store in the 1930s. You used to find these rural islands in the middle of many big cities, but now they are a part of disappearing Texas.

But on my chicken-fried steak trek I discovered that the CFS is not only alive and well in the country, but also innovative cooks in small-town Texas restaurants were creating some delectable new versions of the old classic.

At Perini Ranch Steakhouse in Buffalo Gap, just outside of Abilene, Tom Perini makes his CFS once a week for Sunday brunch. He uses rib-eye steak trim. The pieces of beef are dipped in southern-style egg batter, pounded out into medallions, fried, and served with cream gravy on the side.

At the Beehive in Albany, Amanda Pearson, a former navy cook, tenderizes top sirloin butt and dips it in a blend of flour and bread crumbs. Her awesome chicken-fried steak tastes like a cross between a German schnitzel and a West Texas panfried steak. Pearson beats the flour into the steak with such force that the crust appears to be welded to the meat.

On the Saturday night when I stopped in at the Cliff House Restaurant in Stamford, the kitchen was serving panfried steaks with the inspired topping of sautéed green peppers and onions. It tasted like an Italian-style CFS—or would that be a Milanese CFS?

My wanderings confirmed that within the confines of the Chicken-Fried Steak Belt (wherever that is exactly) the CFS is an immutable classic.

ROUND STEAK, TOP SIRLOIN BUTT, OR EYE OF ROUND?

★ ★ ★ ★ ★ ★ ★ ★ ★ ★ ★ ★ ★ ★ ★ ★ ★ ★

TENDERIZED ROUND STEAK is the traditional choice for chicken-fried steak. Round steaks are big. When you see a giant CFS flopping off the plate in all directions, it's probably made with round steak. Bottom sirloin butt, a slightly higher-quality cut, can also be pounded out for CFS. Top sirloin butt is popular as well.

Eye-of-round steaks are a lot smaller than the big cuts. These little ovals average around a quarter pound apiece and are often served two to a portion. They are a favorite for home cooks because they fit nicely in a cast-iron skillet.

You can pound any of these cuts out with a meat mallet, or "Jaccardize" them with one of those multineedle tenderizer tools. But the easiest way to get tenderized beef is to buy cube steaks or ask the butcher to run your steaks through the tenderizing machine.

SOUTHERN-STYLE CHICKEN-FRIED STEAK

"Chicken-fried steak is considered a Southern staple," according to the *Tulsa World*. Food historians who argue that the CFS is a Southern invention, rather than a cowboy or German-inspired dish, point to the fried chicken connection and the fact that recipes for steaks dipped in batter can be found in Southern cookbooks going back to the early 1800s. Aficionados of this style wax poetic about the crunchy crust. It should look just like the coating on a piece of southern fried chicken. See photo on page 192.

SERVES 6 TO 12

Peanut oil, for frying

2 cups seasoned flour (recipe follows)

1 cup buttermilk, evaporated milk, or milk

1 egg, lightly beaten

12 tenderized eye-of-round steaks (about
    3 pounds total)

Onion Gravy (page 201), Black Pepper Gravy
    (page 201), or your favorite gravy, for serving

Pour the oil to a depth of 1 inch into a deep cast-iron skillet and heat to 370°F.

While the oil is heating, put the flour in a large, shallow bowl. In a separate shallow bowl, whisk together the buttermilk and egg. Dredge each steak in the flour, shaking off the excess; dip it into the buttermilk mixture, allowing the excess to drip off; and then dredge again in the flour, evenly coating the batter so it is dry on the outside.

Slide 2 or 3 steaks into the hot oil, being careful not to crowd them. The temperature of the oil will fall the moment the meat is added, so you will need to adjust the heat. As the steaks cook, try to keep the oil at around 350°F. If it gets too hot, the steaks will burn before they are cooked through. If it is not hot enough, the batter will be soggy. Cook the steaks for 3 to 5 minutes, until the batter is crisp and brown and the meat is cooked through. Using a wire skimmer,

transfer the steaks to paper towels to drain and keep in a warm oven until all of the batches are done.

Serve the steaks with the gravy. Plan on 2 steaks for a typical serving; children and dainty eaters will probably want only 1 steak.

SEASONED FLOUR

You can season chicken-fried steaks directly and then use plain flour if you like, but I prefer a spicy batter. It sounds like a lot of seasonings, but only a tiny bit sticks to the meat.

MAKES ABOUT 3 CUPS

2½ cups all-purpose flour

2 tablespoons chili powder, homemade
    (page 110) or store-bought; New Mexico
    chile powder; or hot paprika

1 tablespoon salt

1 tablespoon pepper

1 tablespoon onion powder

1 tablespoon garlic powder

In a bowl, stir together all of the ingredients, mixing well. You will have more seasoned flour than you need for most recipes. Set aside the balance for making gravy, or store in a tightly capped jar in a cupboard for another time. Discard any flour in which you have dipped raw meat.

BEEHIVE PANFRIED STEAK

"Chicken-fried steak probably originated on the range," wrote Dotty Griffith in the 1986 *Restaurants of Dallas*. "It is hypothesized that cowboys on trail drives would fry pieces of meat from a slaughtered steer in grease-filled skillets over an open fire. This proved a very quick and easy way to cook meat, perfect for men on the move eating out of a chuck wagon."

If the point was cooking a steak "quick and easy," then why wouldn't cowboy cooks grill their steaks directly over the coals, instead of messing with frying pans and grease and flour? Tom Perini, a cowboy cooking historian and owner of Perini Ranch Steakhouse in Buffalo Gap, explained that dried buffalo manure, a.k.a. buffalo chips, was the only fuel available on the earliest trail drives. There were no trees on the prairie. Imagine what a steak grilled over buffalo dung would taste like, Perini said. Suddenly the idea of cowboys chicken-frying their steaks makes a lot more sense.

SERVES 6 TO 12

12 tenderized eye-of-round steaks (about
    3 pounds total)
Salt and pepper
2 cups buttermilk
Peanut oil, for frying
2 cups seasoned flour (page 198)
Onion Gravy (page 201), Black Pepper Gravy
    (page 201), or your favorite gravy, for serving

Season the steaks with salt and pepper, put them in a large, shallow bowl, and pour in the buttermilk. Put a weight on top of the steaks if necessary to keep them submerged. Let stand at room temperature for at least 1 hour or up to 2 hours.

Pour the oil to a depth of 1 inch into a deep cast-iron skillet and heat to 370°F.

While the oil is heating, put the flour in a large, shallow bowl. Remove each steak from the buttermilk, allow the excess to drip off, then dredge in the flour, coating thoroughly. Put the flour-coated meat on a cutting board and beat the flour into the meat with your fist or the heel of your palm. Add more flour to the bare spots and beat it in. This helps more of the flour stick to the steak. Allow the floured steaks to dry for 10 minutes to help the batter adhere.

Slide 2 or 3 steaks into the hot oil, being careful not to crowd them. The temperature of the oil will fall the moment the meat is added, so you will need to adjust the heat. As the steaks cook, try to keep the oil at around 350°F. If it gets too hot, the steaks will burn before they are cooked through. If it is not hot enough, the batter will be soggy. Cook the steaks for 3 to 5 minutes, until the batter is crisp and brown and the meat is cooked through. Using a wire skimmer, transfer the steaks to paper towels to drain and keep in a warm oven until all of the batches are done.

Serve the steaks with the gravy. Plan on 2 steaks for a typical serving; children and dainty eaters will probably want only 1 steak.

Plain Panfried Steak: Omit the buttermilk. Dip the steak in the flour and proceed as directed.

THE GREAT GOD BEEF DISH

★ ★ ★ ★ ★ ★ ★ ★ ★ ★ ★ ★ ★ ★ ★ ★ ★ ★

FORT WORTH STAR-TELEGRAM travel editor and CFS correspondent Jerry Flemmons used to say that Texas had three major food groups: barbecue, Tex-Mex, and chicken-fried steak. But he was prejudiced in favor of the CFS.

"As splendid and noble as barbecue and Tex-Mex are, both pale before the Great God Beef dish, chicken-fried steak," Flemmons once wrote. "No single food better defines the Texas character; it has, in fact, become a kind of nutritive metaphor for the romanticized, prairie-hardened personality of Texas."

CHICKEN-FRIED SCHNITZEL

In *Eat Your Way Across the U.S.A.*, Jane and Michael Stern speculated that "the chicken-fried steak was a Depression-era invention of Hill Country German-Texans." A 1994 *Dallas Morning News* article titled "Plate Teutonics" took the same view: "German immigrants brought the breaded and fried cutlet to the Texas frontier, where it was quickly copied—with less finesse—by chuck-wagon cooks and farm wives. . . . The author goes on to say that even "the gravy ladled on top has Teutonic roots: Rahmschnitzel is garnished with cream sauce."

SERVES 6 TO 12

Peanut oil, for frying

2 cups seasoned flour (page 198)

12 tenderized eye-of-round steaks (about 3 pounds total)

1 cup dried bread crumbs or cracker crumbs

2 cups buttermilk, evaporated milk, or milk

Onion Gravy (page 201), Black Pepper Gravy (page 201), or your favorite gravy, for serving

Pour the oil to a depth of 1 inch into a deep cast-iron skillet and heat to 370°F. While the oil is heating, put the flour in a shallow bowl. Dredge each steak in the flour, coating thoroughly and shaking off the excess. Set aside. Spread the bread crumbs on a large plate, pour the leftover flour from the first dredging

THREE WAYS TO MESS UP A CFS

★ ★

SERVING AS A JUDGE of chicken-fried steak at the National Championship Chuckwagon Cookoff in Amarillo gave me some new perspectives on the dish. In the final round of the competition, the judges at my table sampled twelve entries. Although each chuck-wagon team was given the exact same meat, flour, and oil to work with, we gave the finished products very different scores. Successful chicken-frying requires a perfect marriage of meat, batter, and grease. Here are the three most common mistakes:

1. Over- and Underseasoning

Seasoning the steaks with salt and pepper first sounds like a good idea. But if you use a salty seasoned flour for the batter, the steaks end up too salty. Underseasoning is just as bad. The batter on even a perfectly cooked chicken-fried steak can taste pasty if it isn't seasoned. That's why I prefer to season the flour for the batter.

2. Too Much Tenderizing

The ratio of batter to meat is crucial, and it's determined by the thickness of the meat. If you pound the meat too flat, the chicken-fried steak is all batter and the meat gets overcooked by the time the crust is done. The best chicken-fried steaks are tenderized a little, but the meat remains thick enough to stay juicy and slightly pink when the crust is perfectly cooked.

3. Overheating the Oil

To cook a chicken-fried steak so the crust is golden and the meat is cooked through, it is critical to keep the temperature of the oil at around 350°F (as opposed to the 375°F used in some recipes). At this lower frying temperature, the meat is done but still juicy and tender by the time the batter is brown. If it is much lower than 350°F, the crust gets soggy.

over the crumbs, and mix together. Pour the buttermilk into a shallow bowl. Dip each steak into the buttermilk and then into the flour and bread crumb mixture, evenly coating the batter so it is dry on the outside.

Slide 2 or 3 steaks into the hot oil, being careful not to crowd them. The temperature of the oil will fall the moment the meat is added, so you will need to adjust the heat. As the steaks cook, try to keep the oil at around 350°F. If it gets too hot, the steaks will burn before they are cooked through. If it is not hot enough, the batter will be soggy. Cook the steaks for 3 to 5 minutes, until the batter is crisp and brown and the meat is cooked through. Using a wire skimmer, transfer the steaks to paper towels to drain and keep in a warm oven until all of the batches are done.

Serve the steaks with the gravy. Plan on 2 steaks for a typical serving; children and dainty eaters will probably want only 1 steak.

BLACK PEPPER GRAVY

This traditional cream gravy is the ultimate topping for chicken-fried steak and mashed potatoes. See photo on page 192.

MAKES ABOUT 3 CUPS
¼ cup unsalted butter
5 tablespoons all-purpose flour
2½ cups milk
2 teaspoons kosher salt
4 teaspoons coarsely ground pepper

In a heavy saucepan, melt the butter over medium-low heat. Whisk the flour into the butter and continue to whisk for about 5 minutes, until the mixture is ivory-colored and smooth. Slowly add the milk while stirring constantly, then continue to stir until free of lumps. Add the salt and pepper and simmer, stirring often, for about 10 minutes, until the gravy has thickened and reduced. Serve hot.

ONION GRAVY

The sweet flavor of this cream gravy comes from slowly caramelizing the onions, which takes patience but pays off.

MAKES ABOUT 3 CUPS
¼ cup unsalted butter
1 large yellow onion, thinly sliced
5 tablespoons all-purpose flour
2½ cups milk
2 teaspoons salt
1 tablespoon Worcestershire sauce

In a heavy saucepan, melt the butter over medium heat. Add the onion, cover, and cook for about 15 minutes, until the onion is soft. Remove the lid and continue to cook the onion for about 15 minutes longer, until most of the liquid evaporates and the onion has caramelized.

Whisk the flour into the onion and continue to cook, whisking constantly, for about 3 minutes, until the mixture is a smooth, light brown. Slowly add the milk while stirring constantly, then continue to stir until free of lumps. Add the salt and Worcestershire sauce and simmer, stirring often, for about 10 minutes, until the gravy has thickened and reduced. Serve hot.

MASHED POTATOES

Grated Parmesan cheese, garlic powder, onion powder, and prepared horseradish are among the ingredients that great cooks add to mashed potatoes. Feel free to experiment. See photo on page 192.

SERVES 4

2 pounds russet potatoes, peeled and cut into
   1½-inch chunks
6 tablespoons unsalted butter
¾ cup milk or half-and-half
Salt and pepper

In a large, heavy saucepan, combine the potatoes with water to cover by 1½ inches and bring to a boil over high heat. Decrease the heat to medium, cover, and cook for about 20 minutes, until the potatoes are just soft when tested with the tip of a knife.

While the potatoes are cooking, in a small saucepan, melt the butter in the milk over medium heat and bring to a simmer.

When the potatoes are cooked, drain them and return them to the pan. Place the pan back on the heat for 1 minute, shaking the potatoes to cook off any remaining water. Add the milk and butter and mash with a potato masher to the desired consistency. Season to taste with salt and pepper. Serve immediately.

Green Onion Mashed Potatoes: Instead of combining the butter and milk, melt the butter in a small sauté pan over medium heat. Add 3 green onions, including the green tops, minced, and cook, stirring often, for 1 to 2 minutes, until soft. Bring the milk to a simmer in a saucepan and add the green onions and butter to the milk. Proceed as directed.

RANCH DRESSING

Once you learn how to make your own ranch dressing, you'll save yourself a fortune on the stuff. And it's really easy. Add some minced herbs from your garden if you like. Chives are another great addition.

MAKES ABOUT 3 CUPS

1 cup sour cream or plain yogurt
¾ cup buttermilk
½ cup mayonnaise
3 tablespoons minced red bell pepper
2 tablespoons minced yellow onion
2 tablespoons minced fresh cilantro
1 tablespoon minced garlic
½ teaspoon salt
½ teaspoon freshly ground pepper

In a bowl, stir together the sour cream, buttermilk, and mayonnaise until smooth. Add the bell pepper, onion, cilantro, garlic, salt, and pepper and mix well. Use immediately, or cover tightly and store in the refrigerator for up to 1 week.

National Championship Chuckwagon Cookoff in Amarillo.

KING RANCH CASSEROLE

Here's one last "ranch" classic. This recipe has absolutely nothing to do with the South Texas ranch of the same name, but it was the comfort food and potluck companion of a generation of Texans. No one knows who actually invented it, but the canned soups suggest that it originated not long after World War II.

SERVES 6 TO 8

4 to 6 bone-in, skin-on chicken breasts

2 cloves garlic, crushed

2 bay leaves

1 tablespoon vegetable oil

1 large yellow onion, diced

1 green bell pepper, seeded and diced

2 (10¾-ounce) cans condensed cream of chicken
  soup

1 (10¾-ounce) can condensed cream of
  mushroom or celery soup

1 (10-ounce) can RO*TEL diced tomatoes and
  green chiles, with juice

12 corn tortillas, torn into quarters

1 pound Cheddar cheese, shredded

In a soup pot, combine the chicken breasts with water just to cover and bring to a boil over high heat. Add the garlic and bay leaves, decrease the heat to a simmer, and cook for 20 minutes, until the chicken is opaque throughout.

Remove the chicken from the broth and reserve the broth. When the chicken is cool enough to handle, remove the meat from the bones, discarding the skin and bones, and shred the meat into pieces. Set aside.

Preheat the oven to 375°F. Butter the bottom of a 9½ by 13½-inch baking dish.

In a large saucepan, heat the oil over medium heat. Add the onion and green pepper and sauté for 5 to 7 minutes, or until soft. Add the soups, RO*TEL tomatoes, ½ cup of the reserved broth (reserve the remaining broth for another use), and the shredded chicken and mix well.

Cover the bottom of the prepared baking dish with half of the tortillas. Spoon half of the chicken mixture evenly over the tortillas, then sprinkle half of the Cheddar cheese over the chicken mixture. Repeat the layers.

Bake for 30 minutes, until the cheese bubbles. Let cool for 10 minutes before serving.

RANCH DRESSING

★ ★

SOME CLASSIC CHICKEN-FRIED STEAKS, like the one at the long-shuttered Stallion in Austin, were served with French fries and salad on the same plate. There was something magical about the combination of the chicken-fried steak and the ranch dressing on the salad.

So how did ranch dressing become such a phenomenon in Texas? One West Texas chef told me it took off when restaurants began serving whipped low-fat spreads instead of real butter. Cowboys craving butterfat responded by dunking their bread and biscuits in the buttermilk dressing instead of using the low-fat spreads. And pretty soon they were dunking their chicken-fried steaks, onion rings, French fries, pizza, and chicken wings in it, too. Wherever the trend got started, it has taken hold of the condiment industry. In 1992, ranch dressing was reportedly the most popular salad dressing in America.

The invention of ranch dressing is generally credited to Steve and Gayle Henson, the couple who owned Hidden Valley Ranch, a dude ranch near Santa Barbara, California. Their salad dressing was so popular that the Hensons started handing out the recipe. Later they sold spice packets that consumers mixed with buttermilk and mayonnaise. In 1972, the Hensons sold their recipe to Clorox, which marketed the dressing in a shelf-stable formula.

The Hensons and Clorox may have given us the name, but the recipe is much older. Although Hidden Valley Ranch dressing was shortened to ranch dressing in popular parlance, the same stuff was once called buttermilk dressing and has long been a western favorite, perhaps with its origin in cowboy cooking.

Here's a recipe that appeared in the *San Antonio Light* on November 3, 1937, long before Hidden Valley Ranch welcomed its first would-be cowboy:

Buttermilk Dressing
MAKES ABOUT 1¹/₂ CUPS

1/2 cup homemade mayonnaise
Juice of 1/2 onion
1/2 teaspoon fresh lemon juice
1/4 teaspoon dry mustard
1/8 teaspoon white pepper
1/8 teaspoon paprika
1 cup thick buttermilk

Stir all of the ingredients into the unbeaten buttermilk.

Plantation BBQ trailer, Richmond.

The Open Air Bar-B-Q on Fredericksburg Road in San Antonio, 1949.

CHAPTER 18

SHADE TREE BARBECUE

★★★★★★★★★★★★★★★★★★★★★★★★★★★★

William Little is famous for his brisket sandwich. The last time I tried one, the meat was incredibly smoky and very tender and the sandwich was loaded with a huge amount of the meat. Barbecue sauce had been drizzled on the bun and the whole thing was topped with raw onions and dill pickles.

Little's Bar B Que is a camper-trailer with a smoker welded into the trailer's frame. The firebox is on the outside of the camper and the doors of the smoker open into the camper's kitchen. The back of the pickup truck that pulls the trailer is loaded with oak and pecan logs. William Little has been working out of this trailer six days a week for the past twenty years. He usually sets up along Highway 3 in Dickinson, near the Kemah Boardwalk and Galveston Bay. But some days he goes to events, like the rodeo in Pasadena. "Did you ever think of entering the cook-off at the Houston rodeo?" I once asked him.

"Nah, I can't afford it," he scoffed, but he doubted he could win anyway. "Black people know how to cook brisket, but the rules for judging are not really about how it tastes. It's all about how pretty it looks. I've eaten brisket cooked by a team that won, and it was nothin' special," Little said, as he handed the coveted sandwich through the little window.

At first I thought it was strange to be eating barbecue with the trunk of my car as a table and traffic whizzing by. But then I started to contemplate the purity of the experience. The smoker was sitting right in front of me. I didn't have to ask what kind of wood was used. It was in full view in the back of the pickup. And there weren't any assistants or waitstaff to filter my questions. There was just me and the barbecue man. I have since become a shade tree barbecue connoisseur. And as I learned more about barbecue history, I came to understand that shade tree barbecue was where it all started.

After the Civil War, makeshift barbecue stands supplied the best barbecue in Texas and the Old South. And because of the fame of some black barbecuers, "whites, in a strange reversal of Jim Crow traditions, made stealthy excursions for take-out orders," according to the *Encyclopedia of Southern Culture*.

In the late 1800s, street-food vendors of all kinds were common across the country. But around 1907, the tamale carts, barbecue stands, and produce wagons began to disappear in Texas and the rest of the country, falling to the reforms of the Progressive Era. With the licensing and inspecting of food-service establishments, Texas barbecue moved into restaurants. Jim Crow laws separating the races gave white-owned barbecue businesses major advantages. Whites opened profitable barbecue restaurants and hired black pit masters to come work for them.

Today, Texas is home to many excellent barbecue restaurants. They use traditional wood-fired barbecue pits and the cooks lovingly prod, baste, and turn the cuts of meat to perfection. These are the places that regularly top every Best Barbecue list.

But many other modern barbecue restaurants have replaced the traditional pits with gas-fired stainless-steel barbecue ovens. The operator fills the oven with meat, pushes a button, and goes home. Not surprisingly, the smoke flavor is minimal. But no matter how it tastes, barbecue produced in a push-button, gas-fired oven is not a part of the artisanal tradition of Texas barbecue.

Push-button barbecue ovens have caused a decline in the average quality of Texas barbecue, but they have also sparked a revival in old-fashioned shade tree barbecue. The popularity of food trucks has inspired many entrepreneurs—black, white, and Hispanic—to install barbecue smokers in mobile food trucks and trailers.

The barbecue you eat on the side of the road ranges in quality from dismal to stellar, but the batting average is surprisingly high. The charm it delivers is the combination of enthusiastic proprietors and old-fashioned methodology. Shade tree barbecue is invariably cooked in wood-burning contraptions manned by barbecue zealots.

Some of these mobile roadside stands carry health-department permits, and some are flying under the radar. I remember spotting a smoker entering a convenience-store parking lot in north Houston one Friday evening around six. Some of the customers hung around and joked with the guys passing out the rib and sausage plates. One eater sipped a beer and joined in the conversation from the open driver's side window without getting out of his car.

Alsatian barbecue at Castroville, 1900.

I walked over to the smoker with my camera and wallet out. "How much is a rib plate?" I asked. Wrong question. "I'll make you a plate and you can give me a donation," the guy doing the cooking said. When I asked the guy his name and raised my camera, he handed me my food, took my money, and told me to go away.

I kept trying to make a joke out of the whole thing. Finally, two large friends of the barbecue man walked over and said, "You best leave now." The ribs were sensational. But I'm afraid if I told you where to find the barbecue man, he and his friends would have to kill me.

"If you want to take pictures, drive over to the next stoplight and take pictures of Chef Ray. He won't care," the barbecue man said, pointing east down Pinemont Street. Chef Ray Latson had an elaborate trailer at the corner of Pinemont and Shepherd that evening. Sadly, when I got to Chef Ray's place, all of his brisket was gone. All I got to taste were some crispy rib tips. "They call me Chef Ray. I cook in the Astros clubhouse," Latson told me. "I barbecue for the sport of it. I come out here on Friday and Saturday evening at nine o'clock and serve until I run out."

A guy walked up to the smoker and waved some money around. "If you want to make a contribution to the church, I am happy to take your money and pass it along," Ray said, pointing at the structure across the street. "I only have one plate of barbecue left."

★ ★ ★

Church picnics and fundraisers are another reliable source of great shade tree barbecue. Out in front of McCoy's Lumber on Avenue H in Rosenberg, a church group sets up folding tables and chairs under a blue plastic–roofed tent with a sign in front that reads "Barbecue Sale." The pit boss, Reverend Leroy Hodge, and his group have been selling barbecue there one Sunday a month for the past five years.

There was only one item on the menu of the New Hope Missionary Baptist Church Building Fund Barbecue stand: a three-meat plate loaded with falling-apart tender sliced brisket, crunchy rib chunks, and thin, lengthwise slices of sausage. The meat was cooked on a big double trailer parked alongside the tent. The reverend selected some choice cuts for me.

"Brisket? Ribs? Sausage?" inquired church secretary Lillie Brown as she assembled my dinner. The meat was sliced and piled high in a square Styrofoam to-go box. "Barbecue sauce?" she asked with the ladle poised.

Pickles, onions, jalapeños, and white bread were all available as options for those inclined to make sandwiches. The side orders were homemade baked beans and mashed potato salad with yellow mustard dished up out of plastic containers the church ladies had brought from home. Tea cakes and other bake-sale items were also displayed. Nobody said anything about money, so I made a donation of twenty dollars, ten bucks for the barbecue plate and ten bucks for two bags of tea cakes.

★ ★ ★

One of my favorite breakfast spots is the Plantation barbecue and taco truck in front of Lev's Auto Body Shop on 90A near Richmond. The breakfast taco menu includes a smoked brisket and scrambled egg taco.

The stand is run by Lolo Garcia and his wife, Rose. Lolo carved the barbecued brisket and Rose chopped the meat up and tossed it on the griddle until it got crisp. Then she mixed it with scrambled eggs and salt and pepper. A fluffy flour tortilla was generously stuffed with the brisket and eggs and topped with pico de gallo. Then the whole thing was wrapped in aluminum foil so you could eat it in the car.

But I wasn't in a hurry. I sat down at the little picnic table surrounded by chairs made out of tree trunk slices. I also sampled a taco with nothing but barbecued brisket and pico de gallo. The tender smoked brisket was sensational. I loved the whole idea of this barbecue–Tex-Mex taco truck fusion cuisine.

"I bought this barbecue trailer in 1989," Lolo Garcia told me. "Back in the sixties, I was the first one to sell breakfast tacos in Victoria. My place was called Taco Village. Then the economy went bust in the 1980s and I was going under. So I sold my taco places. I decided to get into barbecue because so many people were coming up here from Mexico and opening taco stands. I wanted to do something different. We started selling brisket and egg tacos to use up the rest of the barbecue meat. In the summer we sell a lot of breakfast tacos. That's what keeps us going." Lolo opens at six thirty in the morning and closes at two in the summer. "It gets too hot in the afternoon," he said.

★ ★ ★

By my definition, weekend-only barbecue establishments like Gil's Bar-B-Que Shack on Highway 71 near Ellinger also fall under the category of shade tree barbecue. Gil's is housed in a storage hut sort of structure; inside you'll find a couple of tables, a fridge for the drinks, and the cash register. When I stopped by one Sunday afternoon at two o'clock, Mary Vrazel was reading the Sunday paper and Gil Vrazel was next door at the house napping.

When I asked if there was any barbecue left, Mary took me around back to the old smoker that is sheltered inside a rickety screened-in porch. There wasn't any brisket left, but there was the end of a smoked pork butt and some Czech sausage. I asked for a little of each. I paid for the food and then went to sit at the picnic table under the giant live oaks in the backyard. The pork was moist with fat and nicely smoked; the fatty homemade Czech sausage was coarsely ground and flavored with mustard seeds and garlic.

Gil came out of the house looking sheepish and sat down with me. I told him that I had been driving by this place for decades. I always stopped next door

Gil Vrazel's Bar-B-Que Shack is only open on weekends.

at Hruska's Store & Bakery. Hruska's sells gas, bakes excellent poppy seed kolaches, and makes a serious hand-formed, half-pound hamburger. And Hruska's is open seven days a week.

"Barbecue is just a hobby," Gil Vrazel said. "We are open only on weekends. I work at the livestock auction barn in Columbus on weekdays." Gil said business was really good during football season, when Longhorn fans from Houston drive by on their way to the game in Austin. "We used to have a whole bunch of picnic tables back here under the trees." I asked Gil why he discontinued the picnic grove.

"Too much trouble," he said. "One time these people in really fancy clothes came back here to eat. I'll never forget this one lady had on a big white coat. They put their barbecue plates down, and then they all sat down on the same side of the picnic table. The table tipped over and the barbecue slid off into their laps. That lady's white coat got barbecue sauce all over it. She was furious." Gil decided life was too short to waste time teaching people how to use a picnic table.

One day while I was checking out a grocery store that sells cracklings, I saw a large cloud of smoke rising from a parked vehicle on Laura Koppe Road near the corner of Homestead in the verdant outer reaches of Houston's Fifth Ward. It was lunchtime, so I pulled over and got in line at Gregory Carter's Bar-B-Que Done Right trailer. When I asked for some brisket, Carter scowled at me from behind the window and said, "No brisket."

"You don't cook brisket?" I asked.

"Oh, I cook brisket all right," he said. "But I don't sell it until it's done. Come back around two." I settled for some African American–style beef links. These are made with finely ground beef, lots of tallow, and spices. In the old days, when beef links were made with more fat, you would squeeze the bright orange sausage stuffing out onto a slice of Wonder bread, decorate the spicy goo with raw onion slices and pickles, and eat it like a sandwich. Gregory Carter's beef links aren't quite that fatty, but they are close.

IN HIS OWN WORDS: GREGORY CARTER

★ ★

I WAS A ROUTE SALESMAN FOR Blue Bell ice cream for twenty-four years. I made good money at it. But I had a passion for barbecue. I started competing in barbecue cook-offs about ten years ago. I was on the Los Planos barbecue team. As you can tell by the name, it was a mostly Hispanic gang. Everybody had a specialty. One guy did beans, one guy did chicken. I was the brisket specialist. I took third place in brisket at the Fort Bend barbecue cook-off in 2004.

I had my own barbecue trailer that I used for cook-offs and catering jobs. Then in 2006, I bought this truck. I parked it in the garage for a while, until I had enough money to fix it up. When I got it going, I started taking it out on Saturday night and setting up in the parking lot in front on my uncle's bar, The High Steppers Lounge at the corner of Lanewood and Laura Koppe.

I made my own potato salad and pinto beans. The only things I had to buy were bread and pickles. I sell two hundred plates at an average of eight dollars a plate. That's good money. Pretty soon I decided to quit the ice cream business and just do barbecue for a living.

Now I work Wednesday, Friday, and Saturday. I always park at the same corner on Laura Koppe where I started out. I do ribs and old-fashioned beef links for lunch. The brisket isn't ready until dinnertime. I won't sell any brisket that isn't all the way done, and I like to smoke my brisket for at least twelve hours. Most of my business is at two in the morning, after the bar closes. I sell out every night. It's a pretty rough crowd. The first thing you learn is not to keep all your money in one place.

I started experimenting with specials. Like I do stuffed pork chops sometimes. I buy a whole pork loin and make double-thick chops. Then I cut a pocket in each chop and fill the pockets with boudin. Then I rub the outside of the chops with olive oil so they don't stick to the grill and I smoke them for a couple of hours. You'd be amazed at all the different kind of food you can cook on a barbecue smoker.

His sides were sensational. The homemade pinto beans had big chunks of pork and lots of fresh chiles in them. The creamy mashed potato salad was seasoned with yellow mustard and pickle relish.

★ ★ ★

The story of Franklin Barbecue in Austin is a barbecue trailer rags-to-riches tale. When I first met Aaron Franklin he was running a two-trailer operation in the parking lot of a former Texaco gas station in East Austin. His brisket became justly famous in a short time. The wonderful smoky flavor and perfect moist texture put it in the ethereal category.

The Franklin Barbecue trailer was once counted among the top food trailers in Austin's vibrant street-food scene. Young entrepreneurs who can't afford to open full-on restaurants are creating some intriguing fare in less expensive mobile eateries. The low prices and picnic-grove ambience fit perfectly with Austin's college-town lifestyle.

Franklin Barbecue opened in December 2009. On the Sunday morning I stopped by, twenty-four patrons were waiting when the chain-link gate opened at eleven. By one thirty, all of the meat was sold out. An hour and a half after he had opened it, Aaron Franklin slipped the padlock on the gate and closed his shade tree barbecue operation with a full cash register and no leftovers.

"My first memory of barbecue was sitting on my grandpa's knee while he played dominoes at Martin's Barbecue in Bryan," Franklin told me. "Martin was my grandpa's friend. When I was nine or ten years old, my parents bought a place called Ben's Bar-B-Que in Bryan. I worked there all the time. I didn't graduate from high school. I moved to Austin and joined a band. I am a drummer. I have been in lots of rock and roll bands. We got gigs, but it never went anywhere."

In 2004, Aaron Franklin bought a cheap smoker and started cooking briskets. "It was a nostalgia rush after all the years I spent smelling barbecue." His first brisket was a disaster, but he kept cooking them. "I started getting real nerdy with it, tweaking this and that. I got pretty good," Franklin said.

After cooking barbecue in his backyard, Franklin got a job at John Mueller's Barbecue on Manor Road. When Mueller went out of business, he bought his steel cylinder barbecue pit for a thousand dollars. He started his barbecue trailer business with ten thousand dollars he inherited from his grandmother.

"Our grand-opening party was December 6, 2009," Franklin said. "When we opened, I had twenty-eight cents in the bank. We used the money we made the first day to buy the next day's groceries. There were a lot of food bloggers at the party. They started getting the word out pretty fast. It got really busy, really quick."

Franklin Barbecue is now located in a brick-and-mortar building at 900 East Eleventh Street, the former home of Ben's Long Branch BBQ. Franklin still opens at eleven o'clock in the morning and closes the place when he runs out of barbecue. The line begins forming before ten. He sometimes sells out before noon.

"I always wanted a real barbecue restaurant," Franklin told me with a smile. Now he has the most popular barbecue joint in Austin.

SHADE TREE RIBS

Make an effort to find a small (less than 4 pounds) rack of spareribs before you fire up the smoker. If you start with the typical 4- to 5-pound racks sold in supermarkets, you will need to braise them first.

SERVES 2 TO 4
1 (3½-pound) rack spareribs or baby back ribs
1 cup Hog Rub (page 213)

Trim the ribs (see box below), then season both sides with the rub. Wrap the ribs in plastic wrap and refrigerate overnight.

Prepare a fire for indirect-heat cooking (the coals on one side only) in your smoker with a water pan. Use wood chips, chunks, or logs and keep up a good level of smoke. The smoker is ready when the temperature is between 250°F and 300°F.

RIB TWEAKING

★ ★ ★ ★ ★ ★ ★ ★ ★ ★ ★ ★ ★ ★ ★ ★ ★ ★

Trimming Ribs: To trim a rack of spareribs, cut off the breastbone, the loose meat of the back flap, and the tiny lower ribs. This should produce a squared-up rack that fits nicely on the grill. The breastbone is connected to the top few ribs—it runs north and south, unlike the ribs, which run east and west. Removing the breastbone also makes carving the rack at the table easier.

Skinning Ribs: Many cooks also like to remove the membrane on the bone side of the rack. Some argue that removing it speeds cooking time; some say it makes the ribs more tender. I remove the membrane because the ribs look more appetizing without it.

Put the ribs in the smoker on the cool side of the grate and close the lid. Cook for 3 hours, turning the ribs over after the first hour and then every 30 minutes. Add wood as needed to keep the fire burning evenly. The ribs are ready when a toothpick goes through the meat easily or an instant-read thermometer inserted into the meat away from the bone registers 165°F.

Remove the ribs, wrap them in aluminum foil, and then return them to the cool side of the grill grate for 30 minutes, turning once after 15 minutes. Allow the ribs to sit for at least another 15 minutes before serving. The meat should be falling-apart tender. Cut the ribs apart to serve.

GREGORY CARTER'S BOUDIN-STUFFED BBQ PORK CHOPS

These tasty smoked chops are a great bonus meal you can make while you are barbecuing something else.

SERVES 2 TO 4
2 bone-in, double-thick pork loin chops (about 1 pound each)
1 link Cajun boudin (about 8 ounces)
½ cup Hog Rub (recipe follows)

Prepare a fire for indirect-heat cooking (the coals on one side only) in your smoker with a water pan. Use wood chips, chunks, or logs and keep up a good level of smoke. The smoker is ready when the temperature is between 275°F and 325°F.

While the smoker is heating, prepare the chops. Insert a sharp paring knife into the side of the meaty part of the pork chop all the way to the bone, and then carefully cut in each direction to create a cavity for the stuffing. Squeeze the boudin out of its casing. Divide the sausage in half, and stuff half of it into the pocket in each pork chop. Sprinkle both sides of each chop with the rub. Spray the chops lightly with nonstick cooking spray so the meat won't stick to the grill.

Place the chops in the smoker directly over the fire and sear briefly on both sides to make good-looking grill marks. Move the chops to the cool side of the grate and close the lid. Cook for about 2 hours, adding wood every hour as needed to keep the fire burning evenly, until an instant-read thermometer inserted into the center of a chop away from the stuffing and bone registers 145°F for medium.

Let the chops rest for 15 minutes before carving and serving.

HOG RUB

A little bit of brown sugar is what makes it a pork rub. If you're looking for a shortcut, just add brown sugar to your favorite barbecue rub.

MAKES ABOUT 1 CUP
¼ cup kosher salt
¼ cup chili powder, homemade (page 110) or store-bought
2 tablespoons light brown sugar
2 tablespoons coarsely ground black pepper
2 tablespoons garlic powder
2 tablespoons onion powder
1 tablespoon cayenne pepper

In a small bowl, stir together all of the ingredients, mixing well. Store the rub in a tightly capped shaker jar or regular jar. It will keep in a cool cupboard for a couple of months.

BASIC BBQ RUB

The German Texan barbecue rub is the most basic: just salt and pepper with a pinch of cayenne. Czech Texans like a lot of garlic, Polish Texans add garlic and marjoram, Alsatian Texans love coriander, Lebanese Texans put cinnamon in their rubs, and the Tejanos have to have both chile powder and cumin. Have fun!

MAKES ABOUT ½ CUP
3 tablespoons sea salt
2 tablespoons granulated garlic
2 tablespoons coarsely ground black pepper
Pinch of cayenne pepper
1 teaspoon ground dried herb of your choice
(optional)

In a small bowl, stir together all of the ingredients, mixing well. Be sure to break up any lumps. Store the rub in a tightly capped jar. It will keep in a cool cupboard for a couple of months. Shake or stir well again before use.

AARON FRANKLIN'S BUTCHER PAPER BRISKET

At Franklin Barbecue, Aaron Franklin seasons USDA Prime briskets with nothing but salt and pepper and puts them fat side up in the smoker. He starts the next day's briskets in the evening, smoking them with post oak or live oak for 6 to 8 hours and cooks them to the unheard-of internal temperature of 201°F to 203°F. They get a light spray of diluted Worcestershire sauce about 2 hours before they are ready, to keep them moist.

SERVES 10
1 (8- to 10-pound) first-quality beef brisket, untrimmed
Salt and coarsely ground pepper
¼ cup Worcestershire sauce
¼ cup water

Sprinkle the brisket on both sides with salt and pepper. Combine the Worcestershire sauce and water in a mister.

Prepare a fire for indirect-heat cooking in your smoker (the coals on one side only) with a water pan. Use wood chips, chunks, or logs and keep up a good level of smoke. The smoker is ready when the temperature is between 275°F and 300°F.

Put the brisket in the smoker on the cool side of the grate and close the lid. Cook for 6 hours, adding wood as needed to keep the fire burning evenly. At this point, test the brisket with an instant-read thermometer; the internal temperature should be 165°F.

Remove the brisket from the smoker. Spray it with some of the Worcestershire solution (there will be a lot left over), wrap it in butcher paper, and return it to the smoker. Let it cook in the paper for 2 hours longer.

Remove the wrapped brisket from the smoker and place it in an empty cooler or a 200°F oven for 3 or 4 hours. The brisket is done when a toothpick passes effortlessly through the fat or an instant-read thermometer inserted into the center registers at least 185°F (but preferably as high as 203°F).

To ensure the brisket remains moist, do not trim away the fat cap before serving. Slice only as much brisket as needed and serve immediately. The remainder will keep well wrapped in the refrigerator for up to 1 week.

FRANKLIN'S ESPRESSO BBQ SAUCE

Aaron Franklin's barbecue trailer used to be located behind a friend's coffee-roasting operation. Because freshly made espresso was always available, Aaron Franklin started making this distinctive espresso barbecue sauce. He recommends it with his brisket.

MAKES ABOUT 7 CUPS

4 cups ketchup

1 cup water

½ cup cider vinegar

½ cup distilled white vinegar

6 tablespoons brewed espresso

¼ cup Worcestershire sauce

2 tablespoons chili powder, homemade (page 110) or store-bought

1 tablespoon kosher salt

1 tablespoon coarsely ground pepper

In a saucepan, combine all of the ingredients, stir well, and bring to a simmer over medium heat. Simmer gently for 20 minutes to blend the flavors.

Use immediately, or let cool, cover, and store in the refrigerator for up to 3 weeks.

CHIPOTLE BBQ SAUCE

The flavor of the chipotles makes this sauce taste smoky before you even light the fire. Use the sauce to add barbecue flavor to food that wasn't actually smoked, such as grilled hamburgers or pork chops.

MAKES ABOUT 8 CUPS

1 (7-ounce) can chipotle chiles in adobo sauce

2 tablespoons unsalted butter

1 cup minced yellow onions

4 cloves garlic, minced

3 cups ketchup

1 cup water

1 cup orange juice

1 cup cider vinegar

¼ cup light molasses or cane syrup

1½ cups firmly packed light brown sugar

1 tablespoon Worcestershire sauce

1 tablespoon salt

Seed the chiles and put them in a blender with the sauce from the can. Process until smooth.

In a skillet, melt the butter over medium heat. Add the onions and sauté for 5 minutes, until beginning to soften. Add the garlic and continue to sauté for 5 minutes longer, until the onions and garlic are soft. Add the pureed chiles, ketchup, water, orange juice, vinegar, molasses, brown sugar, Worcestershire sauce, and salt and stir well. Bring to a simmer and cook gently for 15 minutes to blend the flavors.

Use immediately, or let cool, cover, and store in the refrigerator for up to 3 weeks.

PULLED PORK

A whole hog was the original Southern barbecue meat, but Boston butt, another name for pork shoulder, has largely replaced it. It's a lot easier to handle 5-pound pork shoulder roasts than a 100-pound pig. Pork shoulder roasts are easy to cook—the cut is loaded with fat and very forgiving—as long as you don't undercook it or burn it, it will probably taste great. If you opt to shred the cooked pork, rather than slice it, serve it on sandwiches with your favorite barbecue sauce.

SERVES 8 TO 10
1 (4- to 5-pound) bone-in pork shoulder roast
6 tablespoons Hog Rub (page 213)
2 yellow onions, halved
3 cups Barbecue Mop (recipe follows)

Season the pork roast with the rub, pressing the spice mix into the meat. Wrap in plastic wrap and refrigerate overnight.

Prepare a fire for indirect-heat cooking (the coals on one side only) in your smoker with a water pan. Put the onion halves in the water pan. Use wood chips, chunks, or logs and keep up a good level of smoke. The smoker is ready when the temperature is between 210°F and 250°F

Put the pork roast in the smoker on the cool side of the grate and close the lid. Mop the pork every 30 minutes with the mop sauce, turning the roast at the same time so it cooks evenly. Add wood as needed to keep the fire burning evenly. The meat should be ready in 4 to 5 hours. It is done when the Y bone protrudes. Don't worry about overcooking it, however. It will just keep getting better. When an instant-read thermometer inserted into the center of the roast away from the bone registers 175°F, you can serve the meat in slices. For pulled pork, you need to leave the roast in the smoker until the temperature registers 190°F or preferably 200°F.

To serve, slice or pull the pork from the bone, removing the big chunks of fat as you go. To make pulled pork, shred the meat by hand.

BARBECUE MOP

A mop sauce is not a barbecue sauce that you eat. It is a basting sauce to keep the barbecue moist during cooking. Wish-Bone Italian Dressing is a popular mop sauce because it contains oil, vinegar, garlic, and seasonings, which is basically what you are looking for in a good mop sauce. Start with beef broth if you are basting beef, or use chicken broth for chicken or pork, and use a small cotton mop to swab it on the meat.

MAKES ABOUT 3 CUPS
2 cups beef or chicken broth
¼ cup cider vinegar
5 bay leaves
1 teaspoon ground dried oregano
1 cup olive oil
2 tablespoons unsalted butter
½ cup chopped yellow onions
¼ cup minced garlic
2 tablespoons Basic BBQ Rub (page 214)
1 teaspoon dry mustard
1 teaspoon salt
1 teaspoon pepper
Grated zest and juice of 2 lemons
2 tablespoons soy sauce

In a saucepan, bring the broth to a boil over high heat. Add the vinegar, bay leaves, and oregano and decrease the heat to a gentle simmer.

In a skillet, heat the oil and butter over medium-high heat. When the butter melts, add the onions, garlic, BBQ rub, mustard, salt, and pepper and cook for 5 to 7 minutes, until the onions wilt. Add the onion mixture, lemon zest and juice, and soy sauce to the broth mixture and stir to mix well. Transfer the pan to the barbecue firebox and keep at a gentle simmer while using.

THE LAST OF THE OPEN PITS

★ ★

AT THE TURN OF THE LAST CENTURY, barbecue was prepared for large gatherings in long earthen pits. Walter Jetton, the barbecue impresario who catered Lyndon Johnson's barbecues at the LBJ Ranch also cooked on an open pit. The idea of enclosing the pit to capture the smoke was crazy in Jetton's opinion. The open pit was very popular with health department inspectors.

I thought that the old open pit barbecue method had disappeared until I met the folks at Texas Dance Hall Preservation, a group that that is trying to preserve the old structures. The dance halls were built by German *Verein* societies—secular organizations dedicated to choral singing, marksmanship, or some other activity. The Germans and later some Czech groups built over a thousand dance halls in Texas—some five hundred still exist.

Almost every hall had a barbecue pit, and some of them still have the Southern-style open pit design that dates back several centuries.

At a dance hall symposium where I gave a talk about barbecue, I was invited to attend several open pit barbecues that are still held as annual events at old German dance halls and Sons of Hermann Lodges. At the first one I attended at the Millheim Verein Hall, I was astonished to witness an open pit loaded with hundreds of pounds of beef, pork, and mutton. The barbecue "gravy" was also prepared in the traditional way—in a cast iron wash tub stirred with a paddle. The barbecued meats were delicious.

BEEF LINKS

Don't skimp on the beef fat. It is what makes the links juicy.

SERVES 12
3½ pounds boneless beef chuck
1½ pounds beef fat
½ cup paprika
¼ cup salt
2 tablespoons pepper
1 tablespoon garlic powder
Several lengths large-size natural hog casings

Cut the beef and fat into strips, trimming away any gristle or other tough pieces. In a small bowl or cup, stir together the paprika, salt, pepper, and garlic powder. Fit a meat grinder with the fine plate. Pass the beef and fat through the grinder, capturing them in a large bowl. Add a little of the spice mixture to the grinder as you go so the spices will become well incorporated with the meat. Transfer the ground meat to a stand mixer fitted with the paddle attachment and beat on low speed until the spices are

thoroughly incorporated. Cover the mixture and refrigerate for about 3 or 4 hours, until cold.

Soak the hog casings in lukewarm water. Then, using a sausage stuffer or a pastry bag fitted with a ½-inch plain tip, stuff the casings with the meat mixture. As each casing length is filled, tie off one end with kitchen twine, then twist the filled casing into 4- to 6-inch links, forcing out any air bubbles and making the links tight. Finally, tie off the other end. Wrap well and store in the refrigerator for up to 4 days or freeze for up to 2 months.

To smoke the sausages, prepare a fire for indirect-heat cooking (the coals on one side only) in your smoker. Use wood chips, chunks, or logs and keep up a good level of smoke. The smoker is ready when the temperature is about 250°F.

Put the sausage links in the smoker on the cool side of the grill grate and close the lid. Cook, turning as needed to cook evenly, for 35 to 45 minutes, until cooked through. Serve hot.

LOLO'S BRISKET TACOS

This fusion of Texas barbecue and Tex-Mex taco truck cooking is a natural.

SERVES 4
6 to 8 ounces barbecued brisket (3 or 4 slices)
1 tablespoon vegetable oil
¼ cup chopped yellow onions
¼ cup chopped green bell peppers
Salt and pepper
4 corn tortillas, warmed
**Homegrown Tomato Pico de Gallo (page 220),
  for garnish**

Trim any gristle from the brisket, but leave the fat intact. In a skillet, heat the oil over medium heat. Add the brisket slices and cook, turning often, for about 5 minutes, until the meat is lightly browned and the fat melts. Remove from the heat and transfer the brisket to a cutting board. Trim away the excess

fat, if desired. Chop the brisket into bite-size pieces and return them to the pan.

Return the skillet to medium-high heat, add the onions and peppers and sauté for 3 to 5 minutes, until the vegetables are soft and the meat is crispy. Season with salt and pepper.

Divide the brisket mixture evenly among the tortillas. Garnish with the pico de gallo and serve at once.

PLANTATION BRISKET BREAKFAST TACOS

I don't know why I never thought of this ingenious use for leftover brisket before I visited the Plantation BBQ trailer, but it's a favorite at my house now. Sometimes I use my own leftover brisket, and sometimes I use the brisket I carried home in a doggy bag from a barbecue stand.

SERVES 4

6 to 8 ounces barbecued brisket (3 or 4 slices)
1 tablespoon vegetable oil
¼ cup chopped yellow onions
4 eggs
1 tablespoon milk
Salt and pepper
4 flour tortillas, warmed
Tabasco or other red hot-pepper sauce, for
    serving

Trim any gristle from the brisket, but leave the fat intact. In a skillet, heat the oil over medium heat. Add the brisket slices and cook, turning often, for about 5 minutes, until the meat is lightly browned and the fat melts. Remove from the heat and transfer the brisket to a cutting board. Trim away the excess fat, if desired. Chop the brisket into bite-size pieces and return them to the pan.

Return the skillet to medium heat, add the onions, and sauté for 3 to 5 minutes, until the onions

(Continued)

are soft and the meat is crispy. Remove from the heat and reserve.

In a bowl, beat together the eggs and milk and season with salt and pepper. Pour a little of the fat from the skillet containing the onions into your favorite egg pan. Place the egg pan over medium heat and add the eggs. When the eggs begin to set, add the brisket and onions. Incorporate the meat as you scramble the eggs, keeping the long curds of cooked egg intact.

When the eggs are ready, divide the egg and brisket mixture evenly among the tortillas. Season with the Tabasco, wrap the tortilla around the filling, and serve at once.

Potato Variation: Add ½ cup diced cooked potatoes to the pan when you add the brisket and onions to the eggs.

Chile Variation: Add ½ serrano chile, chopped, when you add the brisket and onions to the eggs.

Refried Beans Variation: Smear each tortilla with 1 tablespoon Refried Beans (page 143) before topping with the scrambled eggs and brisket.

HOMEGROWN TOMATO PICO DE GALLO

Homegrown tomatoes make the best pico de gallo. Soaking the onion in lime juice "cooks" it a little (think of ceviche).

MAKES ABOUT 2 CUPS
½ cup minced white onions
Juice of 2 limes
1 large serrano chile
1½ cups finely chopped homegrown tomatoes
1 clove garlic, minced
Sea salt
¼ cup chopped fresh cilantro

In a small bowl, combine the onion and lime juice and let stand for at least 10 minutes. Stem the chile and halve lengthwise. Remove the seeds and ribs if you want a milder salsa and leave them intact if you like it hot. Mince the chile.

In a bowl, combine the onion and lime juice, chile, tomatoes, and garlic and stir well. Season with salt. Cover and refrigerate for 30 minutes to allow the flavors to blend. Stir in the cilantro just before serving.

BOCK-BRINED BBQ CHICKEN

To keep barbecued chicken moist, you need to brine it or marinate it before you put it in the smoker. Here's an easy marinade that starts with a bottle of Shiner Bock (see page 150).

SERVES 4
8 cups hot water
1 (12-ounce) bottle Shiner Bock or beer of your choice
½ cup sea salt
2 tablespoons hot-pepper sauce
1 tablespoon freshly ground pepper
1 teaspoon ground dried thyme
1 (3- to 4-pound) whole chicken
½ cup Basic BBQ Rub (page 214)
1 (16-ounce) bottle Italian salad dressing

Select a container that will fit in your refrigerator and is large enough to hold the chicken and the brine. Pour the hot water and beer into the container, add the salt, hot-pepper sauce, pepper, and thyme, and stir until all of the salt has dissolved. Refrigerate the brine to cool completely.

If the giblets have been included with the chicken, remove them and reserve them for another use. Place the chicken on a cutting board, back side up. Using a sharp knife or poultry shears, and starting at the cavity end, cut along one side of the backbone. Pull the chicken open and cut along the other side of the backbone and remove the back. Put the chicken in the cooled brine, and place a weight on top of the chicken to keep it submerged. Cover and refrigerate for 24 hours.

Prepare a fire for indirect-heat cooking (the coals on one side only) in your smoker with a water pan. Use wood chips, chunks, or logs and keep up a good level of smoke. The smoker is ready when the temperature is between 225°F and 275°F.

Remove the chicken from the brine and pat dry, then rub the chicken all over with the rub. Put the butterflied chicken, bone side down, in the smoker on the cool side of the grate and cook for 3 hours, mopping it with the Italian dressing every 30 minutes. Add wood as needed to keep the fire burning evenly. To test for doneness, insert an instant-read thermometer into the thickest part of a thigh away from the bone; it should register 155°F. Alternatively, insert a knife tip into the thickest part of the thigh; the chicken is ready if the juices run clear.

To serve, cut the chicken into 6 to 8 pieces (for 6 pieces you'll want 2 drumsticks, 2 thighs, and 2 breasts with wings, or for 8 pieces, cut the breasts in half) and serve hot with your favorite barbecue sauce on the side.

BRINED HONEY-THYME PORK LOIN

You can experiment with all sorts of sweet flavors when brining pork. Cooking a pork loin is different from cooking a pork shoulder. Pork shoulder keeps getting better with longer cooking. But pork loin should be cooked just until it is done and then removed quickly from the heat before it dries out.

SERVES 8 TO 12

8 cups hot water
½ cup sea salt
¾ cup Texas honey
3 cloves garlic, minced
2 tablespoons Tabasco sauce
1 tablespoon pepper
1 teaspoon ground dried thyme
1 (4- to 6-pound) boneless pork loin roast
½ cup Hog Rub (page 213)

Select a container that will fit in your refrigerator and is large enough to hold the pork roast and the brine. Pour the hot water into the container, add the salt, honey, garlic, Tabasco sauce, pepper, and thyme, and stir until all of the salt has dissolved. Refrigerate the brine to cool completely.

Put the pork roast in the cooled brine, and place a weight on top of the roast to keep it submerged. Cover and refrigerate for 36 hours. To test if it is ready, slice off a little piece of the pork and fry it to see if it tastes right to you. If it is overcured, it will taste salty; if it is undercured, it won't have much flavor. The average brining time for a pork loin roast is 36 to 48 hours.

Prepare a fire for indirect-heat cooking (the coals on one side only) in your smoker with a water pan. Use wood chips, chunks, or logs and keep up a good level of smoke. The smoker is ready when the temperature is between 275°F and 325°F.

Remove the pork from the brine and pat dry, then rub the pork all over with the rub. Put the roast in the smoker on the cool side of the grill and cook for about 3 hours, adding wood as needed to keep the fire burning evenly. The roast is ready when an instant-read thermometer inserted into the center of the roast registers 145°F.

Let the roast rest for 15 minutes before carving and serving.

Jimi's Frontier Drive-In, San Antonio, 1954.

CHAPTER 19

HAMBURGERS AND CARHOPS

★★★★★★★★★★★★★★★★★★★★★★★★

The burger was a monster—well over a pound of ground meat scorched to a forbidding-looking shade of black, with charred bits on the outside that crunched between your molars. The dark crust was a delightful contrast to the rosy pink interior that literally oozed juices. The homemade bun was decorated with the traditional Texas garnishes: pickles, onions, lettuce, and tomato, with mustard and mayo spread on the bun. I gave this purist's rendition of the Texas hamburger a perfect ten on my ballot. But when the results of the Uncle Fletch Hamburger Cook-off were announced, this awesome classic burger didn't even make the top three.

The contest was held in Athens, an East Texas town that calls itself the Original Home of the Hamburger. In a field of fifteen contestants, I awarded three perfect tens. Maybe my standards were too lenient. Or, maybe after years of eating cooked-to-death hamburgers made from frozen patties, I was just overjoyed to see so many old-fashioned hand-formed burgers all in one place.

When I heard that the Athens hamburger cook-off had been revived in 2005, I called the organizers and talked them into letting me be a judge. I was the restaurant critic of the *Houston Press* at the time, and although I was exaggerating when I told them I was a burger expert, I promised myself I would mitigate my half-truth by using the intervening months to "cram."

In preparation for my stint as a burger judge, I set off on a tour of Texas burgers. For my remedial eating, I sought out the state's famous burgers I had read about but never tried. Between early April and the June 11 cook-off, I sampled sixty-five Texas hamburgers. I was following in the footsteps of other notable food journalists.

In 1998, *New York Times* food writer William Grimes drove around the state sampling burgers both famous and unheralded. In his article, "The Pride of Texas on a Bun," Grimes concluded, "What the croissant is to France, what goulash is to Hungary, what pickled herring is to Sweden, the hamburger is to Texas. It is a symbol, a necessity and a triumph, a part of the cultural patrimony so tightly woven into the fabric of Texas life that Texans themselves do not even remark on it."

The roots of the hamburger are so deep in Texas culture, Grimes postulates, "that even the forces of modernization can't quite pull them up." It's why Texans still prefer big honking beef patties, why they place more trust in greasy side-of-the road joints than national chains, and how they instinctively know that "all the way" means pickles, onions, lettuce, and tomato, with mustard and mayo—but never ketchup.

The ultimate Texas hamburger, according to Grimes, is found at a joint called Arnold's in Amarillo. Embarrassed that I had never been there, I caught a plane to the Panhandle city to check out the place. It was a sorry dump with cracked concrete floors, eight tables, and an air conditioner that barely functioned.

But if you're looking for icons, it's hard to top the Texas-shaped hamburger at Arnold's. A three-quarter-pound patty pressed flat on a griddle and cooked well done, the burger is served on a Texas-shaped bun with pickles, onions, lettuce, and tomato, plus mustard and mayo. You have to take several bites of plain meat that spread out beyond the borders of the bun before you get to the Rio Grande and the condiments beyond it, but if you like beef, that's not all bad.

While I sat and ate my burger, owner Gayla Arnold berated members of the local high-school football team when they attempted to order three-quarter-pound burgers. Growing boys needed double-meat burgers, with a pound and half of meat, Gayla Arnold contended. Two of the linemen followed her advice.

"I thought the burger patty itself would be shaped liked Texas," I told Arnold.

"Well sometimes it is," she admitted, looking over at the griddle beside her. "It depends on how much we've got going on."

At the moment, the griddle was crowded because it held one of Arnold's giant "family burgers." It's an eighteen-inch, ten-pound patty served on a giant bread round and it feeds ten to twelve people. They also have a twenty-four-inch version, which claims to be the biggest burger in Texas. Arnold's is a lot of fun. But I think the ultimate Texas hamburger is something a little less self-conscious. Maybe something like the tostada burger at Chris Madrid's in San Antonio.

The tostada burger starts with a hamburger patty that's been whacked flat with a spatula on the griddle and cooked well done and crispy. The flattened patty is so wide that it extends beyond the toasted bun on all sides. It comes slathered with refried beans and layered with tortilla chips. Jalapeños are fifty cents extra, but, in my opinion, indispensable. The crowning glory, and Chris Madrid's trademark, is a mound of Cheddar cheese melted on top of the burger, beans, and chips until it flows over the edge of the patty and solidifies on the plate beneath it. It looks like a Cheddar cheese waterfall on a bun.

Chris Madrid's, a roomy Blanco Street icehouse and burger emporium, frequently ranks at the top of San Antonio Best Burger surveys. Although my basis for comparison was limited to the four San Antonio hamburger joints I had made it to that day, Chris Madrid's was my favorite.

The tostada burger is one of several variations on an old San Antonio tradition called a bean burger. Invented near Fort Sam Houston in the 1950s at a joint called Sill's Snack Shop, the original bean burger was a regular beef patty on a bun, topped with refried beans, Fritos corn chips, and a dollop of Cheez Whiz. Lots of burger joints in San Antonio serve the old version. Upscale variations include bean burgers made with black beans or with guacamole added.

In his book *Hamburgers and Fries*, author John T. Edge postulates that America is experiencing a burger renaissance. He spends an entire chapter on the bean burger, comparing its sense of place with that of cedar-planked salmon in Washington.

If a burger renaissance means a return to the style of an earlier time, there is no better place to sample the burger's classic era than Texas. Folks like Edge who come here to sample such oddities as the 1950s-era bean burger invariably end up amazed at the wealth of classic artisanal burgers they find in icehouses, bars, bowling alleys, and grocery stores all over the state.

★ ★ ★

The ascendance of the hamburger in Texas started with the rise of the drive-in restaurant. In 1921, Jesse G. Kirby, who noticed that Texans like to eat in their cars, opened the nation's first drive-in in Dallas. His restaurant, the Pig Stand, was named after the chain's signature offering, a barbecued pork sandwich. Meals were delivered by young men in bow ties called "carhops," named for their practice of hopping onto the running board of approaching automobiles before they came to a stop.

In 1929, Doug Prince opened a drive-in in Dallas serving hamburgers and named it Prince's. In the beginning, Prince was the cook, dishwasher, and carhop. But eventually he hired attractive young women to be his carhops and glamorized the occupation by

Prince's carhop competing in the Galveston Carhop Pageant, 1960s.

giving the girls majorette costumes complete with boots and high hats. Prince's combination of hamburgers and hotties took Texas by storm.

Five years later, Prince's opened its legendary South Main location in Houston. The gorgeous carhops inspired Galveston Island, home of the world's first beauty pageant, to revive the tradition with a carhop pageant. In 1941, the pageant winner, Jeanette Hill of Prince's Hamburgers, appeared in a story about Prince's and the drive-in phenomenon in *Life* magazine.

During the 1980s oil bust, Prince's went from eighteen locations to one. The ruined owner handed his keys to manager and former carhop Elizabeth Flores in gratitude for her long service and walked away. Flores was working at Prince's one night in 1950 when Elvis Presley stopped in for a burger after performing in a concert. In 1990, the famous Prince's drive-in on South Main closed for good. Flores gave the business to a creditor, a meat vendor named John Broussard.

In 1993, Broussard opened an upscale hamburger restaurant in Houston called Prince's. The new Prince's didn't have carhops, but the retro burger-joint decor paid homage to the original with displays of historic photos from the South Main location, old menus, vinyl booths, and classic Formica tables. The nostalgic menu included items from the old Prince's, like the chocolate malted and a hamburger that featured Prince's version of special sauce, a slurry of pureed fresh tomatoes. Big eaters went for the Elvis-inspired King's Favorite, a half-pound patty with chili, cheese, and grilled onion on top and lettuce, tomato, pickles, mustard, and mayo on the bottom. There are currently four Prince's locations in Houston. None of them is a drive-in.

* * *

Driving north up Interstate 45, on my way to judge the 2005 Uncle Fletch Hamburger Cook-off, I hit on the brilliant strategy of stopping somewhere and eating a burger for lunch. The random burger would serve as my benchmark. Or, maybe it was just an excuse. I was pretty hungry.

When I missed the exit for Highway 19, the road to Athens, I took a Huntsville exit and drove east hoping to hook up with the north-south road. I was quite lost when I went by Mister Hamburger, a dilapidated drive-in on Eleventh Street. I might have kept going if it hadn't been for the scary clown. The clown sign in Mister Hamburger's parking lot looked like it belonged in a cheap horror movie. I pulled in immediately.

The long awnings where cars once parked to wait for the gorgeous carhops were no longer in use. I walked up to the window and bantered with the aging employees. They revealed that Mister Hamburger has been serving burgers to Sam Houston State students for more than fifty years.

"Cruising for burgers" is a familiar phrase from the era between the late 1940s and the 1970s that described the dual infatuations of driving around aimlessly in our cars and eating hamburgers at drive-ins where our peers hung out. It was also code for looking for attractive members of the opposite sex.

THE FIRST UNCLE FLETCH HAMBURGER cook-off was held in 1984, to publicize Athens as the Original Home of the Hamburger. One of the organizers was Dallas newspaperman Frank X. Tolbert, who attempted to prove that it was an Athens café owner named Fletcher Davis who first put a cooked ground meat patty between two slices of bread in the late 1880s, and subsequently at the St. Louis World's Fair in 1904.

Both the clown and another old hand-painted sign under the eaves of the building recommended the unusually named Killer Burger. Because the Texas penitentiary at Huntsville houses the state's execution chamber, I wondered whether the burger was a come-on for visitors in town to protest the death penalty. Conscious or not, the irony was too rich to ignore. I ordered a Killer Burger with fries and a soda.

What I got was a shiny oversized bun wrapped in tissue paper. Inside were two huge patties of loose ground meat that had been pressed into free-form shapes and griddled to a dark brown with lots of delectable cracks and fissures. The monstrous patties were stacked with a slice of American cheese between them. Adornments included pickles, onion, lettuce, tomato, mustard, mayo, and jalapeños. From the meat to the condiments to the ramshackle joint that turns it out, this was a Texas classic. I congratulated myself on stumbling on the perfect benchmark of a Texas hamburger—suitably served in a 1950s-era drive-in.

I wish I could recommend that you go and try the classic sandwich at Mister Hamburger, but it's too late. Like Prince's and other 1950s-era drive-ins all over the state, Mister Hamburger was bulldozed to make way for something new.

* * *

The Uncle Fletch Hamburger Cook-off was suspended in 1999, after the Hudson Foods hamburger patty recall prompted the United States Department of Agriculture (USDA) to tell consumers to cook burgers well done.

But the Athens, Texas, hamburger creation story persisted. Frank X. Tolbert was said to have produced a *New York Herald* story on the 1904 St. Louis World's Fair that referred to a "hamburger sandwich" being served. Tolbert claimed that the guy who served the burger was Fletcher Davis.

In 2004, the Athens story gained widespread acceptance during the meat industry's celebration of the one hundredth anniversary of the hamburger.

The National Cattlemen's Beef Association head-quarters in Colorado issued press releases pinpointing the hamburger's birth date to the St. Louis World's Fair and crediting Fletcher Davis as the inventor.

Thanks to all the attention Athens was getting, the Uncle Fletch Hamburger Cook-off was resumed in 2005, the year I served as a judge. It was held on the shores of scenic Lake Athens, and a five-dollar admission ticket got you a hamburger lunch and an opportunity to wander among the competitors.

The judging was held in an air-conditioned activity room at the marina. Nine judges considered fifteen burgers that had been cut into neat pieces. We graded the burgers on a scale of one to ten based on the standard cook-off criteria of appearance, taste, aroma, texture, and overall impression.

Two of the top three burgers in the competition, including the winner, were stuffed. Gary Beams headed up the winning team, which came from Trinity Valley Community College (TVCC) in Athens. First, the team baked their own bun, which was covered with various seeds and spices

WHATABURGER

★ ★ ★ ★ ★ ★ ★ ★ ★ ★ ★ ★ ★ ★ ★ ★ ★ ★

THE FIRST WHATABURGER opened for business in Corpus Christi in 1950, and it served a burger that was twice as big as the standard fast-food burger. Instead of a previously frozen two-ounce patty on a two-and-half-inch bun with a dash of mustard and ketchup, Whataburger offered a grilled-to-order four-ounce burger of freshly ground beef on a five-inch bun with lettuce, three tomato slices, four dill pickle chips, chopped onions, mustard, and ketchup. It sold for twenty-five cents.

Whataburger remains the benchmark by which Texas burgers are measured. Whenever I try a new burger, the first question I ask myself is, is this really any better than a Whataburger? (My standard order is double meat, double cheese with jalapeños.)

In 2000, Whataburger celebrated its fiftieth anniversary.

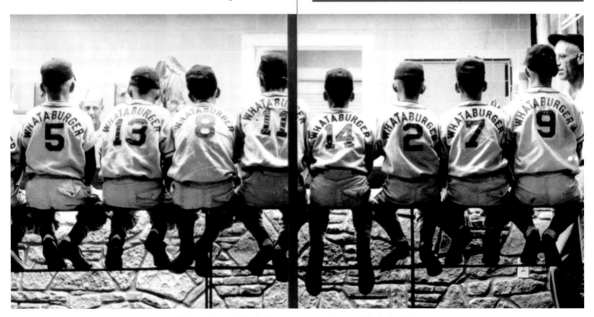

Whataburger Little League team, Corpus Christi, 1950.

and measured more than a foot across. Then Beams, a trained chef, created the patties: He ground the sirloin and chuck mix himself and seasoned it with a combination of spices that remains his secret. He divided the meat into four twelve-ounce patties. He put some pepper Jack cheese between two patties and pinched the edges of the patties together. He made a second giant cheese-sandwich patty with the remaining two patties and more pepper Jack. Finally, Beams grilled the two oversize patties, promptly removing them from the fire when they reached an internal temperature of 146°F. The two patties were stacked on top of each other on the single giant bun.

"The hamburger keeps cooking after you take it off," Beams explained. He hoped the temperature would rise to 150°F by the time the burgers made it to the judging. At this temperature, no pink is visible but the meat is still juicy. It's also ten degrees lower than the 160°F the USDA guidelines allow.

Chefs, home cooks, and burger cook-off contestants are all looking for ways around the USDA's bad cooking advice. Stuffing a hamburger patty with cheese is one way to make it taste moist even when the meat is overcooked, confides Beams, though personally he would rather just cook it less.

Second-place winner Derek Holdredge of Athens mixed ground pork and ground beef to keep the meat juicy. He put his half-pound patties on grocery-store kaiser rolls with the standard pickles, onion, lettuce, tomato, mustard, and mayo. Third-place winner Jan Canterbury, a second-grade teacher from the colorfully named town of Cut and Shoot, stuffed Monterey Jack and grated jalapeños between two big patties, just like the first-place winner.

Gary Beams doesn't think a cheese-stuffed burger will ever make it in Texas restaurants because it is difficult to cook the stuffing to the proper internal temperature. "It's a health-department nightmare," he says. But Beams believes that the American hamburger has turned a corner. According to the burger champion, the once-noble American burger has been in a slump that goes all the way back to the infancy of the fast-food industry.

"Clown burgers" is what Beams calls McDonald's hamburgers, and he blames the company for trying to squeeze more profits out of each sandwich by making the patties smaller and smaller. "Our winning burger weighed three pounds. Clown burgers are now one-tenth of a pound per patty!"

Homemade hamburgers, which were always the burger lover's alternative to the fast-food chains, began their own decline in the 1990s. "I think the integrity of the burger got lost when we couldn't cook them medium-rare anymore," Beams said. "*E. coli* dealt the burger a blow at a time when beef already had a bad rap."

GRIND YOUR OWN

★ ★ ★ ★ ★ ★ ★ ★ ★ ★ ★ ★ ★ ★ ★ ★ ★ ★

GRINDING YOUR OWN MEAT has two big advantages. First, you can sterilize the exterior of the beef cut by submerging it in boiling water for a couple of minutes before grinding it. If you also sterilize your meat grinder and work surfaces, you can make your ground meat safer to eat if cooked rare (or used in Parisa, page 159).

Second, you can use better-quality beef and supplement the fat content. Ground beef generally has a meat to fat ratio of 80 percent meat to 20 percent fat. To make a juicy burger, most chefs recommend a meat to fat ratio of 70 percent meat to 30 percent fat. Chuck, round, and sirloin are fine for homemade ground beef, but they don't come close to the ideal meat to fat ratio, which means you will probably want to supplement the fat content if you grind your own beef. You can do this by adding beef fat, salt pork, or even duck fat. But my favorite method for boosting the fat was devised by the late great Tookie's, a hamburger joint in Dickinson that was closed by Hurricane Ike. Tookie's put bacon through the grinder.

But the new popularity of outdoor cooking may have halted the decline. "Burgers are coming back," Beams said. And the revival is being led by the consumer. "The burger chains are taking their cues from the backyard barbecue craze."

Athens's claim to fame as the Original Home of the Hamburger may not be as lucky as the burger itself. It suffered a setback when the archives of the *New York Herald* were digitized and made available to researchers. No mention of the "hamburger sandwich" was found in the paper's coverage of the 1904 St. Louis World's Fair.

Meanwhile, earlier mentions of hamburgers in other towns and cities in Texas turned up in newly digitized newspaper archives, including an April 12, 1894, item in the *Shiner Gazette*: "Hamburger steak sandwiches every day of the week at Barny's saloon, Moulton."

In 2009, the Uncle Fletch Hamburger Cook-off was cancelled and it hasn't been held since.

TOOKIE'S "SQUEALER"

Tookie's was one of the best burger joints in Texas before Hurricane Ike put them out of business. They ground bacon along with the beef when they ground their hamburger meat. It's easy enough to put a few slices of bacon through the grinder if you are grinding up your own hamburger meat anyway. And you'll love the flavor.

MAKES ABOUT 2 POUNDS
2 pounds beef chuck, round, or sirloin
6 ounces sliced bacon

Cut the beef into strips, trimming away any gristle or other tough pieces. Fit a meat grinder with the fine plate. Pass the beef and bacon through the grinder, capturing them in a bowl. Then combine them well with your hands to spread the fat evenly through the beef.

Use immediately, keep tightly wrapped in the refrigerator for up to a few days, or freeze for up to a month.

TEXAS BURGER PATTIES

Start with ground chuck or ground round with at least 20 percent fat. Shape the burgers by hand and don't compress them too much or try too hard to make them perfectly round. A patty with a few uneven edges produces a burger with an interesting texture.

MAKES 4 (8-OUNCE) OR 6 (5½-OUNCE) PATTIES
2 pounds ground beef
2 tablespoons grated yellow onion
1 tablespoon minced garlic
1 tablespoon minced serrano chile
1 tablespoon Worcestershire sauce
1 teaspoon salt

In a bowl, combine all of the ingredients and mix well by hand. Divide into 4 or 6 equal portions, shape each portion into a ball, and then form each ball into a patty about ½ inch thick.

Cook immediately, or refrigerate for up to 2 days. If you want to freeze the patties, separate them with squares of freezer paper so you can easily remove as many as you need. The patties can be frozen for up to 3 months.

Cheeseburger Patties: Add 1 cup shredded Jack, Cheddar, or other cheese to the meat with the other ingredients and proceed as directed.

GARY BEAMS'S STUFFED BURGERS

This recipe was inspired by the winning entry in the Uncle Fletch Hamburger Cook-off that I judged. It's not the exact recipe, but it's a close approximation.

SERVES 4

4 (8-ounce) Texas Burger Patties (page 229)

1½ cups shredded pepper Jack cheese

1 teaspoon minced pickled jalapeño chile (optional)

4 hamburger buns

Burger condiments of choice

Prepare a hot fire for direct-heat grilling in a charcoal or gas grill.

Prepare the meat mixture for the patties as directed, but don't form it into patties. In a bowl, toss the cheese with the chile. Divide the meat mixture into 4 equal portions and form each portion into a ball. With your thumb, create a pocket in the center of a ball. Force one-quarter of the cheese into the pocket, seal the meat around the stuffing, and flatten the ball into a patty about ½ inch thick. Make sure the cheese is completely encased or it will run out as it melts. Repeat with the remaining 3 balls and cheese.

GARY BEAMS, HAMBURGER HELPER

★ ★ ★ ★ ★ ★ ★ ★ ★ ★ ★ ★ ★ ★ ★ ★ ★ ★

FOR GREAT HOMEMADE BURGERS, Gary Beams recommends that you hand pack well-seasoned, fatty ground meat at the last minute, keep flipping to a minimum, and, most important, resist the temptation to press down on the patty with a spatula as it cooks. If you really want to get serious, you should grind your own meat and try making stuffed burgers.

Place the patties on the grill grate directly over the fire and cook until done to your taste, flipping the patties as little as possible to keep the cheese from escaping through any cracks that may form in the patties. During the last couple of minutes, place the buns, cut side down, on the grate to toast lightly.

Transfer the patties to a platter and let cool for a couple of minutes, then test one to make sure the melted cheese isn't so hot that it will squirt out and burn the diner. Serve the stuffed burger patties on the toasted buns. Pass the condiments at the table.

EL REAL BURGER

The bean burger and its Tex-Mex embellishments "define the burger as Texan, while paying homage to the Mexican roots of the state's people," wrote John T. Edge. At El Real Tex-Mex Cafe in Houston, we have our own version of the San Antonio bean burger. Some folks add pickled jalapeño slices, some remove the tomato, and others douse the burger with hot sauce before chowing down.

SERVES 2

2 (8-ounce) Texas Burger Patties (page 229)

2 pats unsalted butter

2 hamburger buns or kaiser rolls, split

1 cup Refried Beans (page 143), heated

1 medium-size bag Fritos corn chips

¼ yellow onion, finely chopped

½ cup roasted poblano chile strips (page 129)

1 cup chile con queso (page 121)

½ cup Guacamole (page 142)

4 thin tomato slices

Preheat a griddle or the flat-top area of a gas grill to medium. Place the patties on the hot surface to cook. Resist the temptation to press down on the patties with a spatula, which will squeeze out all the juices and result in dry burgers.

(Continued)

A classic Texas burger.

When the burgers are halfway done, butter the cut sides of the buns; place them on the griddle or grill, buttered side down, and toast until nicely browned along the edges. Then place the tops of the buns on top of the burgers to absorb the juices. The burgers will be cooked to medium after 12 to 15 minutes. Check for doneness with an instant-read thermometer; it should register 140°F. (Or, cook to desired doneness; the USDA recommends that ground meat be cooked well done, or to 160°F, for safety's sake.)

Remove the burgers from the heat. Spread ½ cup of the beans on the bottom of each bun and add a handful of corn chips. Top with the burgers. Sprinkle half of the onion over each burger and then add half of the poblano strips and half of the queso. Spread the crown of each bun with half of the guacamole and top with 2 tomato slices. Serve open-faced so the diner can doctor the burger before combining the two halves.

JALAPEÑO CHEESEBURGERS

I seldom eat a hamburger without cheese. Some Texans like the tang of pepper Jack on their burgers. Others prefer the sharpness of Cheddar. American cheese singles are much maligned in the food world, but they are hard to beat at holding jalapeño slices in place on a jalapeño cheeseburger.

SERVES 2

2 (8-ounce) Texas Burger Patties (page 229)

2 pats unsalted butter

2 hamburger buns or kaiser rolls, split

2 slices American, Cheddar, or Jack cheese

12 pickled jalapeño chile slices

1 tablespoon Creole or Dijon mustard

1 tablespoon mayonnaise

2 large, thin Texas 1015 onion slices

2 large, thick tomato slices

2 iceberg lettuce leaves

Preheat a griddle or the flat-top area of a gas grill to medium. Place the patties on the hot surface to cook. Resist the temptation to press down on the patties with a spatula, which will squeeze out all the juices and result in dry burgers.

When the burgers are halfway done, butter the cut sides of the buns; place them on the griddle or grill, buttered side down, and toast until nicely browned along the edges. Then place the tops of the buns on top of the burgers to absorb the juices. The burgers will be cooked to medium after 12 to 15 minutes. Check for doneness with an instant-read thermometer; it should register 140°F. (Or, cook to desired doneness; the USDA recommends that ground meat be cooked well done, or to 160°F, for safety's sake.) Turn the patties, place the cheese on top of the hot meat, and cook for a few minutes longer, until melted.

Remove the burgers from the heat and push 6 jalapeño slices into the cheese on each burger. Spread ½ tablespoon mustard on each bun bottom and ½ tablespoon mayonnaise on each bun top. Place 1 onion slice on each bottom bun, then top with a burger. Put a tomato slice and a lettuce leaf on top of each patty and finish with the crown half of the bun. Serve immediately.

GUY'S BBQ BURGER

Tuesdays through Fridays, Guy's Meat Market on Old Spanish Trail in Houston smokes two hundred burger patties in its barbecue pit. They go on sale at eleven o'clock in the morning and often sell out before noon. The secret to enjoying Guy's barbecued burger is to skip the lettuce and tomato and top it instead with barbecue sauce.

It's not worth firing up the smoker to make a few hamburgers, but these are easy to make when you are smoking something else. Try them for dinner when you are barbecuing a brisket. The hamburgers are done in less than an hour and then you can let the brisket smoke overnight.

SERVES 2

2 (8-ounce) Texas Burger Patties (page 229)

2 pats unsalted butter

2 hamburger buns or kaiser rolls, split

4 tablespoons of your favorite barbecue sauce

2 large, thin Texas 1015 onion slices

8 dill pickle chips, or 12 pickled jalapeño slices (optional)

Prepare a fire for indirect-heat cooking (the coals on one side only) in your smoker with a water pan. Use wood chips, chunks, or logs and keep up a good level of smoke. The smoker is ready when the temperature is between 275°F and 325°F.

Place the burgers directly over the fire and sear, turning once. Resist the temptation to press down on the patties with a spatula, which will squeeze out all the juices and result in dry burgers. When the burgers are browned just a little, move them to the cooler part of the grill grate and close the lid. Cook the burgers for about 1 hour, until an instant-read thermometer inserted into the center registers 155°F. (Or, cook to desired doneness; the USDA recommends that ground meat be cooked well done, or to 160°F, for safety's sake.) When the burgers are nearly ready, butter the cut sides of the buns; place them on the grate, buttered side down, and toast until nicely browned along the edges.

Remove the burgers from the smoker. Spread 1 tablespoon of the barbecue sauce on each bun half. Place 1 onion slice on each bun bottom and top with the burgers. Then put the pickle slices on top of the burgers and add the crown halves of the buns. Serve immediately.

OPEN-FACED CHILI BURGER

This kind of chili burger is eaten with a knife and fork. You get more chili that way. When my dad went on a low-carb diet, he used to eat burger patties topped with chili in a bowl heaped with onions and cheese, but without a bun.

SERVES 4

4 Texas Burger Patties (page 229), any size

1 tablespoon unsalted butter

4 hamburger buns, split

4 cups Chili con Carne Sauce (page 112)

1 cup Crock-Pot Chile con Queso (page 121), Cheez Whiz, or grated Jack or Cheddar cheese (optional)

¼ yellow onion, minced

Fritos corn chips, for serving

Pickled jalapeño chiles, for serving

Preheat a griddle or the flat-top area of a gas grill to medium. Place the patties on the hot surface to cook. Resist the temptation to press down on the patties with a spatula, which will squeeze out all the juices and result in dry burgers. Cook the burgers to your preferred degree of doneness. (The USDA recommends that ground meat be cooked well done, or to 160°F, for safety's sake.)

When the burgers are nearly done, butter the cut sides of the buns; place them on the griddle or grill, buttered side down, and toast until nicely browned along the edges. Put both halves of each bun, buttered side up, on a plate. Place a burger on top, overlapping both bun halves. Ladle 1 cup of the sauce over each burger and bun, then top with ¼ cup of the queso. Garnish with the onion. Serve the corn chips and jalapeños on the side.

CHILI DOGS (CONEYS)

At James Coney Island, the oldest hot dog chain in Houston, chili cheese dogs are called Coneys, just like they are in the Midwest. The restaurant chain was founded by two Greek immigrants, James and Tom Papadakis, in 1923.

SERVES 4
4 all-beef hot dogs
4 thin slices bacon
4 torpedo rolls
1 cup Chili con Carne Sauce (page 112)
1 cup Crock-Pot Chile con Queso (page 121)
1 cup chopped yellow onions
Fritos corn chips, for serving

Wrap each hot dog with a bacon slice so the sausage is completely covered. Heat a skillet, griddle, or *comal* (flat cast-iron pan) over medium heat. Place the hot dogs on the hot surface and cook, turning as needed, for about 4 minutes, until the bacon is cooked.

While the hot dogs are cooking, cut a pocket in each roll and place the rolls on top of the hot dogs to steam. When the hot dogs are ready, slip a hot dog into the pocket in each roll. Spoon ¼ cup chili sauce down one side of each bun and ¼ cup queso down the other until the pocket is nearly full. Top with onions and serve immediately with corn chips.

ONION RINGS

You can serve these onion rings with ketchup, if you want, but real cowboys dip them in ranch dressing.

MAKES ABOUT 28 RINGS; SERVES 4
2 large sweet onions (such as Texas 1015, Vidalia, or Maui)
Peanut oil, for deep-frying

Flour Mixture
1½ cups all-purpose flour
1 tablespoon paprika
2 teaspoons salt
2 teaspoons pepper

Egg Mixture
4 eggs, lightly beaten
1 cup buttermilk
1 cup beer
1 teaspoon salt

Cut the onions crosswise into slices about 1½ inches thick. Remove the very center of each slice and discard it or use it in stock along with the ends of the onions. Separate the slices into rings and set aside.

Pour the oil to a depth of 2 inches into a deep, heavy saucepan or deep fryer and heat to 350°F.

While the oil is heating, prepare the onion rings for frying. To prepare the flour mixture, in a shallow bowl, stir together the flour, paprika, salt, and pepper. To prepare the egg mixture, in another bowl, whisk together the eggs, buttermilk, beer, and salt, mixing well. Dip each onion ring into the egg mixture, allowing the excess to drip off, then dredge in the flour, shaking off the excess. Then repeat the dipping, first in the egg mixture and then in the flour. Allow the floured onion rings to dry for 10 minutes so the batter sticks better.

Preheat the oven to 250°F. Line a large baking dish or baking sheet with paper towels. Working in small batches, slide the battered rings into the hot oil and fry, adjusting the heat as needed to keep the oil at 350°F, for about 5 minutes, until the rings are golden brown. Using a wire skimmer or slotted spoon, transfer the rings to the towel-lined dish to drain and place in the warm oven to keep hot. When all of the rings are ready, serve immediately.

CHEESE FRIES

Here is a quintessential Texas side dish that combines classic American fries with Tex-Mex chile con queso. Serve with extra napkins.

SERVES 4

2 pounds russet potatoes

2½ cups peanut oil

1 yellow onion, sliced

Salt

1 cup Crock-Pot Chile con Queso (page 121)

2 jalapeño chiles, seeded and sliced

Peel the potatoes and cut lengthwise into ½-inch-thick sticks. Rinse the sticks with cold running water and pat dry with paper towels. Pour the oil into a 12-inch skillet. Add the potatoes, packing them in tightly until the cold oil almost covers them.

Place the pan over medium heat and cook the potatoes, shaking the pan to keep them from sticking, for about 10 minutes, until they start to turn a pale gold. Stop shaking the pan and cook the potatoes for another 8 to 10 minutes, until they are cooked through.

Scatter the onion evenly over the top of the potatoes. Increase the heat to medium-high and start turning the potatoes, constantly moving them around to ensure even browning, for 2 or 3 minutes, until the onions are brown. Drain the fries in a colander, then toss them in a bowl with salt.

Divide the fries among 4 bowls. Drizzle ¼ cup of the queso over each serving and top with the sliced jalapeños. Serve immediately.

Chili Cheese Fries: Top the fries half and half with queso and Chili con Carne Sauce (page 112).

CHILI DOGS AND CHILI BURGERS

CHILI DOGS AND CHILI BURGERS first became popular in various parts of the United States in the 1930s. The chili dog (sometimes known as a Coney Island hot dog) looks pretty much the same wherever you go: a hot dog topped with chili, sometimes with cheese and raw onions added. But the Texas chili burger has several permutations. Some published recipes direct you to add chili powder and other seasonings to ground meat and then form patties. The result is supposed to taste like chili. Other recipes call for serving chili con carne on a bun, creating a sandwich that looks like a Sloppy Joe.

Most Texans think of a chili burger as a patty on a bun with chili on top. That's the way they serve them at Christian's Totem, a Houston hamburger joint. The chili burgers there are served open-faced with chili con carne poured over the top, and they are eaten with a knife and fork.

Rebecca Rather's Ancho Brownies (page 245)
with Homemade Vanilla Ice Cream (page 240).

Blue Bell delivery truck, 1936.

CHAPTER 20
ICE CREAM SOCIALS

★★★★★★★★★★★★★★★★★★★★★★

In front of the Blue Bell ice cream plant visitors' center in Brenham, kids stood on the running boards of a 1930s-era Blue Bell delivery truck while their parents snapped photos. Inside, next to the ticket counter, there was a display case full of the company's cardboard ice cream packages from the early part of the century. Tickets for a tour of the plant cost three dollars for adults and two dollars for kids and seniors. That's a bargain by any standard, but especially considering the tour includes all the ice cream you can eat.

Blue Bell is the iconic ice cream of Texas. The plant in Brenham gets an average of one thousand visitors every weekday. No surprise considering the tour ends at the Blue Bell ice cream parlor. In the late summer, when the thermometer hovers at the one hundred mark day after day, some eighteen hundred people show up at the plant every morning, Blue Bell's Bill Weiss said.

The Brenham Creamery was founded in 1907 by a co-op of German farmers looking to make a little extra money by turning their excess cream into butter. Starting in 1911, ice cream was made at the creamery—two gallons at a time.

E. F. Kruse took over as manager of the failing company in 1919, and turned the butter-making operation into an ice cream plant. His family ran it for several generations

237

and changed the name to Blue Bell, after an indigenous wildflower that blooms in midsummer (not to be confused with the spring wildflower, the bluebonnet.).

Blue Bell bought its first continuous freezer in 1936, the same year the company bought the first refrigerated delivery truck, the same ones the kids like to climb on out front.

★ ★ ★

Ice cream ceased to be a novelty and became a part of everyday life during Prohibition, when the soda fountain replaced the tavern as a gathering place and the ice cream social became a common party theme. For half of the counties in Texas, Prohibition never ended, and in those "dry" counties, ice cream socials are still very popular.

On the drive out to Brenham, photographer Paul S. Howell told me about the role that ice cream played in his life. "My mother is a Kelton; the cowboy poet, Elmer Kelton, was her cousin. At every Kelton family reunion, we make ice cream." Paul's father was a Baptist minister, so alcohol was always taboo. "I grew up in Mesquite, which was dry. The Keltons' ranches are in Andrews County in West Texas, which is also dry. You couldn't have a cold beer at the end of the day. So when people got together to relax, ice cream was usually involved."

In East Texas, the ice cream socials were often held at church halls. But in West Texas, they were held at the ranch house, Paul explained. "At times like roundup, when several families gathered to brand cattle, there would be thirty or forty people. They got together in the afternoon. There would be four or five hand-cranked ice cream makers going. We always had several tubs of vanilla, usually some butter pecan, and strawberry or peach if the fruit was in season. If we were short on time, somebody would just run to the store and buy some Blue Bell. The ice cream was seldom served all by itself. Pound cake, chocolate layer cake, cookies, brownies, and peach cobbler were served with it, warm from the oven," Paul said.

WHERE TO GET BLUE BELL ICE CREAM

★ ★ ★ ★ ★ ★ ★ ★ ★ ★ ★ ★ ★ ★ ★ ★ ★

UNTIL THE 1970S, Blue Bell ice cream was only sold in the greater Houston area. In 2006, the company held a 62 percent market share in Houston and sold $400 million worth of ice cream. Although it is only distributed in seventeen Southern states, Blue Bell is the third best-selling ice cream in the nation, behind the West Coast's Dreyer's and the East Coast's Breyers. Why doesn't it expand to national distribution?

"It's a cinch by the inch, but it's hard by the yard," is a favorite Kruse family saying. The quality of any ice cream deteriorates quickly if it isn't stored and transported carefully, especially in a hot climate. If it melts and refreezes, ice crystals ruin the texture. By maintaining tight control over every aspect of production, transportation, and distribution, the Kruse family has kept the quality of Blue Bell exceptionally high. But that total control makes national distribution next to impossible.

The ice cream social was the most practical way to eat ice cream until the home freezer became available in the 1950s. That's when the market for Blue Bell ice cream soared. In 1969, Howard Kruse, a graduate of the dairy science program at Texas A&M and the son of Blue Bell's manager E. F. Kruse, came up with the formula for Blue Bell's Homemade Vanilla. It was intended to replicate the flavor of hand-cranked ice cream. It has remained the most popular flavor in the Blue Bell line for more than forty years.

Bill Weiss led Paul Howell and me on a tour of the Blue Bell plant that started in the "milk bay," where the production of fifty thousand dairy cows is received every day and rigorously tested for milk fat, milk solids, and flavor before being piped into the plant. As you might imagine, an ice cream factory is a blessedly cold place to be on a hot summer day. We lingered beside the sixty-gallon Cherry-Burrell freezers longer than necessary.

Blue Bell employees are allowed to eat free ice cream on breaks. I asked every employee I met which flavor was his or her favorite. Banana Split was very popular, but the overwhelming favorite, even among employees, was Homemade Vanilla. Blue Bell makes four vanilla varieties. I used to buy Natural Vanilla Bean, until I learned that the flecks of bean in the ice cream are purely cosmetic. All of their flavor has been extracted before they are added. Now I buy Homemade Vanilla.

The number two Blue Bell flavor is Cookies 'n Cream, made with imitation Oreo cookies. Number three is Dutch Chocolate, made with chocolate imported from the Netherlands. The number four flavor, "The Great Divide," is a tub with Homemade Vanilla on one side and Dutch Chocolate on the other. "When we're done with the tour, I'll let you taste some Homemade Vanilla right out of the freezer," Bill Weiss promised.

Ice cream tastes best when it first emerges from the freezer, Weiss explained. But when held at temperatures just below freezing, ice crystals grow and slowly rob the product of its creamy texture. To preserve the smoothness of freshly made ice cream, manufacturers rush it into a flash freezer, where it is hard-frozen at 40 degrees below zero. To enjoy your ice cream and get the most flavor, you should soften it up a little before you eat it.

I was disappointed that my favorite flavor, Peaches 'n Cream, was not being made that day. And Blue Bell has decided not to make its legendary Cantaloupe 'n Cream, made with melons from Pecos, at all this year.

"We use the best ingredients we can get, and we produce our ice creams based on what's available. If Texas peaches are great, we use Texas peaches. If Georgia peaches are sweeter, we use Georgia peaches," he said. Blue Bell's Buttered Pecan, made with lightly salted pecans, is number six on the hit parade, and Texas pecans are preferred for their superior flavor.

Weiss won't discuss formulas or recipes, but there are some obvious differences between Blue Bell and other commercial ice creams. A half gallon of Blue Bell weighs fifty-two ounces, while a half gallon of Dreyer's weighs forty ounces, suggesting Blue Bell has less overrun (added air). And Blue Bell's butterfat content is around 13 percent, only 1 percent short of the superpremium level occupied by such brands as Häagen-Dazs.

True to his word, Bill Weiss brought us a tub of Homemade Vanilla straight from the freezer after the tour. It was soupy, but it tasted amazing. A Blue Bell customer once wrote a letter to the company confessing that she had filled an old-fashioned hand-cranked ice cream maker with the Blue Bell flavor and taken it to an ice cream social, where it was unanimously acclaimed the best homemade ice cream in town. It's easy to see why.

Weiss shared a surprising memory as we ate the ice cream. "We made vanilla ice cream at home when I was a kid, and we used to dip saltines into it," he said. "Sometimes when I eat Blue Bell Homemade Vanilla at home, I still eat it with saltines."

Earlier in the day, I asked Paul Howell what he remembered most about the flavor of the hand-cranked ice cream made at East Texas ice cream socials. He mentioned the combination of sweet and salty that resulted when the rock salt solution sloshed into the vanilla ice cream.

When I got home, I bought a half gallon of Blue Bell Homemade Vanilla and a box of saltines and tried the combination. I liked it almost as much as Dutch Chocolate with pretzels.

HOMEMADE VANILLA ICE CREAM

This is the mother of all ice cream flavors. In the days before home freezers were common, soft, hand-cranked vanilla was the definition of ice cream. You could add peaches or other fruit, syrup or toppings, but it all started with plain vanilla. See photo on page 236.

MAKES ABOUT 2 QUARTS

2½ cups half-and-half

1 cup sugar

4 eggs, lightly beaten

2½ cups heavy cream

4 teaspoons vanilla extract

⅛ teaspoon salt, or more to taste

In a saucepan, heat the half-and-half over medium-high heat, stirring often, until the mixture is steaming. Remove from the heat. Gradually add the sugar while stirring constantly, then continue stirring until fully dissolved. Stir in the eggs, mixing well. Return the pan to medium-high heat and heat, stirring often, just until the mixture is steaming.

Transfer the half-and-half mixture to a pitcher or a bowl with a spout. Stir in the cream, vanilla, and salt. Cover and refrigerate for at least 3 hours, until well chilled.

Transfer the custard to an ice cream maker and freeze according to the manufacturer's instructions. If the ice cream is still loose, finish freezing it in your freezer before serving.

BUTTER PECAN ICE CREAM

Texas is one of the nation's largest producers of pecans. In the 1880s, Mexican families around San Antonio made a living picking up free native pecans, turning them into pralines and other candies, and selling them on the street. The flavor of this easy uncooked version of butter pecan ice cream is reminiscent of Tex-Mex pecan pralines.

MAKES 2 GENEROUS QUARTS

1 (14-ounce) can sweetened condensed milk

1½ cups lightly salted roasted pecans, chopped

3 tablespoons unsalted butter, melted

1 tablespoon maple syrup

3 tablespoons bottled cajeta (Mexican thick caramel sauce) or dulce de leche (caramel sauce)

2 cups half-and-half

2 cups heavy cream

In a pitcher or a bowl with a spout, combine the milk, pecans, butter, and maple syrup and mix well. Stir in the *cajeta*, half-and-half, and cream until thoroughly combined. Cover and refrigerate for at least 3 hours, until well chilled.

Transfer the mixture to an ice cream maker and freeze according to the manufacturer's instructions. If the ice cream is still loose, finish freezing it in your freezer before serving.

PAUL HOWELL'S CHOCOLATE POUND CAKE

"I have been making this cake since I was eight. I got the original recipe out of a Shreveport Junior League cookbook," Paul Howell told me. "But I messed around with it. I know a pound cake is supposed to have a whole pound of butter, but I think that's too much. It makes the cake taste greasy. I serve this cake with Blue Bell Homemade Vanilla and fresh raspberries."

SERVES 8 TO 12

½ cup unsweetened cocoa powder, plus some
   for the pan
3 cups cake flour
1 teaspoon baking powder
½ teaspoon salt
1 cup half-and-half
1 tablespoon vanilla extract
1½ cups unsalted butter, at room temperature
3 cups sugar
5 eggs, at room temperature
Homemade Vanilla Ice Cream (page 240),
   for serving

Preheat the oven to 325°F. Butter a 9-inch Bundt pan and dust it with cocoa powder.

In a bowl, sift together the flour, cocoa powder, baking powder, and salt. Measure the half-and-half and add the vanilla to it.

In a stand mixer fitted with the paddle attachment, or in a large bowl with a handheld mixer, cream the butter on medium-high speed. Gradually add the sugar and continue to beat for about 1 minute, until light and fluffy. Scrape down the sides of the bowl. Add the eggs, one at a time, beating well after each addition. On low speed, add the dry ingredients in 3 batches, alternating with the half-and-half in 2 batches, beginning and ending with the dry ingredients. Beat just until combined.

Pour the batter into the prepared Bundt pan. Bake for 1 hour and 20 minutes, until a toothpick inserted near the center comes out clean. Let cool in the pan on a wire rack for 10 minutes, then invert onto the rack.

Serve the cake warm with ice cream. Store tightly covered at room temperature for up to 3 days.

1-2-3-4 CAKE

This was once the most common cake in Texas, probably because it is so easy to memorize the recipe. The name is a meme for the main ingredients: 1 cup butter, 2 cups sugar, 3 cups flour, and 4 eggs. The cake can be baked in a Bundt pan or a loaf pan and served plain or with Confectioners' Sugar Glaze (page 243). Or, you can bake it in two layer cake pans, then fill and frost it like a traditional layer cake.

SERVES 8 TO 12

3 cups cake flour
1 tablespoon baking powder
½ teaspoon salt
1 cup milk
1 teaspoon vanilla extract
½ teaspoon almond extract
1 cup unsalted butter, at room temperature
2 cups superfine sugar
4 eggs, at room temperature

Preheat the oven to 350°F.

In a bowl, sift together the flour, baking powder, and salt. Measure the milk and add the vanilla and almond extracts to it.

In a stand mixer fitted with the paddle attachment, or in a large bowl with a handheld mixer, cream the butter on medium-high speed. Gradually add the sugar and continue to beat for about 1 minute, until light and fluffy. Scrape down the sides of the bowl. Add the eggs, one at a time, beating well

(Continued)

after each addition. On low speed, add the dry ingredients in 3 batches, alternately with the milk in 2 batches, beginning and ending with the dry ingredients. Beat just until combined.

To make a layer cake: Butter and flour three 9-inch round cake pans. Divide the batter evenly among the pans. Bake for 25 to 30 minutes, until golden brown and a toothpick inserted into the center of a cake layer comes out clean. Let cool in the pans on wire racks for 10 minutes, then invert the cakes onto the racks and let cool completely before frosting. Fill and frost as desired.

To make a Bundt cake: Butter and flour a 9-inch Bundt pan. Pour the batter into the pan. Bake for 1 hour and 15 minutes, until golden brown and a toothpick inserted near the center comes out clean. Let cool in the pan on a wire rack for 10 minutes, then invert the cake onto the rack. If desired, pour Confectioners' Sugar Glaze (page 243) over the top while the cake is still warm, allowing the glaze to drip down the sides. Let cool completely before serving.

To make a jelly layer cake: Make the batter as directed, but reduce the baking powder to 2 teaspoons and omit the almond extract. Butter and flour four or five 8-inch cake pans. Divide the batter evenly among the pans. Bake for 15 to 18 minutes, until golden brown and a toothpick inserted into the center of a cake layer comes out clean. Let cool in the pans on wire racks for 10 minutes, then invert the cakes onto the racks and let cool completely. Stack the layers, spreading homemade jelly or other preserves between the layers and on top.

NANNIE'S POUND CAKE

Custom-cake professional Jody Stevens grew up in Corpus Christi. A framed recipe for this cake and a picture of her grandma hung in the family kitchen when she was growing up.

SERVES 8 TO 12
1½ cups unsalted butter, at room temperature
1 (1-pound) box confectioners' sugar, sifted
6 eggs, at room temperature
3½ cups cake flour, sifted
1 teaspoon vanilla extract
1 teaspoon grated lemon zest
Confectioners' Sugar Glaze (page 243; optional)
Your favorite ice cream, for serving

Preheat the oven to 350°F. Butter and flour a 9- or 10-inch Bundt pan.

In a stand mixer fitted with the paddle attachment, or in a large bowl with a handheld mixer, cream the butter on medium-high speed. Gradually add the sugar and continue to beat for about 1 minute, until light and fluffy. Scrape down the sides of the bowl. Add the eggs, one at a time, beating well after each addition. On low speed, add the flour and beat until the flour is thoroughly incorporated, then continue to beat for 15 to 30 seconds. Add the vanilla and lemon zest and beat just until combined.

Pour the batter into the prepared pan and smooth the top with a rubber spatula. Gently tap the bottom of the pan on a countertop to remove any bubbles. Bake for 1 hour and 15 minutes to 1 hour and 25 minutes, until the top is golden brown and cracked and a toothpick inserted into the center of the cake comes out clean. Let cool in the pan on a wire rack for 10 minutes, then invert the cake onto the rack.

Glaze the cake with Confectioner's Sugar Glaze while it's still warm, or serve the cake immediately with ice cream.

CONFECTIONERS' SUGAR GLAZE

Pouring this simple glaze over pound cakes or other plain cakes dresses them up.

MAKES ABOUT 6 TABLESPOONS, ENOUGH FOR 1 CAKE

1 cup confectioners' sugar, sifted
2 tablespoons milk

In a bowl, whisk together the sugar and milk until completely blended and smooth. Use immediately.

GERMAN CHOCOLATE CAKE WITH COCONUT-PECAN FROSTING

If you thought this was a cake that German bakers brought over from the old country, you are not alone. But in fact, the cake first appeared in a Dallas newspaper in 1957. It was a reader's recipe mailed into food editor Julie Bennell, and it was named after German's Sweet Chocolate, a bittersweet baking chocolate. Samuel German, who came up with the baking chocolate, worked for Walter Baker & Company, a Civil War–era chocolate maker that was later acquired by General Foods.

The cake was so good, the publication of the recipe created a huge demand for German's Sweet Chocolate in Texas. Sensing an opportunity, the General Foods test kitchens rewrote the recipe to include Baker's Angel Flake Coconut, another General Foods brand. Since 1958, the recipe for German's Sweet Chocolate Cake (and its new coconut-pecan icing) has appeared on the wrapper of every bar of German's Sweet Chocolate, which is now owned by Kraft.

SERVES 8 TO 12

1 (4-ounce) bar German's Sweet baking chocolate
½ cup water
2 cups all-purpose flour
1 teaspoon baking soda
¼ teaspoon salt
4 eggs, separated
1 cup unsalted butter, at room temperature
2 cups sugar
1 teaspoon vanilla extract
1 cup buttermilk

Coconut-Pecan Frosting
4 egg yolks
1 (12-ounce) can evaporated milk
1½ teaspoons vanilla extract
1½ cups sugar
¾ cup unsalted butter
1 (7-ounce) package sweetened flaked coconut (about 2⅔ cups)
1½ cups chopped pecans

Preheat the oven to 350°F. Cover the bottoms of three 9-inch round cake pans with parchment paper and spray the pan sides with nonstick cooking spray.

Put the chocolate and water in a large microwave-safe bowl and microwave on high for 2 minutes, stirring after 1 minute, until the chocolate is almost melted. Stir until the chocolate is completely melted and the mixture is smooth. Alternatively, combine the chocolate and water in the top pan of a double boiler, place over (not touching) barely simmering water in the bottom pan, and heat, stirring occasionally, until the chocolate is melted and the mixture is smooth. Let cool.

In a bowl, sift together the flour, baking soda, and salt. Set aside. In another bowl, using an electric mixer on high speed, beat the egg whites until stiff peaks form. Set aside.

In another bowl, using the electric mixer on medium-high speed, beat together the butter and

(Continued)

243

sugar until light and fluffy. Add the egg yolks, one at a time, beating well after each addition. Beat in the chocolate and vanilla. On low speed, add the dry ingredients in 3 batches, alternating with the buttermilk in 2 batches, beginning and ending with the dry ingredients. Beat just until combined. Add the egg whites and fold gently until well blended.

Divide the batter evenly among the prepared pans. Bake for 30 minutes, until a toothpick inserted into the center of a cake comes out clean. Transfer the pans to wire racks and immediately run a small metal spatula around the inside of each pan to loosen the cake sides. Let the cakes cool in the pans for 15 minutes, then invert onto wire racks and let cool completely.

To make the frosting, in a saucepan, whisk together the egg yolks, milk, and vanilla until well blended. Add the sugar and butter, place the pan over medium heat, and cook, stirring constantly, for about 12 minutes, until thickened and golden brown. Remove from the heat. Add the coconut and pecans and mix well. Let cool to room temperature before using.

To frost the cake, stack the cake layers on a serving plate, spreading one-third of the frosting between the layer and the final third on top.

TEA CAKES

Tea cakes are round, slightly sweet individual rolls that are served with tea or coffee. They are an old tradition in East Texas.

MAKES ABOUT 60 SMALL CAKES

3 cups all-purpose flour

½ teaspoon baking soda

½ teaspoon salt

¼ teaspoon ground nutmeg

1 cup unsalted butter, at room temperature

1¾ cups sugar

2 eggs, at room temperature

1 teaspoon vanilla extract

In a bowl, sift together the flour, baking soda, salt, and nutmeg. Set aside.

In a stand mixer fitted with the paddle attachment, or in a large bowl with a handheld mixer, cream the butter on medium-high speed. Gradually add the sugar and continue to beat for about 1 minute, until light and fluffy. Scrape down the sides of the bowl. Add the eggs, one at a time, beating well after each addition. Add the vanilla and beat until combined. Add the dry ingredients and stir with a wood spoon until thoroughly incorporated.

Turn the dough out onto a floured work surface. The dough may be sticky. Knead it until it comes together in a smooth ball. Transfer the dough to a clean bowl, cover, and refrigerate for 1 hour or until chilled.

Preheat the oven to 325°F. Have ready 2 ungreased baking sheets.

On a floured work surface, roll out the dough into a large round ¼ inch thick. Using a 1½-inch round biscuit or similar cutter, cut out as many rounds as possible. Transfer the rounds to the baking sheets, spacing them 1 inch apart. Gather up the dough scraps, reroll, cut out more rounds, and add to the baking sheets.

Bake the cakes, rotating the pans back to front midway through the baking time to ensure even baking, for 8 to 10 minutes, until lightly browned. Transfer the cakes to wire racks and let cool completely. The cakes will keep in an airtight container at room temperature for up to 1 week.

Pecan Tea Cakes: Mix ¾ cup chopped pecans into the dough after adding the vanilla and proceed as directed.

SOCK IT TO ME CAKE

As you have probably already deduced, Sock It to Me Cake is a 1970s creation inspired by a rock and roll catchphrase.

SERVES 8 TO 12

Streusel
2 tablespoons light brown sugar
2 teaspoons ground cinnamon
1 cup pecans, toasted

Batter
2¼ cups all-purpose flour
3½ teaspoons baking powder
1 teaspoon salt
1¼ cups milk
1 teaspoon vanilla extract
½ cup unsalted butter, at room temperature
1½ cups granulated sugar
3 eggs, at room temperature

Confectioners' Sugar Glaze (page 243)

Preheat the oven to 350°F. Butter and flour a 9 by 13-inch baking pan.

To make the streusel, in a small bowl, stir together all of the ingredients. Set aside.

To make the batter, in another bowl, sift together the flour, baking powder, and salt. Measure the milk and add the vanilla to it.

In a stand mixer fitted with the paddle attachment, or in a large bowl with a handheld mixer, cream the butter on medium-high speed. Gradually add the granulated sugar and continue to beat for about 1 minute, until light and fluffy. Scrape down the sides of the bowl. Add the eggs, one at a time, beating well after each addition. On low speed, add the dry ingredients in 3 batches, alternating with the milk in 2 batches, beginning and ending with the dry ingredients. Beat just until combined.

Evenly spread almost half of the batter in the bottom of the prepared pan. Sprinkle the streusel evenly over the batter. Cover the streusel with the remaining cake batter and smooth the top with a rubber spatula. Bake for 35 to 40 minutes, until springy to the touch and a toothpick inserted into the center comes out clean. Let cool completely on a wire rack.

Pour the glaze over the top of the cake, then cut into squares to serve.

REBECCA RATHER'S ANCHO BROWNIES

The Hill Country Pastry Queen, Rebecca Rather, makes these gooey, slightly spicy brownies with toasted pine nuts. But I usually substitute pecans because I have them handy. If you like a lot of spice, you can increase the ancho chile powder. See photo on page 236.

MAKES 12 BROWNIES
1 pound semisweet chocolate, coarsely chopped
1 pound unsalted butter, cut into small pieces
8 eggs, at room temperature
3 cups sugar
2 cups all-purpose flour
1½ tablespoons ancho chile powder
1 cup semisweet chocolate chips
1 cup pine nuts or pecans, toasted
Homemade Vanilla Ice Cream (page 240),
    for serving

Preheat the oven to 325°F. Butter a 9 by 13-inch baking pan.

Combine the chocolate and butter in the top pan of a double boiler, place over (not touching) barely simmering water in the bottom pan, and heat, stirring occasionally, until the chocolate and butter have melted and the mixture is smooth. Remove from the heat.

(Continued)

In a large bowl, whisk together the eggs and sugar until thickened and smooth. Add the flour, ancho powder, chocolate chips, and nuts and stir until thoroughly combined.

Pour the batter evenly into the prepared pan. Bake for 20 to 25 minutes, until a knife inserted into the center comes out clean. Let cool in the pan on a wire rack. Cut into 12 squares. Serve with the ice cream.

PECAN TORTE WITH CARAMEL TOPPING

Pecan torte was a favorite in the Big Thicket boardinghouses. Spreading caramel on top allows you to decorate the dessert with pecan halves. The mix of caramel and pecan creates a flavor that is reminiscent of *glorias*, the popular candies made in Monterrey, Mexico.

SERVES 8 TO 12

Torte
4 eggs, well beaten
2¼ cups firmly packed brown sugar
1 cup all-purpose flour
1½ teaspoons baking powder
1 cup chopped pecans
1 teaspoon vanilla extract

Filling
1 tablespoon unsalted butter
2 teaspoons all-purpose flour
1 cup heavy cream
5 teaspoons sugar
1 cup chopped pecans

Topping
1 cup bottled cajeta (Mexican thick caramel syrup) or dulce de leche (caramel sauce)
1½ cups pecan halves, toasted

Preheat the oven to 325°F. Butter and flour two 9-inch round cake pans.

To make the torte, in a bowl, stir together all of the ingredients, mixing well. Divide the batter between the prepared pans. Bake for 30 to 35 minutes, until a toothpick inserted into the center of a cake layer comes out clean. Let cool completely in the pans on wire racks, then invert the cakes onto the racks. The cakes will be thin and fragile, so work carefully.

To make the filling, melt the butter in the top pan of a double boiler placed over (not touching) simmering water. Stir in the flour, blending well, and then stir in the cream and cook, stirring often, for about 10 minutes, or until the mixture thickens. Remove the pan from the heat and let the mixture cool completely. Add the sugar, mixing well, and then stir in the chopped pecans.

Place 1 cake layer on a serving plate and spread the filling evenly over the top. Top with the second cake layer. Spread the top layer with the *cajeta* and then decorate with the pecan halves. Serve immediately, or refrigerate and serve cold.

MOM'S PECAN SANDIES

This recipe for the state's famous buttery pecan cookies comes from professional cake baker Jody Stevens, who borrowed it from her mom.

MAKES ABOUT 24 COOKIES
1 cup unsalted butter
¼ cup granulated sugar
2 teaspoons vanilla extract
2 cups all-purpose flour
1 cup chopped pecans
¼ cup confectioners' sugar

Preheat the oven to 325°F. Have ready an ungreased baking sheet.

In a stand mixer fitted with the paddle attachment, or in a bowl with a handheld mixer, cream the butter on medium-high speed. Add the granulated sugar and continue to beat for about 1 minute, until light and fluffy. Scrape down the sides of the bowl, and then beat in the vanilla. Using a wooden spoon, stir in the flour and pecans just until combined.

To shape each cookie, scoop up a spoonful of the dough and roll between your palms into a 1-inch ball. Arrange the balls on the baking sheet, spacing them 1 inch apart.

Bake the cookies, rotating the pan back to front midway through the baking time to ensure even baking, for about 20 minutes, until golden brown. Transfer the cookies to wire racks and let cool.

While the cookies are still a little warm, put the confectioners' sugar in a bag, add a few cookies, and shake the bag to coat the cookies. Repeat until all of the cookies are coated, then store in an airtight container at room temperature for up to 1 week.

COWBOY COOKIES

These are oatmeal cookies with various add-ins. Some folks call them ranger cookies or Texas Ranger cookies. There are lots of versions, all of which seem to include a different kind of breakfast cereal. Here's the recipe Laura Bush gave out as Governor's Mansion Cowboy Cookies when her husband, George W. Bush, was governor of Texas.

MAKES ABOUT 24 LARGE COOKIES

2 cups all-purpose flour

2 teaspoons baking powder

2 teaspoons baking soda

2 teaspoons ground cinnamon

⅔ teaspoon salt

1 cup unsalted butter, at room temperature

1 cup granulated sugar

1 cup firmly packed light brown sugar

2 eggs

2 teaspoons vanilla extract

2 cups semisweet chocolate chips

2 cups old-fashioned rolled oats

1 cup sweetened flaked coconut

1⅓ cups chopped pecans

Preheat the oven to 350°F. Have ready 2 ungreased baking sheets

In a bowl, stir together the flour, baking powder, baking soda, cinnamon, and salt. In a large bowl, using an electric mixer on medium speed, beat the butter for about 1 minute, until smooth and creamy. Gradually add both sugars and beat for about 2 minutes, until well combined. Add the eggs, one at a time, beating well after each addition. Beat in the vanilla. Using a wooden spoon, stir in the flour mixture just until combined. Add the chocolate chips, oats, coconut, and pecans and stir to distribute evenly.

To shape each cookie, scoop up ¼ cup of the dough and drop it onto a baking sheet, spacing the cookies about 3 inches apart. Bake the cookies, rotating the pans back to front midway through the baking time to ensure even baking, for 17 to 19 minutes, until the edges are lightly browned. Transfer the cookies to wire racks and let cool completely. Store in an airtight container at room temperature for up to 1 week.

NANNIE'S WHISKEY BALLS

This is another recipe from Jody Stevens's grandmother. Teetotalers are generally willing to overlook the modest alcohol content of these tasty cookies, which makes them popular at ice cream socials.

MAKES ABOUT 24 BALLS

3 cups fine crumbs from crushed vanilla wafers

1 cup confectioners' sugar, plus more for rolling

1 cup finely chopped pecans

3 tablespoons natural unsweetened cocoa powder

2 jiggers whiskey or rum

1½ teaspoons cane syrup

(Continued)

In a bowl, using a wooden spoon, stir together the wafer crumbs, 1 cup confectioners' sugar, pecans, cocoa powder, whiskey, and cane syrup until well mixed. If the mixture doesn't hold together, add a little more syrup.

To shape each ball, scoop up a small spoonful of the mixture and roll between your palms into a 1-inch ball. When all of the balls have been formed, spread confectioners' sugar in a small, shallow bowl and roll each ball in the sugar, coating evenly. Place in a covered container and refrigerate for about 2 hours, until set. Serve cool or at room temperature.

OLD-FASHIONED BISCUIT-STYLE PEACH COBBLER

Chuck-wagon cooks had only canned or dried peaches, but you can use stewed fresh peaches if they are in season. The biscuits are baked on top of the peaches in this recipe, so the crust will never get too soggy. Peach cobbler tastes great with vanilla ice cream.

SERVES 10 TO 12

Filling
6 cups peeled sliced peaches
¾ cup granulated sugar
¾ cup firmly packed light brown sugar
¼ cup all-purpose flour
½ teaspoon ground cinnamon
¼ teaspoon ground nutmeg
⅛ teaspoon salt
½ cup water
¼ cup bourbon (optional)
2 teaspoons freshly squeezed lemon juice
3 tablespoons unsalted butter

Boardinghouse Biscuits (page 71)

To make the filling, in a Dutch oven or other deep, heavy pot, combine all of the filling ingredients and mix well. Place over medium-high heat and cook, stirring occasionally, for about 15 minutes, until the mixture begins to thicken and stick to the sides of the pot. Remove from the heat and scrape down the sides and along the bottom of the pot until all of the filling has been loosened. Pour the mixture into a 9½ by 13-inch baking pan and set aside.

Position a rack in the lower third of the oven and preheat the oven to 350°F.

Prepare the biscuit dough. Then, using a large spoon or ice cream scoop, drop the dough on top of the peach mixture, covering it completely.

Bake the cobbler for about 30 minutes, until the biscuits begin to brown and the peach mixture is lightly bubbling. Serve warm.

TONY LAMB ON PEACH COBBLER

★ ★ ★ ★ ★ ★ ★ ★ ★ ★ ★ ★ ★ ★ ★ ★ ★ ★

"SAM'S CLUB STARTED SELLING peach cobbler with a pie crust on it, so now everybody expects peach cobbler to have a pie crust," complained Tony Lamb, a chuck-wagon cook and working cowboy at the Frying Pan Ranch, an historic cattle operation located northwest of Amarillo. Lamb and the Frying Pan Ranch team won the peach cobbler category at the National Championship Chuckwagon Cookoff four years in a row with a sourdough cobbler. "Then the organizers changed the dessert to banana pudding," he said with disgust. (There weren't many bananas in the Old West.) "When they switched back to peach cobbler, the pie-crust kind started winning."

Lamb still makes his authentic cobbler by cooking canned peaches with sugar and nutmeg, then dropping sourdough batter sweetened with brown sugar on top of the peaches before baking. The result is an old-fashioned cobbler with a biscuitlike top crust.

NOAH BARTOS'S BUTTERMILK PIE

This is the recipe for a buttermilk pie that was entered in the student division of the Moulton Pie Contest by Noah Bartos in 2006. It's an easy-to-make Texas classic.

SERVES 8

½ cup unsalted butter, at room temperature

1½ cups sugar

3 tablespoons all-purpose flour

3 eggs, beaten

1 cup buttermilk

1 teaspoon vanilla extract

Pinch of ground nutmeg

9-inch unbaked pie shell

Preheat the oven to 350°F.

In a bowl, using a wooden spoon, cream together the butter and sugar until smooth. Add the flour and eggs and beat thoroughly combined. Stir in the buttermilk, vanilla, and nutmeg, mixing well.

Pour the filling into the pie shell. Bake the pie for 40 to 45 minutes, until the custard has completely set. Let cool completely on a wire rack before serving.

Pie Scholarships in Moulton

The Moulton Pie Contest and Auction is held every July during the Moulton Town & Country Jamboree. Contestants submit pies for judging and then the pies are auctioned off. Thousands of dollars are raised each year. The proceeds benefit a college scholarship for local high-school graduates. Several of Moulton's most promising students have attended college thanks to the pie money.

TEXAS PEACH PIE

Because of high local demand, Texas peaches aren't marketed outside of the state. Use the sweetest, ripest peaches you can find, preferably freestones.

SERVES 8

6 cups peeled, pitted, and sliced peaches
    (about 8 peaches)
¾ cup granulated sugar
¾ cup firmly packed light brown sugar
3 tablespoons minute tapioca
3 tablespoons unsalted butter, cut into
    ¼-inch cubes
2 teaspoons freshly squeezed lemon juice
¼ teaspoon ground nutmeg
⅛ teaspoon salt
Pastry for double-crust pie (page 251)
1 egg white, lightly beaten
Homemade Vanilla Ice Cream (page 240),
    for serving

In a large bowl, toss the peaches with both sugars, the tapioca, butter, lemon juice, nutmeg, and salt, mixing well. Cover the fruit mixture with a sheet of plastic wrap, pressing it directly onto the surface to prevent oxidation, and refrigerate for 30 minutes.

Position a rack in the lower third of the oven and preheat the oven to 400°F.

Divide the pastry dough in half. On a lightly floured work surface, roll out each half into a 13-inch round about ⅛ inch thick. Drape 1 round around the rolling pin, carefully transfer it to a 10-inch pie pan, and fit it into the bottom and sides of the pan. Trim the overhang to the edge of the pan. Brush the bottom and sides of the crust with the egg white. Pour the fruit mixture into the pie shell, being careful not to fill the shell more than even with the rim of the pan. Cover the fruit with the second round of dough and tuck the overhang underneath the edges of the bottom crust. Use your fingers or a fork to crimp the edges, and brush with the remaining egg white.

Using a small, sharp knife, cut 3 or 4 steam vents in the top crust.

Bake the pie for about 1 hour, until the crust is golden brown. Let cool completely on a wire rack. Serve with ice cream.

CANE SYRUP PECAN PIE

If you like regular pecan pie made with corn syrup, wait until you taste old-fashioned pecan pie made with cane syrup—the difference is astonishing!

SERVES 8

Pastry for single-crust pie (recipe follows)

5 tablespoons unsalted butter

1 cup cane syrup

1 cup firmly packed light brown sugar

½ teaspoon salt

3 eggs, lightly beaten

2½ tablespoons rum or bourbon

1 teaspoon vanilla extract

½ cup chopped pecans, plus 1 cup pecan halves

Preheat the oven to 450°F.

On a lightly floured work surface, roll out the pastry dough into a 12-inch round about ⅛ inch thick. Drape the round around the rolling pin, carefully transfer it to a 9-inch pie pan, and fit it into the bottom and sides of the pan. Trim the excess to about 1 inch beyond the pan edge, then fold the overhang under and crimp or flute the edge.

Bake the pie shell for 5 minutes, until light brown. Let cool on a wire rack. Lower the oven temperature to 375°F.

In a saucepan, melt the butter over low heat. Add the cane syrup, brown sugar, and salt and stir for about 5 minutes, or until well mixed and smooth. Transfer to the bowl of a stand mixer or a large bowl and let cool.

Fit the stand mixer with the paddle attachment or have ready a handheld mixer. Add the eggs, rum, and vanilla and beat on medium-high speed for about 10 minutes, until fluffy and smooth. On low speed, add the chopped pecans and beat just until well mixed.

Pour the filling into the cooled pie shell. Arrange the pecan halves attractively on the top. Bake for 50 minutes, until the crust is golden brown. Let cool on a wire rack until the filling is well set before serving.

PIE CRUST

This is a relatively easy pie pastry recipe that comes out nice and flaky if you chill the dough well before you roll it out.

MAKES PASTRY FOR 1 (9- OR 10-INCH) SINGLE- OR DOUBLE-CRUST PIE

Pastry for Single-Crust Pie

2 cups all-purpose flour

¼ teaspoon salt

⅔ cup solid vegetable shortening

¼ cup ice water

Pastry for Double-Crust Pie

1½ cups all-purpose flour

⅛ teaspoon salt

½ cup solid vegetable shortening

3 tablespoons ice water

In a bowl, stir together the flour and salt. Using a pastry blender or a fork, cut the shortening into the flour mixture until the mixture is the texture of coarse meal. Add the water, 1 tablespoon at a time, and stir and toss with a fork to moisten evenly. Gently gather the dough into a ball, then flatten slightly. Wrap with plastic wrap and refrigerate for 30 minutes before rolling out.

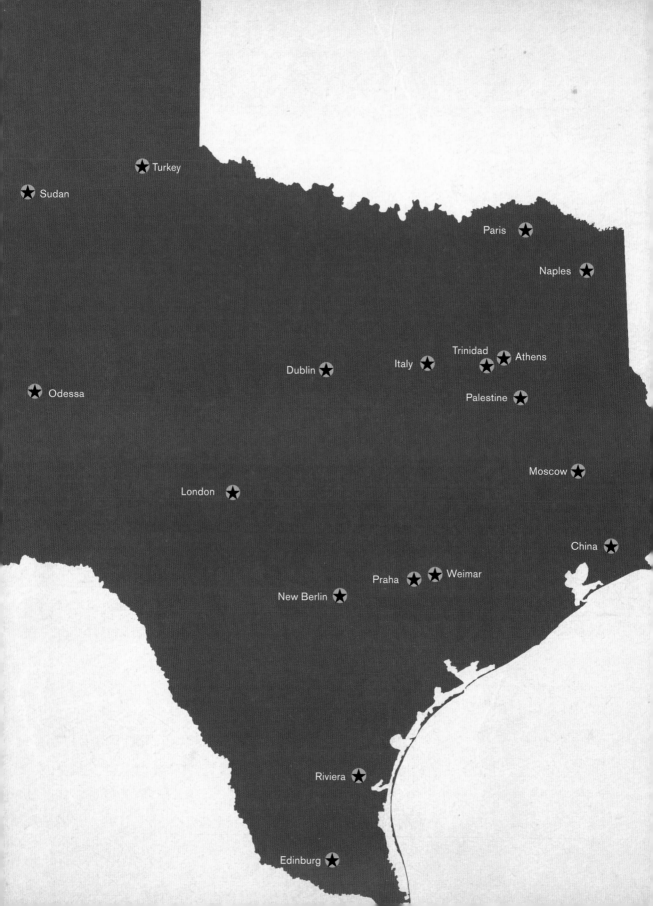

PART VI

NEW TEXAS CREOLE

Multicultural Texas

You don't have to leave Texas to visit Praha, Paris, or Dublin. Athens, Roma, and Moscow are all in-state destinations as well. Immigrants seem to find comfort in naming their new towns and cities after the places they left behind. And it's only a matter of time before more recent immigrants found Texas municipalities named after their homelands, too. Bet on Mumbai, Texas; Saigon, Texas; and Beirut, Texas to be added to the map soon.

Spaghetti and meatballs at the Sacred Heart Society's spaghetti lunch in Houston.

CHAPTER 21

SPAGHETTI WESTERN

★★★★★★★★★★★★★★★★★★★★★★

One and one," Frank Mancuso told the man in front of the spaghetti sauces. The white-haired chef reached into two adjacent pans and lifted out one link of well-cooked Italian sausage and one large meatball and placed them on top of Frank's spaghetti. "And a little extra *sugo*," said Frank. *Sugo* is Sicilian for gravy, and the sauce man obediently doused the whole plate with the hot "red gravy." I parroted Frank's sausage and meatball order.

The Sacred Heart Society's spaghetti lunch is held just north of downtown Houston every Thursday in a hall built specially for the event. Saint Arnold beer sales rep Frank Mancuso showed me the ropes. Baked chicken was on the short menu for those who don't want spaghetti.

Attending the Thursday spaghetti lunch when you don't want spaghetti would be my definition of an eating disorder. The menu also lists pig's feet and pork chops. "Pig's feet?" I muttered in surprise. "They put the pig's feet in the bottom of the sauce pot," Frank explained. "By the time they are done cooking the red sauce, the pig's feet are falling apart." I have never heard of putting pig's feet in red sauce, but it sounded so good, my mouth was watering.

We filed by the cash register and paid up. Then we wandered around the enormous dining hall looking for spots at one of the long tables. The hall seats five or six hundred people and it was more than half full. It looked like the cafeteria at a big high school, except most of the people had white hair. One table had a glass map of the state of Texas with "Fourth Ward Table" engraved on it. Not far away was another placard for the First Ward. Companies and clubs also bring their own little reservation markers and stake out tables.

Frank and I found a place to sit down near a rowdy bunch of Italian American men in their sixties and seventies. The guy sitting next to me was in the avocado business. I asked him how he got started. He explained that his family had been farming and selling vegetables on the Gulf Coast for three generations.

Italians are the sixth largest ethnic group in Texas. The first Italians came to Texas with the Spanish. Several Italians followed Coronado as he crossed the Llano Estacado in 1541, looking for the fabled cities of gold. Italian-born Prospero Bernardi was a soldier

THE NEW CREOLE

★ ★

GUMBO, THE LOUISIANA SOUP that blends African, European, and Native American cultures, is often used to illustrate the process of cultural blending known as creolization. In the 1800s, New Orleans, once the largest port on the Gulf Coast and the commercial hub of the Caribbean basin, was the birthplace of a multicultural cuisine that its residents call Creole.

Houston and Galveston had fewer immigrants than New Orleans did in the late 1800s, but they experienced their own style of creolization. Houston's Market Square was a multicultural bazaar where German farmers brought wagonloads of produce from the outlying settlements, Chinese merchants sold Asian specialties, Italians peddled imported fruit along with fresh fish and wild game, African Texans offered garden vegetables and figs from local orchards, and Tejanos provided hot tamales, chili con carne, and other prepared foods. Houstonians of every social level visited the market on Saturday nights just to take in the colorful scene.

Today, Houston is the largest port and commercial hub of the Gulf Coast. And America's fourth largest city has become a magnet for new immigrants from all over the world. Changes in the immigration laws in the 1960s resulted in more immigration from Central America, India, Pakistan, and Southeast Asia. The vibrant job market in Houston was a big draw for folks from these areas—and so was the hot weather and spicy food.

In the past twenty years, a new wave of creolization featuring such delicacies as Viet Cajun crawfish, Pakistani masala fajitas, and Arab Texan jalapeño falafels joined the existing lineup of Houston multicultural food favorites. But the real change is illustrated by the odd combination of ingredients found on Houston's refrigerator doors. Mainstream Houstonians have become accustomed to squirting Sriracha sauce on their sandwiches and spooning chutney over their pork chops.

Chef Bryan Caswell grew up eating Vietnamese, Indian, and Italian food in Houston, then after completing his training at the Culinary Institute of America, he traveled the world cooking in famed French chef Jean-Georges Vongerichten's restaurants. When he opened his first restaurant, Reef, he wanted to serve food that combined the flavors he grew up with in Houston.

To Caswell, it seemed only natural to make oysters Rockefeller with a dash of Indian lime pickle (see page 280) and to update old-fashioned New Orleans rémoulade with Sriracha sauce. At his "Texas-Tuscan" restaurant Stella Sola ("Lone Star" in Italian), he slathers jalapeño pesto (see page 260) on grilled steaks.

At Houston's now-shuttered Catalan restaurant, chef Chris Shepherd served Mexican, Thai, Vietnamese, and Korean street food dishes side by side. At Haven, Randy Evans combines southern, European, and Latin flavors in dishes like crawfish tails with gnocchi and Mexican marigold mint. Haven serves Gulf soft-shell crabs with vegetables and *nuoc cham*, the Vietnamese dipping sauce.

In the past ten years, new immigrants and their cuisines have spread farther and wider across the state. I've been served pho by a Hmong American at a noodle shop in College Station, eaten kolaches baked by Korean Americans in Dallas doughnut shops, and admired the gardens planted on the grounds of South Asian–owned motels in the far corners of Texas.

This multicultural wave is only beginning and the new Creole cooking is evolving before our eyes.

in Houston's army at the Battle of San Jacinto in 1836. But the largest wave of Italian immigrants entered Texas between 1880 and 1920. Whereas people from northern Italy headed for Brooklyn and the Northeast, the Sicilians gravitated toward the subtropical climates of New Orleans and Galveston. Filling a labor gap, the Sicilian immigrants found work as stevedores, agricultural workers, and railroad workers. But they quickly got into the grocery business.

Many Sicilians established small neighborhood corner groceries. In 1900, Galveston Island alone had more than a hundred corner stores. At Houston's bustling Market Square, Italian farmers packed their stalls with freshly harvested vegetables and fruits and Italian grocers stocked their stores with the produce. Today, the same Italian families still own the buildings of the Farmer's Marketing Association on Airline Drive. The Sacred Heart Society spaghetti lunch is held close by.

Once we were settled, Frank and I dug into our spaghetti. It was cooked perfectly. The meatball was a touch too dense. But the sausage was awesome and so was the *sugo*, or red gravy as it is known in Texas and Louisiana. It was comfort food at its best. Spaghetti and meatballs, pizza, and lasagna were still very foreign to mainstream Texans in the middle of the last century. Campisi's in Dallas, which opened as Campisi's Egyptian Lounge, may be the oldest extant Italian restaurant in the state. It opened in 1946, and remains justly famous for its pizza.

I sprinkled a blizzard of Parmesan and a healthy dose of red pepper flakes over the pile of spaghetti

Tony Leago.

from the shaker bottles in front of me. About halfway through my meal, I reached for a plastic pitcher in the middle of the table, thinking it contained water. Instead, it turned out to be full of *sugo*. As long as I had it in my hand, I splashed more sauce on my plate.

"We are a living tradition," said Tony Leago, the Sacred Heart Society's unofficial greeter and goodwill ambassador. After lunch, Tony, also known as The Man in Black for his monochromatic wardrobe, gave us a tour of the Sacred Heart Society's headquarters. We saw photos of the past presidents going back to the 1950s, we stopped by the card room and billiards room, and we admired the many awards the group has won for their charitable deeds. The proceeds of the spaghetti lunch and other events go to the St. Vincent de Paul Society to feed the poor. "We come here once a week to eat a meal with family and preserve our culture—and it's a nice pasta and sauce and all homemade," Tony said.

The lunch has been held every Thursday since 1953. Frank grew up eating here. His father, Frank Octavius Mancuso, was a popular Houston city councilman. He presided over "the Italian city council table," his son explained.

"This is the most popular lunch spot in the city for politicians during election season," Frank told me. "But we have rules. The politicians are only allowed to talk for three minutes. And before they can get up on the podium, they have to buy a glass of wine for everybody in the hall." I assumed he was kidding at first. But then I realized he was serious. I can't wait to go back at election time.

FRANK MANCUSO'S TEXAS SUGO

This is Frank Mancuso's family *sugo* recipe. It includes sausages, but you can add meatballs instead, if you prefer. The grated Parmesan and Romano cheeses are essential to smooth out the flavor of the sauce, but if you add them too early, the sauce will stick to the bottom of the pot and burn. Add the cheeses just before serving—and don't add any to the sauce you plan to save and reheat.

MAKES ABOUT 6 CUPS SAUCE

2 tablespoons extra-virgin olive oil
½ yellow onion, chopped
3 cloves garlic, chopped
1 jalapeño chile, minced (optional)
1 cup very finely chopped, peeled carrots
1 cup sliced mushrooms
2 (28-ounce) cans Roma tomatoes, with juice
¼ cup chopped fresh flat-leaf parsley
¼ cup chopped fresh basil
1 (6-ounce) can tomato paste
¼ cup dry red wine
2 pounds Italian sausages or meatballs
¼ cup mixed grated Parmesan and Romano
   cheeses, in equal parts
Salt

In a heavy, 4- to 5-quart pot, heat the oil over medium-high heat. Add the onion and cook, stirring, for 2 minutes. Add the garlic and chile and cook, stirring, for 1 minute. Add the carrots and mushrooms and cook, stirring, for 2 minutes. Add the tomatoes and their juice and stir together. Add the parsley and basil, stir well, and then crush the tomatoes with a potato masher for about 5 minutes, until the sauce starts to thicken. Add the tomato paste and wine and stir to blend. Lower the heat to a gentle simmer and cook, stirring occasionally, for an hour or until the sauce has darkened in color and thickened.

Meanwhile, cook the sausages in a skillet over medium heat on the stove top or in a 350°F oven until they are cooked through. Add the cooked sausages to the sauce and continue to simmer, stirring occasionally, for 15 minutes, until the sausage or meatballs are well done. Stir gently so you do not break up the sausages or meatballs.

Just before serving, in a saucepan over low heat, add the Parmesan mixture to as much *sugo* as you intend to use right away. Stir continuously so the cheese doesn't stick to the bottom of the pot. Season with salt.

Use the *sugo* to make spaghetti and meatballs, lasagna, hot baked meatball or sausage sandwiches, or your favorite Italian-American creations.

TEXAS OLIVE OIL

★ ★ ★ ★ ★ ★ ★ ★ ★ ★ ★ ★ ★ ★ ★ ★ ★ ★ ★

TEXAS OLIVE OILS are high quality and have a bold, peppery flavor. But Texas hasn't been in the olive oil business very long. Olive trees require warm days and cool nights and are easily damaged by frost, and only a few areas in the state offer such conditions. Olive groves planted in Carrizo Springs, near the Mexican border at Piedras Negras, and Elmendorf, south of San Antonio, are currently bearing olives.

In 2010, five hundred tons of olives were harvested, according to the Texas Olive Oil Council. More trees are currently being planted, with the state projecting more than a million trees under cultivation by 2012, weather permitting.

SPAGHETTI AND EGGPLANT

The hot climate of Sicily, like the hot climate of Texas, is well suited to growing basil, eggplants, and peppers. This simple pasta dish is one of Sicily's most typical combinations. It's perfect for a Texas summer supper, too.

SERVES 6

½ cup olive oil

2 cloves garlic, minced

1 large eggplant (about 1 pound), peeled and cut into 1-inch cubes

1 pound Roma tomatoes, peeled and coarsely chopped

1 pound spaghetti

¼ cup torn fresh basil leaves

24 Sicilian black olives, pitted and chopped

Red pepper flakes, for seasoning

Sea salt

Dry red wine, for moistening

½ cup grated Romano cheese

In a large sauté pan, heat the oil over medium-high heat. Add the garlic and stir for 1 to 2 minutes, until lightly browned. Add the eggplant and tomatoes, stir well, and simmer, stirring occasionally, for about 20 minutes, until the eggplant is tender.

Bring a large pot of salted water to a boil. Add the spaghetti and cook until al dente, following the instructions on the package.

Just before the pasta is ready, mash the eggplant and tomatoes together, stir in the basil and olives, and season with red pepper flakes and salt. Moisten with a little wine if needed to thin and cook for 5 minutes longer.

Drain the spaghetti and transfer to a serving bowl. Spoon the sauce over the top and sprinkle with the cheese. Serve immediately.

SICILIAN CAULIFLOWER SALAD

Cauliflower and broccoli were exotic vegetables unknown to most Americans until Italian immigrants began growing them and selling them at local markets. The Sicilians also introduced eggplant and pimento. Like the Mexicans, they had a fondness for prickly pear fruit.

SERVES 6

3 quarts water

2 tablespoons table salt

1 large head cauliflower, cut into florets (about 2½ pounds florets)

¼ cup high-quality extra-virgin olive oil

2 tablespoons red wine vinegar

½ teaspoon sea salt

½ cup pitted black Sicilian olives, minced

¼ cup capers, drained

¼ cup sweet pickle relish

1 tablespoon anchovy paste

1 cup finely chopped red bell peppers

1 tablespoon minced fresh flat-leaf parsley

2 hard-boiled eggs, chopped

In a large saucepan, bring the water and table salt to a boil, add the cauliflower, and boil for 3 to 5 minutes, until the florets are tender-crisp. Drain the cauliflower in a colander, then immerse in a bowl of ice water until cool. Drain well again.

In a large bowl, whisk together the oil, vinegar, and sea salt. Add the olives, capers, pickle relish, and anchovy paste and mix well. Add the cauliflower, red peppers, and parsley and toss to mix well. Cover and place in the refrigerator to marinate for a few hours, tossing occasionally.

A few minutes before serving, remove the salad from the refrigerator. Sprinkle with the eggs just before serving.

CAVATELLI AND BROCCOLI

This Italian favorite got my kids to eat broccoli. Cavatelli, small, irregularly shaped ovals with rolled edges, is the traditional pasta for this dish, but it is hard to find. Other short, thick pasta shapes work equally well. My kids like it with wagon wheel pasta.

SERVES 4

2 heads broccoli (about 18 ounces), cut into
    florets
3 tablespoons olive oil
3 cloves garlic, minced
1 pound cavatelli or other short pasta
½ teaspoon salt
½ teaspoon red pepper flakes
2 tablespoons grated Parmesan cheese

Bring a large saucepan of water to a boil. Add the broccoli and parboil for about 5 minutes, until half cooked. Drain well and set aside.

In a large skillet, heat the oil over medium heat. Add the garlic and sauté for 1 to 2 minutes, until lightly golden. Be careful it does not burn. Add the broccoli and sauté, stirring occasionally, for about 10 minutes, until tender yet still crisp to the bite.

Meanwhile, bring a large pot of salted water to a boil. Add the pasta and cook until al dente, following the instructions on the package.

Drain the pasta, and transfer to a serving bowl. Pour the contents of the skillet over the top and toss well. Season with the salt and red pepper flakes, sprinkle with the cheese, and serve immediately.

STELLA SOLA'S JALAPEÑO PESTO

Owner-chef Bryan Caswell likes to combine Italian techniques and Texas ingredients at Stella Sola, his Houston restaurant. This cross-cultural fusion sounds new, but it actually goes back to the city's early Sicilian immigrants. Toss this pesto with spaghetti and serve with Italian sausages, or use the pesto to give a nice fiery kick to vegetable dishes.

MAKES 4 CUPS

1 jalapeño chile, roasted (page 129), peeled,
    seeded, and chopped
1 cup packed fresh flat-leaf parsley leaves
1 cup packed fresh basil leaves
⅛ cup grated pecorino cheese
¼ cup pine nuts, toasted
1 small clove garlic, coarsely chopped
1 small shallot, coarsely chopped
2 cups extra-virgin olive oil
Salt and freshly ground pepper
Grated lemon zest, for seasoning

In a blender, combine the chile, parsley, basil, cheese, pine nuts, garlic, and shallot. Add ¼ cup of the oil and turn on the blender. Once a puree starts to form, slowly stream in the remaining 1¾ cups oil and then continue to process until you have a smooth puree. Season the pesto with salt, pepper, and lemon zest to taste. Use immediately, or transfer to a tightly covered container and refrigerate for up to a week, or freeze for up to 3 months.

GULF CIOPPINO

Gumbo is the native fish stew of the Gulf Coast, but some Italian Texans make cioppino with the local seafood. Cioppino is an Italian American seafood stew that was originally made aboard fishing boats with whatever fish was available. The name comes from the Ligurian dialect word *ciuppin*, which is used for a seafood soup or stew.

SERVES 4

2 pounds heads-on shrimp

2 pounds redfish or other small whole fish, with heads intact, cleaned

1 yellow onion

2 stalks celery

8 cups water

4 live blue crabs

¼ cup olive oil

2 teaspoons salt

2 large cloves garlic, finely chopped

1 jalapeño chile, minced

1 (6-ounce) can tomato paste

1 (28-ounce) can diced tomatoes, with juice

1 cup dry white wine

Juice of 1 lemon

Juice of 1 orange

3 bay leaves

1 tablespoon paprika

Hot pepper sauce, for seasoning (optional)

Peel and devein the shrimp and put the shells and heads in a stockpot. Fillet the fish and add the bones and heads to the stockpot. Refrigerate the shrimp and fish fillets. Peel the onion and trim the celery, then add the peelings and trimmings to the stockpot. Chop the onion and celery and set aside.

Add the water to the stockpot and bring to a boil over high heat. Add the crabs and cook for about 10 minutes, until they turn red. Scoop the crabs out of the pot and lower the heat to a simmer. When the crabs are cool enough to handle, remove the top shell, apron, and gills and other innards from each crab and add them to the stockpot. Set the crab bodies, with claws attached, aside. Simmer the stock, uncovered, for a total of 30 minutes, adding water as needed to maintain the original level. Remove from the heat and strain the stock through a fine-mesh sieve placed over a bowl. Set aside.

In a soup pot, heat 3 tablespoons of the oil over medium heat. Add the onion, celery, and salt and sauté for about 5 minutes, until the onion is soft. Add the garlic and jalapeño and sauté for 2 minutes. Stir in the tomato paste and then add the strained stock, tomatoes and their juice, wine, citrus juices, and bay leaves. Decrease the heat to medium-low, cover, and simmer for about 30 minutes to blend the flavors.

Cut the fish fillets into 2-inch chunks and toss with the paprika. In a skillet, heat the remaining 1 tablespoon oil over medium heat. Add the fish chunks and cook, turning as needed with a spatula, for about 4 minutes, until the fish flakes easily. Add the fish to the soup pot, then return the skillet to medium heat, add a little of the tomato broth from the soup, and deglaze the pan, scraping up any brown bits on the pan bottom. Dump the contents of the skillet into the soup pot and add the shrimp. Simmer gently until the shrimp are just cooked through. Taste and adjust the seasoning with salt, then season with pepper sauce.

Ladle the soup into 4 bowls. Hang a crab body on the rim of each bowl, with the body in the soup and a claw extending beyond the rim of the bowl. Serve immediately with nutcrackers for cracking the claws.

Banh Mi Xiu Mai, page 269.

Carl Han's Vietnamese and French ancestors in Handi.

CHAPTER 22
BANH MI ON THE BAYOU

★★★★★★★★★★★★★★★★★★★★★★★★★★★★

The first time I ate at the original Pho Binh on Beamer Road in South Houston was a cold, foggy Saturday morning. The single-wide trailer that's home to the Vietnamese restaurant was packed. Everyone seemed to be eating *pho* (pronounced "fuh"). The hot beef broth and hearty rice noodle bowl is a favorite Vietnamese breakfast, especially in cold weather.

The place was cramped and tiny. By leaning around the corner behind the cashier, I could see the giant pots of beef broth simmering on the range in the kitchen. Chunks of beef and whole onions were floating on the surface of the broth.

On that first visit, I ordered the #6 *pho*, which came with rare steak, brisket, and crispy fat. The beef broth was rich and salty and heady with spicy aromas. *Pho* is traditionally made with lots of onions and star anise, but my breakfast companion speculated that the kitchen changed the spice blend from summer to winter. She thought she detected more cinnamon in the winter broth.

The soup comes with an herb plate. I tore the basil leaves off their stems and added them to the bowl along with a couple of wheels of jalapeño and most of the bean sprouts. Then I squeezed a couple of lime wedges over the top. The crispy fat was a slice of fatty beef that had been fried. It wasn't really all that crispy after it was submerged in the soup. The soup had a deep, satisfying homemade flavor.

Opened in the early 1980s, the Pho Binh on Beamer Road is said to be the first *pho* restaurant in Houston (and possibly the rest of Texas). Some rickety buildings had been tacked onto the original trailer, and the whole place overlooks a swampy bayou.

Outside the front door that Saturday morning, several men were crowded around a picnic table eating their breakfast noodles and smoking cigarettes. It reminded me of descriptions I have heard of the *pho* stands in Hanoi, where the dish originated. There, the soup is often eaten at long common tables where workers sit side by side slurping their breakfast noodles.

"*Pho* is a North Vietnamese dish," Vietnamese food expert Carl Han told me. The history of the dish is recent and somewhat controversial. "It wasn't introduced to the southern part of Vietnam until the 1950s. Some scholars think that the word is a mispronunciation of *feu*, French for 'fire,'" Han told me.

A symposium on the origins of *pho* was held in Hanoi in 2003. Didier Corlou, a French chef who has spent many years cooking in the city, presented the theory that the soup was inspired by the French pot-au-feu. To support his argument, he pointed out that although oxen were long used as beasts of burden in Vietnam, beef wasn't eaten there until the French arrived. He also observed that both pot-au-feu and the stock for *pho* are made with marrowbones. Plus, the theory that *pho* is related to pot-au-feu makes sense in light of other Vietnamese borrowings.

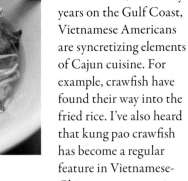

Texas Pho, page 265.

"The Vietnamese, who were under the Chinese for a thousand years and a French colony for a hundred and fifty, have a long tradition of culinary syncretism," Dr. Carl Bankston, an associate professor of sociology and Asian studies at Tulane University, told me. Noodles were borrowed from the Chinese. The Vietnamese baguette, with its component of rice flour, is a distinctly Vietnamese version of French bread. "The Vietnamese have learned to adapt to outside domination by taking foreign influences and making them their own," said Bankston. And the results of these innovations are authentically Vietnamese.

And now, after forty years on the Gulf Coast, Vietnamese Americans are syncretizing elements of Cajun cuisine. For example, crawfish have found their way into the fried rice. I've also heard that kung pao crawfish has become a regular feature in Vietnamese-Chinese restaurants in Baton Rouge. But as odd as Vietnamese-Cajun fusion might sound at first, it's actually a natural.

The two cuisines have a lot in common. Rice is the basic staple of both Vietnamese and Louisianan cookery, and both kitchens rely heavily on fresh seafood and chiles. And since both were also once French colonies, they speak the same language in the kitchen: baguettes, beignets, and café au lait are as well known in Ho Chi Minh City as in New Orleans. Po'boys and *banh mi* (Vietnamese sandwiches) are remarkably similar, despite the fact that they evolved half a world apart from each other.

Vietnamese Cajun isn't a hybrid. It's a clear case of syncretism—the absorption of one culture's traditions by another. The Vietnamese are borrowing

Cajun food traditions to suit themselves. What Cajuns or other Americans think of this new fusion food doesn't concern them.

Texans seem to love a few Vietnamese dishes, whether they are intended for them or not. *Bo luc loc*, a dish of medium-rare grilled beef tenderloin chunks served over a salad, is nicknamed rock and roll beef in Texas. *Bo nuong xa*, grilled beef and herbs that the diner rolls up in rice paper sheets at the table, is better known as Vietnamese fajitas. And *pho* restaurants are popping up everywhere, including in such bastions of meat and potatoes as College Station and Wichita Falls. Vietnamese sandwiches are popular, too. My favorite is *banh mi xui mai*, which is stuffed with meatballs.

But when you eat at a typical Gulf Coast Vietnamese restaurant, you don't see the kind of Americanized dishes that Chinese and Mexican restaurant owners came up with to satisfy the American palate. So why aren't the Vietnamese trying to cater to the mainstream?

The Vietnamese were attracted to the Gulf Coast partly because of the warm weather, Carl Bankston observed, but mainly to seek employment in the seafood industry. And the Vietnamese here continue to be disproportionately employed in fishing, shrimping, and seafood processing, he said. Unlike Chinese and Mexican immigrants, the Vietnamese don't rely on restaurants as a primary means of supporting themselves. So until they start trying to appeal to mainstream customers, there is no point in diluting their cuisine.

"It's the same with Vietnamese Creole food," said Bankston. "It's designed to appeal to new generations of Vietnamese. It's not a cuisine for the masses."

But the Vietnamese have become a part of the new creolized culture of Texas anyway. If you want culinary evidence, witness the *banh mi* burgers that are popping up in Texas burger joints. Texans are so fond of crunchy, spicy *banh mi* sandwiches that they are adopting the Vietnamese form to fit the native burger. And once you taste a burger with pickled daikon and Sriracha mayo, you'll understand why.

TEXAS PHO

I like to roast the bones first to get some color in the stock, but this step is not authentic. "Fuel was too expensive to cook the soup any longer than absolutely necessary," a Vietnamese friend explained. "On special occasions, my mom would add a raw egg to each bowl and gently pour the hot broth over it to poach it," he said. Fresh *banh pho* noodles are available at any Vietnamese market, but you can use dried rice noodles if you can't find them.

MAKES 6 REGULAR BOWLS OR 4 BIG BOWLS

3 pounds beef neck bones
1 pound beef brisket, trimmed
2 shallots, sliced
2 ounces fresh ginger, thickly sliced
1 star anise
1 black cardamom pod
1 cinnamon stick
**½ cup sliced jalapeño chiles, plus more
   for serving**
Fish sauce, for seasoning and serving
Sea salt and freshly ground pepper
4 green onions
**Assorted fresh herbs (such as mint, cilantro,
   and basil), for garnish and serving**
1 pound flat rice noodles (*banh pho*)
3 limes, cut into wedges
Sriracha sauce, for serving

Preheat the oven to 400°F. Rinse the bones and brisket and place in a roasting pan. Roast, turning the bones and meat several times, for about 20 minutes, until well browned.

Meanwhile, in a small, dry skillet, toast the shallot and ginger slices over medium heat until lightly charred. Transfer to a small bowl and reserve. Add the star anise and cardamom to the same pan and toast over medium heat until aromatic. Remove from the heat and crush lightly. Place the star anise,

(Continued)

cardamom, and cinnamon stick on a square of cheesecloth, bring together the corners of the square, and tie securely with kitchen twine. Reserve the bundle.

When the bones and meat are ready, transfer them to a stockpot and add water to cover by (8 to 10 cups). Bring to a boil over high heat, skimming off any scum that forms on the surface. Add the charred ginger and shallot slices, the spice bundle, and the ½ cup chiles and season with fish sauce, salt, and pepper. Decrease the heat to low and simmer for 2½ hours, adding water as needed to maintain the original level.

Remove the spice bundle and beef bones and discard. Remove the beef and set aside. Keep the stock at a gentle simmer and taste and adjust the seasoning with salt and pepper.

Bring a large pot filled with water to a boil. While the water is heating, trim and slice the green onions and herbs and slice the brisket into bite-size pieces pieces. If using fresh noodles, drop the noodles into the boiling water for 30 seconds and then drain. If using dried noodles, cook for 2 to 3 minutes, until just tender, then drain.

Divide the noodles evenly among individual serving bowls. Arrange an equal amount of the meat over the noodles in each bowl, then top with some of the herbs and green onions. Ladle the simmering stock over the noodles and meat. Arrange the remaining herbs and green onions on a plate with the lime wedges and chile slices. Serve the soup immediately, accompanied with the plate of garnishes, Sriracha sauce, and fish sauce.

FAUX PHO

When you don't have a few hours to make the broth, you can make fake *pho* in minutes by adding star anise, cinnamon, and other spices to store-bought beef broth. Filet mignon is easier to slice frozen than at room temperature.

SERVES 2 GENEROUSLY

1 (8-ounce) filet mignon
2 ounces fresh ginger, halved
1 shallot, sliced
1 tablespoon soy sauce
1 star anise
1 black cardamom pod
1 cinnamon stick
4 cups beef broth
½ cup sliced jalapeño chiles
Fish sauce, for seasoning and serving
Sea salt and freshly ground pepper
8 ounces dried rice noodles (banh pho)
Assorted fresh herbs (such as mint, cilantro, and basil), coarsely chopped, for garnish and serving
4 green onions, chopped
2 limes, cut into wedges
Sriracha sauce, for serving

Using a meat slicer or a sharp knife, cut the filet mignon into paper-thin slices and place in a bowl. Peel and mince half of the ginger and add to the beef slices along with the soy sauce. Set aside to marinate.

Cut the remaining ginger into 2 thick slices. In a small, dry skillet, toast the ginger and shallot slices over medium heat until lightly charred. Transfer to a small bowl and reserve. Add the star anise and cardamom to the same pan and toast over medium heat until aromatic. Remove from the heat and crush lightly. Place the star anise, cardamom, and cinnamon stick on a square of cheesecloth, bring together the corners of the square, and tie securely with kitchen twine.

In a saucepan, bring the broth to a boil over high heat. Add the charred ginger and shallot slices, the spice bundle, and half of the chiles and season with fish sauce, salt, and pepper. Decrease the heat to low and simmer for 30 minutes.

Remove the spice bundle and discard. Keep the broth at a gentle simmer and taste and adjust the seasoning with salt and pepper. Bring a large saucepan filled with water to a boil. Drop the noodles into the boiling water and cook for 2 to 3 minutes, until just tender, then drain.

Divide the noodles evenly between 2 individual serving bowls. Arrange an equal amount of the beef slices over the noodles in each bowl, then top with some of the herbs and green onions and half of the remaining chiles. Ladle the simmering broth over the noodles and meat. Arrange the remaining herbs, green onions, and chiles on a plate with the lime wedges. Serve the soup immediately, accompanied with the plate of garnishes, Sriracha sauce, and fish sauce.

BO LUC LAC (ROCK AND ROLL BEEF)

Marinated tenderloin chunks shaken in a hot wok until medium-rare and served over a salad is one of the most popular Vietnamese dishes in Texas. The name translates to "shaken beef," a reference to the action of the wok, but Texans call the dish "rock and roll beef."

According to Vietnamese food expert Andrea Nguyen, the version of this dish we eat in the United States is not authentic. In Vietnam, cattle are never grain fed and slaughtered at older ages. To achieve the more authentic chewiness of real *bo luc lac*, Nguyen's recommends using cheaper, tougher beef cuts. If authenticity is important to you, go for it. I'll stick with the filet mignon.

SERVES 3 OR 4

Marinated Steak
2 cloves garlic, minced
2 tablespoons oyster sauce
2 tablespoons soy sauce
1 teaspoon fish sauce
2 teaspoons sugar
½ teaspoon freshly cracked pepper
1 pound filet mignon, cut into 1-inch cubes

Salad
2 tablespoons rice vinegar
1 tablespoon hot water
2 teaspoons sugar
Sea salt and freshly ground black pepper
1 shallot, thinly sliced
4 cups salad greens
2 tomatoes, sliced

2 tablespoons peanut oil
Pickled Vietnamese Vegetables (page 268), for garnish
Fresh herb leaves (such as cilantro, basil, and mint), for serving
Steamed long-grain white rice, for serving

To prepare the steak, in a bowl, combine the garlic, oyster sauce, soy sauce, fish sauce, sugar, and pepper and mix well. Add the beef and toss to coat well. Set aside to marinate for 1 to 2 hours.

To make the salad, in a large bowl, combine the vinegar, hot water, sugar, and salt and pepper to taste and whisk until the sugar has dissolved. Add the shallot. Reserve the greens and tomatoes.

In a wok or large skillet, heat the oil over high heat. Drain the beef from the marinade, add to the hot oil, and sear for about 1 minute on the first side. Turn the cubes and sear on the second side for about 1 minute. Continue to cook the beef for about 5 minutes, until medium-rare.

Just before the beef is ready, add the salad greens to the dressing and toss to coat well. Arrange the dressed greens on a platter and arrange the tomatoes on top. When the beef is done, spoon it on top of the salad and garnish with the pickled vegetables. Serve immediately with the herbs and rice on the side.

XIU MAI (MEATBALLS)

Vietnamese meatballs are a popular addition to a bowl of *pho*, as well as the filling for my favorite *banh mi*. Traditionally steamed, they are a little rubbery to many Texans, so I have included a variation that calls for browning the meatballs and finishing them in the oven.

MAKES 16 MEATBALLS, ENOUGH FOR 4 SANDWICHES

1 pound ground pork
½ cup minced jicama
2 tablespoons finely chopped fresh basil
2 tablespoons finely chopped green onions (white and green parts)
1 tablespoon chopped garlic
1 egg
1 tablespoon fish sauce or soy sauce
1 tablespoon Sriracha sauce
1 tablespoon sugar
2 teaspoons cornstarch
1 teaspoon freshly ground pepper
1 teaspoon kosher salt

In a bowl, combine all of the ingredients and mix well with your hands. Divide the mixture into 16 balls, rolling them between your palms. Arrange the balls in a shallow heatproof bowl or a bamboo or metal basket that will fit in your steamer.

Bring water to a boil in the bottom of a steamer pan, place the bowl of meatballs on the steamer rack, cover, and steam for about 20 minutes, or until the meatballs are cooked through. To test for doneness, cut open a meatball. Serve hot.

Panfrying and Baking Variation: Preheat the oven to 350°F. In an ovenproof cast-iron skillet, heat 1 tablespoon peanut oil over medium-high heat. Add the meatballs and brown well on all sides. Transfer the skillet to the oven and bake for 5 to 10 minutes, until cooked through.

SPICY VIET-TEX MAYO

This mayo is good on all kinds of sandwiches, so you may want to make a double batch.

MAKES ABOUT 1 CUP

1 cup mayonnaise
3 green onions (white and green parts), finely chopped
1 teaspoon minced jalapeño chile
1 tablespoon Sriracha sauce
Salt

In a bowl, stir together the mayonnaise, onions, chile, and Sriracha sauce. Season to taste with salt. Use immediately, or cover and refrigerate for up to 1 week.

PICKLED VIETNAMESE VEGETABLES

Daikon can be hard to find in Texas, so jicama is often substituted for it in these pickled vegetables. (It can sometimes fill in for water chestnuts, too.)

MAKES ABOUT 6 CUPS

½ cup rice vinegar
½ cup sugar
1 tablespoon Asian sesame oil
1 teaspoon kosher salt
2 cups julienned, peeled carrots
2 cups julienned, peeled daikon or jicama
2 jalapeño chiles, seeded and thinly sliced

In a saucepan, combine the vinegar, sugar, sesame oil, and salt over medium heat and cook, stirring to dissolve the sugar, for about 5 minutes, until steaming. Add the carrots, daikon, and chiles, decrease the heat to low, and simmer for 4 or 5 minutes, until soft.

Remove from the heat and let cool. Transfer to a covered container and refrigerate. The vegetables will keep for up to several weeks.

BANH MI XIU MAI (MEATBALL SANDWICHES)

The term *banh mi* actually refers to the French-style bread the sandwich is served on. *Banh mi thit*, which translates to "meat sandwich," is the generic name for Vietnamese sandwiches. *Xiu mai* is the word for meatballs.

Vietnamese sandwiches are becoming a popular lunch item in Texas. Some people don't like the Vietnamese pâté or some of the cold cuts that are traditionally used in them. For them, I recommend this meatball sandwich. It is also the easiest one to make at home. See photo on page 262.

SERVES 4

4 banh mi rolls or 10-inch baguette lengths, split
½ cup Spicy Viet-Tex Mayo (page 268)
12 cilantro sprigs
16 Xiu Mai (page 268), hot
About 2 cups drained Pickled Vietnamese Vegetables (page 268), or to taste

In a toaster oven or a broiler, toast the cut sides of the roll halves until crispy. Spread the cut sides with the mayo, and then arrange 3 cilantro sprigs on the bottom half of each roll. Cut the meatballs in half, and divide the meatballs evenly among the bottom halves of the rolls. Arrange the pickled vegetables on top of the meatballs. Close the sandwiches with the top halves of the rolls and serve immediately.

BANH MI SLIDERS

These burgers are popping up all over the place. Sometimes they are made on *banh mi* rolls and sometimes on regular buns. The menu at Burger Guys, a Houston gourmet burger joint, includes the Saigon burger, which is a hamburger dressed with pâté, Vietnamese pickled vegetables, jalapeños, and mayonnaise.

These Vietnamese sliders are similar to the meatball sandwiches at left. But instead of steaming small Vietnamese meatballs, you make large meatballs and flatten them into sliders.

SERVES 4

Burgers
8 ounces ground sirloin
8 ounces ground pork
2 tablespoons chopped garlic
3 tablespoons finely chopped fresh basil
3 tablespoons finely chopped green onions
1 egg
1 tablespoon fish sauce or soy sauce
1 tablespoon Sriracha sauce
1 teaspoon freshly ground pepper
1 teaspoon sea salt

4 banh mi rolls or 10-inch baguette lengths, split
½ cup Spicy Viet-Tex Mayo (page 268)
2 tablespoons liver pâté (optional)
About 2 cups drained Pickled Vietnamese Vegetables (page 268), or to taste
12 cilantro sprigs

To make the burgers, in a bowl, combine all of the burger ingredients and mix well with your hands. Divide the meat mixture into 8 equal portions. Shape each portion into a ball and then flatten into a 3-inch patty.

Cook the patties on a charcoal or gas grill over a hot fire, on a griddle heated to medium, or in a skillet over medium heat to desired doneness.

In a toaster oven or a broiler, toast the cut sides of the roll halves until crispy. Spread the cut sides with the mayo, then spread ½ tablespoon of the pâté on the bottom half of each roll. Lay 2 burgers along the bottom half of each roll and top with the pickled vegetables and 3 cilantro sprigs. Close the sandwiches with the top halves of the rolls. Cut the sandwiches in half between the burgers and serve immediately.

Kaiser's Steak Tikka, page 276
(also known as Pakistani fajitas).

CHAPTER 23
INDIAN COWBOYS

★★★★★★★★★★★★★★★★★★★★★

Abdul picked up the Styrofoam bowl and began eating the spicy pink yogurt with a plastic spoon, so I followed his lead. The cold yogurt had minced tomato and cucumber in it, along with an intriguing combination of spices. I detected cumin and black pepper, but there were some others I couldn't identify. I was just getting into the cold yogurt soup when Abdul threw me a curveball. He put the soup bowl back down on the table and started throwing lettuce, tomatoes, and onions into the yogurt. The soup had suddenly become the salad dressing. He smiled as he swished the vegetables around in the liquid and ate them with his fingers. I did what Abdul did.

Abdul Rasheed happened to be first in line as I approached the taxi stand at Hobby Airport. He stood about five foot four and had black hair, dark eyes, and a strange red stain on his teeth. I asked him where he was from and he answered Pakistan. Then I asked him if he knew a good Pakistani restaurant in Houston. When he said he did, I offered to buy him lunch and got into his taxi.

He drove me to a stretch of Bissonett between Highway 59 and the Sam Houston Tollway. "This is the center of the Pakistani community," he said. We passed several shopping centers with Pakistani businesses, including a couple of interesting-looking restaurants, before we pulled into the parking lot at Ali Baba's B. B. Q. and Grill at 11887 Bissonett, a small freestanding restaurant on a "pad" out in front of a shopping center. (The restaurant has since closed.)

It was an odd scene. Abdul explained that the location had been an American breakfast restaurant and that the new owners had done very little to change the place. The booths and the Formica counter said Steak and Egg Kitchen, but the menu hanging above the grill featured brain masala. Instead of bacon and coffee, we smelled curry and mutton. Abdul liked the quail, so I ordered the *batair boti* (grilled quail). We also asked for a barbecue combination plate and an order of *karahi gosht* (stewed beef).

We were the last customers for lunch at around two in the afternoon, and the restaurant had grown quiet while we waited for our orders. Abdul had gone to the washroom, so I got up and strolled into the kitchen and asked a man in an apron what the spices in the yogurt were. He pointed to a rack that contained some large plastic jars.

"We grind these together to make our own masala," he said. Two of the jars on the shelf contained black peppercorns and cumin seeds, as I expected. Another held cloves and the fourth was filled with pods that looked like miniature Brazil nuts. I fish one out of the jar, scraped it with my thumbnail, and sniffed it. It was cardamom.

Abdul returned and our food arrived. The quail was crispy brown and flecked with spices. The bird was very hot and I burnt my fingers pulling it apart. It was really too hot to eat, but I tore off a big rosy piece of juicy breast and popped it in my mouth anyway. I had never had barbecue with such an exotic aroma before. Cumin, cloves, and garlic make quite a grill rub, and they combine stunningly with the slight gaminess of quail. Abdul watched me eat my little bird with wide eyes and a big smile.

He was focused on the little, hot metal pot that contained the *karahi gosht*, which turned out to be a sort of Pakistani pot roast. The well-cooked piece of beef fell apart easily under the small plastic knife. The meat was cooked in a spicy tomato sauce that combined the familiar tomato sauce elements of green onions, jalapeños, and garlic with the South Asian zing of fresh ginger and aromatic masala. Abdul ate his meat and sauce folded in little pieces of naan.

The barbecue plate was a disappointment because the kebabs had been made with frozen ground meat. The guy at the table beside us was polishing off a plate of *masala kebab*, hamburger meat cooked with masala spices and served in a little hot pot with fluffy naan on the side—a Pakistani Sloppy Joe. For three bucks, the kitchen also served bun kebab, better known in the rest of Houston as a hamburger on a bun.

Abdul said that when it's hot outside and you have eaten a big meal like we had, you should always finish off with a big glass of *lassi*, a yogurt drink, to prevent heartburn. I followed his advice. He then handed me a strange little package he bought from the kiosk at the front of the restaurant. He called it *paan* and said it was a betel nut chew. Mine was flavored with aniseeds and sweetened lentils, and his was a mix of betel nut and tobacco. We drove away in silence as I ruminated in the back seat.

The *batair boti* was the best grilled quail for the money I have ever eaten. In *An Invitation to Indian Cooking*, published in 1973, Indian cooking authority Madhur Jaffrey wrote that the food served at Indian restaurants in the United States was a bland, watered-down version of real Indian cuisine. But the huge numbers of Indian immigrants that have arrived since the book was published have changed that. And with its hot climate and excellent job market, Texas is particularly attractive to immigrants from the Indian subcontinent. Texas is on the same latitude as the Punjab region of India and much of Pakistan. The Indian food in Texas is as authentic as you want it to be.

Brain masala and many of the other dishes served at Ali Baba's and places like it reflect the preferences of Houston's Pakistani population. These foods are too authentic for mainstream tastes. But for exactly that reason, they offer culinary adventurers a ticket to Pakistan for the price of a five-dollar lunch.

★ ★ ★

Harris County, where Houston and its suburbs are located, no longer has a majority culture. Hispanics make up about 38 percent of the population, Anglos account for 36 percent, people of African descent are 18 percent, and people of Asian descent are around 8 percent.

"Food traditions are particularly intriguing because they are some of the most persistent of traditions," writes Louisiana cultural anthropologist Maida Owens. "As a result, food often becomes closely tied to cultural identity and can reveal cultural processes such as blending, diffusion, or maintenance." If changes in what we eat really reflect who we are, then a steady influx of immigrants over the past fifty years has changed the fabric of Texan culture.

In Dallas and in much of the rest of the state, Korean nationals and their offspring, following in the successful footsteps of a few early Korean immigrants, have taken over the doughnut business. But because doughnut shops in Texas also sell kolaches, the Koreans have had to master the intricacies of the Czech Texan pastry with its Eastern European poppy seed and sausage fillings. Just across the border in Lake Charles, Louisiana, I visited a shop called Happy Donuts where the Korean owners came up with a new twist, kolaches stuffed with Cajun boudin. The boudin kolaches are now catching on in Houston.

In the rural Brazos Valley, hotel owners from the Indian subcontinent, *taqueros* from Latin America, and noodle-shop proprietors from Southeast Asia are part of the new cultural landscape. In College Station, a Hmong American named Kevin served me Vietnamese egg rolls in a restaurant called Rosie's Pho, which also offered Singapore-style noodles and Japanese udon.

As a result of our new population statistics, some social scientists are reporting a shift away from our former "food neophobic" instincts. That aversion to new foods limited the human palate, of course, but it also protected our forebears from food poisoning. But in a multicultural society, where we see other ethnicities safely eating their foods, we feel free to try them, too. This has led to a new "food neophilic" trend in Texas, a desire to try new things to eat.

Maybe I was staring too intently at the hot foie gras and sweet fig chutney appetizer my tablemate ordered at Indika, Anita Jaisinghani's upscale Indian restaurant on Westheimer in Houston. He was dying to dig in, but instead he sat back and invited me to go ahead and have a bite. Politeness would have dictated that I insist he try some first. But, manners be damned, I reached across the table and cut off a big hunk with my fork. The chutney supplied little more than a sweet glaze on my palate as the hot unctuous liver melted in my mouth. It was heavenly.

My other tablemate was eating something called "duck almond kofta curry, onion pakora salad," a surprising bowl of cool greens and onion fritter croutons with big duck meatballs in it. I stabbed one of the meatballs and cut it up on the side of my plate. The duck meat wasn't ground. Instead, the sphere was made by binding nice-size chunks of duck meat together.

Having helped myself to major forkfuls of each tablemate's appetizer, I offered them each a taste of mine. But they weren't interested. When you order goat brain masala for a starter, you stand a good chance of eating it all by yourself.

Brains and eggs was once a popular Southern breakfast. That dish called for pig's brains instead of goat's brains and grits instead of roti (flat bread). The most unappetizing thing about brains (beyond the psychological) is the pasty color, which Indian cooks solve by simmering the brains in turmeric-laced water, turning them a pleasant yellow. At Indika, the brains are then cooked with a pungent masala (spice blend), mixed with bits of potato in a yogurt sauce, and spooned over flat bread.

My shrimp vindaloo main course, a pile of juicy sautéed shrimp in a deep brown sauce, tasted like an extra-spicy Indian gumbo with masala instead of filé

IN HIS OWN WORDS: KAISER LASHKARI

★ ★

MY MOTHER IS INDIAN and my father is Pakistani. I grew up in Karachi and came to Houston to go to college in 1981. When I first got to Texas, I was amazed by the food. The flavor that most impressed me was the smoked meat. We had charcoal braziers in Pakistan, so I knew the flavor of charcoal-cooked meat, but we never cooked with wood. I am Muslim, so I never ate pork barbecue, but I thought the Texas barbecue brisket was just fantastic. I couldn't get enough.

When Pakistanis first arrive in Texas, they go crazy over the beef. Goat is the most common meat in Pakistan; beef is very expensive. And beef isn't graded in Pakistan. At the market, you have no idea what you are getting. A good steak at a Karachi hotel will cost you around 400 rupees [about twenty-five dollars]—that's a lot of money in Pakistan. The beef here is much better quality and much more affordable.

I love Tex-Mex, too. Fajitas are just like grilled beef dishes we have at home. Chili con carne tastes like *keema*, only with ground beef instead of ground goat. Chili powder, cumin, garlic—these are seasonings that Texas and Pakistan have in common. There are a lot of other similarities. I ate a lot of quesadillas when I was a student. Flour tortillas are just like chapati. It's the same recipe.

I got a degree from the University of Houston Conrad Hilton School of Hotel and Restaurant Management. I thought I wanted to be a hotel food and beverage manager. But I changed my mind. I did a six-month internship at the Intercontinental Hotel

Kaiser Lashkari: owner, Himalaya Restaurant, Houston.

in Karachi. Cooking was the only part of the job that made me happy.

From 1994 to 2003, I had a restaurant called Kaiser's in West Houston. It was a tiny place with mostly takeout. Then I opened Himalaya in 2004. A lot of my customers are Muslims from India and Pakistan. I don't serve any alcoholic beverages, but you can bring your own bottle—except during Ramadan.

There are more than one hundred thousand Indians, Pakistanis, Bangladeshis, and Sri Lankans in Houston. Many non-Indians also come to the restaurant. And then some great Houston chefs started coming here, and they put me on a culinary tour. They bring people here and feed them steak tikka.

My steak tikka is a Pakistani version of fajitas. The seasonings are similar to Tex-Mex fajitas, but I use a masala. We have something like pastrami in Pakistan, which is called hunter's beef, and I serve mine with a mustard curry sauce.

My *keema* is really Pakistani chili con carne made with ground goat.

The chefs like Himalaya because I grind all of my own spices fresh and make my own spice mixes, and I don't use any processed stuff. There are no shortcuts here, just a lot of hard work. I have eaten at some of their restaurants, too.

We get many younger American customers at Himalaya now. Give them hot, spicy, give them goat, or offal, it doesn't matter, they will eat it. It's amazing. I think the young Americans have the most adventurous palates in the world.

powder. Both of my tablemates got even with me for ordering brains by chowing down on several of my shrimp. In fact, the spicy shrimp were so sensational that I almost sent the waiter back for another plate.

Indika's owner and head chef, Anita Jaisinghani, earned a doctorate in microbiology in her native India and then spent ten years in Canada before moving to Houston and changing careers. She worked as a pastry chef at one of the city's leading restaurants for nearly two years before opening the original Indika on Memorial. The *New York Times*, *Gourmet* magazine, and a host of other publications soon lauded the restaurant for its startlingly fresh take on Indian cuisine. In 2011, Jaisinghani opened a second restaurant in Houston, Pondicherry.

Bombay-born chef Neela Paniz is generally credited with introducing the new style of Indian cooking to Americans at her Bombay Café in Los Angeles, which she opened with a partner in 1989. From the beginning, she adapted the traditional

Shubhra Ramineni's spice tiffin.

techniques and spices of the Indian kitchen to the fresh ingredients available in Southern California. For example, in the past in India, only people living in the country's coastal areas ate seafood because of the lack of refrigeration, and irrigation-intensive crops like lettuce were seldom seen. Paniz put lots of local fresh fish and salad greens on her menu from the earliest days of the restaurant.

Today, a new breed of Indian chefs is continuing to stretch the envelope. At Indika, mulligatawny is one of the regular menu items, but Jaisinghani has replaced the traditional meat with seafood. I have also sampled her "Idaho trout stuffed with nuts and herbs, saffron coconut curry, sweet potato, and lentil purée," which combines an iconic American fish and Texas pecans with a heady Indian coconut milk curry.

At Pondicherry, Jaisinghani has made it a goal to teach Westerners about *chaat*, India's popular savory snacks. *Chaat*, which generally includes some kind of starch and a variety of condiments, can be anything from a fruit salad (see page 279) to puffed rice and vegetables with tamarind sauce to spicy potato croquettes. But Jaisinghani also embraces familiar Western forms on her *chaat* menu, including a juicy, sweet, and cheesy "grilled chicken naan sandwich with spinach, goat cheese, and mango chutney."

But as brilliant as she is, Anita Jaisinghani owes part of the credit for her success to the palates of Houstonians. Innovative Indian restaurants in New York will never be able to make the food as spicy as it should be because most New Yorkers are cautious when it comes to chiles. And I imagine innovative Indian restaurants in other parts of the country face the same restraints.

What makes Jaisinghani's food great is that it is not only among the most creative takes on Indian cuisine in the country, but it is also *muy picante* when it is supposed to be—thanks to the "bring it on" palates of jalapeño-happy Texans.

KAISER'S STEAK TIKKA

Marinated skirt steak is sold as "beef for fajitas" in Texas grocery stores. It is marinated at the meat plant in a process that's impossible to duplicate at home, unless you have a vacuum tumbler. But you can substitute flat-iron steak, hanger steak, sirloin flap, or any of the other popular "bistro steak" cuts if you want. Just grill the masala-seasoned meat, and cut it into thin strips against the grain. Then wrap up the spicy beef strips in some flour tortillas and moisten with some chutney for a wild Pakistani Texan flavor ride. See photo on page 270.

MAKES 6 TACOS
- **1 pound marinated inside skirt steak, outside skirt steak, flat-iron steak, hanger steak, or sirloin flap**
- **¼ cup Shubhra's Garam Masala (page 277)**
- **Salt**
- **Juice 1 lime**
- **6 flour tortillas, warmed**
- **Mint Chutney (page 278)**
- **Mango-Habanero Chutney (page 278)**
- **Refried Dal (recipe follows)**
- **Raita (page 278)**

Rub the meat generously on both sides with the garam masala and set aside at room temperature while the grill is heating.

Prepare a hot fire for direct-heat grilling in a charcoal or gas grill. When the coals are covered with white ash, place the meat directly over the fire and cook, turning once or twice, for 12 to 15 minutes, until nicely browned on the outside and still pink in the center.

Transfer the steak to a cutting board. If you are using fajita meat, cut it with the grain into 4-inch-wide pieces. Then cut across the grain into ½-inch-wide strips. Sprinkle with salt and the lime juice. Divide the meat evenly among the tortillas, then add as much of the chutneys and dal as you like. Alternatively, serve on a sizzling *comal* with the chutneys on the side and allow your diners to roll their own tacos. Serve at once. Pass the raita at the table.

REFRIED DAL

If you are in a hurry, you can cook the split peas in a pressure cooker. Or, you can cook the peas in a slow cooker overnight so you don't have to watch them.

MAKES ABOUT 5 CUPS; SERVES 10
- **5 cups water**
- **1 cup dried yellow split peas**
- **2 tablespoons unsalted butter**
- **4 cloves garlic, minced**
- **¾ teaspoon cumin seeds, toasted in a dry skillet until aromatic**
- **¾ teaspoon mustard seeds**
- **½ teaspoon ground turmeric**
- **½ teaspoon ground cinnamon**
- **¼ teaspoon salt, or more to taste**
- **¼ teaspoon black pepper**
- **Pinch of cayenne pepper, or to taste**

In a saucepan, bring the water to a boil over high heat. Add the split peas, decrease the heat to low, cover, and cook for 2 to 3 hours, until the peas are very soft. Remove from the heat. Drain the peas and reserve the liquid.

In a large skillet, melt the butter over medium heat. Watch closely so it does not burn. Add the garlic, cumin, mustard seeds, turmeric, and cinnamon while stirring constantly. Add the cooked peas and a splash of their liquid and mash all of the ingredients together with a potato masher until the mixture is nearly smooth. While continuing to stir constantly, add more cooking liquid, a little at a time, until the mixture is creamy but not soupy. Season with the salt, black pepper, and cayenne, then decrease the heat to low and cook, stirring often, for 5 minutes to blend the flavors. Serve hot.

SHUBHRA RAMINENI'S FLOUR TORTILLA SAMOSAS

Shubhra Ramineni was born in India and moved to Houston as a small child. In her Houston home, her mother made Indian food with local ingredients. Shubhra went on to college and graduate school and is now a busy young professional and a new mom. But she still wanted to cook Indian food at home. That's how Shubhra's easy Indian cookbook, *Entice with Spice*, came about. The recipes are made with ingredients you can find at the supermarket and the techniques include some wonderful shortcuts. Shubhra showed me the easy way to make cocktail samosas from flour tortillas.

MAKES 8 SMALL SAMOSAS
Peanut oil, for deep-frying
4 large flour tortillas
1 tablespoon flour dissolved in 2 tablespoons water
1 cup filling of choice (such as keema or chili con carne)
Mint Chutney (page 278), for serving

Pour the oil to a depth of about 3 inches into a deep, heavy pot or deep fryer and heat to 350°F.

While the oil is heating, lay 1 tortilla on a cutting board and cut the tortilla in half. Holding the right point of the half-moon, fold half of the tortilla down and paint the edge with the flour-and-water "glue." Now paint the straight edge from the left point of the half-moon to the middle with the glue. Press the two wet edges together to form a cone. Fill the cone halfway with 2 tablespoons of the filling. Paint the top edge of the cone with some glue and press it together to seal. Repeat with the remaining tortilla half and then with the remaining tortillas and filling to make 8 samosas total.

Working in small batches, drop the samosas into the hot oil and fry for about 2 minutes, until golden brown. Using a wire skimmer or slotted spoon, transfer the samosas to paper towels to drain. Serve hot.

SHUBHRA'S GARAM MASALA

On the same day Shubhra Ramineni showed me how to make her easy version of samosas (at left), she showed me how to make this equally easy masala. The flavor of freshly toasted spices is well worth the effort. Shubhra's version also includes a few whole cloves, which I have omitted because the aroma reminds me of a toothache remedy.

MAKES ABOUT 1/2 CUP
1/2 cup coriander seeds
6 whole green cardamom pods
1 tablespoon cumin seeds
1/4 teaspoon peppercorns
1 cinnamon stick

In a small, dry skillet, toast the coriander seeds over medium heat, shaking the pan often, for about 2 minutes, until fragrant. Transfer to a bowl. Then toast the cardamom, cumin, peppercorns, and cinnamon together in the skillet for about 1 minute, until fragrant. Add the spices to the bowl and let cool completely.

Grind the cooled spices in a spice grinder or clean coffee grinder into a powder. Use immediately, or store in an airtight container at room temperature for up to 2 weeks.

MINT CHUTNEY

This is an incredibly refreshing relish. If you have mint in your garden, this is a perfect way to use up a lot of it. Serve with grilled meats, samosas, or other Indian dishes.

MAKES ABOUT 2 CUPS
1 cup chopped yellow onions
1½ cups packed fresh mint leaves
½ serrano chile, with seeds
Juice of 1 lime
½ teaspoon salt
¼ teaspoon black pepper
Pinch of cayenne pepper

In a food processor, combine all of the ingredients and pulse until the mixture is almost smooth. The color of the chutney darkens after a few hours, but it will keep in a tightly covered container in the refrigerator for a few days.

MANGO-HABANERO CHUTNEY

Overripe mangoes go on sale at the end of the summer. That's the perfect time to pick up a couple of boxes of fruit and make a big batch of chutney. Two habaneros make a spicy chutney, so you can tone it down if you like—or you can add more if you're chile crazed.

MAKES ABOUT 12 PINTS
3 cups cider vinegar
3 cups firmly packed dark brown sugar
10 cups diced ripe mangoes
3 cups raisins
2 cups chopped red bell peppers
1 cup chopped yellow onions
1 cup finely chopped, peeled fresh ginger
3 small lemons, thinly sliced
2 habanero chiles, seeded and minced
4 cloves garlic, minced
1 teaspoon kosher salt
Freshly ground black pepper

In a large saucepan, combine the vinegar and brown sugar and bring to a boil, stirring to dissolve the sugar. Add the mangoes, raisins, bell peppers, onions, ginger, lemon, chiles, garlic, salt, and pepper and stir well. When the mixture returns to a simmer, remove from the heat and set aside for 30 minutes or more, until the fruit absorbs the flavors.

Return the pan to low heat, bring to a simmer, and cook, stirring constantly, for about 15 minutes, until the chutney is thick. Remove from the heat, let cool, and transfer to airtight containers. The chutney will keep for up to 2 weeks in the refrigerator. For longer storage, follow the directions in Water-Bath Canning on Your Home Stove (page 95).

RAITA

Raita is supposed to be a simple side dish that you eat to cool your mouth off after consuming spicy food. But this unassuming cucumber salad is so tasty, it often steals the show.

MAKES ABOUT 4 CUPS
2 cups plain yogurt
2 cups grated, unpeeled cucumber
1 clove garlic, minced
Leaves from 4 mint sprigs, finely minced
1 teaspoon kosher salt
½ teaspoon ground cumin
¼ teaspoon freshly ground black pepper
Pinch of cayenne pepper

In a bowl, whisk the yogurt until smooth. Add the cucumber, garlic, mint, salt, cumin, black pepper, and cayenne and stir well. Cover and refrigerate for about 2 hours, until well chilled, before serving.

TEXAS PEACH LASSI

This quick and easy Indian yogurt drink is ideal for the end of summer when sweet, juicy Texas peaches are arriving at local farmers' markets. It can be served for breakfast, to accompany appetizers, as a dessert, or whenever you're thirsty on a hot day.

SERVES 4

4 Texas peaches
1 cup plain yogurt
¼ cup sugar
30 ice cubes, plus more for serving
¼ teaspoon freshly ground cardamom (optional)

Halve and pit the unpeeled peaches, then chop. You should have about 2 cups. In a blender, combine half of the peaches, ½ cup of the yogurt, 2 tablespoons of the sugar, and 15 ice cubes and process until the ice is slushy. Transfer to a pitcher. Repeat with the remaining peaches, yogurt, sugar, and ice cubes, then add to the pitcher.

Fill 4 tall glasses with ice cubes. Divide the yogurt mixture evenly among the glasses and garnish each drink with a pinch of the cardamom. Enjoy immediately.

PEPPERY FRUIT CHAAT

The first bite of this salty, peppery fruit salad may be a bit of a shock to your palate. But if you have ever eaten mangoes sprinkled with chile powder at Mexican fruit stands, it will become familiar quickly. Guava and banana are common in the Indian version, but you can make this with any combination of fruits you like.

Fruit *chaat* is often finished with black salt, a mineral-rich unrefined salt that smells like hard-boiled eggs. If you want to try it, you can find it in Indian food stores. Personally, I prefer *fleur de sel*.

MAKES 8 CUPS

1 cup chopped, peeled apples
1 cup chopped, peeled pears
1 cup grapes
1 cup watermelon chunks
1 cup peach chunks
1 cup banana slices
1 cup guava pieces
1 cup nectarine chunks
Juice of 3 lemons
½ teaspoon cayenne pepper
½ teaspoon black pepper
1 teaspoon sea salt or black salt

In a large bowl, combine all of the fruit. Drizzle with the lemon juice and sprinkle with the cayenne, black pepper, and salt and mix well. You can serve the salad right way, or you can cover and chill it for up to 3 hours before serving.

BRYAN CASWELL'S BAKED OYSTERS WITH LIME PICKLE

Bryan Caswell came up with this modern variation on Oysters Rockefeller at Reef, his Gulf seafood restaurant in Houston.

SERVES 4

16 Gulf oysters, shucked and on the half shell, with liquor reserved

Topping

1 large bunch Swiss chard leaves
2 tablespoons unsalted butter
2½ tablespoons all-purpose flour
1 shallot, minced
½ Thai chile, seeded and minced
¼ teaspoon cayenne pepper
¼ teaspoon white pepper
¼ teaspoon kosher salt
¾ cup bottled clam juice
¼ cup milk
4½ tablespoons mascarpone cheese
1½ tablespoons pureed lime pickle

Bread Crumbs

2 tablespoons salted butter
1 cup panko (Japanese bread crumbs)
¼ cup shredded Asiago cheese

1 (5-pound) box rock salt
16 to 20 allspice berries
4 whole cloves

Shuck the oysters, removing and discarding the top shell and leaving each meat resting in the bottom shell. As you work, capture the liquor and then set it aside for using in the topping. Refrigerate the oysters until needed.

To make the topping, trim off the stems from the Swiss chard leaves and discard or reserve for another use. Bring a large pot of water to a boil, add the chard leaves, and blanch for 1 minute. Drain and immediately immerse in ice water to halt the cooking. Drain again and then chop finely. Measure 2 cups and set aside.

In a large sauté pan, melt the butter over medium-high heat and allow it to foam and brown but not burn. Sprinkle in the flour, increase the heat to high, and whisk constantly for about 30 seconds, until a loose paste forms. Add the shallot, chile, cayenne, white pepper, and salt and whisk constantly for 2 to 3 minutes, until the shallot is translucent.

Slowly add the clam juice, milk, and reserved oyster liquor while whisking constantly, then continue to whisk until the mixture comes to a boil. Lower the heat to a gentle simmer and cook, stirring often, for about 10 minutes, until the mixture has thickened and the flour taste is "cooked out." Stir in the Swiss chard and heat through. Remove from the heat and stir in the mascarpone and lime pickle until thoroughly incorporated. Set aside.

To prepare the bread crumbs, in a small skillet or sauté pan, melt the butter over medium-high heat and allow it to foam and brown but not burn. Add the bread crumbs, toss to coat evenly with the hot butter, and remove from the heat. Let cool and fold in the cheese. Set aside.

Preheat the oven to 400°F. Fill a baking pan large enough to hold the oysters in a single layer half full with rock salt. Place it in the preheated oven for about 15 minutes.

Top each oyster with 1 to 1½ tablespoons of the chard topping (the amount will depend on the size of the oysters), then sprinkle with about 1 tablespoon of the bread crumbs. Transfer to the prepared baking pan and bake for about 8 minutes, until bread the crumbs are golden brown and slightly bubbling.

To serve, have ready 4 shallow bowls or rimmed serving plates. Line each bowl with rock salt mixed with 4 or 5 allspice berries and 1 whole clove. As soon as the oysters are ready, transfer them to the bowls and serve immediately.

RESOURCES

Chiles and Spices

Adams Extract & Spice
Spice experts and mail-order source for ancho chile powder, chipotle powder, whole dried chile pequin peppers, New Mexican chile powder, New Mexican green chile flakes, granulated jalapeño, and cracked black pepper. www.adamsextract.com

Goode Company
Spice mixes and seasonings, charcoal starter chimneys, all kinds of barbecue tools, and Texas gifts—call for a catalog. www.goodecompany.com

Hatch Chile Express
Fresh and frozen New Mexican green chiles and red chile powder. www.hatch-chile.com

Pendery's
Molcajetes, chiles, cumin, chili powders, Mexican oregano, and hard to find spices—ask for a catalog. www.penderys.com

Cornmeal and Grits

Anson Mills
Mail-order source for cornmeal and grits from white, yellow, and blue corn varieties ground on an old-fashioned stone mill in South Carolina. www.ansonmills.com

Bob's Red Mill
Cornmeal, organic cornmeal, *masa harina*, biscuit flour, and a wide variety of other grains, meals, and flours. www.bobsredmill.com

War Eagle Mill
Organic white and yellow cornmeals from a refurbished undershot waterwheel mill in Arkansas. www.wareaglemill.com

Seafood, Meat, and Sausage

Bellville Meat Market
A country meat market that sells an award-winning jalapeño cheddar summer sausage, excellent dried sausage products, and lots of spice blends. www.bellvillemeatmarket.com

Broken Arrow Ranch
Venison, wild boar, and game meats. www.brokenarrowranch.com

The Gumbo Pages
Internet directory of Louisiana food products, including sources for mail-order crawfish, frozen turtle meat and seafoods, Cajun spice mixes, andouille, and tasso. www.gumbopages.com

Janak's Country Market
Mail-order source for smoked meats, sauerkraut, and Czech sausages. www.janakpacking.com

Cookware and Equipment

Allied Kenco
Meat grinders, sausage stuffers, fermenting crocks, dehydrators, smokers, slicers, home butcher supplies, and instructional materials. If you can make it to the store, ask Cody for help. www.alliedkenco.com

Lodge Cast Iron
Cast-iron skillets, Dutch ovens, and chicken frying kettles. www.lodgemfg.com

PHOTO CREDITS

ii: Laurie Smith

iv: Laurie Smith

vi: Paul S. Howell

2: Laurie Smith (fish and tartar sauce courtesy Jimmy G's)

3: Courtesy the Rosenberg Library, Galveston, Texas

4: (left) Courtesy the Rosenberg Library, Galveston, Texas

4: (right) Courtesy the Rosenberg Library, Galveston, Texas

5: Paul S. Howell

6: Robb Walsh

7: Courtesy the Rosenberg Library, Galveston, Texas

10: Jody Horton (sea bream courtesy Reef)

12: Laurie Smith (grilled oysters courtesy Jimmy G's)

13: Courtesy the Rosenberg Library, Galveston, Texas

16: Jody Horton (oyster tasting courtesy Gaido's)

18: Robb Walsh

21: UTSA Libraries Special Collections, San Antonio Light Collection

24: Laurie Smith

25: Robb Walsh

27: Jody Horton

28: Laurie Smith

31: Laurie Smith

34: Robb Walsh

36: Laurie Smith

39: (top left and center) Laurie Smith

39: (top right) Robb Walsh

43: Laurie Smith

46: Laurie Smith

48: Laurie Smith

51: Robb Walsh

57: Laurie Smith

62: Laurie Smith

63: UTSA Libraries Special Collections, San Antonio Light Collection

70: Laurie Smith

73: Laurie Smith

76: Laurie Smith

80: Laurie Smith

82: Robb Walsh

84: Julia Walsh

89: Laurie Smith

90: Laurie Smith

92: Laurie Smith

93: Paul S. Howell

94: Paul S. Howell

95: UTSA Libraries Special Collections, courtesy Ruth Higdon

97: Laurie Smith

98: Laurie Smith

101: Paul S. Howell

104: Laurie Smith

105: Collection of Robb Walsh

107: Courtesy Palmetto Inn

108: Courtesy Palmetto Inn

109: Collection of Robb Walsh

116: Laurie Smith

117: Courtesy Felix Tijerina Jr.

118: Courtesy Felix Tijerina Jr.

120: Courtesy Felix Tijerina Jr.

123: UTSA Libraries Special Collections

124: Laurie Smith

128: Robb Walsh

134: Laurie Smith

135: Robb Walsh

136: Laurie Smith

139: Laurie Smith

146: Laurie Smith

147: UTSA Libraries Special Collections, courtesy Vic Fritze

149: Comfort Museum, copy courtesy UTSA Libraries Special Collections

150: Robb Walsh

151: Dan Bryant

153: Laurie Smith

158: UTSA Libraries Special Collections, courtesy Vic Fritze

160: Laurie Smith

161: UTSA Libraries Special Collections, courtesy Natalie McLain

162: Robb Walsh

164: Laurie Smith

165: Robb Walsh

170: Laurie Smith

171: UTSA Libraries Special Collections, courtesy Pioneer Flour Mills

173: UTSA Libraries Special Collections, courtesy Florence C. Ayres

175: *Harper's Weekly Illustrated Magazine*, copy courtesy UTSA Libraries Special Collections

180: Laurie Smith

184: Courtesy Ronnie Bermann

185: Courtesy Ronnie Bermann

189: Laurie Smith (chicken-fried steak courtesy Frank's Chop House)

193: UTSA Libraries Special Collections, San Antonio Light Collection

196: Robb Walsh

202: Robb Walsh

206: Laurie Smith

207: UTSA Libraries Special Collections, Zintgraff Collection

208: UTSA Libraries Special Collections, courtesy Dr. M. W. Sharp

210: Robb Walsh

214: Robb Walsh

217: (left) Robb Walsh

217: (top right) Texas State Archives

217: (bottom right) Jody Horton

218: Laurie Smith

219: Laurie Smith

221: Laurie Smith

222: UTSA Libraries Special Collections, Zintgraff Collection

225: Courtesy the Rosenberg Library, Galveston, Texas

227: Courtesy Whataburger Restaurants

231: Laurie Smith (hamburger courtesy Christian's Totem)

236: Laurie Smith

237: Courtesy Blue Bell Creamery

249: Paul S. Howell

250: Laurie Smith

257: Laurie Smith

261: Laurie Smith

262: Courtesy family of Carl Han

264: Robb Walsh

270: Laurie Smith

272: Robb Walsh

274: Robb Walsh

275: Robb Walsh

279: Laurie Smith

281: Laurie Smith (oysters courtesy Reef)

292: Laurie Smith

BIBLIOGRAPHY

Andrews, Jean. *Peppers: The Domesticated Capsicums.* Austin: University of Texas Press, 1984.

Bridges, Bill. *The Great American Chili Book.* New York: Rawson, Wade 1981.

Brittin, Phil, and Joseph Daniel. *Texas on the Halfshell: A Cookbook of Tex-Mex, Barbecue, Chili, and Lone Star Delights.* New York: Doubleday, 1982.

Cabeza de Vaca, Álvar Núñez. *The Account: Álvar Núñez Cabeza de Vaca's Relación* (1542). Translated by Martin Favata and José Fernández. Houston, TX: Arte Publico Press, 1993.

Cauble, Bill, and Cliff Teinert. *Barbecue Biscuits & Beans: Chuck Wagon Cooking.* Houston, TX: Bright Sky Press, 2002.

Cunningham, Sue, and Jean Cates. *More Chuckwagon Recipes and Others.* Lenexa, KS: Cookbook Publishers, Inc., 1999.

Denker, Joel. *The World on a Plate: A Tour through the History of America's Ethnic Cuisine.* Boulder, CO: Westview Press, 2003.

Dobie, J. Frank, and John D. Young. *A Vaquero of the Brush Country.* Austin: University of Texas Press, 1998.

Dybala, Barbara, and Helen Macik. *Generation to Generation: Czech Foods, Customs, and Traditions, Texas Style.* Dallas, TX: Historical Society of the Czech Club, 1980.

Edge, John T. *Hamburgers & Fries: An American Story.* New York: G. P. Putnam's Sons, 2005.

Fehrenbach, T. R. *Lone Star: A History of Texas and the Texans.* New York: American Legacy Press, 1983.

Fernández-Armesto, Felipe. *Near a Thousand Tables: A History of Food.* New York: The Free Press, 2002.

Flemmons, Jerry. *Jerry Flemmons' More Texas Siftings: Another Bold and Uncommon Celebration of the Lone Star State.* Fort Worth: Texas Christian University Press, 1997.

Foley, Neil. *The White Scourge: Mexicans, Blacks, and Poor Whites in Texas Cotton Culture.* Berkeley: University of California Press, 1997.

Gabaccia, Donna. *We Are What We Eat: Ethnic Food and the Making of Americans.* Cambridge: Harvard University Press, 1998.

Graham, Don. *Kings of Texas: The 150-Year Saga of an American Ranching Empire.* New York: John Wiley & Sons, Inc., 2002.

Groves, Helen Kleberg. *Bob and Helen Kleberg of King Ranch.* Austin, TX: Pentagram, 2004.

Hidalgo County Historical Museum. *Mesquite Country: Tastes and Traditions from the Tip of Texas.* Memphis, TN: Wimmer Cookbooks, 1996.

Jordan-Bychov, Terry G. *North American Cattle-Ranching Frontiers: Origins, Diffusion, and Differentiation.* Albuquerque: University of New Mexico Press, 1994.

_____. *Trails to Texas: Southern Roots of Western Cattle Ranching.* Lincoln: University of Nebraska Press, 1981.

Koock, Mary Faulk. *The Texas Cookbook: From Barbecue to Banquet—an Informal View of Dining and Entertaining the Texas Way.* Denton: University of North Texas Press, 1965.

Kuh, Patric. *The Last Days of Haute Cuisine: The Coming of Age of American Restaurants.* New York: Viking Penguin, 2001.

Landrey, Wanda A. *Boardin' in the Thicket: Recipes and Reminiscences of Early Big Thicket Boarding Houses.* Denton: University of North Texas Press, 1998.

Lanning, Jim, and Judy Lanning. *Texas Cowboys: Memories of the Early Days.* College Station: Texas A&M University Press, 1984.

Linck, Ernestine Sewell, and Joyce Gibson Roach. *EATS: A Folk History of Texas Foods.* Forth Worth: Texas Christian University Press, 1989.

Love, Tim. *Tim Love on the Lonesome Dove Trail: Recipes of Urban Western Cuisine.* Dallas, TX: Dockery House Publishing, 2002.

Luchetti, Cathy. *Home on the Range: A Culinary History of the American West.* New York: Villard, 1993.

Massey, Sara R. *Black Cowboys of Texas.* College Station: Texas A&M University Press, 2000.

Olmsted, Frederick Law. *The Cotton Kingdom: A Traveller's Observations on Cotton and Slavery in the American Slave States. Based Upon Three Former Volumes of Journeys and Investigations.* New York: Mason Brothers, 1862.

_____. *A Journey Through Texas: Or, a Saddle-Trip on the Southwestern Frontier, with a Statistical Appendix.* New York, London: Dix, Edwards & Co., 1857.

Perini, Tom. *Texas Cowboy Cooking.* Buffalo Gap, TX: Comanche Moon Publishing, 2000.

Peyton, James W. *La Cocina de la Frontera: Mexican-American Cooking from the Southwest.* Santa Fe, NM: Red Crane Books, 1994.

_____. *Jim Peyton's New Cooking from Old Mexico.* Santa Fe, NM: Red Crane Books, 1999.

_____. *El Norte: The Cuisine of Northern Mexico.* Santa Fe, NM: Red Crane Books, 1995.

Price, B. Byron. *National Hall of Fame Chuck Wagon Cookbook: Authentic Recipes from the Ranch and the Range.* New York: Hearst Books, 1995.

Prudhomme, Paul. *Chef Paul Prudhomme's Louisiana Kitchen.* New York: William Morrow, 1984.

Ragsdale, Kenneth B. *The Year America Discovered Texas: Centennial '36.* College Station: Texas A&M University Press, 1987.

Reinhart, Peter. *The Bread Baker's Apprentice: Mastering the Art of Extraordinary Bread.* Berkeley, CA: Ten Speed Press, 2001.

Root, Waverly. *Food: An Authoritative and Visual History and Dictionary of the Foods of the World.* New York: Smithmark, 1996.

Root, Waverly, and Richard de Rochemont. *Eating in America: A History.* Hopewell, NJ: The Ecco Press, 1976.

Southern Living. *Southern Living Cookbook: Vegetables.* Birmingham, AL: Southern Living Magazine, 1982.

Stephenson, Patricia, and Alice Young. *Discovering Mexican Cooking.* San Antonio, TX: The Naylor Company, 1958.

Thames, Delma Cothran, ed. *A Pinch of This and a Handful of That.* Austin, TX: Eakin Press, 1988.

Thompson-Anderson, Terry. *Cajun-Creole Cooking.* Los Angeles: HP Books, 1986.

Thorne, John. *Serious Pig: An American Cook in Search of His Roots.* New York: North Point Press, 1996.

Tijerina, Andrés. *Tejanos and Texas under the Mexican Flag, 1821–1836.* College Station: Texas A&M University Press, 1994.

Tolbert, Frank X. *A Bowl of Red.* New York: Doubleday, 1967.

Wagner, Candy, and Sandra Marquez. *Cooking Texas Style: A Heritage of Traditional Recipes.* Austin: University of Texas Press, 1983.

Weatherford, Jack. *Indian Givers: How the Indians of the Americas Transformed the World.* New York: Fawcett Columbine, 1988.

Wilson, Eddie. *Threadgill's: The Cookbook.* Marietta, GA: Longstreet Press, 1996.

Zamora, Emilio, Cynthia Orozco, and Rodolfo Rocha. *Mexican Americans in Texas History, Selected Essays.* Austin: Texas State Historical Association, 2000.

INDEX

Ten Speed Press and the Ten Speed Press colophon are registered
trademarks of Random House, Inc.

Portions of this work were originally published in different form in the
following: "I Love Chicken Fried Steak," "Texas Burger Binge," and "We Want
Beer" in the *Houston Press* (or on houstonpress.com), a Village Voice Media
publication. "Juneteenth Jamboree" in *Gourmet* magazine (June 2007).

All photographs are by Laurie Smith except those attributed to other sources as
listed on page 283.

Library of Congress Cataloging-in-Publication Data
    Walsh, Robb, 1952–
    Texas eats : the new lone star heritage cookbook, with more
than 200 recipes / Robb Walsh.
        p. cm.
    Includes bibliographical references.
1. Cooking, American—Southwestern style. 2. Cooking—Texas. I. Title.
    TX715.2.S69W363 2012
    641.59764—dc23

                    2011035094

ISBN 978-0-7679-2150-3
eISBN 978-1-60774-113-8

Printed in China

Design by Katy Brown

10 9 8 7 6 5 4 3 2 1

First Edition